Advanced Topics in Science and Technology in China

Volume 58

Zhejiang University is one of the leading universities in China. In Advanced Topics in Science and Technology in China, Zhejiang University Press and Springer jointly publish monographs by Chinese scholars and professors, as well as invited authors and editors from abroad who are outstanding experts and scholars in their fields. This series will be of interest to researchers, lecturers, and graduate students alike.

Advanced Topics in Science and Technology in China aims to present the latest and most cutting-edge theories, techniques, and methodologies in various research areas in China. It covers all disciplines in the fields of natural science and technology, including but not limited to, computer science, materials science, the life sciences, engineering, environmental sciences, mathematics, and physics.

If you are interested in publishing your book in the series, please contact:
Dr. Mengchu Huang, E-mail: mengchu.huang@springer.com

This book series is index by the SCOPUS database.

More information about this series at http://www.springer.com/series/7887

Shuiguang Deng · Hongyue Wu ·
Jianwei Yin

Mobile Service Computing

Shuiguang Deng
College of Computer Science
and Technology
Zhejiang University
Huangzhou, Zhejiang, China

Hongyue Wu
College of Intelligence and Computing
Tianjin University
Tianjin, Hebei, China

Jianwei Yin
College of Computer Science
and Technology
Zhejiang University
Hangzhou, Zhejiang, China

ISSN 1995-6819   ISSN 1995-6827   (electronic)
Advanced Topics in Science and Technology in China
ISBN 978-981-15-5923-5   ISBN 978-981-15-5921-1   (eBook)
https://doi.org/10.1007/978-981-15-5921-1

Jointly published with Zhejiang University Press
The print edition is not for sale in China Mainland. Customers from China Mainland please order the print book from: Zhejiang University Press.

This Springer imprint is published by the registered company Springer Nature Singapore Pte Ltd.
The registered company address is: 152 Beach Road, #21-01/04 Gateway East, Singapore 189721, Singapore

Preface

The last two decades have witnessed the rapid development and application of services computing, which includes all the service-oriented methodologies and technologies arising from software engineering, distributed computing, and collaboration computing, etc. With the flourishment of the technologies including cloud computing, Internet of thing, as well as software-defined everything, all the software functions, hardware resources, and equipment capabilities could be utilized and shared as services. This brings an extensive application prospect for services computing.

In recent years, the popularization of mobile devices and the vigorous development of mobile communication technology bring great opportunities for services computing into the mobile environment. Services are no longer limited to traditional contexts and platforms, but they can be deployed on mobile devices and delivered over wireless networks. Although services computing and mobile computing have been studied for many years, respectively, their combination (mobile services computing) has not been widely researched. It is not doubtful that mobile services computing has enabled us to provide and access services anytime and anywhere, which greatly facilitates our life, work, and study. However, the application of mobile services computing still faces challenges due to the constant mobility of users, limited capability, and restricted power of mobile devices, which bring great challenges for both services provision and consumption in the mobile environment.

To our knowledge, this book is the first one to focus on the topic of mobile services computing. It aims to give a comprehensive introduction of mobile services computing, clarify its concept, opportunities, and challenges, and also discuss its main research topics including mobile services selection, recommendation, composition, deployment, offloading, and provision. With the development of mobile technologies as well as communication technologies especially edge computing, we believe that mobile services computing will embrace more and more real application scenarios both from industry and our daily life.

This book would not have been possible without many contributors whose names did not make it to the cover. We would like to give our special thanks to Dr. Longtao Huang who graduated from our research group already but contributed a lot in the research of mobile services computing, as well as some Ph.D. candidates in our group including Mr. Zhengzhe Xiang, Mr. Cheng Zhang, Ms. Yishan Chen, Mr. Guanjie Cheng, and Mr. Hailiang Zhao. For a long time already, it has been our pleasure to do research with them in mobile services computing. They have devoted their energy and enthusiasm to this area and relevant research projects.

The work in this book was mainly supported by the National Key Research and Development Program of China (No. 2017YFB1400601), National Science Foundation of China (No. 61772461), and Natural Science Foundation of Zhejiang Province (No. LR18F020003).

Hangzhou, China　　　　　　　　　　　　　　　　　　　　Shuiguang Deng
January 2020　　　　　　　　　　　　　　　　　　　　　　Hongyue Wu
　　　　　　　　　　　　　　　　　　　　　　　　　　　　　Jianwei Yin

Contents

Chapter 1
Services Computing: A Brief Overview

Abstract Services computing provides techniques for the construction, operation and management of large-scale internet service systems. It represents the frontier development direction of software engineering and distributed computing; thus, it has always been a research hotspot and attracted increasing attention from both industry and academia. This chapter introduces the concepts and perspectives, research framework and evolution history of services computing, and gives a preliminary introduction for mobile services computing.

1.1 Concepts and Perspectives

1.1.1 Concepts of Services Computing

Although services computing has developed for such a long period, it has not a unified concept. As it is in a continuously developing process, its definition and connotation are also ever-changing. Experts and scholars have different understandings for services computing from different perspectives.

IEEE, from the discipline perspective, defines services computing as "Services computing is a basic discipline that crosses computers, information technology, commercial management and consultation services. Its objective is to use service science and service technology to eliminate the gap between commercial services and information technology services [1]."

Maria E. Orlowska and Sanjiva Weerawarana, from the distributed computing perspective, think that "Services computing is a kind of distributed computing paradigm evolved from object-oriented and component-oriented computing. It makes different commercial application systems that are distributed within the enterprises or across the border of enterprises achieving rapid, flexible seamless integration and cooperation [2]."

© Zhejiang University Press and Springer Nature Singapore Pte Ltd. 2020
S. Deng et al., *Mobile Service Computing*, Advanced Topics in Science
and Technology in China 58, https://doi.org/10.1007/978-981-15-5921-1_1

Mike P. Papazoglou, from the software design and development perspective, thinks that "Services computing is a way of developing application systems with services as the basic elements [3]."

Munindar P. Singh and Michael N. Huhns, from the application of services technology, think that "Services computing is the set of technologies that combine service concept, service system architecture, service technology and service infrastructure together to guide how to use these services [4]."

In 2017, 24 well-known scholars in services computing area published "A Service Computing Manifesto" in *Communications of the Acm*. They defined services computing as the discipline that seeks to develop computational abstractions, architectures, techniques, and tools to support services broadly. Services computing is a service orientation that seeks to transform physical, hardware and software assets into a paradigm in which users and assets establish on-demand interactions, binding resources and operations, providing an abstraction layer that shifts the focus from infrastructure and operations to services [5].

The definitions above were formed from different perspectives and in different developmental periods of services computing. To sum up, we think that services computing is put forward in terms of dynamic, versatile, and complex internet environments. It is a new computing discipline with web service and service-oriented system architecture as the basic supporting technology, service composition as the main software development approach, and service-oriented software analysis and design principles as the basic ideas [6]. Service is the most important and core concept in the technical framework of services computing.

1.1.2 Two Perspectives of Understanding Services Computing

From the perspective of software engineering, services computing is a software methodology system, with services as the core and service-oriented architecture as the main technology. In this methodology system, services are the basic elements to construct large-scale and complex software. Here services refer to software entities that are based on the network environment and characterized by adaptive ability, self-description, modularity, and good interoperability. Service-oriented architecture lays the most important technical foundation for the software methodology system. It is a loose, flexible, scalable, distributed software architecture scheme that is formed to be adapted to the dynamic, distributed, autonomous, and transparent services computing environment.

From the perspective of distributed computing, services computing is a kind of computing paradigm to achieve distributed cooperation. In services computing environment, all kinds of computing devices and software resources are highly distributed and autonomous. Services computing models them as adaptive, modular, interoperable and loosely coupled function modules, i.e. services, and applies service-oriented architecture and service composition technologies to integrate and compose them to large-scale software systems, and thus to realize distributed cooperation. In this way, services computing achieves rapid, flexible and seamless integration and cooperation for distributed software and application systems.

1.2   Research Frameworks and Hotspots

1.2.1   Technology System of Services Computing

Services computing, as an independent computing discipline, involves a series of key technologies and research issues, which together form the technical framework of services computing. IBM (International Business Machines Corporation) proposed the technology system of services computing, shown as Fig. 1.1, which contains three parts: key technologies of services computing, supporting technologies and industrial applications.

Among the key technologies of services computing, Service-Oriented Architecture (SOA) is a widely adopted architectural pattern. Web services and business process management are commonly used technologies to implement this architecture and to enable IT services and computing technology to perform business services more efficiently and effectively. Web services standards (W3C) and business process standards (OASIS) are the common standards for Web services and business process

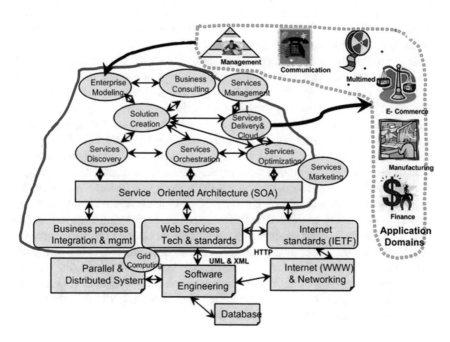

Fig. 1.1 Technology system of services computing

management, respectively. Services computing technologies are involved throughout the whole lifecycle of service innovation research, including business consulting, enterprise modeling, solution creation, services discovery, services orchestration, services delivery, services marketing, services optimization, as well as services management.

Services computing is closely related to the Internet (WWW) and networking technologies, parallel & distributed system technologies, software engineering, database technologies, etc. These technologies serve as technical support platforms for services computing.

Services computing technologies can be used to serve multiple industries, including management, communication, multimedia, e-commerce, manufacturing, finance application, etc. Currently, the modern service industry mainly focuses on these vertical industries. For example, manufacturing, as one of the application areas of services computing, can use the systematic technology and methods of services computing to improve existing manufacturing services, as well as to create new manufacturing service systems.

1.2.2   Research Road Map of Services Computing

Mike P. Papazoglou extended the basic SOA to a research road map [7], shown in Fig. 1.2, which separates the functionality of services computing into three planes: service description and basic operations at the bottom, service composition in the middle, and service management on the top.

This layered architecture utilizes the basic SOA as its bottom layer, which involves the roles (service provider, service client and service aggregator), basic operations (publication, discovery, selection, and binding), descriptions (capability, interface, behavior and QoS), and the relationships among them.

The service composition layer encompasses necessary techniques and functions for the coordination, conformance, monitoring and QoS description of composite services. Specifically, coordination controls the execution of component services and manages the dataflow among them to make them work together in an efficient and organized way. Conformance ensures the integrity of composite services by matching parameters and interfaces between component services to ensure successful interactions, as well as perform data fusion activities. Monitoring aims to find and report events or exceptions produced by component services, in order to ensure the correctness and overall functionality of composite services, and thus to forecast, avoid and handle risks in time. QoS describes the overall QoS values of composite services by aggregating the QoS of their component services according to their composite structures, e.g. sequence, choice and parallel. Common QoS criteria include cost, response time, security, reliability and so on.

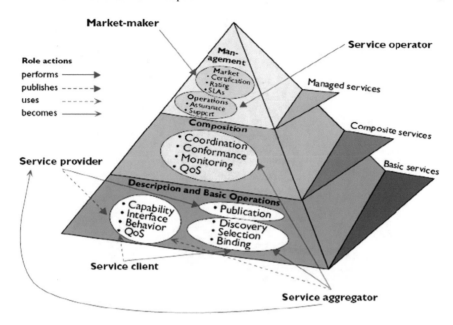

Fig. 1.2   Research road map of services computing

The top layer of the research road map is management, which consists of two components: market and operations. The service market aims at providing market-places for service suppliers and consumers, as well as performing marketplace functions. The purpose is to offer a comprehensive range of trading techniques, including service certification and service rating, and manage the negotiation and enforcement of service level agreements (SLAs). Another aim of the service management layer is to provide operation functionality for service management. In particular, SOA's operation management aims at supporting the management of the service platform, the deployment of services and the applications. Operation management functionality assure that service transactions go through successfully and service activities are implemented normally.

1.2.3   Technical Framework of Services Computing

The technical framework of services computing is proposed in [6]. It provides technical support for service development, service convergence, service application and service system design. Accordingly, these issues can be divided into four layers from bottom to top: service resource layer, service convergence layer, service application layer, and service system layer, as shown in Fig. 1.3.

The service resource layer is the bottom layer of the framework. This layer realizes the service standardization of various heterogeneous data and software resources.

Fig. 1.3 Technical framework of services computing

It provides basic techniques to build data and software resources into services. Through the service resource layer, heterogeneous data and software resources can be transformed into standard services, ensuring services invoked in a convenient, rapid, and transparent way. Service resource layer mainly involves the necessary standards, techniques, and methods for services, such as service standard, service language, service protocol, etc., and the techniques for service realization, such as service development, service encapsulation, service testing, service deployment, service publication, etc., among which, service deployment is a research hotspot of services computing. Service deployment aims to deploy standard services on devices, servers or platforms, thus allowing users to invoke these services seamlessly and conveniently.

The second layer is the service convergence layer. The purpose of this layer is to promote the integration, cooperation and composition of standard services. To this end, this layer provides a series of standards, technologies, and methods for the collaboration of services, as well as the management of service flows that consist of many services. The involved techniques in this layer include service integration, service coordination, service composition, service orchestration, service choreography, service relationship and service flow. Specifically, service composition is a research hotspot in services computing area. Service composition is adopted particularly when a single service cannot fulfill users' requests, to compose several services to a large-grained composite service to fulfill users' complex requests.

The service application layer offers the basic technical and methodological support for service invocations. The technologies involved in this layer are the most popular technologies in current services computing research and development. Specifically, it consists of technologies including service selection, service recommendation, service computation offloading, service provisioning, etc. Service selection is used to select the most suitable services for service requests when there is more than one available candidate service. Service recommendation aims to predict the preference of service users and recommend the most suitable services for users. Service computation offloading is a technique to offload service execution to other devices, servers or platforms in order to save time, energy or resources. It is used mostly when services are executed on resource-limited devices. Service provisioning addresses the problems in service provisioning processes with the objective of facilitating service provisioning and improving service quality.

The service system layer is the top layer of the services computing framework. Based on the techniques in the service application layer, the service system layer is a set of standards, techniques, and methods to guide the design, development, operation, and management of service-oriented software systems under service-oriented computing environment [6]. Issues in this layer include service adaption, service management, enterprise service bus and service-oriented architecture (SOA). These techniques have been researched for more than one decade and are relatively mature now.

1.2.4 Key Knowledge Areas of Services Computing

In 2008, ACM (Association for Computing Machinery) summarized the research points of services computing as 14 key knowledge areas, shown in Fig. 1.4. Generally, these knowledge areas can be categorized into four categories [8].

Principle of Services (M1)	Business Grid and Cloud Computing (M8)
Services Lifecycle (M2)	Enterprise Modeling and Management (M9)
Web Services (M3)	Service-Oriented Consulting Methodology (M10)
Service-Oriented Architecture (M4)	Services Delivery Platform and Methodology (M11)
Services Relationships (M5)	Application Services and Standards (M12)
Services Composition (M6)	Security, Privacy, and Trust in Services Computing (M13)
Business Process Management & Integration (M7)	Services Management (M14)

Fig. 1.4 Key knowledge areas of services computing

The first category is about services and service systems. It consists of the principle of services (M1) and the services lifecycle (M2). In detail, the principle of services involves the principles of services systems, services models, services technologies, services architectures, and optimization of services systems. Services lifecycle includes six phases: consulting and strategic planning, services engagement, services delivery, services operation, services billing, and services management.

The second category is service technologies. It contains Web services (M3), service-oriented architecture (M4), services relationships (M5), services composition (M6), and business process management & integration (M7). The knowledge areas of Web services include Web services modeling, Web services communication protocols, Web services binding, Web services registry, stateful Web services, and Web services interoperability, etc. Service-oriented architecture (SOA) involves services invocation, bridging business and IT architecture, solution lifecycle, and solution reference architecture. The knowledge area of services relationships covers Web services relationship language and service-oriented relationship modeling. Services composition involves services integration framework, and services value chain collaboration. The knowledge area of business process management and integration includes business process modeling, service-oriented business process management, and flexible business process integration.

The third category is services consulting and delivery. It consists of business grid and cloud computing (M8), enterprise modeling and management (M9), service-oriented consulting methodology (M10), and services delivery platform and methodology (M11). Business grid and cloud computing include service-oriented grid computing, business grid solution framework, cloud computing, logical grid infrastructure, and business grid solution development. The enterprise modeling and management area includes dynamics of services ecosystem, requirements for enterprise modeling, methodologies for enterprise modeling, and enterprise performance management. The knowledge area of service-oriented consulting methodology includes consulting method for strategic change, consulting method for IT strategic plan and service-oriented business consulting. Services delivery platform and methodology include services delivery mechanisms, services delivery platform, services delivery methodology, software as a service, and services as software.

The fourth category is service solutioning and management. It covers application services and standards (M12), security, privacy, and trust in services computing (M13), and services management (M14). Specifically, the application services and standards area includes solution-level quality of services, data architecture framework, QoS management modeling, Web services standard stack, and industry-specific standards. The security, privacy, and trust in services areas include access control in services systems, security enablement in services systems, privacy management in services systems, concerns of service-oriented solutions, privacy concerns of service-oriented solutions, and trust in service-oriented solutions. The knowledge area of IT services management includes management of services design, management of services delivery, application management in services, infrastructure management in services, and business and IT aligned management services.

1.2.5   Research Hotspots in Services Computing

With the continuous development of computer-related technologies, the research hotspots of services computing have also shown a specific variation trend. In order to grasp the research hotspots of services computing in the past years, we selected 21 conferences and 20 journals that are most representative and authoritative in services computing area and conducted a statistic on all papers published there from 2005 to 2019.

First, we depict the topics of these papers by word cloud, shown as Fig. 1.5. from which, we can see that the service system, service model and Web services are the most popular research topics in the past years. Moreover, service application, service framework, service network, service analysis and dynamic services also attracted a lot of attention. The rest topics varies widely: some topics are classical service problems, such as modeling, management, composition, etc.; some topics are services related technologies, including scheduling, prediction, clustering, etc.; some topics are about service performance, such as efficient, adaptive, dynamic, real-time, automatic, secure, etc.

Furthermore, we counted the appearance number of hot keywords that appeared in these papers. The result is shown in Fig. 1.6, from which, we can see that "web services" and "web services" are the most popular keywords that are far ahead of others. "Sensor networks", "real-time", "large scale" and "service composition" appeared as keywords more than 400 times, followed by "big data", "cloud computing" and "wireless sensor", which are appeared as keywords more than 200 times.

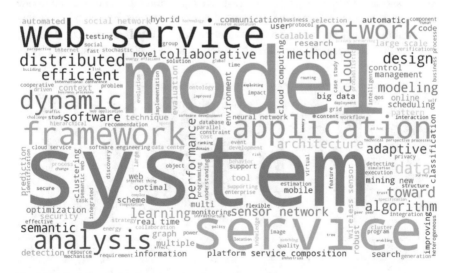

Fig. 1.5 Word cloud of topics of services computing

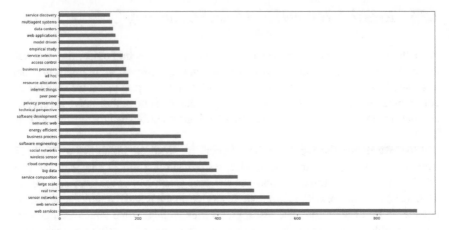

Fig. 1.6 Appearance number of hot key words

For the sake of a deeper analysis of the research trend of services computing, we selected 20 research topics based on the statistical results above and recorded the yearly popularity of these focuses. The heat of each research focus is calculated on the number they appeared in the title, abstract or keywords of given papers. According to the statistics based on this rule, we drew a violin plot to show the variation trend of these research topics, as shown in Fig. 1.7.

In Fig. 1.7, the width of violins represents the heat of corresponding research focus, data of the red violins are original data, and data of the blue and green violins are five and ten times to original data, respectively. From the result, we can divide these research hotspots into three categories: hotspots that just begun, hotspots that are continuing, and hotspots that have already faded. Topics in the first category are becoming increasingly popular. These topics include cloud service, quality of

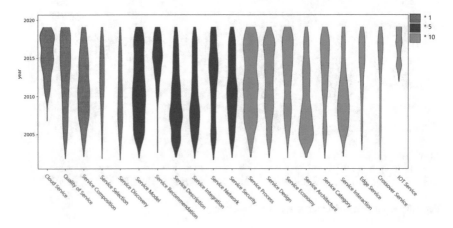

Fig. 1.7 Violin plot of research topics

services, service economy, edge services and IoT services, etc. Topics in the second category include service composition, service model, service network, etc. These topics are still hot topics and their heat is still continuing. The heat of topics in the third category is decreasing. These topics consist of service discovery, service integration, service architecture, etc.

Gartner, the world's biggest IT consultancy, has come up with Gartner Hype Cycle, illustrating that all new technologies go through five stages after their emergence. The first stage is Innovation Trigger. In this stage, technologies are new concepts and it is hard to assess their commercial potential. The second stage is Peak of Inflated Expectations. It is a phase of overenthusiasm and unrealistic projections, which results in some successes but more failures as the technology is pushed to its limits. The third stage is Trough of Disillusionment, when the limitations and shortcomings of technologies are gradually exposed, and their interest begins to wane. The fourth stage is Slope of Enlightenment. In this stage, the advantages and disadvantages of technologies become more and more obvious, and the details become clear. The fifth stage is Plateau of Productivity, when technologies become mainstream and technical standards are clearly defined. Based on the characteristics of this model, we can get the Gartner Hype Cycle of topics in services computing area, as shown in Fig. 1.8.

As can be seen from the plot, emerging service technologies and concepts such as crossover service, service network, IoT service, service design and edge service are currently during the innovation trigger stage. That is to say, they have the potential to become hot topics in the coming period. Service security, service economy, service process, cloud service, quality of service and service category are during peak of inflated expectations stage, as they have maintained their research heat for a period of time and formed some theoretical systems and had some applications. These issues will still attract a lot of research attention, meanwhile many theoretical defects will be exposed. As some of the initial research focus in the field of services computing, service composition, service recommendation, service model, service

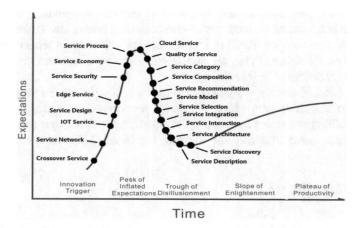

Fig. 1.8 Gartner hype cycle of topics in services computing area

selection, service integration, service architecture, service discovery and service description have achieved lots of research achievements, but it has yet to find a way to integrate fully with industry. At present, the academic research on these issues is gradually decreasing. The next focus is to convert these research results into industrial value and make them enter into the fourth stage, i.e. slope of enlightenment.

1.3   The Evolution with Different Waves and Stages

1.3.1   Seven Waves

In the past years, with the emergence of new techniques such as cloud computing, mobile computing, big data, etc., the research hotspots of services computing are ever-changing. IEEE Fellow, the editor-in-chief of the flagship journal of services computing, *IEEE Transaction on Services Computing*, Ling Liu summarized that the evolution of services computing has undergone seven waves since its birth [9]:

(1) Web services represent the first weave of services computing, where web services are facilitating the eCommerce and eBusiness.
(2) Social computing services represent the second weave of services computing, where social media and online community are facilitating the interactive computing and the social collaboration between people.
(3) Mobile services can be viewed as the third wave of services computing by offering location-based content delivery, location-based entertainment, and location-based advertisement.
(4) Enterprise computing represented by web hosting services and data center computing services represents the fourth wave of services computing where applications are served by stand-alone data centers.
(5) Cloud services represent the fifth wave of services computing, pushing the vision of delivering the hardware infrastructure as a service (IaaS), the software platform as a service (PaaS) and the application software as a service (SaaS).
(6) Big data and data analytics can be viewed as the emerging trend and the sixth wave for services computing.
(7) The vision of making everything as a service will represent the seventh wave of services computing, which will enrich the services computing ecosystem by enabling everything from computing power, network management, business processes, personal interactions to Internet of things (IoT) as a service.

1.3.2   Three Stages

The seven waves represent the research hotspots in the evolution process of services computing from the technical and topical perspective, while from the perspective of

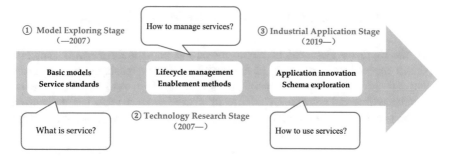

Fig. 1.9 Developmental stages of services computing

research scope and content, the development process of services computing can be divided into three stages, as shown in Fig. 1.9:

(1)   This first stage is the service model exploring stage, which started from the birth of services computing and continues to around 2007. The core problem in this stage is what is service. During this stage, basic service models and standards are addressed mostly. As a result, various industrial standards for web services, semantic Web service models and simple service application methods were proposed.

(2)   The second stage is the service technology research stage, which started from 2007 till now. The core problem of this stage is how to manage services. During this stage, service lifecycle management and enablement methods attracted the most attention. Consequently, a large number of service lifecycle management methods were proposed to resolve problems of service discovery, service recommendation, service composition, service verification, etc.

(3)   The third stage is the service industrial application stage, which just started recently and still in its initial phase. This stage focus on the problem of how to use services. The objective of this stage is bridging the gap among services computing technology, business and economy and application from a multi-discipline perspective, as well as exploring the law of the new service application domain.

Currently, services computing is undergoing the transition from stage 2 to stage 3. Service techniques are becoming increasingly mature, while there are still constantly new techniques proposed to resolve newly emerged problems. Meanwhile, stage 3 has already come. On entering this stage, new service theories and concepts begin to appear, such as service value theory, service pattern computing, service economy, big service, crossover service, experience service, mobile service, etc. In this book, we address services computing problems in mobile environment, which is a cross-discipline and new service application schema.

1.4 When Services Computing Meets Mobile Computing

With the rapid development of cloud computing and mobile networks, mobile systems, especially smartphones, have been playing an increasingly important role in our daily life. The ubiquity of mobile devices has enabled us to access services on the Web anytime and anywhere. Consequently, more and more services are invoked via mobile systems. Therefore, complex and volatile mobile systems have evolved into extremely important services computing platforms.

Although both services computing and mobile computing have been studied for many years, their combination, mobile services computing, hasn't been widely researched. Mobile services computing mainly focuses on services computing problems in mobile environments. In mobile services computing, mobile devices can play the roles of consumers, brokers, and providers simultaneously. That is to say, mobile devices can not only invoke services via wireless networks but also be deployed with services and provide them to others.

Mobile services computing is undoubtedly enabling us to provide and access services easily and conveniently, which greatly facilitates our life, work, and study. However, as we describe here, the application of mobile services computing still faces challenges due to limitations such as constant mobility of users, unstable network environments, and limited resources and capability of mobile service providers.

Currently, some works have been proposed to resolve these problems. Generally, these works are from two perspectives, namely users and providers. From the users' perspective, some research works focus on service selection. As different services have different execution time, input and output parameters, service selection can adjust the location where parameters are transferred. These works aim to select appropriate services to make service parameters transferred in good network condition, and thus to improve the QoS of services, reduce the energy consumption, and lower the risks. Moreover, some researchers pay attention to mobile service offloading, which aims to extend the computing ability and resources of mobile devices by offloading some tasks to the cloud or edge servers. These works can make decisions on whether to offload a specific task and where to offload it. From the perspective of service providers, some researchers address the problem of dynamic service deployment in mobile devices and mobile edge computing systems. Due to limited capability and resources, mobile devices and mobile edge servers can only be deployed with a limited number of services, so current works concentrate on dynamically deploying and replacing services on them to fulfill users' service requirements. Another hot topic of mobile services computing is efficient service provision, which aims to improve the service provisioning ability of resource-limited mobile servers and edge servers. To achieve this goal, researchers have proposed methods and technologies for effective service request selection, request dispatching, service scheduling and resource allocation.

Therefore, in this book, we address those main problems in mobile services computing and introduce related models, theories, technologies and methods to resolve these problems. Specifically, the contents of each chapter are briefly introduced as follows:

This Chapter presents a brief overview of services computing, including the concepts and perspectives, research issues and frameworks, evolution and development process of services computing, and gives a preliminary introduction for mobile services computing.

Chapter 2 introduces mobile services computing in detail from the perspectives of opportunities and challenges. It presents the typical mobile services computing patterns and discusses the main research issues of both service provision and service consumption.

Chapter 3 addresses mobile service selection problems and proposes three service selection methods to resolve three kinds of service selection problems respectively.

Chapter 4 focuses on mobile service recommendation problems and presents three kinds of service recommendation methods.

Chapter 5 aims at mobile service composition problems and introduces three service composition methods with different objectives.

Chapter 6 addresses mobile service deployment problems from the perspective of service providers and proposes three methods for service deployment on edge servers.

Chapter 7 addresses services computation offloading problems in both mobile cloud computing and mobile edge computing and presents corresponding methods.

Chapter 8 focuses on mobile service provisioning with respect to mobile servers and edge servers and introduces three service provisioning methods.

References

1. L. Zhang, J. Zhang et al., in *Services Computing* (Springer, 2007)
2. M.E. Orlowska, S. Weerawarana, et al. (eds.), in *Proceeding of First International Conference on Service-Oriented Computing* (Springer, 2003)
3. M.P. Papazoglou, D. Georgakopoulos, Introduction to a special issue on service-oriented computing. Commun. ACM **46**(10), 24–28 (2003)
4. M.P. Singh, M.N. Huhns, in *Service-Oriented Computing: Semantics, Processes, Agents* (John Wiley & Sons, Ltd., 2005)
5. A. Bouguettaya, M. Singh, M. Huhns et al., A service computing manifesto: the next 10 years. Commun. ACM **4**(64), 72. https://doi.org/10.1145/2983528
6. W. Zhaohui, S. Deng, W. Jian, *Service Computing: Concept, Method and Technology* (Elsevier/Academic Press, Cambridge, 2014)
7. M. P. Papazoglou, D. Georgakopoulos. Service Oriented Computing. Communications of the ACM, October 2003
8. L.-J. Zhang, C.K. Chang, in Towards Services Computing Curriculum. Congress on Services—Part I (SERVICES'08), pp. 23–32 (2008)
9. Ling Liu, Editorial': service computing in the next seven years. IEEE Trans. Serv. Comput. **7**(4), 529 (2014)

Chapter 2
Mobile Services Computing: Opportunities and Challenges

Abstract Services computing offers an overwhelming paradigm for service provision and consumption. It's now embracing new opportunities in the mobile Internet era, which is characterized by ubiquitous wireless connectivity and powerful smart devices enabling us to consume or even provide services anytime and anywhere. This chapter gives an insight into the new generation of services computing paradigm, i.e., mobile services computing. It proposes its application patterns and analyzes the main challenges from both the perspectives of service provision and service consumption as well.

2.1 Introduction

Services computing, which covers the science and technology of bridging the gap between business services and IT services, has attracted more and more attention from both industry and academia [1]. Services are defined as software artifacts that are autonomous, self-described, reusable, and highly portable. They are used as basic units to build rapid, low-cost, secure and reliable applications. Thus, services computing provides such a paradigm that saves the cost of developing new software components each time for a new business process. With the prevalence of emerging techniques such as cloud computing and mobile computing, the provision and consumption of services are changing [2].

Due to the rapid developments in mobile devices and wireless technologies, the use of mobile devices is growing drastically. The huge potential of mobile technology brings great opportunities for traditional services computing into mobile environment. With increased processing power and devices capabilities, mobile devices extend their usage in various application domains. Although services computing and mobile computing have been studied for many years respectively, their combination (mobile services computing) hasn't been widely researched. Thanks to the development and utilization of mobile computing technologies, services are no longer limited to traditional contexts and platforms. They can be deployed on mobile devices or cloud servers and delivered over wireless networks. Mobile devices may play the roles of consumers, brokers, and providers at the same time. Mobile services delivered

© Zhejiang University Press and Springer Nature Singapore Pte Ltd. 2020
S. Deng et al., *Mobile Service Computing*, Advanced Topics in Science
and Technology in China 58, https://doi.org/10.1007/978-981-15-5921-1_2

through mobile techniques are nowadays emerging as a promising technology for the extension of traditional services computing. It is not doubtful that mobile services computing has enabled us to provide and access services anytime and anywhere, which greatly facilitates our life, work and study. However, the application of mobile services computing still faces challenges due to the following main limitations.

- **Constant Mobility**: Mobile devices may frequently change locations, which results in the variation and alteration of wireless networks. For service consumers, the variation may impact the Quality-of-Service (QoS) of invoked mobile services and the alteration may lead to failure. While for service providers, services they provide may become temporarily unreachable due to the failure of wireless connections, and the change of network address may lead to the services cannot be addressed. Thus, how to handle users' mobility is a major challenge for providing reliable mobile services in highly dynamic mobile wireless environments.
- **Limited Capability**: Although the capabilities of mobile devices have improved in terms of processing power, memory space, and embedded sensors, they continue to lag behind other computing devices. Mobile devices (smartphones in particular) are still recognized as resource-constrained computing devices. So, the challenge is how to deploy mobile services on mobile devices and schedule computational resources for them properly in order to make the services performed with high QoS with resource constraints.
- **Restricted Power**: Although the past years have witnessed the advances in battery technology for mobile devices, which improve their stand-by time to a great extent, it is still a big challenge for a user to keep his/her mobile device working as long as possible while using it to deal with business or amusement constantly. Since the energy consumption of mobile devices occurs during the execution of mobile services, it is important to provide an energy saving mechanism to keep mobile devices working as long as possible while using them to provide or access services.
- **Unguaranteed Security**: For mobile service consumers, service invocation through mobile networks are facing the risks of eavesdropping and attacks. While for mobile service providers, they may be troubled by frauds and fake transactions, and their personal privacy data may be stolen by the service consumers.
- **Undetermined willingness**: With the improvement of the capabilities of mobile devices, mobile devices can also perform as service providers to share their computing capability, resource and applications. However, as the capability, battery and resources are limited, and some services are related to personal privacy, mobile providers cannot provide services for some consumers at some time. Therefore, how to predict the willingness of mobile providers and decide whether a mobile service should be provided is still a big challenge.

Compared to the traditional services computing, which is characterized by powerful service hosts, relatively stable networks, and simple interaction patterns, mobile services computing suffering from the above five inherent limitations has completely different application patterns, which bring great challenges for both service provision and consumption.

2.2   Application Patterns of Mobile Services Computing

For traditional services computing, services such as Google and Amazon web services are always deployed on fixed servers. These services are consumed by stationery clients through their specified addresses. The service communication pattern of traditional services is static with the stationery service providers and consumers. However, the traditional pattern and context are broken by mobile devices, which can be used to provide or consume services. According to the mobility of service providers and consumers, we divide the application patterns of mobile services computing into three types (shown as Fig. 2.1): (1) *Cloud-to-Mobile Pattern* (C2M), (2) *Mobile-to-Mobile Pattern* (M2M), and (3) *Hybrid Pattern.*

2.2.1   Cloud-to-Mobile Pattern

The C2M pattern is widely used nowadays, which combines cloud computing and mobile computing together, where services are deployed on no-moving cloud servers and consumed by moving consumers through their mobile devices. For this pattern, mobile devices are linked to the mobile networks through base stations that establish

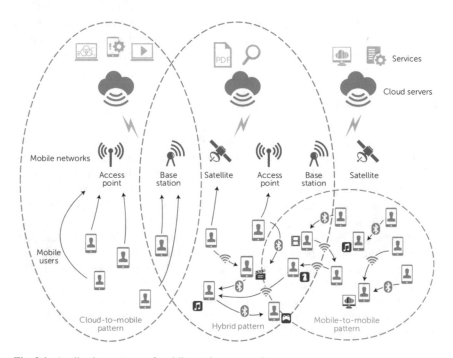

Fig. 2.1 Application patterns of mobile services computing

and manage the connections between mobile devices and networks. Mobile service consumers' requests and information are delivered to a cloud server through the mobile Internet. Then the cloud server processes the requests and provides mobile consumers with the corresponding services. After the execution of the requested services, the results are also returned through mobile networks. For example, Tom wants to invoke a weather forecast service of Amazon through his mobile phone. First, he submits his request through the mobile network to the cloud of Amazon; then the servers on the cloud process this request and generate a result; finally, the result is sent back to the mobile phone of Tom. The C2M pattern utilizes the advantages of both cloud computing and mobile computing (e.g., mobility, computation power, and portability) and has the following three advantages.

- **Context Awareness**: In the C2M pattern, mobile users' real-time contexts (such as location, weather, and activity) can be probed by multiple sensors on mobile devices. Through processing such contextual information by powerful cloud servers, mobile users' requests can be met in diverse contexts and environments.
- **Capability Extension**: Constrained capacity, such as storage and processing, is also a concern for mobile devices. The C2M pattern can support mobile consumers to store/process big data on the cloud through mobile networks. Thus, all the complex computations that cost a long time when executed on mobile devices will be processed fast on the cloud.
- **Energy Saving**: Battery is one of the main concerns for mobile devices. The C2M pattern migrates the large and complex computation tasks from resource-limited mobile devices to powerful cloud servers. This can avoid a long execution time spent on mobile devices and results in a large amount of energy consumption.

2.2.2   Mobile-to-Mobile Pattern

The M2M pattern provides a more Peer-to-Peer framework, where services are deployed on mobile devices and delivered over wireless networks (such as Bluetooth, WLAN, and Near Field Communication), where mobile devices may play the role of consumer or provider. In this case, both the service providers and consumers are moving in a limited range such as a campus or a museum. In this case, they form a temporary ad hoc community and share their services to construct a mobile service sharing paradigm. For example, Peter has developed an air-conditioner control application and installed it on his mobile phone to control the air-conditioner in his house. All his guests can visit his mobile phone through WLAN or Bluetooth and invoke this application to control the air-conditioner.

M2M pattern offers a new set of applications that were not explored much before, mainly due to the limitations of capabilities of traditional mobile devices. It has the following major potential advantages.

- *Internet Independency*: In the M2M pattern, the communication between mobile users is based on free wireless networks such as Bluetooth, WLAN, and Near Field Communication instead of connecting to the Internet. Mobile users can access service from other peer mobile users directly through these communication techniques instead of stationary servers through mobile Internet. Thus, they can save the cost of the mobile Internet fee.
- *Ubiquitous Service Sharing*: The M2M pattern can encourage service sharing among mobile users. Mobile users can share their own services with each other through free wireless communication. They directly pay to each other for the interacted mobile services. For example, a payment strategy can be implemented according to credit rules where users who share services on their own mobile devices can earn credits and consumers pay credit to invoke provided services. Thus, small mobile operators can set up their own mobile service business without resorting to stationary office structures.
- *Emergency Handling*: Under some emergency situations such as earthquakes and storms, the Internet connection is unavailable. With the help of the M2M pattern, mobile users can build a temporary service flow to meet an emergency task through invoking services provided by nearby mobile devices.

2.2.3 Hybrid Pattern

Although the C2M and M2M have their own advantages respectively, purely using either pattern also has some limits. Thus, mobile users should make decisions between the two patterns with the following concerns.

- *Security concern*: In general, the C2M pattern is more secure than the M2M pattern. On one hand, it is more reliable for service consumers to send their data to cloud servers than to other peer mobile users. On the other hand, for a mobile service provider in M2M, it may also bear the risk of receiving malicious service requesting.
- *Communication concern*: In the C2M pattern, it is only available when the network is accessible, and it may generate much cost on communication fee and spend much transmission time if the service consumer sends massive data through the cellular network. However, the communication between nearby mobile devices might take less time and no money cost.
- *Efficiency concern*: Currently, the processing capability of cloud servers is much stronger than mobile devices. If a mobile consumer wants to invoke a computation-intensive service, it is better to choose a service deployed on clouds rather than on a mobile device.

- *Context concern*: Through M2M pattern, mobile service providers are capable of providing various environmental context information collected by embedded sensors, so consumers can obtain some environmental information such as temperature, humidity, atmospheric pressure, which are not obtainable via C2M.

To make a trade-off among the above concerns, a hybrid pattern consisting of both the C2M and M2M patterns can be considered. In the hybrid pattern, a service consumer can switch between C2M and M2M according to his requirements and preferences. Figure 2.1 also gives an example of a hybrid application pattern of mobile services computing, where there exist services provided by cloud servers and mobile devices at the same time and mobile users can request either kind of services. Specifically, if the consumer requires a service with high security, he should choose the C2M pattern; the M2M pattern is better for him, if the network is weak or there is no data traffic left in his plan; if the required service is computation-intensive, he should choose C2M; if the service is context-aware, he can only realize the invocation through M2M.

2.3 Mobile Service Provision

Service provision normally takes place at the side of service providers. It requires providers not only to describe their services with sufficient information to make them discovered and invoked by more consumers, but also to run their services with promised QoS. Service provision in C2M pattern has no difference with it in traditional services computing, as services are deployed on no-moving cloud servers and invoked through the Internet and service provision cannot be influenced by consumers. While for M2M, it becomes different, as services are deployed on mobile devices and invoked via WLAN, Bluetooth or other networks. Therefore, we mainly discuss the challenges for mobile service provision in M2M pattern, which includes the description of mobile services, service provision and energy management for mobile services executed on mobile devices.

2.3.1 How to Describe Mobile Services

In traditional services computing, services are usually described by some definition language, which covers the description of functional and non-functional information of the services. Then service providers would publish their services' description files to a public service repository. Describing a service properly is important because the description can notify users with the existence of such a service and provide all the required information to invoke it. While in mobile services computing, the features of mobile services computing such as uncertain availability of mobile providers and unstable communication in mobile networks present new challenges for mobile service description.

How to describe the availability of services? As mobile providers and consumers are always in constant moving and are likely to move out of the limited communication distance at some time, the availability of their services is difficult to be guaranteed all the time. If a service provider moves out of the available place during the service invocation process, the invocation will fail. Therefore, the description of services provided should contain the description of services themselves and moving information of providers. A mobile model should be constructed to describe the moving information of mobile service providers. The moving information can be provided by the mobile providers themselves or be predicted using the trajectory prediction techniques such as hidden Markov mode [3] and semi-lazy approach [4].

As the resource and capability of mobile devices are always limited, mobile service providers should reject some service requests to ensure the normal operation of themselves. For example, if the CPU of the mobile provider is overload or the battery is low, the provider may reject some computation-intensive service request. Besides, as mobile service providers are always personal devices, some privacy-related services are only accessible to consumers with certain authority. Therefore, the resource usage and battery situations of devices and invocation privilege are also should be involved in the description of mobile services.

With the moving of service providers, the mobile network through which mobile providers connect to the internet may be changed. If a request is sent to a provider after the change of its network address, it will fail to find the provider. Therefore, the moving information, resource usage and battery situations of devices as well as the network information should be updated in time. A reasonable heartbeat mechanism can be adopted to update the situation of mobile service providers [5]. The heartbeat mechanism is to update the real-time network address, the resource conditions and the moving information of mobile service providers regularly. It is hard to determine the frequency of heartbeat mechanism, since a low heartbeat frequency cannot guarantee the real-time information of service providers, while a high heartbeat frequency can lead to high network traffic and energy consumption. Therefore, the heartbeat frequency needs to be dynamically adjusted according to the situation change rate and the resource utilization of service providers. Specifically, if a provider is moving quickly, its situation should be updated more frequently, and if its resources are overloaded or the battery is low, the situation should be updated infrequently.

Through the heartbeat mechanism, the situation of mobile service providers can be updated in time. Service consumers can search the service repository to acquire the information of available services. The availability of services can be reflected through the network conditions, resource utilization situation, battery level, moving information, etc., of mobile service providers. It is intuitive that high network strength implies high availability and low network strength implies low availability. If the required resources of a service request are currently overloaded, it means that the availability of the service is low for that request. The moving information of mobile service providers can reflect the future availability of services provided. If a provider is moving toward locations with poor network or moving far away from the consumer (for communication through Bluetooth or Near Field Communication), the availability of the service is becoming lower for the consumer.

2.3.2 How to Perform Service Provision

With the advance in the capability of mobile devices, it becomes realistic to deploy services on mobile devices, which makes it considered as potential data collector and service provider. Deploying services on mobile devices enables to deliver real-time contextual services, such as location-based and health monitoring services. However, besides the dynamic characteristics of mobile networks, there are many other problems for service provision. Challenges for deploying mobile services are summarized as the following aspects.

Security: Considering that mobile service providers are always personal devices, they may be troubled by frauds and fake transactions and their personal privacy may be invaded by service consumers. Therefore, service consumers should be grouped according to the relationship with the provider or the integrity grade and each group is assigned with an authority to invoke services. Each resource (e.g. album or address book) and service is only accessible to consumers with corresponding authorities. For example, the address book of a provider can only be visited by his relatives.

Lightweight framework: Services provided on mobile devices are considered as value-added functions of mobile holders. They should not impact their main functions such as phone calls, texting, etc., too much. Therefore, lightweight frameworks should be developed to deploy services on mobile devices, which fit well with their resource constraints, such as low CPU occupancy, memory usage and energy consumption. In general, two kinds of approaches can be utilized. One of them is to reduce the complexity of messaging, which can be realized by adopting Representational State Transfer (REST). The other one is to offload the complex computational tasks to the cloud. Furthermore, lightweight protocols can also be helpful, such as Constrained Application Protocol (CoAP) and Bluetooth Low Energy (BTLE).

Willingness decision: In traditional service provision, service requests are seldom rejected, as the capability of the cloud is powerful, and the resources are sufficient. However, the resource and capability of mobile devices are always limited, so mobile service providers should reject some service requests to ensure their normal operation. The willingness for a service request is influenced by the resource condition as well as the required resources of the service. Willingness depends on various factors including the CPU occupancy, battery power, network status, request loads, etc. of the devices and the required resources, authority, etc. of the required services. All these factors should be integrated together to judge whether a request should be accepted or rejected. Moreover, the revenue of the providers should be considered too, as the provider may choose to provide services regardless of the low battery and high overload if the revenue is high enough.

Performance improvement: For mobile service providers, the resources and capability are always limited, so it is more important to perform service scheduling and resource management for mobile service providers. Service scheduling and resource management aim to fulfill the promised QoS and process as many service requests as possible to increase the revenue of service providers. To achieve these goals, a resource management profiler is needed to supervise the resource utilization and to estimate the resource demand of service requests. Based on the resource utilization situation of mobile service providers and the resource demand of incoming requests, decisions can be made to accept or reject service requests as illustrated in *Willingness Decision* part. For example, if the battery is high and the network is heavy, then a computation-intensive service request may be accepted but a connection-intensive service request may be rejected. Besides, service request sequence scheduling also can help to improve the performance of service provision. Service requests that require resources that are currently idle can be removed to the front of the waiting queue and service requests that require resources that are currently overloaded should be delayed. For example, if the battery is high and the network is poor, then connection-intensive service requests should be processed firstly, and computation-intensive service requests should be postponed.

2.3.3 How to Save Energy for Mobile Devices

While mobile devices, especially smart mobile devices, become more and more powerful and multifunctional, energy saving, as the biggest concern, haunts mobile users, device manufactories, and content providers all the time. As running services on mobile devices will produce additional energy consumption, it becomes a more critical issue that mobile users will consider while providing services on their mobile devices. It is intuitive that even slight efforts that reduce energy consumption on mobile devices can greatly reserve energy when providing more repetitively used mobile services. In order to realize energy saving for mobile services, the following issues should be addressed.

A mathematical model should be proposed to best characterize the relationship between energy consumption (measured in Watts) and system properties when continuously processing mobile services on mobile devices. The model should generate the energy consumption profile of a specific mobile service or group of services according to the specific devices on which they are deployed. Some studies have utilized the experimental results and regression method trying to reveal the relationship between energy consumption and mobile services [6]. However, it is not appropriate to evaluate the energy consumption of every service by this method, and the result may vary from different mobile devices. A precise energy consumption profile should evaluate the energy consumption by analyzing the behavior of services, such as the invocation of specific sensors and the execution time of CPU and memory. Energy consumption can be calculated by composing the energy consumed on each operation of device units. Moreover, energy consumption profile should take the operating systems as well as the energy consumption on invoking specific units into consideration, as they vary from different devices. However, it is rather challenging and difficult to realize such an absolutely precise profile. A feasible way is to coarsen service behaviors and obtain an approximate solution, which still deserves a large amount of research.

As illustrated above, absolutely precise profiles are difficult to achieve, and it is feasible to coarsen service behaviors and get approximate profiles. However, it is still hard to measure the energy consumption on certain service behaviors. Therefore, repeatable approaches are needed to estimate the energy consumption on specific service invocations for certain mobile devices. The approach can be realized by constructing and solving the relation equation between energy consumption and operations of mobile devices. A large amount of measurement on multiple service invocations on multiple mobile devices is required to evaluate the energy consumption of mobile services. Some prediction methods such as regression and neural networks can be used to construct the energy consumption models from these equations and measurements [7].

An adaption approach is demanded to make configuration decisions at run time according to the learned energy consumption profile. Based on the energy estimation model, the configuration could decide to adjust the computational parameters instantly when the battery is low, or the mobile network happens to change.

2.4 Mobile Service Consumption

Service consumption is from the perspective of service consumers who discover services to satisfy their requirements, make selection among candidates with similar functionalities, and invoke the selected services. Compared with service consumption in traditional services computing, mobile service consumption has completely different issues that should be considered due to the constant mobility of users and providers as well. The mobility not only brings location-sensitive experience of service invocation for mobile users, but also complicates the process of service selection. More importantly, another special issue arising from mobile service consumption is about computation offloading for resource-restricted mobile devices.

2.4.1 How to Evaluate Mobile Services

Different from QoS declared by service providers or assessed by third parties, the term Quality of Experience (QoE) emphasizes the evaluation from service consumers that invoke the services. QoE in mobile services computing is more dynamic and uncertain than in traditional services computing because traditional services can provide guaranteed and predictable QoS due to powerful services hosts and stable networks. However, the experience of mobile services is location-sensitive and might be changed to a great extent by different locations where the users are.

In C2M pattern, although the services executed on cloud servers can perform consistently, their actual QoS experienced by mobile consumers might be different with the variation of users' locations. The actual response time experienced by mobile consumers would be affected by the locations of users. This is because users' moving can cause the variation of the signal strength and the data-transmission speed, thus influencing the data-transmission time. Similarly, energy consumption on mobile service invocation is uncertain, because the variation of signal strength can change the energy consumption on service parameter transmission. The reliability of services in mobile environment is also different from it in traditional environment. For service consumers, they may move out of the mobile network coverage, hence services that will be completed by the time he moves out of the mobile network coverage would be more reliable than those that will not be completed.

In M2M pattern, the QoE of services would be more dynamic. The availability of services is uncertain, because if providers move out of the communication coverage or run out of resources, services will become not available. Service cost may be related to the situation of service providers and the relationship between providers and consumers. For example, if the capability, resources and energy of the provider are all sufficient or the provider and consumer are in an intimate relationship, the cost may be lower, otherwise, the cost would be higher. Besides, some metrics, such as response time, reliability and energy, can be affected by not only the location and signal strength of service consumers but also those of service providers, so the evaluation of those metrics is more complicated than in C2M pattern.

To correctly evaluate the experience of mobile services, a proper QoE model for mobile services should be proposed. Existing QoS models do not consider the dynamic and mobile environment too much and cannot be used directly to represent QoE. It is quite necessary to develop a comprehensive QoE model for mobile services with the consideration of both QoS and the feature of mobility.

2.4.2 How to Select and Compose Mobile Services

Service selection becomes a problem for users as the number of available services continuously increases. Traditional service selection methods always select services according to QoS factors such as cost, time or reliability. In mobile services computing, these QoS factors are still important selection criteria. Service cost almost has no difference with it in traditional services computing, while factors of time and reliability are location-sensitive due to different QoE at different locations. With the moving of mobile devices, their location and mobile network strength are changing, so the data transmission time of services is changed, which leads to variation of service response time. Service reliability is also network-related, since poor network can lead to disconnectedness between service providers and consumers. Moreover, mobile service selection should also be energy-concerned due to the limited battery capacity of mobile devices.

In such cases, some tradeoff between them is necessary when selecting proper services for mobile users [7]. Besides, the willingness of service providers must be considered. The services with high QoS may be invoked by many users, so if more requests are sent to these services, they may be rejected, and the invocation fails.

In C2M pattern, the constant mobility of service consumers will result in the variation of the mobile network's signal strength in different locations. As a result, the time and the energy consumption for data transmission between mobile devices and clouds affected a lot by service consumer's moving will be an important factor that should be considered in service selection in terms of good QoE and energy-saving. Traditional QoS-based service selection approaches, which focus more on the properties of services themselves but neglect the mobile context of service consumers, are not suitable for mobile environment anymore.

While in M2M pattern, both service consumers and providers may keep in moving. A successful invocation of a mobile service requires that the consumers and providers stay within the communication distance during the interaction time. Once they move out of the distance during the execution of services, the services would come to execution failures. So, in order to guarantee a successful invocation of a selected service, the selection method should evaluate whether the service is available for the consumer when the consumer sends out the invocation request, but also evaluate its availability when the consumer gets response from the service. Moreover, consumers should consider their authorities and check whether they are qualified to invoke the services that they want. Besides, the status of the providers also should be taken into consideration, because if they are busy or with low battery, they may reject the service requests. Moreover, it must be checked whether the users have authority to invoke the services, because the request by users who do not authority must fail. The willingness of providers also should be considered when performing service selection. If the provider is with low energy and high workload, the possibility that the request will be rejected will be high, so these services should not be preferred to be selected.

The problem of service selection can be more challenging if selecting more than one service to compose a workflow. Specifically, each service composition consists of multiple tasks, and there are multiple candidate services that provide the same functionality for each task. Thus, it needs to select one of these candidate services to perform each task with optimal criteria (e.g. the best QoS and the lowest energy consumption). This is more complicated than the single service selection problem because a different selection result for one task might result in issuing the request for the following task from a different place, which could change the data transmission time and the distance between service requesters and providers in M2M.

The selection problem for mobile services computing relies on efficient mobility modeling and prediction mechanisms, which can predict not only a mobile user's specific future location over time, the estimated time that a mobile user will stay at the specific location [8, 9]. Based on that, we can carry out service selection with the combined consideration of QoS, QoE and energy saving together.

2.4.3 How to Do Computation Offloading

Computation offloading is a useful strategy for C2M pattern to improve the efficiency of service invocation and reduce energy consumption for mobile devices through migrating heavy computation tasks to powerful servers in clouds. A mobile task can be run on a mobile device locally or submitted to the cloud [10]. As an optimization, mobile users can decide whether a task should be executed by invoking the local service or the cloud one. To invoke a service device locally can avoid data transmission but consumes the limited device resource; to invoke a cloud service can utilize the power of cloud but suffers from the cost of data transmission.

There are many factors adversely impacting the efficiency of offloading techniques, especially bandwidth limitation between mobile devices and cloud servers and the volume of data that must be exchanged among them. For mobile services computing, we believe that with the rapid change of mobile applications and increase of their computational complexities, the following concerns should be included for the design and implementation of future offloading strategies.

As users' requirements become more complicated, one single service can hardly satisfy such requirements, and thus multiple services should be composed in a workflow to execute complicated tasks. Each component service in a service workflow can be either executed locally on a mobile device or remotely offloaded to cloud servers. Because of their dependencies, the order of execution is very important here and must be carefully considered before execution. For example, if a service is offloaded, its following component services cannot start their execution until its result is returned, even if local resources are available.

The main characteristic of mobile users is their mobility, and thus offloading strategies must allow users to invoke mobile services whilst roaming in a network. Because of their mobility, mobile network bandwidth and data exchange rates are expected to vary during invocation of mobile services, and thus must be carefully considered to have the least effect on computational performance and energy consumption of mobile devices.

Also because of their roaming, mobile users may occasionally lose their connection during receiving a service. Thus, offloading strategies must be equipped with appropriate fault-tolerant strategies to not only reinitiate lost commutating tasks, but also minimize the extra execution time and energy consumption caused by failures.

Mobile Internet has been remarkably growing during the past years in terms of mobile devices, mobile users and mobile applications/services. It changes our life overwhelmingly through enabling people to share information and services anytime and anywhere. Services computing will benefit from mobile Internet to serve as a more promising paradigm for emprises and personals with great opportunities and challenges as well in the future.

References

1. Z. Wu, S. Deng, J. Wu, *Service Computing: Concepts, Methods and Technology* (Elsevier, Amsterdam, 2014)
2. K. Mitra, C. Ahlund, A mobile cloud computing system for emergency management. IEEE Cloud Comput. **1**(4), 30–38 (2014)
3. S. Qiao, D. Shen, X. Wang et al., A self-adaptive parameter selection trajectory prediction approach via hidden Markov models. IEEE Trans. Intell. Transp. Syst. **16**(1), 284–296 (2015)
4. J. Zhou, A.K.H. Tung, W. Wu, W. Siong Ng, A "Semi-lazy" approach to probabilistic path prediction in dynamic environments, in *ACM International Conference on Knowledge Discovery and Data Mining*, pp. 748–756 (2013)
5. T. Johnson, S. Muthukrishnan, V. Shkapenyuk, O. Spatscheck, A heartbeat mechanism and its application in Gigascope, in *International Conference on Very Large Data Bases*, pp. 1079–1088 (2005)
6. A. Papageorgiou, U. Lampe, D. Schuller, R. Steinmetz, A. Bamis, Invoking web services based on energy consumption models, in *IEEE First International Conference on Mobile Services*, pp. 40–47 (2012)
7. S. Deng, H. Wu, W. Tan, Z. Xiang, Z. Wu, Mobile service selection for composition: an energy consumption perspective. IEEE Trans. Autom. Sci. Eng. (2015). https://doi.org/10.1109/TASE.2015.2438020
8. S. Deng, L. Huang, D. Hu, J.L. Zhao, Z. Wu, Mobility-enabled service selection for composite services. IEEE Trans. Serv. Comput. (2014). https://doi.org/10.1109/TSC.2014.2365799
9. J. Wang, Exploiting mobility prediction for dependable service composition in wireless mobile ad hoc networks. IEEE Trans. Serv. Comput. **4**(1), 44–55 (2011)
10. S. Deng, L. Huang, J. Taheri, A. Zomaya, Computation offloading for service workflow in mobile cloud computing. IEEE Trans. Parallel Distrib. Syst. **26**(12), 3317–33294 (2015)

Chapter 3
Mobile Service Selection

Abstract Service selection has always been a hot topic in services computing area. In mobile environment, the characteristics such as mobility, unpredictability and variation of the signal strength of mobile networks bring great challenges for the selection of optimal services. Traditional QoS-aware methods selecting services with the best QoS may not always result in a best composition as the constant mobility makes the performance of service invocation unpredictable and location-based. Moreover, due to the limits of the battery capacity of all mobile devices, how to select cloud services in order to reduce energy consumption in mobile environments is becoming a critical issue. This chapter addresses the problem of mobile service selection for composition in terms of QoS and energy consumption and proposes the resolving methods respectively.

3.1 Introduction

Quality of service (QoS) describes the non-functional characteristics of Web services. As there may be many available services with the same functionality, traditional service selection methods always differentiate services by QoS; thus, the objective of service selection is to select the optimal service from the candidate service set for each task to optimize the QoS criteria of the composite service.

The invocation of services via mobile systems has provided us many advantages such as convenience and portability, but it brings several difficult problems at the same time. These problems have brought new challenges to service selection [1]. Specifically, how to select the correct service among thousands of applicable service instances in the cloud and satisfy mobile users' quality of service (QoS) requirements, is a challenging problem. As users' requirements become more and more complicated, single services can hardly satisfy their requirements. It needs to utilize service composition technology to compose a complex application by integrating several distributed services that are provided by different service providers [2]. Specifically,

© Zhejiang University Press and Springer Nature Singapore Pte Ltd. 2020
S. Deng et al., *Mobile Service Computing*, Advanced Topics in Science
and Technology in China 58, https://doi.org/10.1007/978-981-15-5921-1_3

each service composition request includes multiple tasks, and for each task, there are multiple services that can provide the same functionality. Thus, we need to choose one of such services to make the whole composition performs with the best QoS. Traditionally service selection methods for composition will select such a service for each task that claims with the best QoS. However, in mobile environment, it becomes more difficult for mobile users to select candidates. It must consider the variation of the signal strength of mobile network in different places when the user is moving.

Another fatal problem is limited energy, which is the primary constraint of all mobile devices. Various studies have identified longer battery lifetime as the most desired feature of mobile systems [3]. Therefore, how to reduce energy consumption in mobile environments has become a critical issue. This objective is difficult to achieve, as the energy consumption of services can be affected by many factors including the location of mobile devices, users' route, the signal strength along that route, the amount of transferred data, the response time of the invoked service, etc. In the process of service selection, all of these factors should be taken into account in order to minimize energy consumption.

Moreover, another important factor for service selection is QoS correlations between services, which may have a significant impact on the overall QoS values in the mobile environment. QoS correlations occur when some QoS attributes of a service are not only dependent on the service itself but correlated to some other services. QoS correlations exist everywhere in mobile environment. For example, if two adjacent tasks in a service plan can be achieved by two individual services deployed on the same provider, then the response time of the composite service will be greatly reduced as the parameter transmission between the two services can be finished inside the server, saving the cost of data transmission in mobile network, with is quite time-consuming. Another example is a sales promotion that claims that a discount on the execution cost will be given if two or more services are used in the same plan. In mobile environment, the reliability of services is relatively lower, so if a user has just successfully invoked a service from Amazon, this implies that other services from Amazon will be more reliable for him. If these relevant QoS correlations are taken into consideration in service selection, the ultimate result will be significantly improved. Nevertheless, this important factor is neglected by most of the existing works.

Therefore, the objective of service selection is not only optimal QoS but also minimal energy consumption, and QoS correlations also have significant impact on service selection in mobile environments. Therefore, in this chapter, we focus on the problem of service selection in terms of QoS, energy consumption and QoS correlations in mobile environments, and propose three service selection methods in Sects. 3.2, 3.3 and 3.4, respectively.

3.2 Qos-Driven Mobile Service Selection

This section proposes a new approach for service selection in mobile environments. We identify the new research problem of service selection for mobile service composition and provide formal definitions to describe this problem. A mobility model is proposed to formally model service invocations in mobile environments. The model consists of two parts: the paths of moving mobile users when they are invoking service compositions and the quality of the mobile network when transmitting data for component services. A mobility-aware QoS computation rule is specified to allow computing mobility-aware QoS for service composition. Our mobility-aware QoS computation can also handle the QoS of structured service compositions with data dependence. Finally, a mobility-aware service selection algorithm is defined by utilizing the teaching-learning-based optimization (TLBO) algorithm. Based on the proposed mobility model, we tailor the operations of TLBO to the problem of service selection for mobile service composition to improve the solution quality and scalability of our algorithm. A series of evaluations are conducted to validate that the global QoS of service compositions obtained by our algorithm is approximately optimal and much better than that of traditional composition approaches. Furthermore, we compare our methods with other population-based optimization methods on both optimality and scalability.

3.2.1 Prerequisite Definitions

In this subsection, we give clear definitions of the key concepts in the scope of service selection for service composition in mobile networks. The formal framework for service composition in [4] is adopted and extended.

Definition 1 (*Service*) A service is modeled as a triple $s = (I, O, Q)$ where:

(1) I is the set of input parameters;
(2) O is the set of output parameters;
(3) Q is an n-tuple $< q_1, q_2, \ldots q_n >$, where each q_i denotes a QoS property of s such as cost, response time, throughput, or availability.

In this section, we only consider one QoS property (response time). In the following parts, the QoS of a service is equivalent to the response time of a service.

Definition 2 (*Service Invocation*) A service invocation is modeled as a triple $ivc = (s, d_i, d_o)$, where:

(1) s is the invoked service;
(2) d_i is the size of the input data of s;
(3) d_o is the size of the output data of s.

Note that a service s may have different service invocations since the input data may be different. Similarly, services with the same I and O may also have different service invocations for the same user request.

Definition 3 (*Service Composition Plan*) A service composition plan is modeled as a 2-tuple $scp = (T, R)$, where:

(1) $T = \{t_1, t_2, \ldots t_n\}$ is a set of tasks, each task t_i can be implemented by a set of candidate services C_i.
(2) $R = \{r(t_i, t_j)|t_i \in T, t_i \in T\}$ is a set of relations between tasks in T. $r(t_i, t_j)$ represents that the inputs of t_j depends on the outputs of t_i. R is used to depict the structure of the service composition plan.

Definition 4 (*Service Composition*) A service composition is modeled as a triple $sc = (p, S, Q)$, where:

(1) p is the service composition plan that sc corresponds to.
(2) S is the set of services in sc. Each $s_i \in S$ corresponds to a $t_i \in p.T$.
(3) Q is the global QoS of sc. There exist many computation methods to achieve the global QoS by integrating the QoS of each service [5–8].

Generally speaking, the process of service composition has three steps as shown in Fig. 3.1:

- **Composition Planning**. The first step is to build the composition plan with multiple tasks (abstract services). Unlike the concrete service, each task is the symbol representing a group of candidate services with similar functions and interfaces. The tasks are orchestrated together by some control statements (such as assignment, switch and loop).

Fig. 3.1 Process of service composition

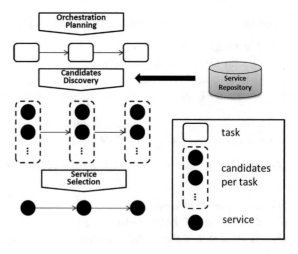

- **Candidates Discovery**. After the composition plan is generated, it should discover suitable candidates for each task. These candidate services have the same functions and interfaces as the task. This step can be implemented through service discovery or service recommendation mechanisms, which discover/recommend first k services for each task in the service repository with some non-functional constraints or personal preferences.
- **Service Selection**. Service selection is a key part of service composition. The optimal service from each candidate service group is selected and replaces the corresponding task in the composition plan. In this study, we focus on how to select concrete services for each task to get the optimal service composition. However, it is also an important issue to guarantee that the services for different tasks are compatible. This issue is beyond the scope of this section and there are many researches on this topic [9, 10]. Therefore, we assume that all candidates for different tasks can interact with each other.

3.2.2 Mobility-Aware Approach

3.2.2.1 Mobility Model

In the mobile scenario, we face the challenge of dealing with users' mobility, that is, users always keep moving when they are invoking a service composition in mobile environment. During users' movement, the mobile network latency for transmitting input/output data for services would vary according to users' locations. Thus, our mobility model consists of two parts: the user's moving path and the quality of mobile network.

Definition 5 (*User's moving path*) User's moving path is modeled as a triple $mp = (Time, Location, M)$, where:

(1) *Time* is the set of continuous time points ranging from t_0 to t_n, t_0 is the time point that the user starts the service composition. t_n is the time point that the user finishes the service composition;
(2) *Location* is the set of the user's locations corresponding to all time points in *Time*;
(3) *M* is a function that mapping time points to users' locations on the moving path. M: *Time* $\rightarrow$ *Location*. The function M can be implemented by the random waypoint mobility model [11].

Definition 6 (*Quality of Mobile Network*) The quality of mobile network (*QoMN*) is to describe the mobile signal strength at a specific location. In this section, we mainly consider the data transmission rate as the quality of mobile network. The function L is used to map locations to *QoMN*, L: *Location* $\rightarrow$ *QoMN*.

By Definition 6, a user's moving path can be mapped into a two-dimension space, and we can get his location at any specific time point by function M. Then we can get the location where he starts to send or receive data for a service invocation by calculating the time points of service invocations. Meanwhile, given a location, we can get the quality of mobile network corresponding to this location. Thus, the mobile network latency of transmitting input/output data can be calculated. After that, the final response time of the whole service composition can be achieved.

To make the mobility model computable, we build an overlay grid on top of the two-dimensional space. Each cell of the grid corresponds to an area where the *QoMN* keeps the same. This is equivalent to the practical situation when the cells are infinitely small. Thus, we can approximately measure the *QoMN* of the area covering the user's moving path and build this grid by distributing different *QoMN* values for each cell. Based on the mobility model, we can define the problem this section targets at.

Definition 7 (*Service selection for service composition in mobile networks*) Given a user's moving path and the *QoMN* within the area covering the path. For a service composition required by the mobile user, select concrete services from service candidates to get the optimal global QoS (the shortest response time).

3.2.2.2 Mobility-Aware QoS Computation

In this section, we first introduce the concept of mobility-aware QoS (MQoS) based on the mobility model. Then we present how to compute the global QoS of the mobile service composition.

Assumption 1 During the time of data transmission of each task, the *QoMN* should keep the same.

The assumption can be explained as follows. On one hand, the data size for a mobile service is normally not so large for the consideration of the Internet fee and energy consumption. Therefore, the time cost for data transmission is short. On the other hand, the covering area of a signal base station for mobile network is usually large enough to guarantee the *QoMN* keeps similar within the covering area. Hence, during the time of data transmission, the mobile user can hardly move to another area with different *QoMN*.

Definition 8 (*Mobility-aware QoS*) Mobility-aware QoS (*MQoS*) is to describe the performance of a component service in a mobile service composition with mobility concern. In this section, we only consider one property of QoS (response time). The *MQoS* of a component service s can be calculated as follows:

$$MQoS_s = t_{d_i} + Q_s + t_{d_o} \tag{3.1}$$

where t_{d_i} is the mobile network latency of transmitting input data, Q_s is the execution time of s, t_{d_o} is the mobile network latency of transmitting output data. t_{d_i} and t_{d_o} can be calculated as follows:

Table 3.1 Integration rules for QoS of service composition

QoS property	ψ_1	ψ_2
Cost	$\sum$	$\sum$
Response time	$\sum$	Max
Throughput	$\sum$	Min
Availably	$\prod$	$\prod$

$$t_{d_i} = \frac{d_i}{QoMN_i}$$

$$t_{d_o} = \frac{d_o}{QoMN_o} \tag{3.2}$$

where d_i is the size of input data and the $QoMN_i$ is corresponding $QoMN$ at the location where the user starts to send the input data. According to the Assumption 1, $QoMN_i$ won't change during t_{d_i}. d_o and $QoMN_o$ are the corresponding variables for the output data.

Definition 9 (*Global QoS*) Global QoS is to describe the performance of the whole service composition. The global response time of a service composition *so* can be calculated as follows:

$$GQoS = \underset{s \in so}{\psi} MQoS_s \tag{3.3}$$

where ψ is a operator which integrates the values of local QoS. We adopt the QoS integration rules in [8] to implement ψ shown in Table 3.1, where ψ_1 is the integration function for QoS of services in a sequence execution path. ψ_2 is the integration for QoS of multiple parallel paths. For the notations in the table, we only use their intuitive mathematic meanings. For example, '$\sum$' means summation, '$\prod$' means product, 'max' means maximum, and 'min' means minimum. The optimal QoS of a composition is the best value obtained from the integration rules from Table 3.1. For simplicity, we only consider a 1-dimensional QoS value (response time) in this section. Still, it is easy to extend to other criteria by aggregating the overall QoS value of the service composition through the mentioned computation rules. If an efficient aggregating function of multiple QoS properties is provided, our proposal can also handle multiple-dimension QoS value.

3.2.2.3 Mobility-Enabled Service Selection

Our selection algorithm is based on the teaching-learning-based optimization algorithm (TLBO), which belongs to the swarm intelligent optimization methods. First, we illustrate how the problem in this section is transformed to an optimization problem. Then, we introduce our service selection algorithm based on TLBO.

An optimization problem of finding the smallest $F(\Theta)$ with a feasible parameter vector Θ, which can be modeled as follows [12]:

$$
\begin{aligned}
\inf \quad & F(\Theta) \\
\text{subject to } & \theta_i \in [1, N] \\
& \theta_i \in Z
\end{aligned}
\tag{3.4}
$$

This means the feasible set of parameter vectors is constrained by $\theta_i \in [1, N]$ and is an integer. The optimal solution $\hat{\Theta}$ satisfies the following conditions:

(1) $\hat{\Theta}$ belongs to the feasible set
(2) $\forall \Theta, F(\hat{\Theta}) \leq F(\Theta)$

The following theorem presents the relationship between this optimization problem with our mobility-aware service selection problem.

Theorem 1 (Optimization Problem) *A mobility-aware service selection problem with user's moving path and the quality of mobile network in this area confirmed is equivalent to the optimization problem described in* (3.4).

Proof For the problem of selecting optimal services with shortest response time with mobility consideration, the vector $\Theta = (\theta_1, \ldots, \theta_m)$ can describe a possible solution as a service composition with m tasks. An element θ_i in Θ corresponds to a selected service from the candidates for the i-th task. The evaluation function for the parameter vector Θ can be implemented by the Eq. (3.3):

$$
F(\Theta) = \underset{\theta_i \in \Theta}{\psi} \ MQoS_{\theta_i}
\tag{3.5}
$$

The target of the mobility-aware service selection problem is to find a Θ to get the smallest $F(\Theta)$. Thus the problem is equivalent to the optimization problem described in (3.4).

The problem in (3.4) is an integer programming problem (IP), which is a famous NP problem. Generally speaking, there is not an algorithm with Non-deterministic Polynomial time complexity. Thus, we propose a method based on the TLBO algorithm to solve this problem which can achieve an approximate optimal solution with polynomial time.

In the following, we firstly give a basic overview of the TLBO algorithm. Then, we introduce the customizations of our algorithm that are targeted at the problem of service selection for mobile service composition.

(1) Overview of TLBO

Teaching-learning-based optimization algorithm was firstly proposed by Rao and Kalyankar [13]. Like other nature-inspired algorithms, TLBO is also a population-based method that uses a population of solutions to proceed to the global solution. For TLBO, the population is considered as a group of learners or a class of learners. For

Table 3.2 Terms matching between TLBO and service composition domain

Terms in TLBO	Terms in service composition domain
Teacher	The optimal service composition
Learner	One feasible service composition
Class	The feasible set of service composition
Subjects	Tasks in the service composition plan
Grade	Fitness (*GQoS*) of a service composition

the mobile service composition problem in this section, each learner in the population corresponds to a feasible service composition. Moreover, different tasks in the service composition plan would be analogous to different subjects offered to learners and the learners' result is analogous to the 'fitness', as in other population-based optimization techniques. The teacher is considered as the best solution obtained so far. Table 3.2 shows the terms match between TLBO and service composition domain.

The process of TLBO consists of two parts: 'Teacher Phase' and 'Learner Phase'. The 'Teacher Phase' means learning from the teacher and the 'Learner Phase' means learning through the interaction between learners (Fig. 3.2).

(2) Initialization Phase

One advantage of TLBO is that there are not so many parameters to be tuned as other population-based methods. Only two basic parameters should be decided in the initialization phase. One is the population size P, and the other is the maximum iteration number I. Then the initial population is generated randomly.

For each learner in the class, $X^i = (x_1^i, x_2^i \ldots x_d^i)$ is generated randomly, where: $i = (1, 2, 3, \ldots, P)$, d is the number of tasks in the service composition plan. x_j^i is the selected candidates for the j-th task in the solution X^i, which is an integer that represents the selected candidate.

(3) Teacher Phase

In the teacher phase of TLBO, every learner X^i ($i = 1, 2, 3, \ldots, P$) in the class learns to the teacher $X_{teacher}$ according to the difference between the teacher $X_{teacher}$ and the mean value of learners *Mean*:

$$X_{new}^i = X_{old}^i + difference \tag{3.6}$$

$$difference = r_i \times (X_{teacher} - TF_i \times Mean) \tag{3.7}$$

where X_{old}^i and X_{new}^i is the i-th learner before learning and after learning to the teacher; $r_i = \text{rand}(0, 1)$ is the learning step-length; $TF_i = \text{round}[1 + \text{rand}(0, 1)]$ is the teaching factor; *Mean* is the average of all learners:

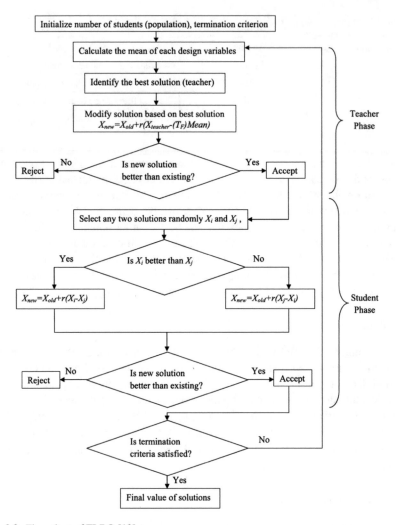

Fig. 3.2 Flow chart of TLBO [13]

$$Mean = \frac{1}{P}\sum_{i=1}^{P}X^{i} \tag{3.8}$$

In our mobile service composition problem, each variable in a solution vector X must be an integer. So we add a *refine* operation for TLBO after each vector operation:

$$\text{def } refine(X^i):$$
$$\quad \text{for } x_j \text{ in } X^i:$$
$$\quad\quad x_j = \text{round}(x_j) \tag{3.9}$$
$$\quad\quad \text{if } x_j > up: x_j = up$$
$$\quad\quad \text{if } x_j < low: x_j = low$$

where up is the upbound of the candidates and low is the low bound.

After learning to the teacher, all learners should update themselves according to the learning result:

$$\text{if } F(X_{new}^i) < F(X_{old}^i):$$
$$X_{old}^i = X_{new}^i \tag{3.10}$$

where the function F is used to calculate the fitness of the leaner according to Eq. (3.5).

(4) Learner Phase

Instead of learning to the teacher, learners would increase their knowledge through interaction between themselves in the learner phase. A learner learns something new if the other learner has more knowledge than him or her. This can keep the diversity of the population, which can avoid the algorithm converging too early to get a good result.

For each learner in the class $X^i = (x_1^i, x_2^i \dots x_d^i)$ will randomly choose a learning target $X^j = (x_1^j, x_2^j \dots x_d^j) \, i \neq j.X^i$ would analyze the difference from X^j and then make the learning decision:

$$X_{new}^i = \begin{cases} X_{old}^i + r_i \cdot (X^i - X^j) & F(X^j) > F(X^j) \\ X_{old}^i + r_i \cdot (X^j - X^i) & F(X^j) < F(X^j) \end{cases} \tag{3.11}$$

where $r_i = \text{rand}(0, 1)$ is the learning step-length.

After learning between learners themselves, learners should also make update as in (3.10).

Suppose the number of population is P, the number of tasks in a service composition plan is d, and the maximum iteration number is I. The process of the proposed method can be summarized as follows:

(1) Initialization: randomly generate P service compositions;
(2) Calculate the fitness of every composition;
    For i = 1:P
(3) Decide the teacher in the class;
    For j = 1:d
(4) Update the candidate for each task by learning to the teacher according to Eqs. (3.6) and (3.10);
(5) Update the candidate for each task by learning to other learners according to Eqs. (3.9) and (3.10);

EndFor
EndFor

(6) If the iteration number reaches I, the algorithm terminates. Otherwise, go back to the step (2).

From the process of the algorithm, we can see that the main computation time is cost by step (4) and step (5): computing the difference between learners and the teacher/learners and then updating the candidates for each task. The time complexity of the two steps is both $O(d)$. Thus, for each learner in the population, the time complexity in teacher phase and leaner phase is $O(d)$. Then the time complexity for the whole population is $O(P * d)$. Finally, the overall time complexity with I iterations is $O(I * P * d)$.

3.2.3   Experiments and Analysis

In this section, we conduct a series of experiments to evaluate and validate our proposed approach. The experiments are aimed at answering the following questions:

(1) Why is it necessary to consider the user mobility when selecting services for service composition in mobile environment? What is the impact of the mobility?
(2) Compared with other metaheuristic algorithm-based methods, can our approach find better optimal result?
(3) Compared with other metaheuristic algorithm-based methods, how does our approach perform on scalability?

3.2.3.1   Setup

The evaluation was run on a machine with an Intel Core i7 CPU with 2.3 GHz. All algorithms were implemented by Python 2.7 and evaluated sequentially and given up to a maximum of 8 GB of memory if needed. We generated our service compositions with randomly inserted tasks and control structures. For each task, we randomly created a number of candidate services with different QoS. To avoid other factors that affect the evaluation results, we set the candidates of the same task to require the same size of input/output data. The execution time of each service was generated according to a uniform distribution

For all the implemented algorithms, the population size $P = 10$, the maximal iteration number is 100 and all the algorithms are independently run 50 times for unprejudiced statistical results.

3.2.3.2 Impact of Mobility

In order to validate the necessity of considering the mobility when making selection for mobile service composition, we compare our method with the standard composition method which only considers services' individual QoS. This method selects the candidate with the optimal execution time for each task without considering the mobile network latency. For the experiments in this section, we generated service compositions with 50 tasks and 100 candidates available per task.

(1) Impact of Variation of Signal Strength

According to the proposed mobility model, the two functions M and L decides the relationship between users' movement and the variation of signal strength. For our experiments, we combined the user moving function: $location = M(time)$ and the mobile signal strength function $QoMN = L(location)$ into one variation function of signal strength: $QoMN = G(time) = L(M(time))$, which plots the signal strength against increasing time. Since there are many factors affecting the variation of signal strength (such as user's moving speed, distance from signal stations, properties of signal station, etc.), the variation of signal strength in practice can hardly be defined by any functions and it is difficult to acquire the real data of signal strength. Therefore, we generated four different variation function of signal strength to simulate the variation of signal strength during users' movement:

G_1: Constant function. We set $G_1 = a$. This function simulated traditional environment and is used to evaluate how our method compare to the standard method for traditional service composition.

G_2: Cosine function. We set $G_2 = a * (cos(b * time) + 1) + 1$, which makes the signal strength vary between 1 and $a + 1$, and the variation cycle is $2\pi/b$. This function can simulate that the user is moving with constant velocity and the signal stations are distributed regularly.

G_3: Piecewise function. We set G_3 as a piecewise function. $G_3 = a : time \in [0, t_1)|b : time \in [0, t_1)|c : time \in [0, t_1)| \ldots$ This function can simulate that the user is various in different period, and the distance is not so long that the signal strength keeps the same during that period.

G_4: Random function. We set $G_4 = random(a, b)$. This function can simulate some unpredictable situations.

Figure 3.3 shows the comparison results with the four variation functions where the x-axis means the iteration number and the y-axis means the response time of the service composition found by the two methods. Figure 3.3a shows that the standard method can find better service composition (with shorter response time) than our method. The reason is that the standard method can guarantee to find the optimal solution with the shortest response time since the mobile network latency is always the same with function G_1. But our method is closely approaching to the optimal result after enough iterations, which validates that our method can find near-optimal solutions.

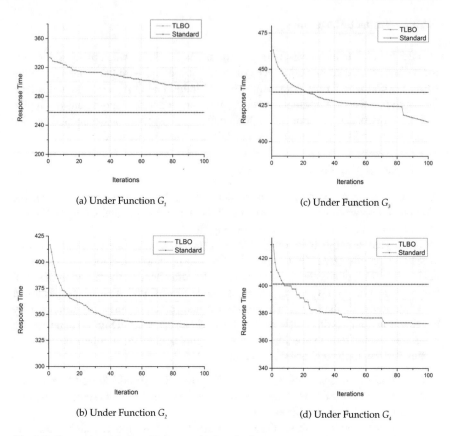

Fig. 3.3 Comparison results with the standard method

Figure 3.3b–d shows that our proposed method outperforms the standard method with the three variation functions of signal strength. This indicates that the standard method is not effective at finding compositions with variation of signal strength in mobile environment. We can also find that our method performs better no matter the signal strength varies regularly or randomly.

(2)   Impact of Amplitude of Variation of Signal Strength

In this experiment, we target at evaluating the impact of the amplitude of the variation of signal strength on the improvement of our approach. To this end, we select the cosine function G_2 as the variation function of signal strength since it is easier to adjust the amplitude of variation through tuning the parameter a in G_2. We set a range from 60 to 120, and $b = 1$. We use the metric *improve_rate* to evaluate the improvement of our method compared to the standard method.

$$improve\_rate = \frac{r_s - r_m}{r_s} \qquad (3.12)$$

Fig. 3.4 Impact of amplitude of variation

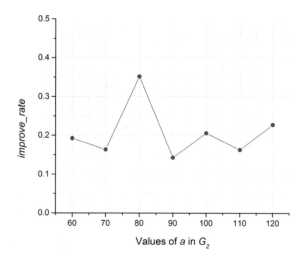

where r_s is the optimal result achieved by the standard method, and r_m is the optimal result from our method.

Figure 3.4 shows the improvement of our method with different values of the amplitude of the variation of signal strength. The average improvement of our method is around 20% compared to the standard composition method. From the results, we can see that as the amplitude of variation increases, there is no obvious regularity how the *improve_rate* value varies with. The result indicates that our method considering mobility outperforms the standard method without considering mobility no matter how the amplitude of variation varies since the values of *improve_rate* are always positive. Furthermore, we can also observe that the improvement fluctuates with different amplitude values. This can be explained that the improvement of the mobile network latency can hardly remain at a fix level all the time.

(3) Impact of Frequency of Variation of Signal Strength

Besides the amplitude, we also evaluate the impact of the frequency of the variation of signal strength on the improvement of our approach. Similarly, we also select the cosine function G_2 as the variation function of signal strength. The frequency is adjusted by tuning the parameter b in G_2. We set b range from 0.5 to 100, and $a = 100$. The metric *improve_rate* is also used to evaluate the improvement of our method compared to the standard method.

Figure 3.5 shows the improvement of our method with different values of the frequency of the variation of signal strength. From the results, we can see that as the frequency of variation increases, the *improve_rate* value increases at first. When the frequency passes over a certain threshold, the *improve_rate* value decreases again. Thus, we can conclude that our method cannot always improve at a stable level with different variation frequency of signal strength. Two reasons cause this observation: (1) The increase of *improve_rate* confirms the intuition that a relatively obvious variation of signal strength leads to better improvement. (2) When the variation

Fig. 3.5 Impact of
frequency of variation

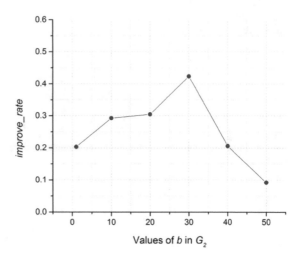

frequency surpasses a certain threshold, it may cause the signal strength varies so
quickly that goes back to the previous value when the user re-issues a data request,
which turns out that there is not so much change on signal strength from the user's
perspective.

3.2.3.3   Optimality Evaluation

Since little work has focused on the problem of service selection for mobile service
composition, we can hardly find existing methods for such a problem to compare
with ours. Because TLBO is a fundamental population-based algorithm, we chose
several other population-based algorithms and compared their optimality with our
method.

Genetic Algorithm (GA). A search heuristic algorithm that mimics the process
of natural selection [14]. It has already been used by existing service composition
approaches [15–17]. We extended it by adding the mobility consideration.

Particle Swarm Optimization (PSO). A computational method that optimizes a
problem by iteratively trying to improve a candidate solution with regard to a given
measure of quality [18]. It has also been widely utilized in service composition area
[19–21].

Negative Selection Algorithm (NSA). NSA belongs to the field of Artificial Immune Systems inspired by theoretical immunology and observed immune
functions, principles and models [22]. It is recently involved in solving service
composition problems and proved high efficiency [23, 24].

To compare the above algorithms with our approach, we tuned the parameters for
each algorithm to achieve their best performance. The most suitable parameters are
shown in Table 3.3. We generated service compositions with sizes between 10 and
100 (in steps of 10). We varied the number of candidate services available per task

Table 3.3 Parameters setting of different algorithms

Algorithms	Parameters setting
GA	cross rate $= 0.7$; mutate rate $= 0.3$
PSO	$c_1 = c_2 = 2$; weight $= 0.8$
NSA	$\alpha = 0.1$; $\beta = 3$; $\rho = 1$

between 100 and 1000 (in steps of 100), which is considerably more than what most of the previous studies have used.

To evaluate the optimality of the algorithms, we plotted the total response time of the service compositions found by all algorithms versus an increasing problem size.

(1) Impact of Different Task Number

Figure 3.6 plots the response time of the optimal service composition achieved by different algorithms against an increasing task size with a fixed number (100) of services available per task.

From the comparison result in Fig. 3.6, we can observe that our method has an outstanding performance on the solution optimality with all different task numbers. The response time of the optimal service composition returned by TLBO is at least 10% than others. And the advantage becomes more obvious with the increasing number of tasks. Thus, we can conclude that our approach manages to keep a good approximation ratio of the optimal solution regardless of the composition size.

(2) Impact of Different Candidate Number

Figure 3.7 shows that the optimal response time decreases slightly as the number of services per task increases. This is because there are more choices available as the number of services increases. We can also observe that our method outperforms the others no matter what the number of candidate services is.

Fig. 3.6 Response time of service composition found with different number of tasks

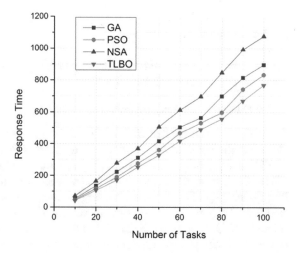

Fig. 3.7 Response time of
service composition found
with different number of
services per task

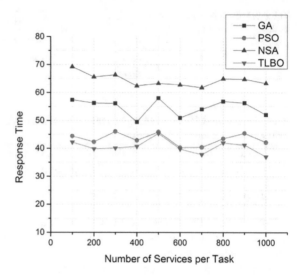

From the comparison results from the experiments in this section and the previous section, we can observe that our approach can keep good performance with large-scale datasets both on tasks and candidates. This is because TLBO can keep the diversity of the population through the learning phase, which can efficiently avoid converging to a suboptimal value too early. PSO performs better than GA because it has an evolution target in each generation, but this can also result in an early convergence. For the problem in this section, NSA performs worst which is not consistent with the previous researches in [23]. This is because NSA-based methods care more about local fitness, which is efficient in traditional service composition problems but not suitable in mobile environment. In summary, our proposed TLBO-based method has the best performance on optimality compared to the other methods.

3.2.3.4   Scalability Evaluation

In this section, we compared the scalability of our approach with the same algorithms under the same settings as for optimality.

(1)   Impact of Different Task Number

In Fig. 3.8, we can see that GA runs fastest compared to the other three algorithms. However, the qualities of the solutions found by GA are much worse than those of PSO and TLBO, which takes much less than 100 ms to compute the results. Therefore, it seems that GA is only faster, because it fails to improve the quality of its solutions significantly, thus, converging more quickly to a bad local optimum. Similarly, NSA also runs faster than PSO and TLBO, but the qualities of solutions found by NSA is even worse than GA. PSO and TLBO can get much better quality of solutions, but they sacrifice some runtime to improve the optimality.

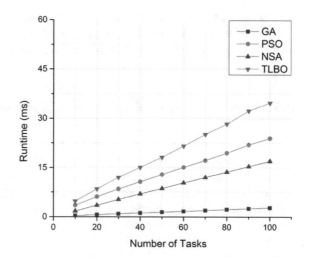

Fig. 3.8 Runtime per iteration with different number of tasks

Furthermore, we can observe that TLBO spends more time than PSO, this is because TLBO adds a learning phase to avoid early convergence which takes a considerable runtime to do so. We can also observe that although TLBO spends a little more runtime than the other algorithm, it has a low algorithmic complexity, which is roughly linear with regard to the composition size. This observation validates the time complexity analysis in Sect. 3.2.2.

(2)   Impact of Different Candidate Number

From Fig. 3.9, we can observe that the runtime of NSA significantly increases as the number of services per task increases. Thus, NSA quickly becomes infeasible for practical purposes; it takes 6 times of the runtime as the other algorithms for 1000

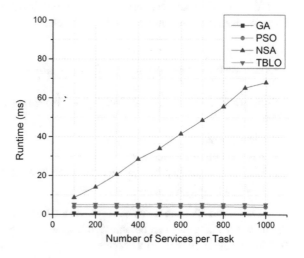

Fig. 3.9 Runtime per iteration with different number of services per task

services per task. On the other hand, the runtime of the other three algorithms does not change so much against the increasing number of services per task. Hence, all of the three algorithms scale well in this regard in our scenario.

3.3   Energy Consumption-Driven Mobile Service Selection

In this section, we focus on the problem of service selection in terms of energy consumption in mobile environments. The problem is how to select the optimal service for each task to minimize the overall energy consumption. Traditional methods try to achieve this objective by simply selecting services with the least response time. These methods can ensure that the composite services have the shortest response time; thus, the least standby energy consumption can be guaranteed. Unfortunately, compared to data transmission energy consumption, standby energy consumption is tiny [25]. In conclusion, traditional methods are not capable of resolving the service selection problem in terms of energy consumption.

Therefore, it is necessary for us to propose a service selection method to effectively reduce the energy consumption of composite services. To achieve this objective, not only should we reduce the standby energy consumption but also, more importantly, we should make the data transmission proceeded under better network conditions as much as possible to reduce the energy consumed by data transmission.

3.3.1   Problem Definition

In this section, we formally describe the energy consumption-aware service composition problem. First, we introduce the basic concepts about Web service including the definitions of Web service, service plan, service invocation and composite service. Then, we formally present the mobility models.

3.3.1.1   Web Service and Service Composition

Definition 10 (*Web Service*) A Web service is represented by a 3-tuple (i, o, QoS), where:

(1) i is the input parameters;
(2) o is the output parameters;
(3) QoS is the quality of the service, including execution cost, response time, reliability, availability, reputation, etc.

In Definition 10, each service is represented by i, o and QoS. The upload data size and download data size can be obtained from i and o, respectively. QoS presents the non-functional properties of a service.

Definition 11 (*Service Plan*) A service plan is a triple (T, P, B), here:

(1) $T = \{t_i\}_{i=1}^{n}$ a set of tasks, including two mutually disjoint subsets FT and CT. FT is the functional task subset, and CT is the control task subset, including two special tasks: a beginning task b and an ending task e;

(2) P is a set of settings in the service plan (e.g., execution probabilities of the branches and loops structures);

(3) B provides the structural information of the service plan, which can be specified by XML-based languages such as BPEL.

A service plan is an abstract description of a business process. For simplicity, we mainly use sequence structure as examples in the hereafter in this section.

Each service plan task can be realized by invoking an individual service. There may be various services, with different input parameters, output parameters and QoS, that can be adopted to fulfill a task. Service selection is the operator that selects the optimal service from the candidate service set for each task. The result of service selection is service invocations, defined as follows.

Definition 12 (*Web Service Invocation*) A Web service invocation can be formalized as a triple (t, s, ic), here:

(1) t is the realized task in the service plan;

(2) s is the service invoked to realize t;

(3) ic is the energy cost during the invocation of s.

A service plan is realized by a set of service invocations. Each task corresponds to one service invocation and one proper service. In our model, we pay attention to the energy consumption on invocations.

Definition 13 (*Composite Service*) A composite service is a triple (S, B, QoS), here:

(1) S is the set of Web services constituting the composite service;

(2) B provides the structural information of the service plan, which is the same as the service plan;

(3) QoS expresses the quality of the composite service.

Composite services are achieved by a set of service invocations, in detail, selecting one proper service for each task in the service plan and composing these services according to the plan structure. In this chapter, we regard the composite service that not only satisfies user's functional requirements but also does so with the lowest energy consumption as the optimal composite service.

Service composition is the process of automatically constructing optimal composite services. In this process, the business process proposed by the user is specified as a service plan; then, service selection is processed to select component services according to the service plan; finally, the selected services are composed according to the plan structure. Service selection is considered as the most pivotal step in the service composition process, as it determines the quality and energy consumption of the composite services.

3.3.1.2 Mobility Model

In mobile environments, the energy consumption of mobile terminals is mainly influenced by mobile paths and network conditions along the route. Therefore, we formally model these two factors in this subsection.

The mobile path is the path user moving along. For the sake of convenient calculation, we break the mobile path up into a set of segments and use segments as the minimum computing units.

Definition 14 (*Mobile Path*) A mobile path is represented by a triple (T, L, F) where:

(1) $T = \{(t_i, t_{i+1})\}_{i=0}^{n-1}$ is a set of discrete time intervals, with t_0 as the start time and t_n as the stop time;
(2) L is a set of discrete location points;
(3) F is a function representing the correspondence between time and location: $\forall t \in (t_0, t_n), F(t) \rightarrow L$.

In Definition 14, function F represents the correspondence between time and location. Actually, it indicates the variable speed while a user moves. Specifically, if the time interval is small, it means the user moves with a high speed in that location; whereas, the user moves slowly.

In our models, signal strength is used to measure network quality. Similarly, we also measure the signal strength with path segments as the basic units, considering that the signal strength in a small region is identical. To compute the energy consumption of mobile devices, we express signal strength with two variables: data transmission rate and radiant power of the mobile terminal. A higher data transmission rate or lower radiant power represents a better network.

Definition 15 (*Signal Strength*) The signal strength of a location point l can be obtained by function $ss = G(l)$. The data transmission rate tr and radiant power rp of a mobile device can be obtained according to functions $tr = H(ss)$ and $rp = R(\text{ss})$, respectively.

By Definitions 14 and 15, the relationships among path segments, time intervals, location points and signal strength are modeled as one-to-one correspondences. Given a time point, we can determine the location of the user by function F and obtain the signal strength of that location by function G. Then we can obtain the data transmission rate and radiant power of the mobile device by functions H and R, respectively. Functions H and R vary for different kinds of mobile devices. With these parameters, we can calculate the energy consumption of a mobile terminal by invoking a specific service. The detailed computation methods are represented in the next section.

3.3.1.3 Energy Consumption Computation Model

For mobile devices, the energy consumed during the service invocation process mainly includes data transmission consumption and standby consumption. In our models, the energy consumption of a service invocation is discomposed into three parts, and we can calculate the total energy consumption by summing these three parts together.

Definition 16 (*Invocation Consumption*) Given a service $s = (i, o, QoS)$ and mobile path $mp = (T, L, F)$, suppose that s is invoked at time t_1; then the energy consumption of the mobile device during the invocation of s is calculated by

$$ic(s) = uc + sc + dc \tag{3.13}$$

where:

(1) ic is the invocation consumption of the mobile device;
(2) uc is the energy consumption on uploading the input parameters, calculated by

$$uc = \frac{D(i)}{H(G(l_1))} \times (R(G(l_1)) + sp) \tag{3.14}$$

where $D(i)$ is the data size of i, which can be obtained by some service retrieval tools; $l_1 = F(t_1)$, as described in Definition 14; $G(l_1).tr$ and $G(l_1).rp$ denote the data transmission rate and radiant power at location l_1, respectively, and these information can be obtained from some existing tools like OpenSignal; sp is the standby power of the mobile device, which is known;

(3) sc is the standby consumption of the device while waiting for the execution of the service, calculated by

$$sc = sp \times rt \tag{3.15}$$

where rt is the response time of s, which can be obtained by some service retrieval tools;

(4) dc is the energy consumption on downloading the results of the invocation, calculated by

$$dc = \frac{D(o)}{H(G(l_2))} \times (R(G(l_2)) + sp) \tag{3.16}$$

where

$$l_2 = F\left(t_1 + \frac{D(i)}{H(G(l_1))} + rt\right) \tag{3.17}$$

Given a time point t_1, we can compute the location of the user with function F and afterwards obtain the signal strength of that location with function G. Then, based on the transferred data size, the uc can be calculated with Eq. (3.14). The sc of an invocation is calculated with Eq. (3.15) according to the response time of the service. The time point when the results are downloaded can be calculated by summing t_1, the duration of uploading the input parameters and the execution time of the invoked service. With the time point, the location where the results are downloaded can be calculated by function F, shown as Eq. (3.17).

The dc can be calculated with Eqs. (3.16) and (3.17). Finally, the whole energy consumption during a service invocation is obtained by summing these three parts together.

Definition 16 presents the computation rules of invocation consumption. Based on the energy consumption of service invocations, we can calculate the energy consumed by a composite service.

Definition 17 (*Composite Consumption*) Given a service plan sp (with n tasks) and its service invocation set $\{si_i\}_{i=1}^{n}$, where $si_i = (t_i, s_i, ic_i)$, the composite consumption of the composite service can be calculated by $agg(sp, \{ic_i\}_{i=1}^{n})$, using the following aggregation rules:

(1) If the services are implemented in sequence, then

$$cc = \sum_{i=1}^{n} ic_i \tag{3.18}$$

(2) If the services are implemented in choice, then

$$cc = \sum_{i=1}^{n} (p_i \times ic_i) \tag{3.19}$$

where $\{p_i\}_{i=1}^{n}$ is the set of branch execution probabilities, with $\sum_{i=1}^{n} p_i = 1$.

(3) If the services are implemented in parallel, then

$$cc = \sum_{i=1}^{n} (ic_i - sc_i) + \max_{i=1}^{n} sc_i \tag{3.20}$$

where sc_i is the standby consumption of ic_i.

(4) If the service is implemented iteratively, then

$$cc = \sum_{j=1}^{m} (p_j \times (ic)^j) \tag{3.21}$$

where $\{p_j\}_{j=1}^{m}$ is the set of probabilities for executing the iteration j times, and m is the maximum iteration time, with $\sum_{j=1}^{m} p_j = 1$.

For these composite services with complex structure, composite service decomposition can be used to decompose the composite services into composite services with single structure. After composite service decomposition, we can calculate the energy consumption of composite services according to the rules in Definition 17.

Definition 18 (*Energy Consumption-aware Service Selection*) Given a service plan *sp* (with *n* tasks), its corresponding candidate service sets $\{css_i\}_{i=1}^n$ and the mobile path *mp*, energy consumption-aware service selection is to select one service from css_i for each task to minimize the composite consumption of the generated composite service.

Definition 18 illustrates the objective of service selection in this chapter. Service selection involves calculating the energy consumption of the composite services according to the given assumed conditions, then selecting the optimal one among them.

3.3.2 Service Selection Methods and Algorithms

In this section, we introduce the details of our approach. The quantity of alternative composite services increases exponentially with the number of tasks increasing, so we adopt the well-known genetic algorithm for service selection. We present how the genetic algorithm is applied to service selection first, and then introduce the detailed algorithm.

This approach works well only when it knows the path of the mobile user and the signal strength along the path as well in advance. For the signal strength for a given path, we can get the signal strength for each point along this path from network-status databases provided by communication companies or the third-party websites like OpenSignal.[1]

3.3.2.1 Energy Consumption-Aware Service Selection as an Optimization Problem

According to Definition 18, the energy consumption-aware service selection problem is an optimization problem that can be modeled as follows:

$$\begin{cases} \min cc(\theta) & 1 \\ cc(\theta) = agg\left(sp, \{ic_{\theta_i}\}_{i=1}^n\right) & 2 \\ \theta_i \in [1, N_i] & 3 \\ \theta_i \in Z & 4 \end{cases} \tag{3.22}$$

---

[1]http://www.opensignal.com.

where $cc(\theta)$ is the composite energy consumption of the composite service generated according to θ, θ is an n-dimensional vector representing the feasible solution, θ_i implies which candidate service is selected for the i-th task. agg is the energy consumption aggregation function defined in Definition 17, sp is the service plan, and ic_{θ_i} is the invocation consumption of the service selected according to θ_i. Given θ, the composite energy consumption is calculated by function agg in (3.22)-2 and its rules in Definition 17. ic_{θ_i} can be calculated by equations in Definition 16. We do not list these equations here to avoid duplication. N_i is the quantity of candidate services for the i-th task. Obviously, relations (3.22)-3 and (3.22)-4 must hold, and they construct the feasible solution set. The optimal solution $\hat{\theta}$ should satisfy the following two conditions:

(1) $\hat{\theta}$ belongs to the feasible solution set;
(2) θ in the feasible solution set, $cc(\theta) \geq cc(\hat{\theta})$.

Therefore, this problem is an integer programming problem. As analyzed above, the objective function contains Eqs. (3.13)–(3.22). In these equations, besides the optimization variable, all of the functions and variables are known, except the locations where the services are invoked. However, these locations are related to the selected services, which is the optimization variable [as shown in Eq. (3.17)]. Given a specific case, all of the locations where the services are invoked can be determined only when all the services have been selected. Therefore, this problem is more complex than traditional integer programming problems where all parameters are known except the optimization variables. Generally speaking, no algorithm can resolve this problem in polynomial time. The complexity of the enumeration method is $O(m^n)$, where m denotes the average number of candidate services for each task and n denotes the number of tasks. The enumeration method becomes not practical with the scale of the problem increasing. Therefore, we propose a genetic algorithm-based method to resolve this problem. It can provide an approximate optimal solution within polynomial time. Moreover, the genetic algorithm has many advantages: it starts with a group of solutions, which makes it robust; it selects randomly points to crossover and mutation, which can avoid local convergence; it works by crossover and mutation, which are simple and quick, but of powerful function.

3.3.2.2 Service Selection Method Based on the Genetic Algorithm

The genetic algorithm is an algorithm model inspired by biological phenomena: in natural evolution, chromosomes with genomes that fit the environment survive. The genetic algorithm encodes specific problems in a chromosome-like structure and simulates the evolution process by applying a fitness function to judge whether a chromosome is predominant. In the following, we illustrate how the genetic algorithm is applied to our energy consumption-aware service selection problem.

(1) Encoding

Table 3.4 presents the corresponding relationships between the genetic algorithm and our service selection problem. In the genetic algorithm, feasible solutions are modeled by chromosomes; thus, chromosomes correspond to composite services. Each chromosome comprises a set of independent genes, so we use genes to represent services. The locus of a gene in a chromosome expresses a task in the service plan. If a chromosome has a high fitness, it implies that the energy consumption of the corresponding composite service is low.

(2) Initialization

At the beginning of the initialization phase, we initialize the algorithm parameters including the population size, namely the quantity of initial chromosomes cq, the maximum iteration times it, the crossover times ct and the mutation times mt.

Then, the initial population is generated randomly. For each chromosome in the population, $s_j = \left(s_j^1, s_j^2, \ldots, s_j^n \right)$ is generated randomly, where n is the quantity of tasks in the service plan and s_j^i implies which candidate service is selected for the i-th task.

(3) Selection

Selection is a process of reserving the superior chromosomes and weeding out the inferior chromosomes. The objective of selection is to transmit the superior chromosomes directly to the next generation or indirectly to the next generation via mutation and crossover operations.

Chromosomes are evaluated by fitness. Fitness is used to describe how well an individual fits the environment. In our model, a chromosome with high fitness implies that the corresponding composite service has low composite energy consumption. Fitness can be calculated according to Eqs. (3.13)–(3.18).

We adopt the well-known roulette wheel method to perform selection. The probability of a chromosome S_j with fitness f_j to be selected out of the population is calculated by:

$$P(S_j) = \frac{f_j}{\sum_{l=1}^n f_l} \tag{3.23}$$

Equation (3.23) guarantees that chromosomes with higher fitness values have a higher probability of being selected.

Table 3.4 Term matching between the genetic algorithm and service selection	Genetic algorithm	Service selection
	Chromosome	Composite service
	Gene	Service
	Locus	Task
	Fitness	Composite energy consumption

(4) Crossover

Crossover is an operation that recombines parent chromosomes to generate new child chromosomes. Crossover plays a central role in the genetic algorithm. Through crossover, new chromosomes are generated, and the fitness of the new generated chromosomes may be higher than that of their parents. The objective of crossover is to generate additional new chromosomes with high fitness to improve the average fitness of the chromosomes in the next generation.

In this chapter, we adopt the standard single-point crossover operator. In the crossover process, a single point of the genome is randomly chosen first; then, two new child chromosomes are generated by holding the genes before that point unchanged and interchanging the genes after the point. Figure 3.10 shows an example of crossover.

From the service selection perspective, crossover is to recombine two composite services by interchanging constituent services that realize the same task to generate two new available composite services. The new generated composite services may have lower energy consumption than their parents. Therefore, through crossover, additional superior composite services are generated for us to select.

(5) Mutation

Mutation is an operator that changes chromosomes slightly in a random way in order to generate chromosomes with higher fitness and avoid early convergence. The function of mutation is as same as crossover.

The mutation process is realized by randomly choosing a gene and randomly changing it to another feasible gene. Figure 3.11 shows an example of mutation, where two new chromosomes are generated.

From the service selection perspective, mutation is to randomly choose a component service in the composite service and randomly choose another service from the same candidate service set to replace it. This operator may generate superior composite services.

Fig. 3.10 Crossover example

Fig. 3.11 Mutation example

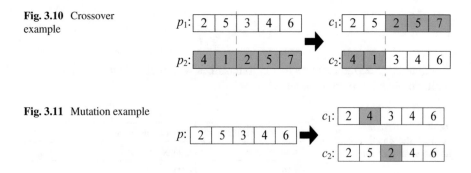

3.3.2.3 Service Selection Algorithm

Given a fitness function, the genetic algorithm could execute iteratively and eventually achieve approximate optimal solutions. In the genetic algorithm, new individuals are generated through constant crossover and mutation. Then, superior individuals are reserved and inferior individuals are weeded out. Thus, superior genes are transmitted to the next generations, making the next generations fit the environment better. The genetic algorithm is summarized in Table 3.5.

The algorithm begins with initialization (line 1), which randomly selects a gene for each locus, generates the initial chromosomes, and put them into the chromosome set *ChrSet*. Then, the pivotal steps crossover (lines 3–4) and mutation (lines 5–6) are processed, by which more new chromosomes are added into the chromosome set. Afterwards, the fitness of all of the chromosomes is calculated (line 7), and the current optimal chromosome is recorded (line 8). Next, the current optimal chromosome is compared with the optimal chromosome that has ever occurred in the history, and the better one is recorded as *OptChr* (lines 9–10). After that, the chromosomes are selected according to the probability calculated by their fitness (line 11). This process is repeated until the given iteration times *it* is reached. Finally, *OptChr* is returned as the optimal chromosome (line 12).

Table 3.5 Service selection algorithm based on the genetic algorithm

Input parameters	Quantity of chromosomes *cq*, iteration times *it*, crossover times *ct* and mutation times *mt*
Output result	The chromosome with the highest fitness

1:	randomly compose *cq* chromosomes in *ChrSet*
2:	**for** *i*=1 to *it*
3:	**for** *j*=1 to *ct*
4:	randomly choose two chromosomes, crossover them, and put the new generated chromosomes in *ChrSet*
5:	**for** *k*=1 to *mt*
6:	randomly choose one chromosome, mutate it, and put the newly generated chromosome in *ChrSet*
7:	Compute the fitness of all of the chromosomes in *ChrSet*
8:	*CurOptChr*←the chromosome with the highest fitness
9:	**if** $f(CurOptChr) > f(OptChr)$
10:	*OptChr*←*CurOptChr*
11:	select *cq* chromosomes and remove others from *ChrSet*
12:	**return** *OptChr*

Obviously, the time complexity of the algorithm is polynomial. Moreover, we can adjust the efficiency by adjusting the input parameters of the algorithm. The result may be better if one or more parameters among cq, it, ct, and mt are increased, but it will cost more time to obtain the result. If these parameters decrease, the efficiency will be improved, but the result may be suboptimal.

3.3.3 Simulation Experiments and Analysis

In order to evaluate the genetic algorithm-based service selection approach proposed in this chapter, we conduct two sets of simulation experiments. The first set of simulations aim to evaluate how much energy can be saved by comparing the energy consumption of composite services generated by our approach with two other methods. The second set of simulations evaluate the efficiency of our method, where we implement the algorithms in different scale scenarios to examine the scalability of the algorithm.

3.3.3.1 Effectiveness Evaluation

In traditional methods, energy consumption has not been considered during the process of service selection. They always suppose that the network condition is constant and the composite services with shorter response times cost less energy. Therefore, to verify the effectiveness of our algorithms, we compare these methods with our genetic algorithm-based algorithm. Moreover, we also compare our method with another famous heuristic algorithm, i.e. Particle Swarm Optimization (PSO) algorithm, to verify the superiority of Genetic Algorithm. Meanwhile, we examine the impact of iteration times, signal strength, mobile speed and the scaling on the results of our method.

All of the simulation experiments are run on a machine with an Intel Xeon E3-1230-V2 CPU at 3.3 GHz, with an available 8 GB of memory if needed. The algorithms are implemented by Python 2.7.6.

In these simulations, the mobile paths are randomly generated on a convex region that is divided into a set of small checks. We use these checks as basic units (points), assuming that the network conditions within a small check are identical. The signal strength of each point is randomly generated by a cosine function.

The mobile paths are generated by the well-known random waypoint mobility model (RWP) [26]. RWP is a most commonly used mobility model, which is widely used for random mobile path generation. We define the RWP model as follows. Given a convex region R, the mobile point stays in the initial point p_0 for a random time $t_0 \in [t_{min}, t_{max}]$. Then, another point p_1 is randomly selected from the surrounding points of p_0. Next, the mobile point moves from p_0 to p_1 and stays in p_1 for a random time $t_1 \in [t_{min}, t_{max}]$. After that, a point p_2 is randomly selected from its surrounding points. This process is repeated until the end.

(1)   Impact of Iteration Times

As in Table 3.5, iteration times are set in the initialization phase. If the genetic algorithm iterates more times, it may generate a better result. This group of simulations is to verify the effectiveness of our method and examine the impact of iteration times at the same time.

To this end, we vary the iteration times and hold other parameters unchanged. RWP is used to generate random mobile paths, where the stay time for the user on each point is randomly generated from 1 to 5. The point number is set as 200, which is big enough to guarantee that the user keeps moving before the tasks are fulfilled, as our method aims at service selection in mobile environment. The signal strength along the route is generated by a cosine function, $ss = 10 \cos x + 35$, where x is randomly generated from 0 to π. The effect of the signal strength on the data transmission rate tr and the radiant power rp of mobile devices varies for different mobile devices. In this section, for simplicity, we assume that $tr = 2.3ss^2 - 114ss + 1424$ and $rp = -3ss + 105$, which are obtained by fitting the data we measured in reality. The task number is set as 10 and the candidate service number for each task is randomly generated from 5 to 25. The input and output data size for each service is randomly generated from 5 to 100 and the response time for each service is randomly generated from 5 to 10. To avoid other factors affecting the simulation results, the input and output data sizes are set equal if two services have the same functionality. All of the three methods are adopted to perform service selection. This process is repeated 100 times, and the average energy consumption is recorded as the result.

Figure 3.12 shows the results. It is obvious that our genetic algorithm significantly outperforms PSO algorithm and traditional methods. With the increasing of iteration times, the mean energy consumption of composite services generated by the genetic algorithm and PSO algorithm decreases stably at first and then converges to a stable value. However, the traditional methods can only generate composite services with higher energy consumption, which verifies the conclusion that traditional methods

Fig. 3.12 Impact of iteration times

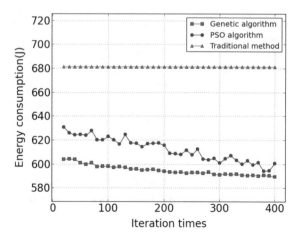

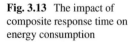

Fig. 3.13 The impact of composite response time on energy consumption

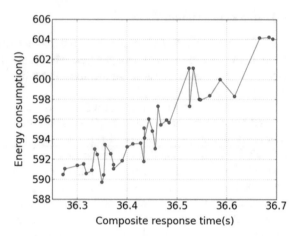

that select services only according to the response time and do not account for the mobile network environment are not capable of achieving the objective of minimal energy consumption. PSO algorithm can get reasonable results, but compared to Genetic Algorithm, it is outshone.

Meanwhile, we also record composite response times in the simulations. In order to reveal the relationship between energy consumption and composite response time, we depict the result in Fig. 3.13. Overall, with the increasing of composite response time, mean energy consumption shows a slow upward trend. This is because the standby consumption is increased. However, energy consumption fluctuates up and down all of the time, implying that shorter response time does not mean low energy consumption. This contradicts traditional methods. Therefore, it is inappropriate to minimize energy consumption by selecting services with the shortest response time.

(2) Impact of Signal Strength

In mobile environments, users are always moving, and network conditions along the route are ever-changing with the movement of mobile devices. As in Sect. 3.3.2, signal strength has a great impact on the energy consumption of mobile devices. In order to examine the impact of variation amplitude and mean value of signal strength, we design the simulation as follows.

The signal strength of each point is set by a cosine function $ss = A\cos x + B$, where x is randomly chosen from $(0, \pi)$. Other experimental parameters are set as the previous simulations. We examine the variation of energy consumption by varying the value of amplitude (A in the cosine function) and offset (B in the cosine function). Each simulation is repeated 100 times and the average values are recorded as the result.

The result of the impact of amplitude is shown in Fig. 3.14. It indicates that the energy consumption of composite services generated by our method is obviously less than traditional methods and PSO algorithm. As amplitude increases, there

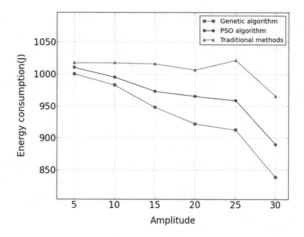

Fig. 3.14 Impact of the amplitude of signal strength

is no evident variation tendency in the consumption of composite services generated by traditional methods because they do not take signal strength into account when selecting services. The consumption of composite services generated by the genetic algorithm and PSO algorithm gradually decreases. Moreover, the discrepancies between the three methods becomes greater. This is because the genetic algorithm can select services to adjust the data transmission locations. If the amplitude increases, it can generally make the data transmission between services and users in locations with stronger signal strength; therefore, the energy consumption is reduced. PSO algorithm also achieve this functionality, but it is still inferior to Genetic Algorithm. This simulation shows that in scenarios where signal strength is constant, the results of the three methods are similar, whereas if the signal strength varies widely, the superiority of our method becomes more evident.

Figure 3.15 shows the result of impact of the offset. It shows that the energy

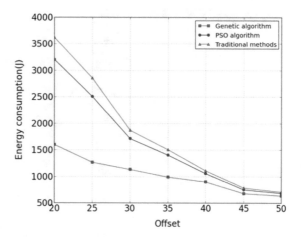

Fig. 3.15 Impact of the offset of signal strength

consumption of composite services generated by our method is always less than traditional methods and PSO algorithm. As the offset increases, the energy consumption of composite services generated by all of the three methods decreases in line with our computation method [Eqs. (3.14) and (3.16)]. However, the gap between the three methods also decreases because the variation amplitude ratio becomes lower with the increase of the mean signal strength.

(3)   Impact of Mobile Speed

Users may move continuously during the invocation of composite services. Users' movement can change the signal strength of service invocation; therefore, their velocity may affect the energy consumption of the composite services. In this simulation, we examine the impact of mobile speed on the energy consumption of the composite services. We also use RWP to randomly generate mobile paths, but vary the moving speed by varying the standing time interval $[t_{min}, t_{max}]$; other parameters are set as before. This simulation is also repeated 100 times, and the average value is recorded as the result shown in Fig. 3.16.

In Fig. 3.16, we can see that with the speed increasing, the consumption of composite services generated by traditional methods shows no evident variation tendency, as they select services only according to response time, whereas the consumption of composite services generated by the genetic algorithm and PSO algorithm is obviously decreasing. When the mobile speed is low, the gap between our method and traditional methods is small, but with increasing speed, it becomes larger. When the speed is very low, the signal strength is nearly constant. Therefore, the results of the three methods are similar. As the velocity increases, the genetic algorithm and PSO algorithm have more opportunities to make data transmission under better network conditions, allowing the superiority to become more evident. In addition, the result of our method is better than that of PSO algorithm.

Fig. 3.16 Impact of moving speed

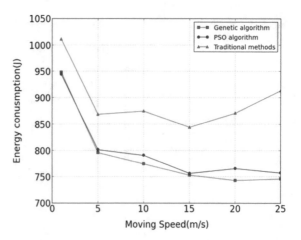

(4) Impact of the Scale

The scale includes the number of tasks in the service plan and the number of candidate services for each task. In this simulation, we vary these two parameters to examine the impact of scale on energy consumption. Other parameters are designed as before.

From Fig. 3.17, we can see that with the increasing task number, the energy consumption of composite services generated by the three methods increases almost linearly, and the gap between them increases, which is in line with our energy consumption calculation rules in Sect. 3.3.2. With the increasing of the task number, energy consumption on both data transmission and standby are increasing; therefore, the total energy consumption is increasing. The genetic algorithm can reduce data transmission consumption by adjusting the data transmission locations; therefore, energy consumption increases more slowly. PSO algorithm also can adjust the data transmission locations, therefore, its result is better than traditional methods. However, the simulation results show us that it is inferior to Genetic Algorithm.

Figure 3.18 shows the impact of candidate service number on energy consumption. Energy consumption of composite services generated by traditional methods decreases while the number of candidate services increases. This is because with the increasing of candidate services, there could be more services with shorter response times. Traditional methods can therefore select them to make the composite response time shorter, so the mean standby consumption decreases. However, the standby consumption constitutes only a small proportion, so the total consumption decreases slowly. With the candidate services increasing, the genetic algorithm and PSO algorithm can select services to make data transmission occur in better locations to decrease data transmission energy consumption. Therefore, with the candidate services increasing, the energy consumption decreases sharply. Moreover, the ability of Genetic Algorithm to select services for energy saving is better than PSO algorithm.

Fig. 3.17 Impact of task number

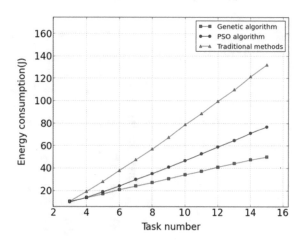

Fig. 3.18 Impact of
candidate service number

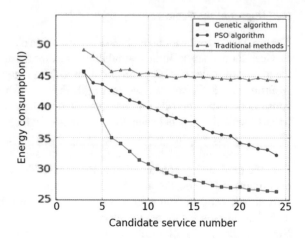

3.3.3.2 Efficiency Evaluation

Our genetic algorithm-based service selection method performs a good scalability.
The following simulations are designed to verify this statement.

(1) Impact of Task Number

In order to examine the impact of task number on the execution time of our algorithm,
we vary the task number to examine the execution time of the algorithm in this
simulation experiment. The RWP model is used to randomly generate the mobile
paths, and other parameters are randomly generated as simulations of Sect. 3.3.3.1.
The task number is changed from 3 to 15. For each task number, the simulation is
repeated 100 times, and the average value is recorded as the result.

The result is shown in Fig. 3.19. The execution time of our algorithm is obviously

Fig. 3.19 Impact of task
number on execution time

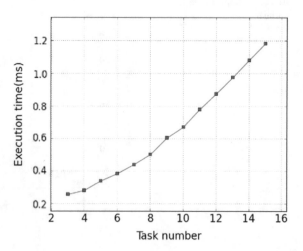

Fig. 3.20 Impact of candidate service number on execution time

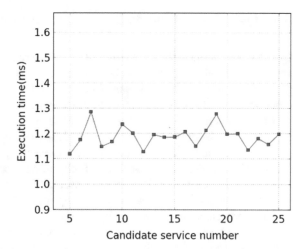

of a low order of magnitude. Moreover, with the increase in task number, it increases almost linearly which, in accordance with energy consumption aggregation roles [Eqs. (3.18)–(3.21)], verifies the good scalability of our service selection method.

(2) Impact of Candidate Service Number

In this step, we vary the number of candidate services to examine the impact of candidate service number on the execution time of our algorithm. All parameters are randomly generated as in the previous simulations. The candidate service number is changed from 5 to 25. For each number, we also repeat the simulation 100 times and record the average value as the result.

The result is shown in Fig. 3.20. We can see that the number of candidate services does not affect the execution time of the genetic algorithm because in the initialization step, the scale of the algorithm is determined, and it is only affected by the algorithm parameters including chromosome number, iteration times, crossover times and mutation times.

From the two above simulations, we can conclude that, with the increasing of task number and candidate service number, the execution time of the genetic algorithm does not increase sharply because the execution time is primarily determined by the algorithm parameters set in the initialization phase. In the real world, to obtain a better result, these algorithm parameters, including chromosome number, iteration times, crossover times and mutation times, should be adjusted appropriately.

3.4   QoS-Correlation Aware Mobile Services Selection

QoS correlations have significant impact on the overall QoS values of the composite services in mobile environments. QoS correlations occur when some QoS attributes of a service are not only dependent on the service itself but correlated to some other services. If these relevant QoS correlations are taken into consideration in service selection, the ultimate result will be significantly improved. Nevertheless, this important factor is neglected by most of the existing works.

In this section, we focus on QoS-aware service composition and take QoS correlations into consideration. To achieve this object, we propose a novel method named Correlation-Aware Service Pruning that reserves the services with QoS correlations and pruning redundancy services step by step (CASP). First, as a component of the CASP approach, a preprocessing algorithm named P4CS (preprocessing for candidate services) is proposed to remove services that cannot contribute to the optimal composite services from the candidate service sets. Then, two CASP algorithms, namely CASP4AT (CASP for service selection with correlations in adjacent tasks) and CASP4NAT (CASP for service selection with correlations in nonadjacent tasks), are proposed for service selection with correlations in adjacent tasks and nonadjacent tasks respectively. Both of them select services for each task in the service plan step by step. In this process, they account for all services that may compose optimal composite services and prune services that are concluded not the optimal candidate services.

3.4.1   Problem Definition

3.4.1.1   Formalization of Service Composition

Definition 19 (*Web Service*) A Web service is represented by a 4-tuple (i, f, b, QoS) (i, o, QoS), where:

(1) i is the unique identifier of the service;
(2) f is the functional description of the service, including the input, output, precondition and result of the service;
(3) b is the basic information of the service, including its name, location, provider, etc.;
(4) QoS is a set of attributes, including execution cost, response time, reliability, availability, reputation, etc.

In Definition 19, each service is identified by i, f describes the function of a service, which is used to aggregate candidate services for tasks in the service plan, and QoS will be defined in detail by Definition 23.

Definition 20 (*Service Plan*) A service plan is a triple (T, P, B), where:

(1) $T = \{t_i\}_{i=1}^{n}$ is a set of tasks;
(2) P is a set of settings in the service plan (e.g., execution probabilities of the branches and loops structures);
(3) B provides the structural information of the service plan, which can be specified by XML-based languages, such as BPEL.

A service plan is an abstract description of a business process. Each service plan task can be realized by invoking an individual service. There may be multiple services with different QoS and providers that can be adopted to fulfill each task.

Definition 21 (*Composite Service*) A composite service is a triple (S, B, QoS), where:

(1) S is the set of Web services composed in the composite service;
(2) B provides the structural information of the service plan, which can be specified by XML-based languages, such as BPEL;
(3) $QoS = \{q_i\}_{i=1}^{n}$, expressing the QoS of the composite service.

Composite services are obtained by selecting one individual service for each task in the service plan and composing them according to the plan structure. We regard the composite service that not only satisfies user's functional requirements but has optimal QoS value as the optimal composite service. In service composition process, the business process proposed by the user is specified as a service plan first; then, service selection is processed to select component services according to the service plan; finally, the selected services are composed according to the plan structure. Service selection is considered the most pivotal step of service composition, as it determines the quality of the composite service.

It is noted that an individual service can also be regarded as a composite service with only one component service. We use the symbol "·" to denote the sequence composition of two services. For example, $s_1 \cdot s_2$ denotes a composite service composed of s_1 and s_2 in sequence.

Definition 22 (*Prefix*) Suppose cs, cs_1 and cs_2 are three composite services, with $cs = cs_1 \cdot cs_2$, then cs_1 is called a prefix of cs.

For example, both cs_1 and $cs_1 \cdot cs_2$ are prefixes of composite service $cs_1 \cdot cs_2 \cdot cs_3$. Service selection can be regarded as a process of lengthening the prefix of the optimal composite service one by one and eventually achieving the optimal composite service.

3.4.1.2 Service QoS Models

In some conditions, some QoS attributes of a service are not only dependent on the service itself but correlated to other services. For simplicity in the rest of the section, we state that a service is correlated to another service instead of saying that a QoS attribute of a service is correlated to another service. QoS attributes of a service may be correlated to more than one service (one-to-many service correlations), and there may be more than one service whose QoS attributes are correlated to one service (many-to-one service correlations). In more complex conditions, a service may be involved in both kinds of service correlations. We have considered all these conditions in this section.

Definition 23 (*QoS*) QoS is a set of attributes, $QoS = \{q_i\}_{i=1}^n$, and each attribute is a 4-tuple, $q_i = (d, c, S_1, S_2)$, where:

(1) d is the default value of q_i of the service;
(2) c is the correlated value of q_i of the service;
(3) S_1 is the set of services that the value of q_i is correlated to;
(4) S_2 is the set of services whose value of q_i is correlated to the service.

Each service may have several QoS attributes, and each QoS attribute is defined by four elements. The default value applies to the service if no services in S_1 are invoked first, while correlated value applies to the service if and only if one or more services in S_1 are invoked first. If one service is selected, then all the services in its S_2 will appear with their correlated value.

Definition 24 (*QoS Correlation*) A QoS correlation is a triple $cor = (q_i, s_1, s_2)$, implying a relationship, that is, the QoS attribute q_i of S_2 is correlated to S_1.

For example, suppose two services S_1 and S_2 with correlation (q_i, s_1, s_2), and S_2 is to be composed with a composite service cs. If cs contains S_1, then the value of $q_i(cs \cdot s_2)$ is the aggregation of $q_i(cs)$ and $s_{2\_}c$, otherwise, $q_i(cs \cdot s_2)$ is the aggregation of $q_i(cs)$ and $s_{2\_}d$.

It is reasonable to assume that all QoS attributes of a service may have QoS correlations with other services. In the rest of this section, we will mainly use response time and execution cost as the example to describe our approach, while it is also suitable for other attributes.

3.4.2   CASP Approach

In this section, we briefly introduce our approach's main operations and algorithms. The candidate service sets are preprocessed. Then the CASP approach is implemented. As correlations can be divided into correlations in adjacent tasks and nonadjacent tasks, we propose two kinds of CASP algorithms accordingly.

3.4.2.1   Preprocessing of Candidate Service Sets

There may be a large number of candidate services for a task in a service plan, and too many redundant services will increase the complexity of the service selection process. In order to decrease the complexity of service selection, Algorithm-P4CS is proposed to remove the redundant services from candidate service sets.

In the candidate services sets, all services free of correlations will be removed except the service with the optimal default QoS value. For two certain tasks, if there is more than one correlation between the corresponding candidate service sets, only the one with optimal composite QoS value is reserved; others will be removed.

The symbols used in this section are defined in Table 3.6.

Each task is a step in Algorithm-P4CS. For each task, the preprocessing on its candidate service set can be generally divided into two steps. The first step (lines 3–10) is to find the service with optimal default value of q and remove all the other services free of correlations. The symbol "$\succ$" is used to represent better than, as for some QoS criterion (reliability, availability, reputation) a higher value is better, while for others (execution cost, response time) a lower value is better. The second step (lines 11–18) is to remove services with non-optimal correlations. As a service may be involved in one-to-many and many-to-one service correlations, if one correlation involving it is worse than another, the algorithm will continue to check if there is any other correlations involving it; if so, it will be reserved, and otherwise be removed.

The time complexity of Algorithm-P4CS is O (mn^2), where m denotes the number of tasks and n denotes the average number of candidate services. Algorithm-P4CS has a low time complexity, but it has great impact on the efficiency of service selection, especially when the number of candidate services is very large, as it significantly decreases the number of candidate services.

Theorem 2 *Let sp be a service plan, q is the QoS value preferred by the user, ocws is the optimal composite service of sp and RS is the set of removed services after the preprocessing of Algorithm-P4CS, then $\forall s \in RS$, s is not contained in ocws.*

Table 3.6 Symbol explanations

Symbols	Explanation
$t \leftarrow b$	Assign variable t with b
$b \rightarrow$ task	The subsequent task of b in the service plan
t_optWS	The service with optimal default QoS value in the candidate service set corresponding to task t
$t\_firstWS$	The first service in the candidate service set corresponding to task t
t_WS	The candidate service set corresponding to task t
$q(s)$	The value of q for service s
$q(s_1) \succ q(s_2)$	The value of q of s_1 is better than that of s_2
s_task	The task that service s corresponds to
s_S_1	The set of services that the QoS of s is correlated to
s_S_2	The set of services whose QoS is correlated to s
$s_1 \cdot s_2$	The composition of services s_1 and s_2 by sequence
$cws (s_1 \rightarrow s_2)$	The composite service obtained by replacing s_1 with s_2 in cws

Proof We adopt reductio ad absurdum to prove this Theorem 2. Assume that $\exists s \in RS$, such that s is contained in *ocws*, then s must be removed from either the first step or the second step of Algorithm-P4CS. If s is removed from the first step, then s must be free of correlations and there must be a service *s'* such that $q(s') \succ q(s)$, so $q(ocws(s \rightarrow s')) \succ q(ocws)$ holds, which is contradictory with the assumption that *ocws* is the optimal composite service of *sp*. If s is removed from the second step, then there must be another service s_1, such that $s \in s_1\_S_2$ (or $s_1 \in s\_S_1$), and s_1 is also contained in *ocws*, otherwise, $q(ocws(s \rightarrow s\_task\_optWS)) \succ q(ocws)$ holds. Moreover, there must be s_2 and s_3, such that $s_3 \in s_2\_S_1$ (or $s_2 \in s_3\_S_2$), $s\_task = s_2\_task$, and $s_1\_task = s_3\_task$, with relationship $q(s \cdot s_1) \prec q(s_2 \cdot s_3)$. Then $q(ocws(s \rightarrow s_2, s_1 \rightarrow s_3)) \succ q(ocws)$ holds, which is contradictory with the assumption. Therefore, $\forall s \in RS$, s is not contained in *ocws*.

Algorithm-P4CS: Preprocessing Algorithm of Candidate Service Sets

---

Input: service plan *sp* with beginning task *b* and ending task *e*, candidate service sets *css*, correlation set *cs* and user preference *q*

Output: candidate service sets after preprocessing

1    $t \leftarrow (b \rightarrow task)$
2   **while** $t @ e$
3        $t\_optWS \leftarrow t\_firstWS$
4   **for** every $s \in t\_WS$
5   **if** $q(s) \succ q(t\_optWS)$
6   **if** t_optWS is free of correlations
7   remove t_optWS from t_WS
8                $t\_optWS \leftarrow s$
9   **else if** $q(s) \prec q(t\_optWS)$ and s is free of correlations
10   remove s from t_WS
11   **for** every $s \in t\_WS$ and $s\_S_i @ \varnothing$
12   **if** $\exists s_i \in s\_S_1, s_j \in s_i\_task\_WS, s_k \in t\_WS$, such that $q(s_i \bullet s) \prec q(s_j \bullet s_k)$
13   **if** $s_i\_S_1 = \varnothing$ and $s\_S_2 = \varnothing$
14   remove the correlation between s_i and s
15   **if** s_i is free of correlations and s_i is not $s_i\_task\_optWS$
16   remove s_i from $s_i\_task\_WS$
17   **if** s is free of correlations and s is not t_optWS
18   remove s from t_WS
19        $t \leftarrow (t \rightarrow task)$
20   **return** *css* and *cs*

After preprocessing of candidate service sets, a large number of services are removed, and only the services with optimal default QoS value and the services with excellent correlations are reserved. Therefore, Algorithm-P4CS significantly reduces service searching space and decreases the difficulty of generating the optimal composite services. As the number of tasks in a service plan will not be too large, the number of candidate services after preprocessing is smaller than a determined value, which is related to the task number.

3.4.2.2 CASP for Service Selection with Correlations in Adjacent Tasks

In some cases, correlations only exist in services corresponding to adjacent tasks. In these cases, we can reserve all composite services that may be the prefix of the optimal composite service and prune the composite services the first time they are determined not the prefix of the optimal composite service. In other words, service composition can be viewed as a process of generating possible prefixes of the optimal composite service and pruning those that do not meet the requirement, shown as Algorithm-CASP4AT.

Algorithm-CASP4AT: Algorithm for Service Selection with Correlations in Adjacent Tasks

Input: service plan sp with beginning task b and ending task e, candidate service sets css, correlation set cs and user preference q

Output: composite service with optimal value of q

1    $optCWS \leftarrow$ null
2    $CorCWSSet \leftarrow \varnothing$
3    $t \leftarrow (b \rightarrow \text{task})$
4   **while** $t @ e$
5   creat $newCorCWSSet$
6   **for** every $s \in t\_WS$ and $s\_S_2 @ \varnothing$
7   add $optCWS \bullet s$ to $newCorCWS$
8       $optCWS \leftarrow optCWS \bullet t\_optWS$
9   **for** every $cws \in CorCWSSet$
10   remark the service correlated to cws as s
11   **if** $q(cws \bullet s) \succ q(optCWS)$
12              $optCWS \leftarrow cws \bullet s$
13   **if** $s\_S_2 @ \varnothing$
14   add $cws \bullet s$ to $newCorCWS$
15       $CorCWSSet \leftarrow newCorCWSSet$
16       $t \leftarrow (t \rightarrow \text{task})$
17   **return** $optCWS$

Before the algorithm starts, the current optimal composite service is set as null (line 1). *CorCWSSet* (line 2) is the set of composite services that contain one or more services correlated with subsequent services. The algorithm begins with the first task (line 3). For a task, it composes the current optimal composite service with all the services that are correlated with subsequent services and adds them to *CorCWSSet* (lines 6 and 7). Then it chooses the service with the optimal default QoS value, composes it with the current optimal composite service and sets it as the new current optimal composite service (line 8). Each composite service in *CorCWSSet* is composed with the services that correlated to it; then, the new composed composite service will be compared with the current optimal composite service; the better one of the new composed composite service and the current optimal composite service will become the new current optimal composite service and the worse one will be removed (lines 9–12). If the correlated service is also correlated with other services in the following task, the composed service will be added to *CorCWSSet* (lines 13 and 14). The algorithm will go forward like this step by step, finally returning the current optimal composite service as the result (line 17).

The time complexity of Algorithm-CASP4AT is O (mn), where m denotes the number of tasks and n denotes the average number of candidate services. It implies that the execution time of Algorithm-CASP4AT is in a low order of magnitude. It can be proved that Algorithm-CASP4AT can generate the optimal composite service, shown as Theorem 3.

Theorem 3 *Algorithm-CASP4AT can generate the optimal composite service of a service plan where correlations exist in adjacent tasks.*

Proof Assume the current optimal composite service before task t is *optCWS*. When the process goes forward to task t, the current optimal composite service must be either the composition of *optCWS* and the candidate service with optimal default QoS value, or the composition of *optCWS* and a service that is correlated with a subsequent service. So, all composite services that may generate the optimal composite service of the plan are reserved. If a composite service *cws* is removed, there must be $q(optCWS) > q(cws)$ and any service in *cws* is not correlated with a subsequent service, so no matter which service s will be selected in the following, there must be $q(optCWS \cdot s) \succ q(cws \cdot s)$. Therefore, Algorithm-CASP4AT reserves all the composite services that may be the prefix of the optimal composite service and prunes all the composite services that are not the prefix of the optimal composite service, thus it can generate the optimal composite service. □

3.4.2.3   CASP for Service Selection with Correlations in Nonadjacent Tasks

However, correlations can exist in services that are not adjacent. In these cases, the CASP method can also be used to achieve the selection. It reserves all the composite services that may be the prefix of the optimal composite service and prunes the composite services the first time they are determined not as the prefix of the optimal composite service.

Given a composite service cws in the service selection process, we use $cws\_corWSSet$ to represent the set of services that are in cws and correlated with subsequent services. Given two composite services with the same $corWSSet$, we can conclude that the one with lower composite QoS value cannot be the prefix of the optimal composite service, shown as Theorem 4.

Theorem 4 *Let sp be a service plan with sequence structure, q is the QoS user-preferred criterion, and cws_1 and cws_2 are two composite services generated in the process of service selection, if $cws_1\_corWSSet = cws2\_corWSSet$ and $q(cws_1) \succ q(cws_2)$, then cws_2 is not the prefix of the optimal composite service.*

Proof We use reductio ad absurdum to prove this theorem. Assume cws_2 is the prefix of the optimal composite service, and the optimal composite service is $cws_2 \cdot cws_3$. Then $q(cws_2 \cdot cws_3) = q(cws_2) + \Sigma s_1\_c$ ($\exists s \in cws_2\_corWSSet$, such that $s_1 \in s\_S_2 \cap cws_3\_WS) + \Sigma s_2\_d$ ($\neg\exists s \in cws_2\_corWSSet$, such that $s_1 \in s\_S_2 \cap cws_3\_WS$), and $q(cws_1 \circ cws_3) = q(cws_1) + \Sigma s_1\_c$ ($\exists s \in cws_1\_corWSSet$, such that $s_1 \in s\_S_2 \cap cws_3\_WS) + \Sigma s_2\_d$ ($\neg\exists s \in cws_1\_corWSSet$, such that $s_1 \in s\_S_2 \cap cws_3\_WS$). As $cws_1\_corWSSet = cws_2\_corWSSet$, and $q(cws_1) > q(cws_2)$, $q(cws_1 \cdot cws_3) \succ q(cws_2 \cdot cws_3)$ holds, which is contradictory with the assumption. Therefore, cws2 is not the prefix of the optimal composite service. $\square$

Based on Theorem 4, we propose Algorithm-CASP4NAT to achieve service selection with correlations in nonadjacent tasks.

Algorithm-CASP4NAT: Algorithm for Service Selection with Correlations in Nonadjacent Tasks	

Input: service plan with beginning task b and ending task e, candidate service sets css, correlation set cs and user preference q

Output: composite service with optimal value of q

```
1    CWSSet←∅
2    t←(b→task)
3    while t@ e
4        newCWSSet←∅
5        for every cws∈CWSSet
6            add cws• t_optWS to newCWSSet
7            if ∃cwsᵢ∈newCWSSet such that cwsᵢ_corWSSet=cws• t_optWS_corWSSet
8                remove the worse one of cwsᵢ and cws• t_optWS from newCWSSet
9            for every s∈t_WS and s_S₂@∅
10                add cws• s to newCWSSet
11                if ∃cwsᵢ∈newCWSSet such that cwsᵢ_corWSSet=cws• s_corWSSet
12                    then remove the worse one of cwsᵢ and cws• s
13            for every s∈t_WS that ∃sᵢ∈cws_corWSSet such that s∈sᵢ_S₂
14                add cws• s to newCWSSet
15                if ∃cwsᵢ∈newCWSSet such that cwsᵢ_corWSSet=cws• s_corWSSet
16                    remove the worse one of cwsᵢ and cws• s
17        CWSSet←newCWSSet
18        t←(t→task)
19    return cws in CWSSet
```

CWSSet (line 1) is the set of composite services generated in the process of selection. The algorithm starts with the first task (line 2). *newCWSSet* is set as an empty set in the beginning (line 4). For a task, all the services in *CWSSet* are composed with the service with optimal default value of q, and the generated composite service is added to *newCWSSet* (lines 5 and 6). All services in *CWSSet* are composed with all the services that are correlated with subsequent services (lines 9 and 10). Each composite service *in CWSSet* is composed with the services that correlated to it (lines 13 and 14). In this process, if there is a composite service whose *corWSSet* is the same as the newly added composite service in *CWSSet*, then the two services will be compared and the one with worse value of q will be removed (lines 7, 8, 11, 12, 15 and 16). The process will be repeated until it reaches the ending task e. In the last step, all the composite services are with the same *corWSSet* ($\emptyset$), and only the one with optimal value of q is reserved; it will be returned as the optimal composite service (line 19).

The time complexity of Algorithm-CASP4NAT is O (mnl^2), where m denotes the number of tasks, n denotes the average number of candidate services and l denotes the average number of composite services in the generated CWSSet. l has greater effect on the execution time. It is mainly affected by the number of correlations among services.

Theorem 5 *Algorithm-CASP4NAT can generate the optimal composite service of a service plan where correlations exist in nonadjacent tasks.*

Proof Assume that *cws* is a composite service generated before task *t*. The candidate services of *t* can be divided into four categories: (1) the service with optimal default QoS value, (2) services correlated with subsequent services in the candidate service set of the following tasks, (3) services correlated to one or more services in *cws*, (4) other services. Services in category 4 do not have optimal default QoS value, are not correlated with services in the following tasks, and have no correlation with *cws*, so $\forall s \in$ category 4, *cws* · *s* can't be the prefix of the optimal composite service, as for any composite service *cws'* of the following tasks, there must be $q(cws \cdot t\_optWS \cdot cws\prime) > q(cws \cdot s \cdot cws\prime)$ holds. So, Algorithm-CASP4NAT reserves all the composite services that may be the prefix of the optimal composite service. Moreover, all the removed composite services are not the prefix of the optimal composite service (Theorem 4). Therefore, Algorithm-CASP4NAT can generate the optimal composite service of a service plan. □

3.4.3 Experiments

In order to evaluate the effectiveness of the algorithms proposed in this section, we carry out two sets of experiments. The first set of experiments evaluates the QoS improvement by comparing our approach with the methods that do not account for QoS correlations. The second set of experiments evaluates the efficiency of our methods, where we implement the algorithms in different scale scenarios to examine the scalability of the methods.

We have realized the algorithms using Python language. Experiments are implemented on a computer with Pentium(R) Dual-Core CPU 2.50 GHz, 2 GB of RAM and Windows 8 operating system.

We choose response time and execution cost to examine the effectiveness and efficiency of Algorithm-CASP4AT and Algorithm-CASP4NAT respectively, while other QoS attributes are analogous. As there is no standard experimental platform and test data sets, we automatically generate the parameters and use them as the experimental data sets. Each service is assigned an integer as the default QoS value, which is generated randomly from 2 to 10. Correlations are randomly generated. When generating correlations, a random value in (0, 1) is generated for each pair of services from different tasks; if the value is smaller than the given percentage, then a correlation is added between the two services. For each correlation, it is certain that the QoS of the service from the latter task depends on the service from the former task, so there is no cycle in the generated correlations. Besides, the ratio between the correlated value and default value is generated randomly from 0.1 to 0.9.

We focus on the following three variables in the experiments:

1. Correlated service percentage. The percentage of services that are involved with correlations among all services.
2. Candidate service number. The number of candidate services of a task in a service plan.
3. Task number. The number of tasks in a service plan.

As analyzed in Sect. 3.4.2, the complexity and efficiency of the three algorithms are mainly related to these three variables. Correlated service percentage reflects the number of correlations among services, which directly affects the results and efficiency of the algorithms. Candidate service number and task number reflect the scales of candidate service sets and tasks respectively, which are the main factors determining the results and efficiency of the algorithms.

3.4.3.1   Effectiveness Evaluation

To verify the effectiveness of our algorithms, we compare our methods with a greedy algorithm that selects the service with optimal QoS value for each task and does not account for QoS correlations between services in the process of service selection.

(1)   Effectiveness Evaluation of Algorithm-CASP4AT

We design three experiments to evaluate the effectiveness of Algorithm-CASP4AT. These experiments vary the values of correlated service percentage, candidate service number and task number, respectively, to examine the QoS improvement of Algorithm-CASP4AT compared to the greedy algorithm. Response time is chosen as the user preference.

Experiment 1   What is the impact of correlated service percentage on the results of Algorithm-CASP4AT?

In this experiment, the task number is set to 10; integers randomly generated from 5 to 100 are assigned to each task as the candidate service number; each service is assigned an integer randomly generated from 2 to 10 as the default QoS value. The greedy algorithm is utilized to select the optimal service for each task and eventually generate the composite service. Then the correlated service percentage is set to 10; correlations are generated by randomly choosing two services from adjacent tasks; correlated QoS values are randomly generated from 0.1 to 0.9 times of the default QoS value. After that, Algorithm-P4CS and Algorithm-CASP4AT are implemented and the composite QoS value is recorded. Then the correlated service percentage is set to 20, 30, ..., 90, and the experiment is repeated. This process is repeated 1000 times and we adopt the average values.

Results are shown in Fig. 3.21a, where the horizontal coordinate represents the value of correlated service percentage and the vertical coordinate represents the average composite QoS value of 1000 experiments. The average QoS value of the

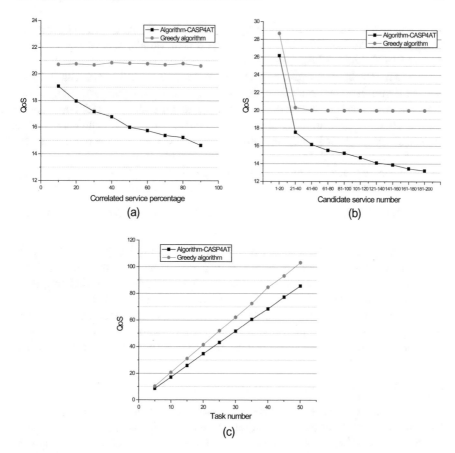

Fig. 3.21 Effectiveness of Algorithm-CASP4AT

composite services generated by the greedy algorithm is about 21. When 10% of the services are correlated, the average composite QoS value decreases to 19.1. When the correlated service percentage increases, the average composite QoS value decreases steadily because there may be more excellent alternative correlations. When the correlated services increase to 90%, the average composite QoS value decreases to 14.6, a more than 30% decrease. We can conclude that the whole QoS value will be significantly improved if correlations are taken into account. Furthermore, the superiority will be more obvious if more correlations are considered.

Experiment 2 What is the impact of candidate service number on the results of Algorithm-CASP4AT?

In this experiment, we set the correlated service percentage to 0.3, and randomly generate integers from 1 to 20 for each task as the candidate service number. Other experimental parameters are set just like Experiment 1. Then we implement Algorithm-CASP4AT and record the composite QoS value. Next, we change all candidate service numbers to randomly generated integers from 21 to 40, from 41 to 60, ..., from 181 to 200, and repeat the experiment. Similarly, each experiment is repeated 1000 times and the average value is adopted.

Figure 3.21b shows the results. It is obvious that the result is significantly better with QoS correlations taken into consideration. As the candidate services increase, there are more services with better QoS values and more services with better correlations, so the results of both algorithms improve. When the candidate service number exceeds 60, the greedy algorithm results do not decrease any more, as all the candidate services reach the lower limit, while the result of Algorithm-CASP4AT decreases continuously, as more correlations are increased. That is, the superiority of Algorithm-CASP4AT will be more obvious with increased candidate services.

Experiment 3 What is the impact of task number on the results of Algorithm-CASP4AT?

In order to examine the impact, we set the task number to 10, 20, ..., 100, respectively, and randomly generate an integer from 5 to 100 for each task as the candidate service number. Other parameters are the same as Experiment 2. Similarly, each experiment is repeated 1000 times and the average value is recorded.

As shown in Fig. 3.21c, Algorithm-CASP4AT performs much better than the greedy algorithm. The superiority will be more obvious with the task number increasing, as more correlations are reserved. Both results are increasing linearly with the task number increasing.

(2)   Effectiveness Evaluation of Algorithm-CASP4NAT

In the following three experiments, we verify the effectiveness of Algorithm-CASP4NAT, and execution cost is chosen as the user preference. These three experiments vary the values of correlated service percentage, candidate service number and task number, respectively, to examine the QoS improvement of Algorithm-CASP4NAT. The experimental data sets are similar to that of Experiments 1, 2 and 3, while the correlations are generated among services from two random tasks that may not be adjacent tasks.

Experiment 4 What is the impact of correlated service percentage on the results of Algorithm-CASP4NAT?

We randomly generate the experimental parameters just like Experiment 1, except that correlations are generated among services from two random nonadjacent tasks. Then Algorithm-P4CS and Algorithm-CASP4NAT are implemented.

The results are shown in Fig. 3.22a, from which we can see that the greedy algorithm result is about 21. When 10% of the services are correlated, the result decreases to 19.1. With increasing correlated service percentage, it decreases steadily, because there may be more excellent alternative correlations. When the correlated services reach 90%, the average composite QoS value decreases to 14.9, a 30% decrease. We can conclude that the result will be significantly improved if correlations are taken into account. The composite QoS value will steadily improve with more correlations considered.

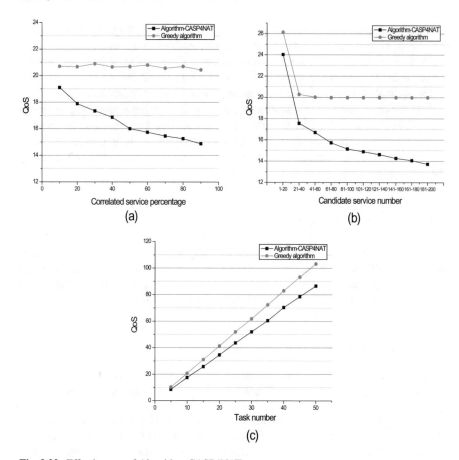

Fig. 3.22   Effectiveness of Algorithm-CASP4NAT

Experiment 5 What is the impact of candidate service number on the results of Algorithm-CASP4NAT?

We repeat Experiment 2 and generate correlations among services from two random tasks. Then we implement Algorithm-P4CS and Algorithm-CASP4NAT.

As shown in Fig. 3.22b, the results of Algorithm-CASP4NAT are far better than the greedy algorithm. With the candidate services increasing, the greedy algorithm results do not decrease as it reaches the lower limit, while the result of Algorithm-CASP4NAT decreases steadily, as there are more excellent alternative correlations. Therefore, the superiority of Algorithm-CASP4NAT will be more obvious with the candidate service number increasing.

Experiment 6 What is the impact of task number on the results of Algorithm-CASP4NAT?

In this experiment, we repeat Experiment 3 to examine the impact of task number. Similarly, we generate correlations among services from two random tasks.

As shown in Fig. 3.22c, the result of Algorithm-CASP4NAT is far better than the greedy algorithm. As the task number increases, there are more correlations involved in the optimal composite service; therefore, the gap will be more obvious.

These experiments have shown that QoS correlations have great impact on the whole QoS value of composite services. If service correlations are taken into account, the QoS value of the composite services will be significantly improved. With the correlated service percentage, candidate service number and task number increasing, the superiority of our methods will be more obvious.

3.4.3.2 Efficiency Evaluation

The following experiments are designed to verify the efficiency of the three algorithms. In order to examine the execution time growth trend with the range of the variables, we fit the experimental results and compute the confidence intervals in the following experiments. Similarly, each experiment is repeated 1000 times and the average value is adopted as the result.

(1) Efficiency Evaluation of Algorithm-P4CS

Experiment 7 How does the efficiency of Algorithm-P4CS change with the correlated service percentage, candidate service number and task number increasing?

In order to examine the efficiency of Algorithm-P4CS, we randomly generate experimental parameters just like Experiments 4, 5 and 6, respectively, and use Algorithm-P4CS to preprocess the candidate service sets. The execution times are shown in Fig. 3.23, where the experimental results are shown along with the fitting curves and confidence intervals including upper confidence limit and lower confidence limit curves.

Algorithm-P4CS's execution time is in a low order of magnitude. As the correlated service percentage, candidate service number or task number increases, the execution time increases at a modest pace. The three groups of experimental results can be fitted by a quadratic function, quadratic function and linear function, respectively. Therefore, the results are in accordance with the complexity of Algorithm-P4CS, $O(mn^2)$.

(2) Efficiency Evaluation of Algorithm-CASP4AT

Experiment 8 How does the efficiency of Algorithm-CASP4AT change with the correlated service percentage, candidate service number and task number increasing?

We repeat Experiments 1, 2 and 3, record the execution time of Algorithm-CASP4AT and adopt the average value of the 10-times repeated experiments. The results are shown in Fig. 3.24. The execution time of Algorithm-CASP4AT is in

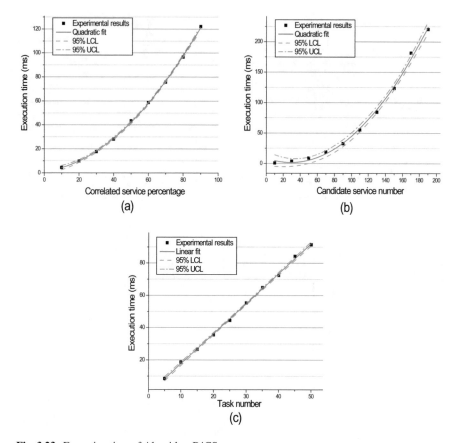

Fig. 3.23 Execution time of Algorithm-P4CS

a low order of magnitude. All of the three groups of experimental results can be approximately fitted by liner functions. Therefore, with the correlated service percentage, candidate service number and task number increasing, the execution time of Algorithm-CASP4AT increases linearly, which is in accordance with the complexity of Algorithm-CASP4AT, $O(mn)$.

(3) Efficiency Evaluation of Algorithm-CASP4NAT

Experiment 9 How does the efficiency of Algorithm-CASP4NAT change with the correlated service percentage, candidate service number and task number increasing?

Experiments 4, 5 and 6 are repeated again and the average execution time of Algorithm-CASP4NAT is recorded, as shown in Fig. 3.25. The execution time of Algorithm-CASP4NAT is in a low order of magnitude. However, all of the three groups of experimental results are fitted by exponential functions. Therefore, all the three parameters have big effect on the execution time of Algorithm-CASP4NAT.

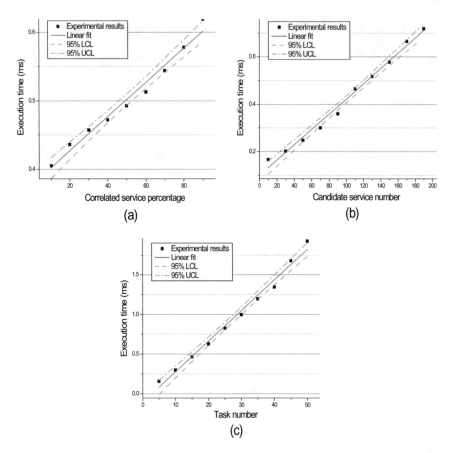

Fig. 3.24 Execution time of Algorithm-CASP4AT

With the growth of correlated service percentage and candidate service number, the execution time of Algorithm-CASP4NAT increases steadily. The number of tasks in the service plan has a larger effect on the execution time of Algorithm-CASP4NAT. It will spend little time if the task number is small. However, if a service plan has a large number of tasks, it will spend enough time for the Algorithm-CASP4NAT to obtain the result. Fortunately, the task number can't be very large in the real life.

According to the experiments above, all three algorithms perform with good scalability. As the experimental scale grows, the execution time of Algorithm-P4CS increases steadily. Algorithm-CASP4AT performs linear relations to all experimental variables. As for Algorithm-CASP4NAT, if the task number is not very large, it will cost little time, while if the task number is large, it may cost a large amount of time, but the task numbers are not very large in real life.

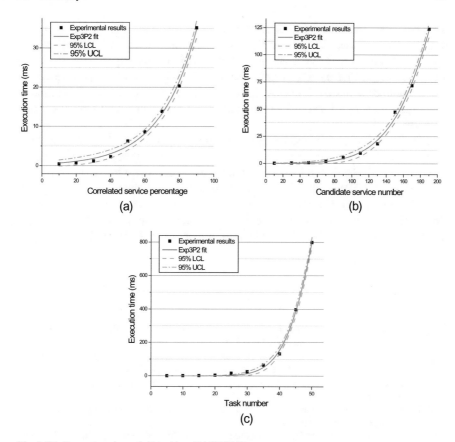

Fig. 3.25 Execution time of Algorithm-CASP4NAT

3.5 Summary

This chapter focused on the problem of service selection in terms of QoS, energy consumption and QoS correlations in mobile environments, and proposed three service selection methods.

Firstly, we proposed a mobility- enabled approach for service composition in a mobile environment, consisting of a mobility model, a mobility- aware QoS computation rule, and a mobility-enabled selection algorithm based on TLBO. The experimental simulation results demonstrate that our approach can obtain better solutions in a mobile environment than current standard composition methods. Furthermore, our approach achieves near-optimal solutions and has roughly linear algorithmic complexity with regard to the problem size.

Then, we focused on service selection in terms of minimizing the energy consumption of mobile devices in mobile environments. This problem is formally modeled, and the energy consumption calculation rules are presented in detail. Furthermore, the structure of composite services is taken into consideration to calculate the composite energy consumption. The genetic algorithm is adopted to achieve the objective of energy consumption-aware service selection. The simulation experiments show that our genetic algorithm-based service selection method significantly outperforms traditional methods in terms of energy consumption. Moreover, the execution time of our algorithm is of a low order of magnitude. It scales well as experimental scales increase.

Finally, we focused on QoS-aware service composition and took QoS correlations between services into account. A novel method, CASP, is proposed to achieve the objective. As QoS correlations have a significant effect on the QoS of the composite services, our CASP method can greatly improve the QoS of the generated composite services by taking QoS correlations into account in the service selection process. We proved that this method can generate the optimal composite service effectively. Our experiments also show the effectiveness and efficiency of the method.

References

1. Z. Shi, R. Gu, A framework for mobile cloud computing selective service system, in *Wireless Telecommunications Symposium (WTS)* (IEEE, 2013), pp. 1–5
2. S. Deng, L. Huang, W. Tan et al., Top-k automatic service composition: a parallel method for large-scale service sets. IEEE Trans. Autom. Sci. Eng. **11**(3), 891–905 (2014)
3. K. Kumar, Y.-H. Lu, Cloud computing for mobile users: can offloading computation save energy? Computer **43**, 51–56 (2010)
4. S. Deng, B. Wu, J. Yin et al., Efficient planning for top-K Web service composition. Knowl. Inf. Syst. **36**(3), 579–605 (2013)
5. S. Haak, B. Blau, Efficient QoS aggregation in service value networks, in *2012 45th Hawaii International Conference on System Science (HICSS)* (IEEE, 2012), pp. 1512–1521
6. M.C. Jaeger, G. Rojec-Goldmann, G. Muhl, Qos aggregation for web service composition using workflow patterns, in *Enterprise Distributed Object Computing Conference, 2004. EDOC 2004. Proceedings. Eighth IEEE International* (IEEE, 2004), pp. 149–159
7. P. Karaenke, J. Leukel, V. Sugumaran, Ontology-based QoS aggregation for composite web services. Wirtschaftsinformatik 84 (2013)
8. L. Zeng, B. Benatallah, A.H.H. Ngu et al., QoS-aware middleware for web services composition. Softw. Eng. IEEE Trans. **30**(5), 311–327 (2004)
9. F. Lecue, N. Mehandjiev, Seeking quality of web service composition in a semantic dimension. Knowl. Data Eng. IEEE Trans. **23**(6), 942–959 (2011)
10. M. Hilila, A. Chibani, K. Djouani et al., *Semantic service composition framework for multidomain ubiquitous computing applications. Service-Oriented Computing* (Springer, Berlin Heidelberg, 2012), pp. 450–467
11. D.B. Johnson, D.A. Maltz, *Dynamic Source Routing in Ad Hoc Wireless Networks. Mobile Computing* (Springer, US, 1996), pp. 153–181
12. F. Glover, Future paths for integer programming and links to artificial intelligence. Comput. Oper. Res. **13**(5), 533– 549 (1986)
13. R.V. Rao, V.J. Savsani, D.P. Vakharia, Teaching–learning-based optimization: a novel method for constrained mechanical design optimization problems. Comput. Aided Des. **43**(3), 303–315 (2011)
14. *Genetic Algorithms and Their Applications: Proceedings of the Second International Conference on Genetic Algorithms* (Psychology Press, 2013)

15. M. Tang, L. Ai, A hybrid genetic algorithm for the optimal constrained web service selection problem in web service composition, in *2010 IEEE Congress on Evolutionary Computation (CEC)* (IEEE, 2010), pp. 1–8

16. Z. Ye, X. Zhou, A. Bouguettaya, *Genetic algorithm based QoS-aware service compositions in cloud computing. Database Systems for Advanced Applications* (Springer, Berlin Heidelberg, 2011), pp. 321–334

17. H. Jiang, X. Yang, K. Yin et al., Multi-path QoS-aware web service composition using variable length chromosome genetic algorithm. Inf. Technol. J. **10**(1), 113–119 (2011)

18. M. Clerc, *Particle Swarm Optimization.* John Wiley & Sons, 2010

19. S. Wang, Q. Sun, H. Zou et al., Particle swarm optimization with skyline operator for fast cloud-based web service composition. Mob. Netw. Appl. **18**(1), 116–121 (2013)

20. G. Kang, J. Liu, M. Tang et al., An effective dynamic Web service selection strategy with global optimal QoS based on particle swarm optimization algorithm, in *Parallel and Distributed Processing Symposium Workshops & Ph.D. Forum (IPDPSW), 2012 IEEE 26th International* (IEEE, 2012), pp. 2280–2285

21. H. Yin, C. Zhang, B. Zhang et al., A hybrid multiobjective discrete particle swarm optimization algorithm for a SLA-aware service composition problem. Math. Probl. Eng. (2014)

22. D. Dasgupta, K. KrishnaKumar, D. Wong et al., *Negative Selection Algorithm for Aircraft Fault Detection. Artificial Immune Systems* (Springer, Berlin Heidelberg, 2004), pp. 1–13

23. X. Zhao, Z. Wen, *QoS-aware Web Service Selection with Negative Selection Algorithm, Knowledge and Information Systems* (2013)

24. S. Deng, L. Huang, Y. Li, J. Yin, Deploying data-intensive service composition with a negative selection algorithm. Int. J. Web Serv. Res. (2014)

25. L.M. Feeney, M. Nilsson, Investigating the energy consumption of a wireless network interface in an ad hoc networking environment, in *INFOCOM 2001. Twentieth Annual Joint Conference of the IEEE Computer and Communications Societies. Proceedings* (IEEE, 2001), pp. 1548–1557

26. C. Bettstetter, H. Hartenstein, X. Pérez-Costa, Stochastic properties of the random waypoint mobility model. Wireless Netw. **10**, 555–567 (2004)

Chapter 4
Mobile Services Recommendation

Abstract The overwhelming amount of services makes it difficult for users to find appropriate services to meet their functional and non-functional requirements. Therefore, the service recommendation technique becomes an important role in helping using services. Besides the typical methods driven by service properties, some external information can also be introduced to improve the recommendation of mobile services. This chapter proposes three different recommendation approaches that consider users' context, trust and social information respectively to improve the recommendation quality.

4.1 Background

Service recommendation is now playing an important role in helping users out of the service overload predicament and automatically recommending proper services for users. Researchers make lots of efforts to solve these problems by proposing plenty of models. The early research on mobile service recommendations mainly focused on users' functional requirements [1, 2]. Srinivasan et al. [3] have created a recommendation system called MobileMiner, they mine the frequent co-occurrence patterns of mobile context and user behavior on mobile phones. Christoffer et al. [4] create a mobile application recommendation system using the first use record, which improves the results in cold start situations. However, they focus on finding new and relevant mobile applications and ignore the influence on selection in different environment. Natarajin et al. [5] adopt Markov graph, personalized PageRank and collaborative filtering methods to predict which app a user will use next. But with the number of services with similar functionalities increasing, researchers turn to QoS-based service recommendations. These QoS-aware service recommendation approaches aim to predict the values of the QoS attributes of mobile services and then make a final recommendation according to the predicted QoS values. Among the existing approaches, collaborative filtering has been widely adopted. Shao et al. proposed a user-based CF algorithm using Pearson correlation coefficient to compute levels of similarity between users [6]. The approach in [7] is based on the premise

© Zhejiang University Press and Springer Nature Singapore Pte Ltd. 2020
S. Deng et al., *Mobile Service Computing*, Advanced Topics in Science
and Technology in China 58, https://doi.org/10.1007/978-981-15-5921-1_4

that two users are similar if two users have similar QoS experiences for the same services.

Besides these, some external information is introduced to improve recommendation accuracy. For example, integrating trust in recommendations can be an enhancement for collaborative filtering-based approaches. Golbeck proposed an extended breadth first search method in the trust network for prediction called TidalTrust [8], which finds all raters with the shortest path distance from the given user and then aggregates their ratings with the trust values between the given user and these raters as weights. MoleTrust is similar with TidalTrust [9], but it only considers the raters with the limit of a given maximum-depth. Ma et al. proposed a matrix factorization approach named STE for social network-based recommendation [10]. STE is based on the intuition that each user's decisions on the items should include both the user's characteristics and the user's trusted friends' recommendations. Comparing to STE, Jamali et al. incorporated the mechanism of trust propagation into their recommendation model [11] and proposed a novel model-based approach named SocialMF. It learns the latent feature vectors of users and items. They also proposed a random walk method named TrustWalker [11] which combined trust-based and item-based recommendation. The random walk model can efficiently avoid the impact of noisy data by considering enough ratings.

4.2 Context-Aware Mobile Services Recommendation

4.2.1 Introduction

Mobile App is deemed to be a sort of monofunctional web service in some service recommendation problems. Though the massive amounts of Apps on smartphones make users' daily life more convenient, the quantity makes it quite inconvenient for smartphone users to select appropriate service from several screens of apps on their smartphones—the simple classification with a named directory cannot satisfy the requirement of fast reaching and it needs the smartphone users to collate apps manually. Besides this, it does not consider the mobile context of mobile users, which distinguishes mobile user from traditional service invoker. Context can be defined as any piece of information that is relevant for a user's interaction with a system like location, time, relation and activity [12]; it describes the environment of the mobile user. It is known that the most remarkable characteristic of smart phone is its mobility and mobile environment. With various sensors of the smart phone collecting personal physical context information real-timely and incessantly, it can obtain the environment information in time. Using the mobile context, we are able to recommend apps in a more rational and personalized way.

To make the results more accurate, we turn to recommend services by considering conditional probability on service selection given the mobile context information as a user preference. This preference will be a valuable reference in a certain circumstance or a certain time period, but it will change when the behavior mode changes. For example, a taxi driver prefers to use taxi apps like Uber[1] in his work time, but when he gets off work from the taxi, he is more likely to use a reading app to read his favorite novels or a game app to play with friends online. Thus, simply listing recently used apps will give the recommendation of taxi apps but not the one he wants. Besides the simple solutions, traditional recommending approach like collaborative-filter still cannot handle this problem well, because (1) the users would not like to share their context information with others on the Internet for their privacy; (2) the installed apps on different smartphones varies, we do not need to recommend an app which the user has never heard of to him in this situation; (3) even under the same context, the behaviors of the users will be different—the driver on a taxi and his passenger would not like to use the same app. And the traditional time series analysis approaches like frequent set mining cannot work well in this situation as well, because we cannot ensure that the mobile device can always collect the user's sequential log data—the user may choose to turn part of the sensors off for saving energy or other reasons, and the time interval may be long.

In this work, we make contributions to solving the problem of recommending mobile services on mobile devices, we build up a user behavior model to describe the changing rule of user states with a deterministic finite automaton. Based on the user behavior model, we build up a generate model to describe how service invocation sequence is generated with the changing of user states. Then, we adopt the hidden Markov model to label the service invocation sequence with the user's current state and estimate the user preference. Finally, using the <mobile context, state> pairs, we train a classifier by adopting the logistic model tree approach to estimate the user state when given the mobile context. Combining the former steps, we create our recommendation system. Besides this, we conduct a series of experiments to evaluate how this recommendation approach improves the user experience and how it improves the accuracy comparing to the baseline approaches.

4.2.2 Models and Definitions

In this section, we will firstly introduce the basic concepts used in this work, and then formally define the context-aware personalized mobile service recommending problem.

4.2.2.1 Mobile Context

Mobile context describes the mobile environment. In this installed app recommending problem, 2 main components—time and location information are involved. Given the time information, we will know whether it is a holiday or festival and

---

[1] https://www.uber.com/.

whether it is morning or afternoon, and given the location information, we will know which kind of district you are in, a shopping area or a working place. From the mobile context, e.g. there is a user staying in the taxi this night, we can infer what the user would like to use. According to the usage record, the taxi driver in this example may use the taxi app.

Now we will define the components formally to make the concepts clear.

Time information

The time information can be presented as a 3–tuple time Info = <date, period, holiday>:

date: it describes the <year, month, day> in the conventional sense.

period: in our work, we separate the time of one day into 1440 parts whose time slot is 1 min.

holiday: the holiday ∈ {*weekday, weekend, festival*} presents what kind of a day it is.

Location information

The location information includes the geography information like latitude, longitude, and altitude, which describes where the user is. The altitude information is not helpful in location feature presentation in this work, because the difference in altitude value does not affect the actual position in a 2D map. Intuitively, we can use a 2-tuple <latitude, longitude> to describe the location information. But the simple 2-tuple location information does not make sense in our model, because it cannot reflect the surrounding environment of the mobile user. Therefore, we turn to the map information. Taking full advantage of Baidu Map API,[2] we can obtain the environment information. Figure 4.4 shows the ambient of the mobile device user who stands in front of computer college building of Yuquan Campus, Zhejiang University, and his location information is (30.2655210000, 120.1275260000).

In Fig. 4.1, the places with blue rectangle are teaching buildings or laboratories, the places with orange rectangles are restaurants or café shops, and the places marked with purple rectangle and black rectangle are shopping malls and government agencies. These appended building and facility classification information are described by the point of interest (POI) label system of the map. In our work, we divide the buildings and facilities in to 14 groups according to the POI label system—{*food, house, enterprise, hotel, finance service, traffic, education, scenery, shopping, entertainment, government, medical service, life service, automobile service*}. In Fig. 4.4 there are 3 red circles around the user location, which means 3 different coverage areas. The subsumed buildings and facilities are different in these 3 areas, but the ones with "education" labels always form the majority of them. This result is congruous with the fact that the user is in a university, thus we can use a 14-dimension vector to present the location information of user u with coverage area whose radius is r.

$$\vec{l}_{u,r} = (l_1, l_2, \ldots, l_{14}) \tag{2.1}$$

---

[2]https://lbsyun.baidu.com/index.php.

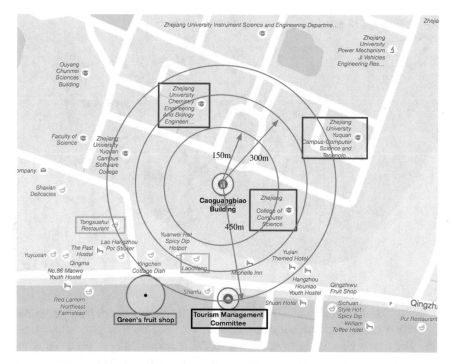

Fig. 4.1 Example of surrounding environment

where $l_i = \sum_j \frac{\zeta}{distance_{ij}+\lambda}$ is the weight of different POI types, the parameters ζ, λ here are the scale factor and the smooth factor, and $distance_{ij}$ means the distance between the user and the j-th building of facility in class i.

In conclusion, we combine the time information and location information together to form the mobile context for user u with cover area whose radius is r:

$$mc_{u,r} = \left(period, holiay, \vec{l}^*_{u,r}\right), \tag{2.2}$$

The $\vec{l}^*_{u,r}$ here means this vector is normalized.

4.2.2.2 User Behavior Pattern

In this work, our usage model is based on the following phenomenon in real life:

(a) A user's behavior depends on his current state. For example, the user can stay in the state "working in the morning in office" or "relaxing at night in house". In the former state, the user prefers to use office apps or communication apps

Fig. 4.2 Example of state transition

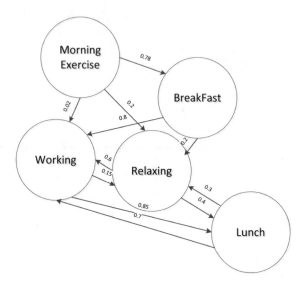

like "Mail Master" while in the latter state, the user tends to play games like "Angry Bird" and "Monument Valley".

(b)   The user's state changes according to the previous state. A userstate is the summary of a user's a series of actions, due to the fact that normal people always live in a well-organized or regular way, the user's state will not change abruptly. Namely, the changing rule of a given user will keep stable over a period of time—the user will most likely go to work after breakfast. No matter he is going to write code in the office or be on business outside, he is going to work. So we can use a deterministic finite automaton to describe the changing rule of the user's state. Figure 4.2 shows a typical user state pattern.

(c)   The user's state changes with time and location. Time information and location information form the mobile context, that means the user's state varies in different mobile context. For example, the user is more likely to be working in the office in the morning rather than sleeping.

The above phenomena are the basements of our user behavior pattern; we now give the formal definition of this pattern. In this work, we use sequential mobile app invocation record to analyze the user's behavior. Figure 4.3 shows a sample of sequential invocation with location and time.

According to above phenomena, we first figure out a generate model, which imitate how the app records are generated, and then estimate the parameters appeared in the generate model by an estimate model. At last, we will show how to recommend app to user when mobile context is collected successfully by the mobile device.

Fig. 4.3 Context and corresponding app invocation

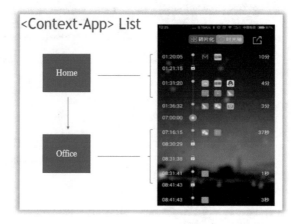

4.2.2.3 Generate Model

According to the user behavior pattern, we assume the sequential history record data is generated as following:

Determine the initial user state q_1 based on π.

Sample app I_j in every state q_i from distribution probability $p_{q_i,1...M}$.

Generate next user state q_{i+1} by sampling from probability distribution $t_{q_i,1...N}$.

There are two problems involved in the generating process, respectively corresponding to the two layers of the hierarchical framework of our generate model shown in Fig. 4.4.

Layer 1: Mobile Context → User State

In this layer, we try to answer the question—given a user's current mobile context, what is the state of the user? This problem is a classification problem.

In this work, we use the logistic model tree (LMT) algorithm to solve the classification problem, because the simple logistic regression method may result in high bias and the tree induction method cannot produce explicit class probability [13]. The LMT algorithm separates the data space in the way the same as C4.5 [14] algorithm does, but instead of giving a user's state class label us_i to every mobile context leaf node mc_i of the decision tree, the LMT algorithm attaches a set of logistic regression functions $\{F_i(x)\}_{i=1}^{N}$ on it. Here N is the total number of user state. Figure 4.5 shows an example of a 2-class logistics model tree.

Given a user's mobile context mc_i, the probability that his user state is q_j is determined by:

$$\Pr\left(\text{UserState} = q_j | \text{MobileContext} = mc_i\right) = \frac{e^{F_j(mc_i)}}{\sum_k e^{F_k(mc_i)}} \quad (2.3)$$

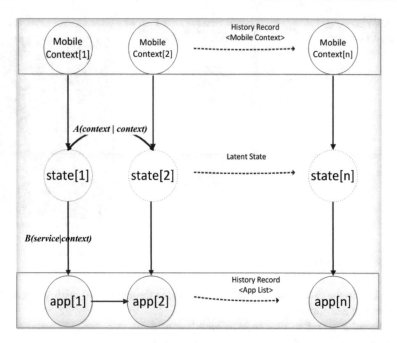

Fig. 4.4 Generate model

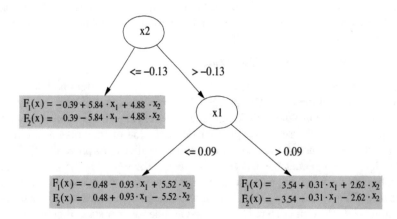

Fig. 4.5 Example of logistic model tree

Layer 2: User State → App

In this layer, we try to answer the question—given a user's state or user state distribution, how to select the top-k appropriate apps to for recommendation.

A direct way to solve this problem is to select app according to the user's preference in his current user state. When the preference matrix P is known, we can use a k-size heap to select top-k apps given a user state q_i.

Input: preference matrix P, user state q_i,
rank number K, App set I
Output: top-k recommendation *recommend*

H := K-size min heap;
recommend := K-size empty list;
M := I->size;
for j := 1 to M:
if   H->size < K:
    H->insert($P_{i,j}$);
else:
    if P_{ij} > H->top():
       H->pop();
       H-> insert($P_{i,j}$);
for k = K to 1:
p := H->pop();
j := index(p);
recommend[k] := I_j;
return recommend;

In the same way, we can select top-k apps when the input is a user state distribution $\varphi_{1 \times N}$.

Input: preference matrix P, user state distribution $\varphi_{1 \times N}$,
rank number K, App set I
Output: top-k recommendation *recommend*

$\theta := \varphi P$;
H := K-size min heap;
recommend := K-size empty list;
for j := 1 to M:
if   H->size < K:
    H->insert(θ_j);
else:
    if θ_j > H->top():
       H->pop();
       H-> insert(θ_j);
for k := K to 1:
p := H->pop();
j := index(p);
recommend[k] := I_j;
return recommend;

4.2.2.4   Estimate Model

In generate model, we have introduced two questions involved in our model and answer them with logistics model tree algorithm and a selection approach. Combine them together, we can easily give the suggestion on app selection. In estimate model, the main task is to estimate the transition matrix T and preference matrix P, which are two core parameters in recommendation.

The generating assumption of the sequential record data indicates the generate process of user state is a first-order Markov process, because

$$\Pr\left(userstate_{t+1} = q_{i_{t+1}} | userstate_t = q_{i_t}, \ldots, userstate_1 = q_{i_1}\right)$$
$$= \Pr\left(userstate_{t+1} = q_{i_{t+1}} | userstate_t = q_{i_t}\right).$$

With the app invocation record data as observation sequence, we can use hidden Markov model [15] to estimate the parameters and then label the corresponding mobile context with hidden user state.

Given the parameter $\mu = \{\pi, T, P\}$, we always expect that the observation app sequence O is the most possible sequence generated from the Markov process, thus we can estimate the parameters by maximize the observation probability $\Pr(O|\pi, T, P)$. Generally, the forward-backward algorithm is used to deal with the optimization problem. We denote a forward vector by $\alpha_t(i)$, which means the probability that the generate process has generated the former t apps $O_1 \ldots O_t$ and the state is q_i in this step. Similarly, we denote a backward vector by $\beta_t(i)$, which means the probability that the generate process produces $O_{t+1} \ldots O_L$ latter when current user state is q_i in the tth step. From the definitions of forward vector and backward vector, we can formulate them recursively:

$$\alpha_t(j) = \left(\sum_{i=1}^{N} \alpha_{t-1}(i)T_{i,j}\right)P_{j,O_t} \tag{2.4}$$

$$\beta_t(i) = \sum_{j=1}^{N} T_{i,j}P_{j,O_{t+1}}\beta_{t+1}(j) \tag{2.5}$$

With forward vector α and backward vector β, the probability $\xi_t(i,j)$ that user state is q_i in the t-th step and user state is q_j in the $t+1$th step can be presented as

$$\xi_t(i,j) = \Pr\left(userstate_t = q_i, userstate_{t+1} = q_j | O, \mu\right)$$
$$= \frac{\Pr\left(userstate_t = q_i, userstate_{t+1} = q_j, O | \mu\right)}{\Pr(O|\mu)}$$
$$= \frac{\alpha_t(i)T_{i,j}P_{j,O_{t+1}}\beta_{t+1}(j)}{\sum_{i=1}^{N}\sum_{j=1}^{N} \alpha_t(i)T_{i,j}P_{j,O_{t+1}}\beta_{t+1}(j)} \tag{2.6}$$

And the probability that the user state is q_i in the tth step is:

$$\gamma_t(i) = \sum_{j=1}^{N} \xi_t(i,j) \tag{2.7}$$

Hence, $\mu = \{\pi, T, P\}$ can be computed by expectation maximization (EM) method:

Input: app sequence O,
total number of user state N,
              total number app M,
              length of app sequence L
Output: $\mu = \{\boldsymbol{\pi}, \mathbf{T}, \mathbf{P}\}$

Initialize $\mu = \{\boldsymbol{\pi}, \mathbf{T}, \mathbf{P}\}$ with constriant $\begin{cases} \sum_{i=1}^{N} \pi_i = 1 \\ \sum_{j=1}^{N} T_{i,j} = 1 \\ \sum_{j=1}^{N} P_{i,j} = 1 \end{cases}$

count := 0
while   count++<MAXITERATION   or μ is   not
convergent:
//E-step
Compute α;
Compute β;
for i := 1 to N:
        for j := 1 to N:
Compute $\xi_t(i,j)$;
Compute $\gamma_t(i)$;
              for i := 1 to N:
$\pi_i := \gamma_t(i)$;
for j := 1 to N:
        $T_{i,j} := \frac{\sum_{t=1}^{L} \xi_t(i,j)}{\sum_{t=1}^{L} \gamma_t(i)}$
for j := 1 to M:
        $P_{i,j} := \frac{\sum_{t=1}^{L} \gamma_t(i) * \delta(O_t, I_j)}{\sum_{t=1}^{L} \gamma_t(i)}$;
$//\delta(O_t, I_j) := (O_t == I_j? 1: 0)$
return $\mu = \{\pi, T, P\}$

Besides these, it is easy to label the tth app sequence with user state q_z where $z = \arg \max \alpha_t(z)$.

4.2.3   *Experiment and Analysis*

In this section, a series of experiments are conducted on user record data collected by the users' Android mobile phone to evaluate the performance of our approach comparing with other approaches and explore the factors that affect the recommendation result.

We install the app developed by ourselves on 30 volunteers' Android cellphones, and this app listens to app launching event by observing the task stack of Android system and records the user behavior with local log file. Finally, we collect 7952 complete sequential record data in format like <userid, date, latitude, longitude, appid> and 1424,453 corresponding location information on map in format like

<latitude, longitude, POI type, distance> from 23 users in 3–12 days, the missing data is caused by network disconnections and GPS errors. The experiments are conducted on a computer with Windows 7 operation system, an 8 GB memory and a 3.2 GHz Intel CPU.

4.2.3.1   Performance Comparison

In this part, we compare our mobile context-aware recommendation approach using sequential record data to typical recommendation approach used in smart phones on the market to validate whether it can make the recommendation result more accurate.

Hit rate and average rank score are two typical metrics in recommendation system to exhibit the performance. A hit means the recommendation list contains the item that the user actually uses, and the rank is the order of that used item in recommendation list. The two metrics are defined individually by:

$$HitRate = \frac{No(hits)}{No(recs)},$$

where:

- *No(hits)* is the number of hit
- *No(recs)* is the total number of recommendation
- *RecSize* is the size of recommendation list
- $RankScore(item) = 1 - \frac{rank(item)}{RecSize}$ *rank*(*item*) is the order of item in recommendation list, it is set to *RecSize* + 1 when fails to recommend.

A large hit rate means the recommendation can always give a satisfying result that matches user's preference, and a large rank score means the user can always find the items he wants in the head of the recommendation list—it ensures a good user experience.

(a)   Frequency Statistics Approach

The frequency statistics approach is a simple but practical approach; it summarizes the using frequency of an app by counting the occurrence number of it in the entire record data and recommends apps with high frequency. If the user spends most of their time on only a few apps, this recommendation can work with high accuracy.

As shown in Fig. 4.6, when recommend list size increases, the average hit rate of frequency statistics approach and context-aware approach both increase as well. Because the frequency statistics approach always recommends the item with high frequency. The first 3 apps frequency are (14.3, 13, 10.3%), if the recommend list size is 2, the hit rate is 27.3%, and when the size changes to 3, the hit rate will be 37.3%. In context-aware approach, the increasing size allows it to recommend items with similar preference, so the hit rate increases as well.

As shown in Fig. 4.6, the average rank score of these two approaches both increases with the increasing to recommend list size, but the growth rate reduces. The average

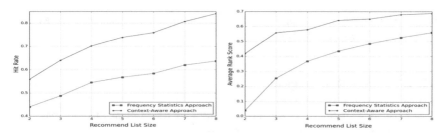

Fig. 4.6 Impact of recommend list size

rank score increases because the missing recommendation results are included. And the reason why the growth rate reduces is the aggregation property of item use, user prefers to use a set of few apps.

(b) KNN Approach

K-nearest neighbor (KNN) algorithm is a frequently-used algorithm in classification problem. In this algorithm, it chooses k nearest points of a given target to present it. The implicit thought of this algorithm is that the points of the same class should be close to each other in the data space. Given a record <mobile context, app>, we label the mobile context vector with the app, and compute the similarity of different mobile context vectors with cosine distance:

$$sim(mc_i, mc_j) = \frac{\sum_k mc_{i,k} * mc_{j,k}}{\sum_k (mc_{i,k} - mc_{j,k})^2} \tag{2.8}$$

After selecting k nearest mobile context vectors by considering the vectors with large similarity with target, we use the voting strategy to determine the label or the possible app.

As shown in Fig. 4.7, the hit rate of KNN approach and context-aware approach both increase with the increasing of recommend list size. From the chart, we can see that the hit rate of KNN approach is lower than the context-aware approach, because even when the mobile contexts are similar, the behavior may change. The factor that

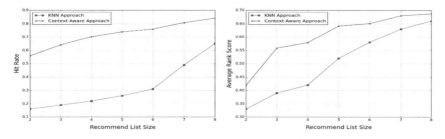

Fig. 4.7 Impact of recommend list on hit rate

keeps stable is the user state. In Fig. 4.7, both of the rank scores increase with the increasing of recommend list size.

4.2.3.2   Performance Influence Factor

In this part, we conduct experiments to investigate the influence factors that affect the performance of the context-aware approach.

(a)   Impact of user state number

The number of user state describes the grouping of a user's behaviors. In Fig. 4.8, it indicates that the approach gets its maximum average hit rate when the number of user state is 3. Because in real life, the number of a normal user's state will not be large, a coarse-grained user state number contributes generalization ability to this approach.

In Fig. 4.8, when the number of user state is 3, the context-aware approach gets its maximum average rank score. Similarly, the increasing number of user state expands the scale of the parameter estimation problem, the EM algorithm needs more data to solve this problem or the locally optimal solution it returns may not be the best.

(b)   Impact of day number

The number of day determines the length of the data. If the number of day equals 3, it means the approach uses sequential record data of 3 days. As shown in Fig. 4.9, the average hit rate and average rank score decreases with the increasing of day number. The average hit rate and average rank score stay acceptable when the day number is less than or equal to 4, but decrease fast contrarily. It means that the user's behavior pattern is cyclical, and the cycle time is about 1–4 days. According to this, we'd better choose sequential data which contains an entire behavior cycle.

(c)   Impact of scale

The parameter scale is the radius of the cover area of the user. It determines the amount of surrounding buildings or facilities information used in the context-aware approach. Figure 4.10 shows that the average hit rate and average rank score almost

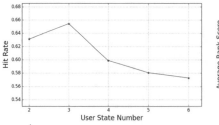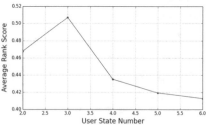

Fig. 4.8 Impact of user state number

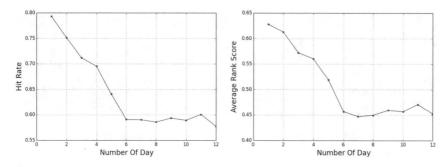

Fig. 4.9   Impact of day number

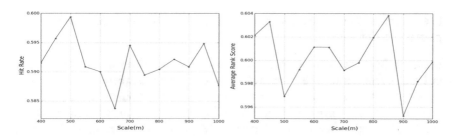

Fig. 4.10   Impact of scale

keep the same individually, while the variance of average hit rate is 1.42×10^{-5} and the variance of average rank score is 5.59×10^{-6}. It means that the attribute of a location computed by weighted distance in our approach is stable, because the closer buildings or facilities are, the more likely they belong to the same type. Using this property, we can set the scale to a smaller one so that the data size can be reduced during mobile context vector computing.

4.3   Trust-Aware Mobile Services Recommendation

4.3.1   Introduction

Although recommender systems have been widely studied, a traditional RS, which purely mines the user-item rating matrix for recommendations, cannot provide sufficiently accurate and reliable predictions. Considerable research has been conducted to address the above problems and new solutions have been proposed accordingly. Among these approaches, a kind of effort is to integrate the side (or complementary) information along with the traditional rating data. In line of this direction, a typical work is called the trust-based RS thanks to the emergence of social networking. The foundation of trusted-based recommendation is the hypothesis that people usually

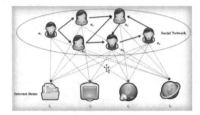

	i_1	i_2	i_3	i_4
u_1	5	5		5
u_2	5		3	4
u_3	3	4		3
u_4			5	3
u_5	5	4	4	5
u_6	5	4	5	5

(a) Real World Internet Item Rating Scenario

(b) User-Item Rating Matrix

Fig. 4.11 A toy example of trust-aware social recommendation

like to refer to their trusted friends' preferences to make decisions rather than the mass population.

Example Suppose a real world Internet item-rating scenario as shown in Fig. 4.11a, in which users can rate items according to their personal experiences. The rating records of items by users are shown in Fig. 4.11b. In this example, a user's missing preference scores, which are the unknown values in the rating matrix such as $<u_4, i_1>$ and $<u_4, i_2>$, can be inferred by referring its neighbor's known ratings via similarity calculation given the whole rating data is reliable and sufficient enough. Suppose that the predicting missing values of $<u_4, i_1>$ and $<u_4, i_2>$ are 4.8 and 3.6, then the item i_1 is better than i_2 for u_4. Users' ratings are not only determined by their neighbor's rating, but also impacted by those of their trusted friends in a certain extent. Another important advantage of trusted-based RS is its capability of dealing with sparsity and cold-start.

Recently, trust-aware recommender systems have attracted lots of attention [11, 16, 17], and the main stream in current approaches is to leverage the empowerment of machine learning exploit the Matrix Factorization (MF) technique to learn latent features for users and items from the observed ratings and trust relationships of users [10, 18] Theoretical and empirical evaluations have verified its superiority compared to other state-of-the-art approaches. In principle, MF can be considered as a prediction model learning process via estimating the model parameters from the observed training data. More concretely, it is indeed an optimization problem of determining the model parameters in order to best approximate the ground truth with the prediction. For an optimization problem, the initialization is sometimes a crucial issue to the quality of optimization. This inspires us to investigate this common difficulty in MF. Hence this work attempts to address these two questions simultaneously: First, it is important to generate a good initialization for the latent features of users and items, which has been sidestepped or overlooked by most matrix factorization based RS. Second, the existing models in the current methods fail to take into account the diversity of user trust networks.

Therefore, we propose a matrix factorization based approach for the trust-aware recommendation in social networks, called DLMF. In this approach, we examine the importance of the initialization of the matrix factorization methods. We propose a deep learning based initialization method in which deep autoencoder is utilized to pre-train the initial values of the parameters for our learning model. For the second limitation, we propose a social trust ensemble learning model which not only considers trusted friends' recommendation but also involves the community effect. Furthermore, we also provide a community detection algorithm to form a community in a trust social network. To evaluate DLMF, we conduct a series of experiments based on the real-world data from Epinions and Flixster. The results show that DLMF can provide better recommendation accuracy than other state-of-the-art approaches.

4.3.2 Problem Definition and Preliminary

As stated in [13], there is a set of users $U = \{u_1, u_2 \ldots u_m\}$ and a set of items $I = \{i_1, i_2 \ldots i_n\}$ in a recommender system. The ratings expressed by users on items are given in a rating matrix $R = [R_{u,i}]_{m \times n}$. In this matrix $R_{u,i}$ denotes the rating of user u on item i. $R_{u,i}$ can be any real number, but often ratings are integers in the range $[1, 5]$. In this work, without loss of generality, we map the ratings $1, \ldots, 5$ to the interval $[0, 1]$ by normalizing the ratings. In a social rating network, each user u has a set S_u of direct neighbors and $t_{u,v}$ denotes the value of social trust u has on v as a real number in $[0, 1]$. Zero means no trust and one means full trust. Binary trust networks are the most common trust networks (Amazon, eBay, …). The trust values are given in a matrix $T = [T_{u,v}]_{m \times m}$. Non-zero elements $T_{u,v}$ in T denote the existence of a social relation from u to v. Note that T is asymmetric in general.

The social rating network can be presented as a graph where there are two types of nodes corresponding to users and items respectively. Edges between users correspond to trust relations between users, and edges between users and items correspond to ratings assigned. An example of a graph representation of social rating network is shown in Fig. 4.11.

Thus, the task of a trust-aware recommender system is: given a user u and an item i for which $R_{u,i}$ is unknown, predict the rating for u on item i using R and T.

In the following, we first briefly review the basic matrix factorization approach for recommendation using only user-item rating matrix. Then in Sect. 4.4, we will introduce our proposed approach DLMF which employs deep learning and matrix factorization for recommendation in social rating networks.

Matrix factorization model is an efficient mechanism for predicting missing values and becomes more and more popular in recommender systems. This model maps both users and items to a joint latent feature space of a low dimension k, so that user-item interactions can be modeled as inner products in that space. The premise behind the matrix factorization technique is that there are only a few key features affecting the user-item interactions, and a user's interactive experience is impacted by how each feature applies to the user. Specifically, each user u corresponds to a column vector $P_u \in \mathbf{R}^k$, and each item i corresponds to a column vector $Q_i \in \mathbf{R}^k$. For a given user u, the elements of P_u measure the extent of interest the user has in items that are high on the corresponding features. For a given item i, the elements of Q_i measure the extent to which the item possesses those features. Then the m users and n items form the user latent feature matrix $P \in \mathbf{R}^{k \times m}$ and item latent feature matrix $Q \in \mathbf{R}^{k \times n}$ respectively. The resulting dot product, $P_u^T Q_i$, models the interaction between user u and item i. Hence, the user-item rating matrix R can be approximately divided into two parts P and Q with k-dimensional features constraints.

$$R \approx P^T Q \tag{3.1}$$

The goal of matrix factorization is to learn these latent variables by minimizing the following term:

$$L(R, P, Q) = \frac{1}{2} \min_{P,Q} \sum_{u=1}^{m} \sum_{i=1}^{n} I_{ui}(R_{u,i} - P_u^T Q_i)$$
$$+ \frac{\lambda_1}{2} \|P\|_F^2 + \frac{\lambda_2}{2} \|Q\|_F^2 \tag{3.2}$$

where I_{ui} is the indicator function that equals to 1 if user u rated item i and equals to 0 otherwise. λ_1 and λ_2 are regularization terms to avoid model over fitting. $\| \cdot \|_F^2$ denotes the Frobenius norm. The initial values of P and Q are always generated randomly or manually. Then in each iteration, P and Q are updated by employing the stochastic gradient descent technique as follows:

$$P_u' = P_u - \gamma_1 \frac{\partial L}{\partial P_u}$$
$$Q_i' = Q_i - \gamma_2 \frac{\partial L}{\partial Q_i} \tag{3.3}$$

where $\gamma_1 > 0$ and $\gamma_2 > 0$ are set as the learning rates. To reduce the model complexity, we set $\gamma_1 = \gamma_2$ in our experiments. Salakhutdinov and Mnih provided a probabilistic foundation for regularizing the learned variables [19] which has been employed by some recent approaches [10, 11].

4.3.3 Trust-Aware Recommendation Approach

This section presents our approach DLMF in detail to incorporate deep learning into a matrix factorization model for trust-aware recommendation in social networks. In our proposed approach DLMF, we utilize deep autoencoder to learn the initial values of latent features of users and items at first, then using the learned results for the learning of minimizing the objective function. For our objective function in the matrix factorization model, we consider both the users' characteristics and their trusted friends' recommendations. Besides, a trust-aware regularization term is added to describe the trust propagation. In the following parts, more details of DLMF are introduced.

4.3.3.1 Pre-training with Deep Autoencoder

In this subsection, we analyze how to employ deep autoencoder to pre-train the rating matrix and learn the initial values of the latent features of users and items.

In the rating matrix $R = [R_{u,i}]_{m \times n}$, each row corresponds to the rating experience on all items from one user. Thus we can denote user vectors by $U_{n \times m} = [U_1, \ldots, U_i, \ldots U_m] = R^T$, in which each vector is denoted by $U_i = [R_{i,1}, \ldots, R_{i,j}, \ldots R_{i,n}]^T$. Similarly, item vectors can be denoted by $I_{m \times n} = [I_1, \ldots, I_i, \ldots I_n]$ where each vector is $I_i = [R_{1,i}, \ldots, R_{j,i}, \ldots R_{m,i}]^T$. In the real world, the number of users and items are both extremely large. Hence, the matrix factorization method maps user vectors and item vectors to a joint latent factor space of a low dimensionally k, i.e. $P_{k \times m}$ and $Q_{k \times n}$. In most current matrix factorization methods, $P_{k \times m}$ and $Q_{k \times n}$ are initialized randomly. After multiple iterations these methods converge to a local optimum that depends on the starting point. In this work, we follow the hypothesis that an appropriate initialization of latent features yields that matrix factorization methods produce more precise feature vectors and therefore provide more accurate predictions.

When investigating the feature vectors of accurate matrix factorization models, we can observe that similar users (e.g. users rating similar scores for the same items) have similar user feature vectors. Based on this observation, we can intuitively conclude that if the initialization of feature vectors characterized the similarities of users and items more precisely, it will result in more appropriate models. Thus, we try to get the initial values of $P_{k \times m}$ and $Q_{k \times n}$ by extracting features from the original user vectors and item vectors $U_{n \times m}$ and $I_{m \times n}$. It is worth to note that the original user vectors and item vectors are typically very sparse and the initial vectors should be compliant with the feature size of the matrix factorization model. Hence, the goal of pre-training turns out to dimensionally reduction or feature extraction.

The autoencoder is an artificial neural network used for learning efficient coding, which aims at learning a compressed representation (encoding) for a set of high-dimensional data. Hinton has developed a pre-training technique for training many-layered deep autoencoders and then using a back propagation technique to fine-tune. The whole system of deep autoencoder is depicted in Fig. 4.12, which consists of an encoder network and a decoder network. The encoder network targets to transform the original data with high dimensionality into a low-dimensional code. And the decoder network, which can be regarded as the inverse process of the encoder network, is to re-construct the original data from the code. The joint part of the two networks is called code layer, which is the core of the whole system and determines the intrinsic dimensions of the original data.

The main working process of deep autoencoder is: start with learning weights for the two networks by using restricted Boltzmann machine (RBM) [20]; then use back propagation of error derivatives to train the two networks together by minimizing

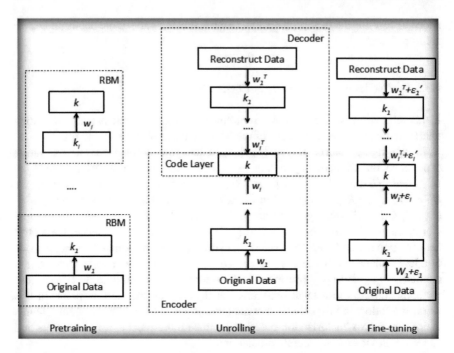

Fig. 4.12 Framework of deep autoencoder

the deviation between the original data and its reconstruction. However, RBM is only applicable for binary data but not ideal for modeling continuous data like the rating matrix in this work. So we utilize Continuous restricted Boltzmann machine (CRBM) for pre training weights.

CRBM consists of a visible layer and a hidden layer, which correspond to input data and output data respectively. Take user vectors as an example, $U_{n \times m}$ is the input and $U'_{p \times m}$ is the output. Thus each n-dimensional user vector is encoded as p-dimensional vectors. And there are n visible units and p hidden units. For a visible unit v_i and a hidden unit h_j, w_{ij} denotes the weight between them and $w_{ij} = w_{ji}$. Then the main steps of encoding stage with CRBM are:

(1) For each data vector v from $U_{n \times m}$, h for the hidden units can be achieved by:

$$h_j = \varphi_j \left(\sum_i w_{ij} v_i + \sigma N_j(0, 1) \right)$$

$$n_j = \sigma N_j(0, 1) \tag{3.4}$$

where the set v_i denotes the set of visible units which contribute to the input of h_j. $N_j(0, 1)$ represents a Gaussian random variable. The constant σ and $N_j(0, 1)$ form a noise input component $n_j = \sigma N_j(0, 1)$ according to a probability distribution:

$$p(n_j) = \frac{1}{\sigma\sqrt{2\pi}} \exp\left(\frac{-n_j^2}{2\sigma^2}\right) \tag{3.5}$$

In Eq. (3.4), $\varphi_j(x)$ is a sigmoid function with asymptotes at θ_L and θ_H:

$$\varphi_j(x) = \theta_L + (\theta_H - \theta_L)\frac{1}{1 + \exp(-a_j x)} \tag{3.6}$$

where a_j controls the slope of the sigmoid function.

(2)   Reconstruct each visible vector as v with the following equation that is similar to Eq. (3.4):

$$v_i' = \varphi_i\left(\sum_j w_{ji} h_j + \sigma N_i(0, 1)\right) \tag{3.7}$$

where the set h_j denotes the hidden set of units which get the output of v_i.

(3)   Re-compute the hidden states as h' using Eq. (3.4) with v' instead of v.

(4)   Update the weights w_{ij} and the noise controllers a_j using Minimizing Contrastive Divergence (MCD).

$$\Delta w_{ij} = \eta_w(v_i h_j - v_i' h_j') \tag{3.8}$$

$$\Delta a_j = \frac{\eta_a}{a_j^2}\left(h_j^2 - h_j'^2\right) \tag{3.9}$$

Actually, there could be multiple CRBMs to encode the n-dimensional user vectors to the final k-dimensional vectors. Each input data of a CRBM is the output of the previous CRBM and the top CRBM reaches the code layer. The fine-tune stage is relatively simple, and back propagation is utilized to minimize the root mean squared reconstruction error $\sqrt{\sum_i (v_i - \hat{v}_i^2)^2}$ until an optimal reconstruction is reached. Finally, the optimal autoencoder is trained, and the k-dimensional vectors of users and items are achieved.

4.3.3.2   Social Trust Ensemble

In this subsection, we investigate how the social trust networks affect users' decisions on selecting items, and extend the basic matrix factorization model by involving the recommendations of trusted friends.

As discussed in the previous section, the trust values are given in a matrix $T = [T_{u,v}]_{m \times m}$. Non-zero elements $T_{u,v}$ in T denote the existence of a social relation from u to v. And we regard the value of $T_{u,v}$ as the trust degree of the user u on the user v, note that $T_{u,v}$ is asymmetric in general. In most existing work, the trust degree is usually assigned by users explicitly. However, in most real-world online social networks (such as Facebook, Epinions, Flixster), there is no explicit value that measures the extent of users' trust relations. Hence, the first we do is to propose a new model of trust degree no matter the trust values are assigned explicitly or not.

Section 4.1 has mentioned that people always prefer to rely on their friends' recommendations because the comments from friends are more trustworthy. However, the recommendation from trusted friends are not absolutely suitable for the target user since they may have different tastes, preferences, or habits. Then we associate the preference similarity to model trust degree $T_{u,v}$ as follows:

$$T_{u,v} = \frac{sim(u, v) \times trust(u, v)}{\sum_{s \in S_u} sim(u, s) \times trust(u, s)} \qquad (3.10)$$

where $sim(u,v)$ is the similarity of the two users by calculating the cosine similarity of their corresponding vectors P_u and P_v. $trust(u,v)$ is the assigned trust value by user u. If the value is not assigned explicitly, it equals 1 if the user u links to the user v and 0 otherwise. S_u is the set of users whom u directly links to. Note that this equation is only applicable for two users which are linked directly. For the users which are not linked directly, we use multiplication as the trust propagation operator to calculate the trust degree. And only the shortest path is taken into consideration if multiple trust propagation paths exist.

After calculating the trust degree of users, we will illustrate how to ensemble the trust degree to the matrix factorization model. In the basic matrix factorization approach, the estimated rating of the item i from the user u is only interpreted by the user's favor on the item as $\hat{R}_{u,i} = P_u^T Q_i$. As the analysis above, recommendations on item i from user u's trusted friends S_u should also be considered. Hence, we extend the form of estimated ratings by considering both above factors as follows:

$$\hat{R}_{u,i} = P_u^T Q_i + \sum_{v \in S_u} T_{u,v}(P_v^T Q_i + \Delta_{u,v} - P_u^T Q_i) \qquad (3.11)$$

In this equation, rather than involving the favors of u's trusted friends directly, we take into consideration the differences of the favors of u's trusted friends and u's favors. This means, u's favor on i $\left(P_u^T Q_i\right)$ is a base term, and is adjusted by the deviations from his trusted friends' favors. $\Delta_{u,v}$ means the average bias on ratings between u and v. For example, user u is a generous rater who always provides high ratings. While v is a critical rater who always gives low ratings and their average bias on ratings are around 2. Then for an item i, the ratings from them are 5 and 3 respectively. It is intuitive that they have different opinions on the item i from the ratings directly. However, if the bias on ratings is taken into consideration, 3 is almost the highest ratings given by user v, then we may conclude that both u and v think the item i is good.

Furthermore, there also exist biases on users and items respectively. For example, suppose that we want to predict user u's rating on the item i. The average rating over all movies avg is 3. Besides, item i is better than an average item and tends to be rated 0.5 higher than the average. On the other hand, user u is a critical rater, who tends to rate 0.3 lower than the average. Thus, the estimate for item i from user u would be 3.2 $(3 + 0.5 - 0.3)$. Thus, the Eq. (3.5) is extended with biases of users and items as follows:

$$\hat{R}_{u,i} = P_u^T Q_i + \sum_{v \in S(u)} T_{u,v}(P_v^T Q_i + \Delta_{u,v} - P_u^T Q_i)$$
$$+ avg + bias_u + bias_i \qquad (3.12)$$

where the parameters $bias_u$ and $bias_i$ indicate the deviations of user u and item i.

4.3.3.3   Regularization with Community Effect

As mentioned above, social networks demonstrate a strong community effect. Users in social networks have a tendency to form groups of closely-knit connections. The groups are also called communities, clusters, or cliques in different context. Furthermore, people in a group tend to trust each other and share common preferences with each other more than those in other groups. Hence, in this subsection we discuss how to incorporate the community effect in a trust social network as regularization terms to revamp the proposed matrix factorization model in detail.

Graph mining techniques have been widely used for community detection in social networks as they are effective in identifying groups that are hidden in the underlying data. One important type of community detection is to identify cliques based on the reachability between actors in a network. Inspired by the existing community structure *n-clique* in social science, we propose the *n-trust-clique* to identify the cliques in a social network based on the trust relationship between users and develop an algorithm TrustCliques to detect cliques. The reason that we choose *n-clique* is that this kind of methods helps to detect overlapping communities. Besides, it is worth to note that the reason that we don't directly apply *n-clique* on the social network is that the link information itself will lead to low detection accuracy, while the trust information helps guarantee good performance. In what follows, we first introduce an important parameter, collectivity, used by the proposed TrustCliques algorithm in Sect. 4.3.1. Then we give the details of the TrustCliques algorithm in Sect. 4.3.2. At last, we present the regularization terms based on community effect in Sect. 4.3.3.

(a)   Key Definitions for Community Detection

The notion of *n-clique* is a typical concept for cliques in social science, which is defined as follows.

Definition 1 (*n-clique*) Given a network G, an *n-clique* is a maximal subgraph in which the largest distance of each pair of nodes is no greater than n. That is,

$$dist(v_i, v_j) \leq n, \forall v_i, v_j \in G$$

Note that the distance is defined in the original network. Thus, the geodesic is not necessarily included in the group structure. So an *n-clique* may have a diameter greater than n or even become disconnected.

In order to extend the notion of *n-clique* to handle the trust relationships in the social network, we propose a parameter collectivity. The definition is as follows.

Definition 2 (*Collectivity*) Given a user trust matrix T and the corresponding trust network G_T, assume that the users have been clustered into a set of cliques C_i. The collectivity of a clique C_i is defined as:

$$Col_i = \frac{\sum_{u,v \in C_i} T_{u,v}}{\sum_{u \in C_i, v \notin C_i} T_{u,v}}$$

Thus the global collectivity of user collection the trust Network is defined as follows:

$$Col = log\left(\frac{\sum_{C_i \in Clqs} Col_i}{|Clqs|}\right)$$

where *Clqs* is the set of cliques and the log operator is employed to ensure that global collectivity decreases linearly with the number of cliques.

Based on the parameter collectivity, we propose a new community structure called *n-trust-clique*, which is defined as follows.

Definition 3 (*n-trust-clique*) Given a trust network G_T, an *n-trust-clique* is a subgraph in which the largest distance of each pair of nodes is no greater than n. At the same time, the generation of cliques in G_T should guarantee the maximum value of the global collectivity *Col*.

To achieve the maximum value of the global collectivity *Col* is an NP-hard problem. So we utilize optimization methods to get approximate *n-trust-cliques* in the follows. The larger value of *Col* means that users in the same clique have higher trust degrees with each other than with users in other cliques. That is, users in the same cliques are more likely to share common preferences and there is greater difference between users in different cliques. Hence, if the clique preference feature is more obvious, the recommendation prediction is more precise.

(b) Algorithm for Community Detection

Based on the previous definitions, we present the details of the proposed algorithm TrustCliques in Algorithm 1. This algorithm is inspired from [21], which combines the greedy techniques and the simulated annealing techniques. Specifically, the algorithm runs l iterations and each iteration produces a partition result $Clqs$, which is initialized as the user set U and each user forms a clique. For each C_i in $Cliqs$, J is the set of C_i's connected vertices. We assume to merge the clique C_i and $v_j \in J$, calculate the ΔCol for the merge and pick the merged clique C_t with the maximum ΔCol (lines 4–14 in Algorithm 1). If $\Delta Col_{max} > 0$, we accept this change and update $Clqs$. Otherwise we give a probability $prob$ to accept this (lines 16–20). This is based on the stimulated annealing technique. For simplification, we just set the probability to a real-valued number between 0 and 1, e.g. 0.3. After i runs over all cliques in each iteration, we get a new partition $Cliqs$. Then we store the partition information and the corresponding collectivity. After l iterations, we get l different partition results. Finally, we choose the partition result with the maximum value of collectivity as the final result (line 24 in Algorithm 1).

Algorithm 1 TrustCliques Algorithm

Require:
    clique size n, iteration limitation l,
    user set U, user trust matrix T;
Ensure:
    cliques collection $Clqs$;
1:   $Clqs = U$, $n_c = |Clqs|$;
2:   **while** $n_c > 1$ or the number of iterations $< l$ **do**
3:     **for** $i = 1$ to n_c **do**
4:        C_i = the ith clique in $Clqs$,
            J = the set of C_i's connected vertices;
5:        $\Delta Col_{max} = 0$;
6:        **for each** $v_j \in J$ **do**
7:           $C_i' = C_i \cup v_j$;
8:           **if** C_i' satisfies the first condition of *n-trust-clique* **then**
9:              calculate ΔCol for the change;
10:             **if** $\Delta Col > \Delta Col_{max}$ **then**
11:                 $\Delta Col_{max} = \Delta Col$;
12:                 $C_t = C_i'$;
13:             **end if**
14:           **end if**
15:        **end for**
16:        **if** $\Delta Col_{max} > 0$ or $Random(0, 1) > prob$ **then**
17:           delete clique C_i from $Clqs$;
18:           add C_t to $Clqs$;
19:           store current partition result $Clqs$ and the corresponding Col;
20:        **end if**
21:     **end for**
22:     $n_c = |Clqs|$, iteration number++;
23: **end while**
24: **return** optimal $Clqs$ with the maximum value of Col;

(c) Regularization with Community Effect

As mentioned above, it is intuitive that users tend to share similar preferences on items with their trusted friends in the same clique. We regard these trusted friends as the neighbors of the given user. These neighbors can contribute more meaningful information to improving prediction accuracy. For a given user u, a set of neighbors $N(u)$ can be defined as follow:

$$N(u) = \{v | v \in C \wedge u \in C, u \neq v\} \tag{3.13}$$

where C is a clique that the given user u belongs to. Note that u may belong to not only one clique, we take all the cliques u belongs to into consideration.

With the help of neighborhood information, we propose a regularization term for ratings prediction. Due to community effect, the behavior of a user u would be affected by his neighbors $N(u)$. This indicates that the difference of user feature vectors in the neighborhood should be minor. Then this idea can be expressed mathematically by minimizing the following form:

$$\left\| P_u - \frac{1}{|N(u)|} \sum_{v \in N(u)} T_{u,v} P_v \right\|_F^2 \tag{3.14}$$

The above regularization term is used to minimize the preferences between a user u and his neighborhood to an average level. That means, if the neighborhood of user u is $N(u)$, then we can assume that u's preferences (feature vector P_u) should be similar to the general preferences of all neighbors in $N(u)$. Then, we add this regularization term in our proposed objective function to revamp the matrix factorization model as follow:

$$L(R, T, P, Q) = \frac{1}{2} \min_{P,Q} \sum_{u=1}^{m} \sum_{i=1}^{n} I_{ui} \left(R_{u,i} - \hat{R}_{u,i} \right)$$

$$+ \frac{\mu}{2} \sum_{u=1}^{m} \left\| P_u - \frac{1}{|N(u)|} \sum_{v \in N(u)} T_{u,v} P_v \right\|_F^2$$

$$+ \frac{\lambda_1}{2} \|P\|_F^2 + \frac{\lambda_2}{2} \|Q\|_F^2 \tag{3.15}$$

where the non-negative parameter μ is used to control the importance of the regularization term. To reduce the model complexity, we set $\lambda_1 = \lambda_2$ in our experiments. We can observe that this objective function takes all the users into consideration, and thus it is aiming at minimizing the global difference within different neighborhoods. Similar to the basic matrix factorization model, the global minimum of L cannot be achieved due to the nature of its inner structure. We can find a local minimum of the objective function by utilizing gradient descent on P_u and Q_i for all users u and all items i.

$$\frac{\partial L}{\partial P_u} = \sum_{i=1}^{n} I_{ui} \left(\hat{R}_{u,i} - R_{u,i} \right) \left(Q_i - \sum_{v \in S(u)} T_{u,v} Q_i \right)$$

$$+ \mu \left(P_u - \frac{1}{|N(u)|} \sum_{v \in N(u)} T_{u,v} P_v \right) + \lambda_1 P_u \tag{3.16}$$

$$\frac{\partial L}{\partial Q_i} = \sum_{u=1}^{m} I_{ui} \left(\hat{R}_{u,i} - R_{u,i} \right) \left(P_u^T + \sum_{v \in S(u)} T_{u,v} \left(P_v^T - P_u^T \right) \right)$$

$$+ \lambda_2 Q_i \tag{3.17}$$

4.3.4 Experiments

In this section, we conduct several experiments to compare the recommendation qualities of our approach with other state-of-the-art trust-aware recommendation methods. Our experiments aim at addressing the following questions. (1) How do the model parameters affect the prediction accuracy? (2) How does the pre-training phase affect the prediction accuracy? (3) How does the community effect affect the perdition accuracy? (4) How does DLMF compare with the existing state-of-the-art trust-aware recommendation algorithms with different sparsity of datasets? (5) Can DLMF perform well with cold start users?

4.3.4.1 Experiment Setup

(a) Dataset

In the trust-aware recommender research domain, there is not much publicly available and suitable test data. In our experiments, we mainly use the following two datasets: the Epinions dataset and the Flixster dataset.

Epinions is a well-known product review website established in 1999 [22]. Users can rate products from 1 to 5 and submit their personal reviews. These ratings and reviews will influence other customers when they make a decision on whether to buy a product. Besides, users are also allowed to specify whom to trust and build a social trust network. In social trust network, reviews and ratings from a user can be consistently found to be valuable by his trustees. Flixster is a social networking service in which users can rate movies. Users can also add some users to their friend list and create a social network. Thus, Epinions and Flixster are both ideal source for our experiments. We use the dataset of Epinions and the dataset of Flixster [11].

Table 4.1 shows the statistics of the two data sources. It shows that the user-item rating matrix of Epinions is much sparser than Flixster. Thus, the Epinions dataset can evaluate the performance of our approach with high sparsity.

(b) Evaluation Metrics

Our experiments are developed by Java and the execution environment is: Intel Core2 P7370 2.0 GHZ with 4 GB RAM, Windows 7, and jdk1.6.0.

We adopt the Root Mean Squared Error (RMSE) to measure the error in recommendation, which has been widely used in recommendation research:

Table 4.1 Statistics of datasets

	Epinions	Flixster
Users	49,290	1049,445
Items	139,738	492,359
Ratings	664,824	8238,597
Trust relations	487,181	26,771,123

$$RMSE = \sqrt{\frac{\sum_{u,i}\left(R_{u,i} - \hat{R}_{u,i}\right)^2}{N}} \qquad (3.18)$$

where $R_{i,j}$ is the actual rating the user u gave to the item i and $\hat{R}_{u,i}$ is the predicted rating the user u gave to the item i. N denotes the number of tested ratings. The smaller the value of RMSE is, the more precisely the recommendation.

Meanwhile, some recommendation mechanisms may not be able to predict all the ratings in test data for the high sparsity of the dataset. Involving trust can enhance the coverage without sacrificing the precision. So we use the metric *coverage* to measure the percentage of pairs of <user, item> that a predicted value can be generated. For a pair of <user, item>, if the recommender cannot find a prediction on the rating, then it means that the recommender cannot cover this pair of <user, item>.

$$coverage = \frac{S}{N} \qquad (3.19)$$

where S denotes the number of predicted ratings, and N denotes the number of tested ratings.

To combine RMSE and *coverage* into a single evaluation metric, we compute the F-Measure. Therefore, we have to convert RMSE into a precision metric in the range [0, 1]. The precision is denoted as follows:

$$precision = 1 - \frac{RMSE}{4} \qquad (3.20)$$

In this equation, 4 is the maximum possible error since the values of ratings are in the range [1, 5].

$$F - Measure = \frac{2 \times precision \times coverage}{precision + coverage} \qquad (3.21)$$

4.3.4.2   Impact of Model Parameter μ

In our DLMF approach, the parameter μ controls how much the trust-aware regularization terms influence to the objective function of Eq. (3.12). Larger value of

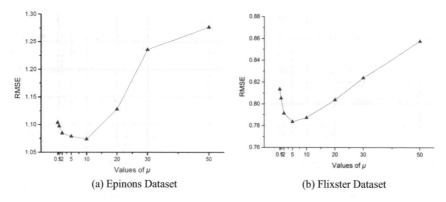

Fig. 4.13 Impact of different values of μ on the prediction accuracy. RMSE decreases at first and increases when μ passes over a certain threshold

μ indicates that the social trust network has more impact on the characteristics of users. Extremely small value of μ makes our model focus on basic matrix factorization model and weaken the impact of the trust-aware regularization terms. However, extremely large value of μ leads to such a model that the social trust information dominates the prediction, which would potentially limit the prediction accuracy. In this section, we study how the changes of μ can impact the prediction accuracy. We change μ from 0 to 50. For other parameters, we utilize the grid-search method to find the best combination values. We set dimensionality $k = 80$, $\lambda_1 = \lambda_2 = 0.1$, $\gamma_1 = \gamma_2 = 0.01$. For the community consideration, *we use 2-trust-cliques.*

Figure 4.13 compares the RMSE of our model with different values of μ. From the results, we can see that as μ increases, the RMSE value decreases at first. When μ passes over a certain threshold, the RMSE value increases again. We observe that the threshold is around $\mu = 10$ for Epinions dataset and $\mu = 5$ for Flixster dataset. Thus, we can conclude that DLMF has its best performance on Epinions with $\mu = 10$ and on Flixster with $\mu = 5$. The results also indicate that solely using matrix factorization and trust relationship cannot lead to better prediction accuracy unless an appropriate combination.

4.3.4.3 Analysis of Pre-training Phase

(a) Impact of Pre-training

In our method, we propose to initialize the latent features of users and items P and Q by utilizing deep autoencoder. While most of existing matrix factorization methods for recommendation use simple initialization, i.e. P and Q are initialized as dense matrices of random numbers. To study the advantages of initialization with deep autoencoder, we compare our initialization method with other four classic methods—*random* initialization, *zero* initialization, *K-means* initialization, and *Normalized-cut* (*Ncut*) initialization. For the learning model, we set $\mu = 10$ for Epinions dataset and

$\mu = 5$ for Flixster dataset, $k=80$. For the community consideration, *we use 2-trust-cliques.* Figure 4.14 shows that our proposed initialization method outperforms the other two. This result is caused by two reasons: (1) our method starts with the original feature vectors to extract features, which are much closer to the global minimum of the learning model; (2) the initial vectors achieved by our method can reflect the original relations of the similarities of users and items better than the other two methods.

Furthermore, we also evaluate the total time cost to learn the prediction model with different initialization method. From the comparison result in Table 4.2, we can observe that our method costs around 20% more time than the others in average. The increased time cost is caused by two reasons: (1) It would take more time to learn the initial values by deep autoencoder than just generating them zero or randomly; (2) The iteration number to converge is increased, which can avoid converging to a bad local optimum too early. However, the time is mainly used to train the prediction model, which can be executed offline. So it won't impact users' interaction experience. But the improvement of prediction accuracy can bring more benefit.

(b)   Impact of Dimensionality k

The purpose of the pre-training phase of our method is to reduce the dimensionality of the user-item matrix and extract features to model the characteristics of users and

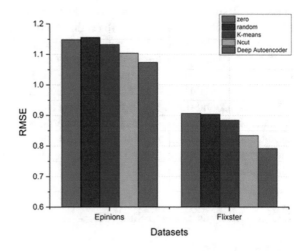

Fig. 4.14 Impact of initialization for learning models. Deep autoencoder can provide better initializations than compared methods

Table 4.2 Total time to learn the parameters of models

Initialization method	Epinions (min)	Flixster (min)
Zero	22	53
Random	21	53
K-means	24	57
Ncut	25	60
Deep autoencoder	27	72

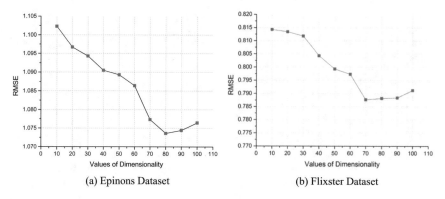

(a) Epinons Dataset   (b) Flixster Dataset

Fig. 4.15 Impact of different values of Dimensionality k on the prediction accuracy. RMSE decreases at first and increases when k passes over a certain threshold

items. Then dimensionality controls the number of factors for matrix factorization. To study the impact of dimensionality, we utilize the grid-search method to find the best combination values. We set $\mu = 10$ for Epinions dataset and $\mu = 5$ for Flixster dataset, $\lambda_1 = \lambda_2 = 0.1$, $\gamma_1 = \gamma_2 = 0.01$. For the community consideration, *we use 2-trust-cliques*. Figure 4.15 shows that with the increase of dimensionality, the value of RMSE dramatically decreases at first. However, the value of RMSE increases when dimensionality goes above a certain threshold (around 80 for Epinions and 70 for Flixster). Two reasons cause this observation: (1) the improvement of prediction accuracy confirms the intuition that a relative larger dimension leads to better results; (2) when the dimensionality surpasses a certain threshold, it may cause the issue of overfitting, which turns out to degrade the prediction accuracy.

(c)   Impact of Pre-training Algorithms

In our proposed method, we utilize deep autoencoder to reduce dimensionality and extract features of users and items from the rating matrix. Actually, there are many classic algorithms for feature extraction such as principal component analysis (PCA), locally linear embedding (LLE) [23], local tangent space alignment (LTSA) [24], Laplacian eigen-map [25], ISOMAP [26]. So in this section, we compare the performance of applying these algorithms with deep autoencoder for pre-training.

Except for PCA, the other algorithms need to specify the parameter K (the number of nearest neighbors). We set $K = 8$ for the experiments, which seems to perform well for the experiments.

For the comparison, we utilize the grid-search method to find the best combination values. We set $\mu = 10$ for Epinions dataset and $\mu = 5$ for Flixster dataset, $\lambda_1 = \lambda_2 = 0.1$, $\gamma_1 = \gamma_2 = 0.01$. For the community consideration, *we use 2-trust-cliques*. And we also tune the dimensionality k from 10 to 100. From the comparison results shown in Fig. 4.16, we can observe that involving pre-training phase can improve the prediction accuracy very much compared to the criterion algorithm. And deep autoencoder can

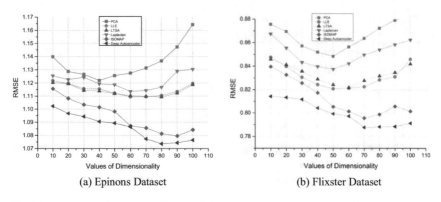

(a) Epinons Dataset   (b) Flixster Dataset

Fig. 4.16 Comparison results of different feature extraction algorithms

provide lower RMSE compared to other feature extraction algorithms. That means deep autoencoder is more suitable for trust-aware recommendation.

4.3.4.4 Impact of Community Effect

For our method, we involve a trust-aware regularization term to incorporate the community effect for recommendation. In order to evaluate the impact of the community effect in the trust social network, we compare the recommendation behavior between the model with and without the proposed regularization term. Besides, we also take the model using *n-clique* to generate cliques for comparison. For our method, we set $\mu = 10$ for Epinions dataset and $\mu = 5$ for Flixster dataset, $k = 80$ for Epinions dataset and $k = 70$ for Flixster dataset. And we generate cliques with *2-clique* and *2-trust-clique* respectively. Figure 4.17 shows the comparison results and we can observe that the model with the proposed regularization

Fig. 4.17 Impact of community effect

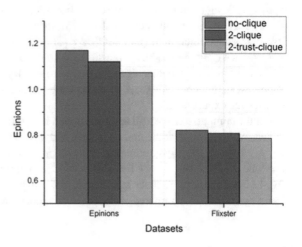

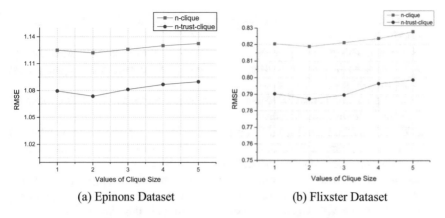

Fig. 4.18 Impact of different values of clique size n on the prediction accuracy

term can provide better recommendation precision. Furthermore, the model using *2-trust-clique* performs better than *2-clique*, which means the generating cliques with the proposed TrustCliques algorithm is more suitable for the trust-aware recommendation problem.

The value of clique size n decides the size of neighbors. If the value of n is quite small, only those neighbors which are quite trustworthy can be identified. If the value of n is quite large, the neighbors would be incorporated to a large extent. We set $\mu = 10$ for Epinions dataset and $\mu = 5$ for Flixster dataset, $k = 80$ for Epinions dataset and $k = 70$ for Flixster dataset. And we tune the clique size n from 1 to 5. Figure 4.18 shows the impact of clique size n on the prediction accuracy. We can find that when n increases, the RMSE value decreases at first. But when n passes over a threshold, the RMSE value increases again. This observation can be explained as when n is smaller than a certain threshold, there are few neighbors contributing to missing ratings predictions, which prevents user to fully absorb the wisdom of crowds. When n is larger than a certain threshold, the neighbors contain much noise even though the sample size is large enough. The above two cases will both lead to lower prediction accuracy.

4.3.4.5   Comparison Results

In order to evaluate the performance improvement of DLMF, we compare our method with the following state-of-the-art methods:

UserCF: This method is the classic user-based collaborative filtering method which makes prediction according to users' similarity.
ItemCF: This method is the classic item-based collaborative filtering method which captures similar item characteristics to make prediction.

TidalTrust: This method generates predictive ratings based on a trust inference algorithm.

MoleTrust: This method predicts the trust score of source user on target user by walking the social network starting from the source user and by propagating trust along trust edges.

BMF: This method is the basic matrix factorization approach which does not take the social network into account.

STE: This method employs the social trust network to make recommendations for users. The parameter α for STE is set as 0.4 in our comparison experiments, which is the optimum value to handle the datasets.

SocialMF: This method incorporates the mechanism of trust propagation into the recommendation model. For our comparison experiments, we set the parameter $\lambda = 5$ for SocialMF, which can provide best results in this experiment.

GWNMF: This method is proposed by Gu et al. [27], which is a collaborative filtering method based on graph regularized weighted nonnegative matrix factorization.

In order to get a fair comparison, we use grid-search method to get the best performance of these compared algorithms when processing the datasets in this work. Thus all the compared algorithms are adjusted to get the best performance with the datasets.

(a) Comparison with all users

In this subsection, we compare the performance of the above methods with ours using different training data. Thus can show the behavior of these methods with different data sparsity. For our method, we set $\mu = 10$ for Epinions dataset and $\mu = 5$ for Flixster dataset, $k = 80$ for Epinions dataset and $k = 70$ for Flixster dataset. From the comparison results shown in Table 4.3, we can conclude that: (1) our method

Table 4.3 Comparison results with all users

	Epinions			Flixster		
Methods	RMSE	Coverage (%)	F-Measure	RMSE	Coverage (%)	F-Measure
UserCF	1.3443	18.32	0.2872	0.8562	64.82	0.7105
ItemCF	1.3682	20.80	0.3161	0.8447	68.56	0.7336
TidalTrust	1.2524	37.84	0.4880	0.8337	75.85	0.7747
MoleTrust	1.2853	37.91	0.4865	0.8243	76.73	0.7804
BMF	1.2136	69.48	0.6957	0.8148	87.13	0.8321
STE	1.1724	78.52	0.7440	0.8023	90.54	0.8491
SocialMF	1.1228	82.15	0.7670	0.7968	90.42	0.8494
GWNMF	1.1045	85.67	0.7847	0.7954	92.34	0.8579
DLMF	**1.0736**	**87.64**	**0.7975**	**0.7853**	**95.84**	**0.8742**

outperforms the other methods with both datasets; (2) the MF extended recommendation methods STE, SocialMF and GWNMF perform better than the BMF which purely uses the rating matrix for recommendations; (3) the trust methods Tidal-Trust and MoleTrust perform worse than the BMF, which shows that solely using trusted friends' opinions to recommend is not appropriate; (4) the classic collaborative filtering methods UserCF and ItemCF perform worst of all methods, which indicates that when the data becomes extremely sparse, these methods are not applicable since the similarity of users or items can be hardly achieved for the missing of most ratings. To sum up, among all these methods, our DLMF method can generally achieve better performance both on precision and coverage. This demonstrates that our method for trust-aware recommendation is reasonable and efficient.

(b) Comparison with cold-start users

A major challenge of recommender systems is that it is difficult to recommend items to cold-start users who have made quite few ratings. Users who have expressed less than 5 ratings are considered as cold start users. In the dataset from Epinions, more than half of users are cold start users. Therefore, it is significant to keep high efficiency for recommender systems to recommend for cold-start users. Hence, to compare our method with the others for cold-start users, we pick out the cold-start users in each test data and predict their ratings. Table 4.4 shows that DLMF also outperforms other methods for cold-start users. We can also observe that the improvement of DLMF compared to other methods for cold-start users is more than the improvement for all users which is introduced in the previous subsection. This indicates that DLMF can handle cold-start users better than other methods.

Table 4.4 Comparison results with cold-start users

Methods	Epinions			Flixster		
	RMSE	Coverage (%)	F-Measure	RMSE	Coverage (%)	F-Measure
UserCF	1.4658	12.57	0.2098	0.9569	55.69	0.6431
ItemCF	1.5433	13.26	0.2181	0.9353	58.78	0.6652
TidalTrust	1.3664	25.45	0.3671	0.9268	68.24	0.7228
MoleTrust	1.3719	27.18	0.3845	0.9148	69.66	0.7320
BMF	1.3258	54.36	0.5996	0.8932	78.96	0.7831
STE	1.2637	67.22	0.6781	0.8556	85.35	0.8184
SocialMF	1.2158	75.83	0.7258	0.8273	86.37	0.8269
GWNMF	1.1854	79.32	0.7457	0.8194	88.62	0.8382
DLMF	**1.1564**	**81.49**	**0.7594**	**0.8043**	**92.46**	**0.8572**

4.4 Social Network-Based Mobile Services Recommendation

4.4.1 Introduction

Driven by social networks, the participation of users has become more abundant and broader. Thus, descriptions of services not only include functional and non-functional attributes but are also enriched by users' feedback information, interaction histories, distances and users' social relationships. Such information can help to mine mobile users' preferences on services, trust relationships between users, and users' influence on others to make personalized service recommendations more accurate and objective. Hence, understanding how to effectively utilize these data to make recommendation more accurate has become a significant challenge.

Currently, most studies on service recommendations mainly rely on the properties of individual services, i.e., Quality of Service (QoS) [6], but overlooking users' views on services. Thus, these methods may fail to capture users' personalized preferences accurately. With the help of social networks, users are more likely to share the feedbacks of services with their friends. Therefore, it is possible to make personalized recommendation by collecting users' feedback. Recommendation methods based on user feedback have been put into practice in many online commercial systems, such as Amazon, and Netflix. Collaborative filtering, as a dominantly used approach in recommender systems, is being extended by researchers to Web service recommendations. However, these methods still suffer the same intrinsic shortcomings like sparsity, cold-start and trustworthiness in traditional recommender systems.

To solve the above problems, some research has proposed trust-enhanced recommendation methods [28, 29]. Instead of referring to the whole population's ratings on objects, such methods mainly consider the trusted friends' ratings to make predictions. The current trust-enhanced recommendation methods are based on 0/1 trust relationships—users who are trusted by the target user can be treated as neighbors equally in making recommendations. In reality, however, the contributions of users with different levels of trustworthy should be differentiated. Hence, we present a novel trust-enhanced service recommendation method based on social networks in this work. We first introduce the concept of trust relevancy, which measures the trustworthiness weight of neighbors in social network. Then, we propose the algorithm RelevantTrustWalker, which uses random walk to make service recommendations in the weighted social network. Finally, we conduct experiments with a real-world dataset to evaluate the accuracy and efficiency of the proposed method. The experimental results validate the improvement of the proposed method.

4.4.2 Problem Definition and Preliminary

Figure 4.19 gives an example of the trust-enhanced service recommendation problem.

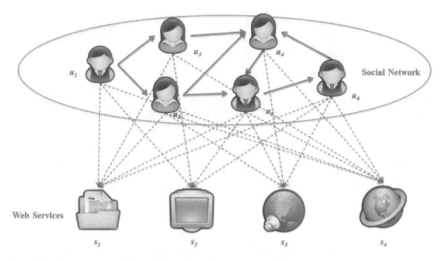

Fig. 4.19 An example of trust-enhanced service recommendations

The trust relations among users form a social network. Each user invokes several web services and rates them according to the interaction experiences. When a user needs recommendations, it predicts the ratings that the user might provide and then recommends services with high predicted ratings. Hence, the target of the recommender system predicts users' ratings on services by analyzing the social network and user-service rating records.

There is a set of users $U = \{u_1, u_2, ..., u_m\}$ and a set of services $S = \{s_1, s_2, ..., s_n\}$ in a trust-enhanced service recommender system. The ratings expressed by users on services are given in a rating matrix $R = [R_{u,s}]_{m \times n}$. In this matrix, $R_{u,s}$ denotes the rating of user u on service s. $R_{u,s}$ can be any real number, but often ratings are integers in the range of [1, 5]. In this work, without loss of generality, we map the ratings 1, ..., 5 to the interval [0, 1] by normalizing the ratings. In a social rating network, each user u has a set S_u of direct neighbors, and $t_{u,v}$ denotes the value of social trust u has on v as a real number in [0, 1]. Zero means no trust, and one means full trust. Binary trust networks are the most common trust networks (Amazon, eBay, etc.). The trust values are given in a matrix $T = [T_{u,v}]_{m \times m}$. Non-zero elements $T_{u,v}$ in T denote the existence of a social relation from u to v. Note that T is asymmetric in general.

Thus, the task of a trust-enhanced service recommender system is as follows: Given a user $u_0 \in U$ and a service $s \in S$ for which $R_{u_0,s}$ is unknown, predict the rating for u_0 on service s using R and T.

4.4.3   Trust-Enhanced Recommendation Approach

This section presents our approach in detail for trust-enhanced service recommendations. First, we define the concept of trust relevancy, on which our recommendation algorithm is based. Then, we introduce the algorithm RelevantTrustWalker. Lastly, the predicted ratings are returned. The main process of our approach is shown in Fig. 4.20.

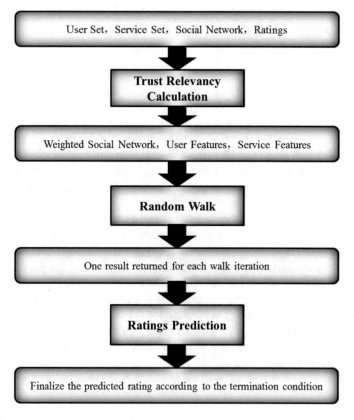

Fig. 4.20 Overview of the proposed method

4.4.3.1   Trust Relevancy

As stated earlier, the direct application of a trust relationship in a social network does not always increase the prediction accuracy. Services recommended from trusted users can only be considered reliable; such recommendations do not absolutely affect the target user's ratings because the target user and trusted users might differ in interests, preferences and perception. Therefore, we propose the concept of trust relevancy, which considers both the trust relations between users together with the similarities between users.

Definition 1 (*Trust Relevancy*) Given user u and v, the trust relevancy between u and v is as follows:

$$tr(u, v) = simU(u, v) * t(u, v),$$

where $simU(u, v)$ is the similarity of users u and v, and $t(u, v)$ is the degree of trust of u towards v. $t(u, v)$ can be explicitly provided by users or calculated based on some algorithms. Because most practical social networks are 0/1 trust networks, the degree of trust between two users usually equals 1. In this work, we obtain the degree of trust directly from the Epinions dataset. If the degree of trust has not been explicitly provided by the dataset, we can calculate the values based on the historic interactions. By computing the trust relevancy between all connected users in a social network, we can obtain a weighted trust network (SN^+), where the weight of each edge is the value of trust relevancy.

In this work, we mainly aim to decompose the user-service rating matrix R. Based on the matrix factorization technique, matrix R can be approximately decomposed into two matrices P and Q:

$$R \approx PQ^T \tag{4.1}$$

where $P \in \mathbf{R}^{m \times d}$ and $Q \in \mathbf{R}^{n \times d}$ represent the latent feature matrices of users and services, respectively. Each line of the respective matrix represents a user or service latent feature vector. After decomposing the matrix, we use the cosine similarity measure to calculate the similarity between two users. Given the latent feature vectors of two users u and v, their similarity calculation is as follows:

$$simU(u, v) = \cos(\mathbf{u}, \mathbf{v}) = \frac{\mathbf{u} \cdot \mathbf{v}}{|\mathbf{u}| \cdot |\mathbf{v}|} \tag{4.2}$$

where $\mathbf{u}$ and $\mathbf{v}$ are the latent feature vectors of the users u and v. The following example is used to clearly illustrate the process of calculating similarity.

Example 1 Given 6 users and 4 services, the user-service rating matrix is as follows:

$$R = \begin{bmatrix} 5\ 5\ 0\ 5 \\ 5\ 0\ 3\ 4 \\ 3\ 4\ 0\ 3 \\ 0\ 0\ 5\ 3 \\ 5\ 4\ 4\ 5 \\ 5\ 4\ 5\ 5 \end{bmatrix}$$

Through the MF technique, the rating matrix R is decomposed into two latent feature matrices, P and Q:

$$p = \begin{bmatrix} -0.4472 & 0.5373 \\ -0.3586 & -0.2461 \\ -0.2925 & 0.4033 \\ -0.2078 & -0.6700 \\ -0.5099 & -0.0597 \\ -0.5316 & -0.1887 \end{bmatrix} \quad Q = \begin{bmatrix} -0.5710 & 0.228 \\ -0.4275 & 0.5172 \\ -0.3846 & -0.8246 \\ -0.5859 & -0.0532 \end{bmatrix}$$

We select the users $\mathbf{u_5}$ $(-0.5099, -0.0597)$ and $\mathbf{u_6}$ $(-0.5316, -0.1887)$. The similarity between the two users can be calculated as 0.9749. From the rating matrix, we can observe that user $\mathbf{u_5}$ and $\mathbf{u_6}$ only rate the third service differently. Therefore, their similarity should approach 1. It can be observed that the method accurately measures the similarity of two users.

4.4.3.2   Recommendation Algorithm

This section introduces the proposed trust-enhanced random walk algorithm, RelevantTrustWalker, in detail. Table 4.5 gives the variables definitions used in the algorithm.

The RelevantTrustWalker algorithm attains a final result through multiple iterations. For each iteration, the random walk starts from the target user u_0 in the weighted trust network SN^+. In the k-th step of the random walk in the trust network, the process will reach a certain node u. If user u has rated the to-be-recommended

Table 4.5   Variables for RelevantTrustWalker

Variables	Description
$r_{u,s}$	The real rating of service s from user u
$p_{u,s}$	The predicted rating of service s from user u
$\varphi_{u,s,k}$	The probability that the random walk stops at user u in the k-th step
TU_u	The set of users that user u trusts
$E_u(v)$	The probability that user v is selected from TU_u as the target of the next step
$simS(s_i, s_j)$	The similarity of services s_i and s_j
RS_u	The set of services that user u has rated
$F_u(s_i)$	The probability that s_i is selected from RS_u to obtain u's rating for s_i

service s, then the rating of s from user u is directly used as the result for the iteration. Otherwise, the process has the following options:

(a) The random walk will stop at the current node u with a certain probability $\varphi_{u,s,k}$. Then, the service s_i is selected from RS_u based on the probability $F_u(s_i)$. The rating of s_i from u is the result for the iteration.

The probability that the random walk stops at user u in the k-th step is affected by the similarity of the services that u has rated and the to-be-recommended service s. The more similar the rated services and s, the greater the probability is to stop. Furthermore, a larger distance between the user u and the target user u_0 can introduce more noise into the prediction. Therefore, $\varphi_{u,s,k}$ should increase when k increases. Thus, the calculation for $\varphi_{u,s,k}$ is as follows:

$$\varphi_{u,s,k} = \max_{s_i \in RS_u} simS(s_i, s) \times \frac{1}{1 + e^{-\frac{k}{2}}}, \tag{4.3}$$

where $simS(s_i, s)$ is the similarity between the services s_i and s. The sigmoid function of k can provide value 1 for big values of k, and a small value for small values of k. Existing methods for calculating the similarity between two services are mostly based on collaborative filtering techniques. However, when two services do not have ratings from mutual users, such approaches cannot calculate their similarity values. Therefore, we propose calculating similarities between services based on the matrix factorization method. In Sect. 4.1, the matrix factorization of the rating matrix can be used to obtain not only the user latent features but the service latent features. Then, each service can be represented as a latent feature vector. Similar to Formula (4.2), for two services s_i and s_j, the similarity calculation is as follows:

$$simS\left(s_i, s_j\right) = \cos\left(\mathbf{s_i}, \mathbf{s_j}\right) = \frac{\mathbf{s_i} \cdot \mathbf{s_j}}{|\mathbf{s_i}| \cdot |\mathbf{s_j}|} \tag{4.4}$$

When it is determined that user u is the terminating point of the walk, the method will need to select one service from RS_u. The rating of s_i from u is the outcome for the iteration. The probability of the chosen service $F_u(s_i)$ is calculated according to the following formula:

$$F_u(s_i) = \frac{simS(s, s_i)}{\sum_{s_j \in RS_u} simS\left(s, s_j\right)} \tag{4.5}$$

The way to select services based on $F_u(s_i)$ is through a roulette-wheel selection, that is, services with higher values of $F_u(s_i)$ are more possible to be selected. Once the service s_i is selected, the rating of s_i from user u is returned as the result of the iteration. The random walk is likely to run and never stop. Therefore, we adopt the concept of "six degrees of separation". The maximum step for a random walk is set to 6.

(b) By contrast, the walk can continue with a probability of $1 - \varphi_{u,s,k}$. A user is selected from the set of users whom the current user u directly trusts as the target node for the next step.

At present, the existing methods usually choose the target node randomly, which means each user whom u trusts has an equal chance of being selected. However, as mentioned above, these users have different reference significance for user u. To distinguish different users' contribution to the recommendation prediction, we propose that the target node v for the next step from the current user u is selected according to the following probability:

$$E_u(v) = \frac{tr(u, v)}{\sum\limits_{x \in TU_u} tr(u, x)}, \tag{4.6}$$

where $tr(u, v)$ is the trust relevancy introduced in Sect. 4.1. The trust relevancy guarantees that each step of the walk will choose the user that is more similar to the current user, making the recommendation more accurate.

The pseudo-code of the RelevantTrustWalker algorithm is as follows:

Algorithm 1. RelevantTrustWalker

Input: *U*(user set), *S*(service set), *R*(rating matrix), SN^+(weighted social network),
          u_0(the target user), *s*(to-be-recommended service)
Output: *r* (predicted rating)

---

1. **set** $k = 1$; //the step of the walk

2. **set** $u = u_0$; //set the start point of the walk as u_0

3. **set** *max-depth* = 6; //the max step of the walk

4. **set** $r = 0$;

5. **while** ($k <=$ *max-depth*){

6. $u = $ ***selectUser***(*u*); // select *v* from TU_u as the target of the next step according to

    the probability $E_u(v)$

7.   **if** (*u* has rated *s*){

8. $r = r_{u,s}$;

9.   **return** *r*;

10.   }

11.   **else**{

12.   **if** (random(0,1)< $\varphi_{u,s,k} \| k ==$ *max-depth*){

        //stop at the current node

13. $s_i = $ ***selectService***(*u*); // service s_i is selected from RS_u according to the

    probability $F_u(s_i)$

14. $r = r_{u,si}$;

15.   **return** *r*;

16.   }

17.   else

18. k++;

19.   }

20. }

21. **return** *r*;

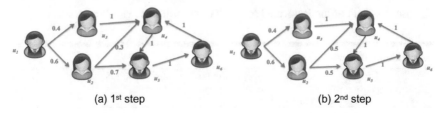

(a) 1st step   (b) 2nd step

Fig. 4.21 Example of RelevantTrustWalker

Example 2 Figure 4.21 shows an example to illustrate the Algorithm 1 clearly. The weight of each edge represents the probability $E_u(v)$ which is calculated according to the Eq. (4.6). Suppose the service s_3 is to be recommended for the user u_1. For the first step of the walk (shown in Fig. 4.21a), u_2 is more likely to be selected as the target node since the value of $E_u(u_2)$ is larger. If u_2 has rated s_3 with the rating r, r will be returned as the result of this walk (Line 7–9). Otherwise, if the termination condition (Line 12) is not reached, the walk would continue. For the second step, u_5 is selected (shown in Fig. 4.21b). It should also check whether u_5 has rated s_3. If u_5 has not rated s_3 but the termination condition is reached, it will select the most similar service to s_3 from the services u_5 has rated (Line 13). The selection probability of each service is according to the Eq. (4.5). Then, the rating of the selected service by u_5 is returned as the result of this walk.

4.4.3.3   Ratings Prediction

The RelevantTrustWalker algorithm attains a final result through multiple iterations. The final predicted rating is obtained by polymerizing the results returned from every iteration:

$$P_{u_0,s} = \frac{1}{n}\sum_{i=1}^{n} r_i \qquad (4.7)$$

where r_i is the result of each iteration, n is the number of iterations. To obtain a stable predict result, the algorithm needs to perform an adequate number of random walks. We can decide the termination condition of the algorithm through the calculation of the variance of the prediction values. The variance of the prediction results after a random walk is denoted as σ^2. The calculation of σ^2 is as follows:

$$\sigma_i^2 = \frac{1}{i}\sum_{j=1}^{i} (r_j - \bar{r})^2 \qquad (4.8)$$

where r_j is the result of every iteration, i is the total number of iterations until the current walk, and σ_i^2 is the variance obtained from the last i iterations, which will eventually tend to a stable value. In this work, when $\left|\sigma_{i+1}^2 - \sigma_i^2\right| \le \varepsilon$, the algorithm terminates ($\varepsilon = 0.0001$).

4.4.4 Evaluation and Analysis

In this section, we conduct several experiments to compare the recommendation quality of the RelevantTrustWalker approach with other state-of-the-art trust-enhanced service recommendation methods.

4.4.4.1 Experiment Setup

In the trust-enhanced recommender research domain, there is not much publicly available and suitable test data. The Epinions dataset is considered the only publicly available social rating network dataset. Hence, in this work, we also choose Epinions as the data source for our experiments on trust-enhanced recommendations. Users can rate products from 1 to 5 and submit their personal reviews. These ratings and reviews influence other customers when they make decisions on whether to buy a product. In addition, users are also allowed to specify whom to trust and build a social trust network.

Table 4.6 shows the statistics of the data source. It consists of 49,290 users, who rated a total of 139,738 different items at least once. The total number of ratings is 664,824. The density of the user-item rating matrix is less than 0.01%. Each user has rated 13.4 items on average. As to the social trust network, the total number of issued trust statements is 487,181. Each user has 9.9 direct trusters on average. We can observe that the user-item rating matrix of Epinions is incredibly large in size and extremely sparse, much sparser than another commonly used collaborative

Table 4.6 Statistics of the Epinions dataset

Users	49,290
Items	139,738
Ratings	664,824
Trust relations	487,181
Avg. ratings per user	13.4
Max. ratings per user	1845
Avg. ratings per item	4.8
Max. ratings per item	6843
Avg. trusters per user	9.9
Max. trusters per user	1587
Avg. trustees per user	9.9
Max. trustees per user	2365

filtering dataset, Movielens, with a density of 4.25%. Thus, the dataset can evaluate the performance of our approach with big data and high sparsity at the same time. They found that those with a service number of fewer than five comments can be identified as cold-start users. Cold-start users and relevant data accounted for more than 50%. Therefore, it is very important to consider cold-start users to enhance the accuracy of recommendations and coverage.

To evaluate the performance improvement of RelevantTrustWalker, we compare our method with the following state-of-the-art methods:

- *UserCF*: This method is the classic user-based collaborative filtering method, which makes prediction merely based on user similarity.
- *ItemCF*: This method is the classic item-based collaborative filtering method, which captures similar item characteristics to make predictions.
- *TidalTrust*: This method generates ratings based on a trust inference algorithm.
- *MoleTrust*: This method predicts the trust score of the source user for the target user by walking through the social network starting from the source user and propagating trust along trust edges.
- *TrustWalker*: This method is a random walk method based on trust and item similarity.
- *CoTrustWalker*: This method is an extension of *TrustWalker* and utilizes a cloud model to compute item similarity.
- *CliquesWalker*: This method is a random walk method that considers social cliques.

4.4.4.2   Evaluation Metrics

Our experiments are developed using Java, and the experimental setting is an Intel Core2 P7370 2.0 GHZ with 4 GB RAM machine with Windows 7 and jdk 6.0.

Leave-One-Out (LOO) is widely used for the evaluation of recommendation methods. In this work, we adopt LOO to evaluate the recommendation algorithms by hiding an actual rating value and predicting its value through the compared recommendation algorithms. Then, we compare the accuracy of the algorithms by analyzing the root mean square error.

We adopt the Root Mean Squared Error (RMSE), which is widely used in recommendation research to measure the error in recommendations:

$$RMSE = \sqrt{\frac{\sum_{u,s}\left(R_{u,s} - \hat{R}_{u,s}\right)^2}{N}}, \tag{4.9}$$

where $R_{u,s}$ is the actual rating the user u gave to the service s and $\hat{R}_{u,s}$ is the predicted rating the user u gave to the service s. N denotes the number of tested ratings. The smaller the value of RMSE is, the more precisely the recommendation algorithm performs.

Some recommendation mechanisms may not be able to predict all the ratings in test data given the high sparsity of the dataset. Involving trust can enhance coverage without sacrificing the precision. Therefore, we use the metric *coverage* to measure the percentage of pairs of <user, service>, for which a predicted value can be generated. For a pair of <user, service>, if the recommender cannot find a prediction on the rating for the reason of lack of enough information to calculate similarity, then the recommender cannot cover this pair of <user, service>.

$$coverage = \frac{S}{N},\qquad(4.10)$$

where S denotes the number of predicted ratings and N denotes the number of tested ratings.

To combine RMSE and *coverage* into a single evaluation metric, we compute the F-Measure. We have to convert RMSE into a precision metric in the range of [0, 1]. The precision is denoted as follows:

$$precision = 1 - \frac{RMSE}{4}.\qquad(4.11)$$

In this equation, 4 is the maximum possible error because the values of the ratings are in the range of [1, 5].

$$F - Measure = \frac{2 \times precision \times coverage}{precision + coverage}.\qquad(4.12)$$

4.4.4.3   Experimental Results

This section presents the results of a different experimental comparison including the recommendation results of all users and cold-start users and a performance comparison of the different algorithms.

From the experimental results in Table 4.7 and Fig. 4.22, we can observe that the accuracy of all the algorithms improves when recommending for all users. This finding is mainly because the user-service rating information is more adequate. From Table 4.7, we can see that the trust-enhanced recommendation algorithms have no absolute advantages in terms of accuracy compared to the User-based CF and the Item-based CF recommendation algorithms because the traditional collaborative filtering methods can calculate user/service similarity with adequate rating information. Several trust-enhanced recommendation algorithms only consider the trust between users, without considering the interests and preferences between users, which would result in the improvement of coverage without sacrificing accuracy. By contrast, the proposed RelevantTrustWalker considers trust relevancy, which

Table 4.7 Comparison
results for all users

Algorithms	RMSE	Coverage (%)	F-Measure
User-based CF	1.141	70.43	0.7095
Item-based CF	1.345	67.58	0.6697
TidalTrust	1.127	84.15	0.7750
MoleTrust	1.164	86.47	0.7791
TrustWalker	1.089	95.13	0.8246
CoTrustWalker	1.074	94.23	0.8236
CliquesWalker	1.045	96.78	0.8379
RelevantTrustWalker	1.012	98.21	0.8486

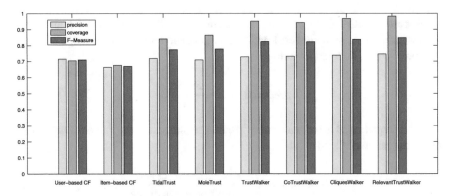

Fig. 4.22 Comparison results for all users

combines the trust degree and user similarity, to improve the accuracy of the recommendation. Thus, the recommendation performance of RelevantTrustWalker is also superior to other algorithms when recommending for all users.

RelevantTrustWalker and other trust-enhanced recommendation algorithms offer the advantage of being able to solve the cold-start problem. It is necessary to assess their performance on recommendations for cold-start users. Table 4.8 and Fig. 4.23

Table 4.8 Comparison
results for cold-start users

Algorithms	RMSE	Coverage (%)	F-Measure
User-based CF	1.485	18.93	0.2910
Item-based CF	1.537	23.14	0.3364
TidalTrust	1.238	60.75	0.6463
MoleTrust	1.397	58.29	0.6150
TrustWalker	1.212	74.36	0.7195
CoTrustWalker	1.204	74.85	0.7229
CliquesWalker	1.187	76.78	0.7341
RelevantTrustWalker	1.143	79.64	0.7531

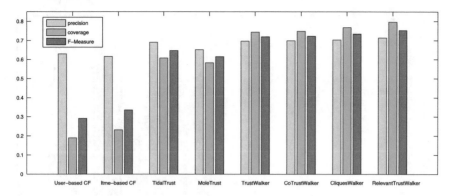

Fig. 4.23 Comparison results for cold-start users

show the comparison results for cold-start users.

From the above experimental results, we can observe that RelevantTrustWalker has a lower error than other recommendation algorithms for cold starts. Two traditional collaborative filtering algorithms, User-based CF and Item-based CF, perform the worst, mainly because the cold-start users rated few mutual services, which means most user/service similarities cannot be calculated accurately. As a result, these two methods perform with the highest RMSE and the lowest coverage compared to other methods. Due to the introduction of the trust relationship between users, Tidal-Trust and MoleTrust can make service recommendations for users without mutual-rated services by utilizing trust relations. Therefore, the coverage improved greatly compared to the previous two algorithms, but the accuracy is not improved significantly. TrustWalker CoTrustWalker, and CliquesWalker have obvious improvements in both accuracy and coverage. Compared to these three random walk methods, RelevantTrustWalker has a lower RMSE because, at each step of the walk, RelevantTrust-Walker chooses to trust more relevant users, rather than random selections, which justifies that not all recommendations from trusted users have equivalent reference values. In addition, the coverage of RelevantTrustWalker is also the highest because, when computing the similarity, we adopt the method of matrix factorization to obtain a service feature vector, which avoids the typical failures of similarity calculations in the absence of mutual-rated services. All in all, from the point of F-Measure, RelevantTrustWalker outperforms the compared algorithms for the cold-start users.

Because the size of the rating data is extremely large, the time cost of service recommendation is also an important evaluation indicator. Figure 4.24 shows the average time cost of different algorithms. We can observe that the User-based CF and Item-based CF cost the least in terms of time, primarily because they only consider the rating relationship between users and services as the algorithm input. By contrast, the other algorithms also add the trust relationship between users as input, which increases the calculation of algorithms. Compared to the other random walk algorithm, RelevantTrustWalker costs much less in terms of time because, at each step of the walk, RelevantTrustWalker selects the target according to trust

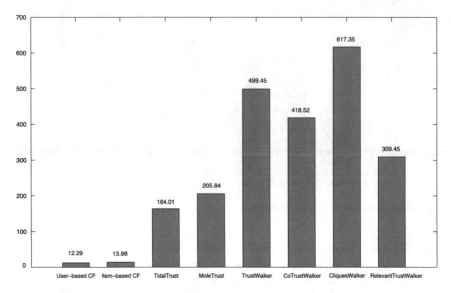

Fig. 4.24 Time costs of different algorithms

relevancy instead of selecting randomly, which makes the recommendation result tend to become stable more quickly to improve the calculation efficiency.

4.5   Summary

Personalized mobile service recommendations from large-scale candidate services have been a heavily researched topic in recent years. Based on the intuition that users' decisions on the Internet items are affected by both their own characteristics and their trusted friends' recommendations, we propose some models to measure the trust and then propose some trust-based recommendation approaches. Based on the behaviors of mobile users, we propose a context-aware mobile service recommendation approach. We believe that these context-based methods still have much room for improvement. For example, we consider the trust relationships between users in the social trust network as invariant. In fact, the trust relationship between users can change with time. In addition, it would be better if the recommendation approach can recommend a suitable topic for users. Besides this, the generate model could be more sophisticated because a user can invoke many services in a user state. What's more, as many kinds of information are collected with the increasing of mobile users, we would like to use some more kinds of contexts to guide the recommendation in the future.

References

1. N. Thio, S. Karunasekera, Web service recommendation based on client-side performance estimation. Aust. Softw. Eng. Conf. 81–89 (2007)
2. M.B. Blak, M.F. Nowlan, A web service recommender system using enhanced syntactical matching. IEEE Int. Conf. Web Serv 575–582 (2007)
3. V. Srinivasan et al., Mobileminer: mining your frequent patterns on your phone, in Proceedings of the 2014 ACM International Joint Conference on Pervasive and Ubiquitous Computing (ACM, 2014), pp. 389–400, https://doi.org/10.1145/2632048.2632052
4. C. Davidsson, S. Moritz, Utilizing implicit feedback and context to recommend mobile applications from first use, in *Proceedings of the 2011 Workshop on Context-awareness in Retrieval and Recommendation* (ACM, 2011), pp. 19–22, https://doi.org/10.1145/1961634.1961639
5. N. Natarajan, D. Shin, I.S. Dhillon, Which app will you use next? Collaborative filtering with interactional context, in *Proceedings of the 7th ACM Conference on Recommender Systems* (ACM, 2013), pp. 201–208, https://doi.org/10.1145/2507157.2507186
6. L. Shao, J. Zhang, Y. Wei et al., Personalized QoS prediction for web services via collaborative filtering. IEEE Int. Conf. Web Serv. 439–446 (2007)
7. Y. Jiang, J. Liu, M. Tang, An effective web service recommendation method based on personalized collaborative filtering. IEEE Int. Conf.Web Serv. 211–218 (2011)
8. J. Golbeck, *Computing and applying trust in web-based social networks*. Ph.D Thesis, University of Maryland (2005)
9. P. Massa, P. Avesani, Trust metrics in recommender systems. in *Computing with Social Trust*, ed. by J. Golbeck (Springer, 2009)
10. H. Ma, I. King, M. Lyu, Learning to recommend with explicit and implicit social relation. ACM Trans. Intell. Syst. Technol. **2**(3), 29–48 (2011)
11. M. Jamali, M. Ester, A matrix factorization technique with trust propagation for recommendation in social networks, in *Proceeding of ACM Conference on Recommender Systems* (2010), pp. 135–142
12. A.K. Dey, Understanding and using context. Personal Ubiquitous Comput **5** (1), 4–7 (2001). https://doi.org/10.1007/s007790170019
13. N. Landwehr, M. Hall, E. Frank, Logistic model trees. Machine Learn. **59**(1), 161–205 (2005). https://doi.org/10.1007/s10994-005-0466-3
14. J.R. Quinlan, C4. 5: Programs for Machine Learning (Elsevier, 2014)
15. H. Yu, C. Hsieh, S. Si, I. Dhillon, Parallel matrix factorization for recommender systems. Knowl. Inf. Syst. **41**(3), 793–819 (2014)
16. P. Avesani, P. Massa, R. Tiella, Moleskiing it: a trust-aware recommender system for ski mountaineering. Int. J. Infonomics **20**(35), 1–19 (2005)
17. P. Massa, P. Avesani, Trust-aware recommender systems, in *Proceeding of ACM Conference on Recommender Systems* (2007), pp. 17–24
18. S. Deng, L. Huang, J. Wu, Z. Wu, Trust-based personalized service recommendation: a network perspective. J. Comput. Sci. Technol. **29**(1), 69–80 (2014)
19. A. Mnih, R. Salakhutdinov, Probabilistic matrix factorization, in *Proceeding of Advances in Neural Information Processing Systems* (2007), pp. 1257–1264
20. R. Salakhutdinov, A. Mnih, G. Hinton, Restricted Boltzmann machines for collaborative filtering, in *Proceeding of International Conference on Machine Learning* (2007), pp. 791–798
21. Z. Zhou, W. Wang, L. Wang, Community detection based on an improved modularity, in *Pattern Recognition* (Springer, Berlin Heidelberg, 2012)
22. Epinions. http://www.epinions.com
23. S. Roweis, L. Saul, Nonlinear dimensionality reduction by locally linear embedding. Science **290**(5500), 2323–2326 (2000)
24. J. Wang, Local tangent space alignment, in *Geometric Structure of High-Dimensional Data and Dimensionality Reduction*, ed. by J. Wang (Springer, 2011)
25. M. Belkin, P. Niyog, Laplacian eigenmaps for dimensionality reduction and data representation. Neural Comput. **15**(6), 1373–1396 (2003)

26. M. Balasubramanian, E. Schwartz, The isomap algorithm and topological stability. Science **295**(5552), 7–7 (2002)
27. Q. Gu, J. Zhou, C. Ding, Collaborative filtering: weighted nonnegative matrix factorization incorporating user and item graphs, in *Proceeding of SIAM International Conference on Data Mining* (2010), pp. 199–210
28. P. Victor, M. Cock, C. Cornelis, Trust and recommendations, in *Recommender Systems Handbook*, ed. by P. Kantor, L. Rokach, F. Ricci, B. Shapira (Springer, 2011)
29. P. Massa, P. Avesani, Trust metrics on controversial users: balancing between Tyranny of the majority. Int. J. Semant. Web Inf. Syst. **3**(1), 39–64 (2007)

Chapter 5
Mobile Service Composition

Abstract Service composition supports and realizes complex business logics through combining multiple single services. However, the mobile environment brings great challenges to the reliability of service composition due to the uncertain services quality and usability. In this chapter, a mobile service provisioning architecture is proposed to tackle the composition in mobile communities. Additionally, a dependable composition model is constructed to reduce the risk of the mobility of both service providers and requesters. Finally, a differential evolutionary for constraint-driven service composition algorithm is designed to ensure the successful composition.

5.1 Introduction

Service-oriented computing (SOC) has become a significant computing paradigm to build and integrate distributed systems, due to its flexibility and ability to be adapted into the dynamic environment [1]. One of the most important issues in SOA is service composition, i.e., to compose a complex application by integrating several distributed services that are provided by several service providers in the network. Under such a situation, a requirement cannot be accomplished by a single service, thus a composite service consisting of multiple single services should be generated to satisfy the requirement [2]. For each service composition request that may include multiple services, finding an appropriate service provider to provide the services is important. In some cases, there are multiple service providers that can provide the same services, and thus we need to choose one of them according to certain criteria.

More and more researchers have focused on service composition in recent years. However, traditional researches on composition are usually based on an assumption that services are deployed on centralized servers and they usually provide computation-intensive functions. Therefore, traditional works of service composition are always stationary and certain. But with the advancement of technologies and newly emerging concepts, this kind of assumption would be broken by services provided by modern mobile devices such as smart phones and tablets, which are equipped with various sensors and computation-powers [3]. The rapid development in mobile devices and wireless technologies has enabled the provisioning of services more flexible and diverse [4]. The manufacturers of mobile devices have made efforts to improve mobile devices' capabilities on memory, storage capacity, and computational power as well as extend their capabilities and functionalities with other integrated devices such as built-in cameras, GPS, and Bluetooth technology [5]. Besides, due to the revolution in wireless communications, the data transmission rates and the spectral efficiency have increased dramatically than before [6]. As a result, services are no longer limited to traditional platforms. With the help of modern smart devices' progress, services can be deployed on mobile devices and delivered over wireless networks. Mobile devices may play the role of service requesters, consumers and providers simultaneously [7].

However, services provided by mobile providers will be quite different from traditional stationary services, which bring in many challenges. The communication among service requesters and providers are based on some wireless communication technologies such as Bluetooth, wireless local-area network, and near field communication [8]. These techniques require the communication must be within a limited range. As service providers in a mobile network can be mobile, the availability time of their services to their consumers is limited to their physical adjacency, i.e., both service requesters and providers are within a connection range. Furthermore, mobility can also be caused by mobile users in a network with static service providers.

Cause it has huge impacts on the execution of tasks, the mobility of users and devices is proposed as a risk model [9]. If a service provider moves out of the sensing distance when the service is being used, the composition fails and a re-composition is needed, which results in a big waste of time and resources. Thus, it's important to select a service provider with enough available time for each service such that the composition can exist and run to execute a complete task. In addition, there are several other challenges involved in building such service compositions in mobile communities. Except for the mobility environment, many other constraints also make the service composition problem dramatically tough, such as local-time constraints and global QoS (quality of services) constraints [10]. Therefore, it's significant to form such a service composition that not only satisfies both the time constraints and QoS constraints in a mobile service composition but also ensures the composition to be executed successfully to the greatest extent in the uncertain mobile environment.

5.2 Mobility-Aware Service Composition

With the rapid development of mobile devices and wireless technology, Web services are becoming more flexible and scalable, thus growing as a main character in service-oriented computing (SOC). However, there exist many challenges in building Web service compositions under mobility environments.

5.2.1 Prerequisites and Problem Definition

5.2.1.1 Mobile Web Service

Mobile Web services are deployed on mobile devices and provisioned over wireless networks. Devices may play the roles of consumers, brokers, or providers. Their role as a Web service requester is fundamental. Shifting such a role from a requester to a provider, however, is feasible only if mobile devices can offer standard Web services with acceptable performance while making a negligible impact on their regular usage. It brought many challenges to traditional services computing techniques mainly due to their technological limitations, summarized as follows.

Mobility: On one hand, mobile users may change their communication networks causally, which causes technological disparity. On the other hand, if the users turn off the network, the services they provide become unreachable immediately. Then the composite service becomes a failure and a re-composition is needed.

Limited Resources: Mobile devices are suffering from various constraints on resources, such as battery power. Recent developments in mobile computing and the growing popularity of mobile applications outpace what current battery technologies can provide.

Addressability: Mobile devices may frequently change their point of connection to the network as they roam. Changing a network provider or network technology typically results in changing a mobile provider's IP address (unless a static IP is assigned). This, in turn, may make the services' binding information invalid if not properly updated when mobile services become stale or inaccessible.

Scalability: Mobile Web services will not meet the requirements under the situation when many mobile users expect to concurrently access the network, because of the limited capacity of mobile devices.

The existing services computing protocols and mechanisms can be hardly utilized for mobile Web services according to the above characteristics. Therefore, it is essential to study new protocols and mechanisms that are more suitable for mobile domains.

5.2.1.2 Service Composition in Mobile Community

As wireless communication technologies such as Bluetooth, Wireless LAN (WLAN), and device-to-device communication are developed, the service interaction between two mobile devices within a limited distance is enabled. The mobile users sharing services within a limited area can form a virtual mobile community. Service composition of multiple mobile Web services is challenging. In such a mobile community, both the user and some service providers may be subject to frequent movements. As service providers in a mobile network can also be mobile, the availability time of their services to their consumers is limited to their physical adjacency, i.e., both service requesters and providers are within a connection range. Furthermore, the mobility can also be caused by mobile users in a network with static service providers. If a service provider moves out of the sensing distance when the service is being used, the composition fails and a re-composition is needed. To avoid frequent re-composition, it's important to select a service provider with enough available time for each service such that the composition can exist and run to complete a user-intended task. The difficulty for getting a valid service composition in such mobile environment is the uncertainty in the mobility of service requesters and service providers.

5.2.1.3   Mobility Services Sharing Community

In order to solve the problem referred above, we propose a novel mobile architecture for service provision called MSSC, which is a virtual community formed by multiple mobile users. Within it, users can share services on their own mobile devices through mobile networks. It has three main characteristics as follows.

Locality: An MSSC is not established on the Internet. It corresponds to a specific region such as a university campus, a company building, and a restaurant. Only mobile users who enter the same region can share services with each other.

Dynamicity: MSSC participants are not stationary. They can enter or leave the community at any time.

Mobility: Services provided by mobile users are not fixed at the same location. Service requesters are also mobile when invoking a mobile service.

We first give a formal definition of an MSSC.

Definition 1 (*Mobile Services Sharing Community*) An MSSC is a 3-tuple

$$mssc = \langle Region, C, U \rangle,$$

where:

(1) *Region* is a region;
(2) C is the set of critical points within *Region*; and
(3) U is the set of mobile users.

For example, Region can be a university campus. A critical point is a fixed place, e.g., teaching buildings in a campus, exhibitions in a museum, and counters in a marketplace, where mobile users can move to/from and stay for specific time periods. Mobile users can be either moving between critical points or stay at a specific critical point. They can be a service requester and provider at the same time.

Figure 5.1 presents the basic architecture of MSSC that is based on the peer-to-peer architecture. MSSC participants are mobile users who can communicate with each other through Bluetooth, WLAN, or device-to-device communication technologies.

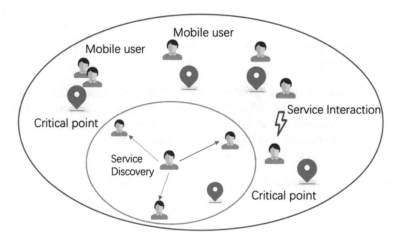

Fig. 5.1 Basic MSSC architecture

Since such wireless communication is limited in distance, each mobile user can only sense and interact with nearby users. They may be moving during interactions. The communication among them may use a wireless implementation of simple object access protocol (SOAP), such as WSOAP, gSOAP, and eSOAP for data exchange across mobile networks.

5.2.1.4 Problem Definition

In order to describe the problem addressed above, we first provide formal definitions of a few key concepts in MSSC, and then present the problem description.

Definition 2 (*Mobile User*) A mobile user is a 4-tuple

$$u = (uid, umt, S, l)$$

where

(1) *uid* is the identification;
(2) *umt* is the moving trajectory;
(3) *S* is a set of mobile services that *u* can provide where *S* can be a null set if *u* does not want to share its own services; and
(4) *l* is the sensing distance of *u*'s mobile device.

Definition 3 (*Mobile Services*) A mobile service is a triple

$$s = (sid, e)$$

where:

(1) *sid* is the identification; and
(2) *e* is the response time.

Service providers publish the information of their services including function and non-function properties. Therefore, the average response time of a service is already known when a requester selects it. For data-intensive services, the response time is a function of the input data. To simplify the explanation, we assume that the response time of a mobile service is a constant.

Definition 4 (*Composition Request*) A composition request is a 2-tuple

$$cr = (T, R)$$

where:

(1) $T = \{t_1, t_2, \ldots, t_n\}$ is a set of tasks
(2) $R = \{r(t_i, t_j) | t_i, t_j \in T\}$ is a set of relations between tasks in T.

Each task t_i can be implemented by a set of candidate services, and $r(t_i, t_j) = 1$ represents that the inputs of t_j depend on the outputs of t_i. R is used to describe the structure of the composition.

Definition 5 (*Mobile Services Composition*) A mobile services composition is a triple

$$msc = (h, S, L),$$

where:

(1) h is the composition request to which *msc* corresponds,
(2) S is the set of services in *msc*;
(3) $L = \bigsqcup_{s \in S} l_s$ is the total response time of *msc*.

Note that each $s_i \in S$ corresponds to a task $t_i \in h$.

Definition 6 (*MSSC Service Composition*) Given a mobile services sharing community *mssc*, and a service composition request h by a mobile user u, select concrete services provided by other mobile users in MSSC to achieve an optimal service composition *msc* with the shortest response time L. Meanwhile, *msc* should guarantee to run successfully when the service requester and the service providers are moving.

Theorem *The service composition problem in MSSC* (Definition 5) *is NP-Hard.*

Proof The standard integer programming problem to find the smallest value of a given objective function $F(\Theta)$ with a feasible parameter vector $\Theta = (\theta_1, \ldots, \theta_n)$ can be modeled as follows:

$$\inf \quad F(\Theta)$$
$$\text{subject to } \theta_i \in \{1, 2, \ldots, N\}$$

(5.1)

This means the feasible set of parameter vectors is constrained by $\theta_i \in \{1, 2, \ldots, N\}$ with integer values. The optimal solution Θ^* satisfies the following conditions:

(1) Θ^* belongs to the feasible set
(2) $\forall \Theta, F(\Theta^*) \leq F(\Theta)$.

For the problem of selecting optimal services with shortest response time while considering mobility, the vector $\Theta = (\theta_1, \ldots, \theta_n)$ can describe a possible solution as a service composition with n tasks. An element θ_i in Θ corresponds to a selected service from the candidates for the i-th task. The evaluation function for the parameter vector Θ is as follows:

$$F(\Theta) = \coprod_{\theta_i} rt_{\theta_i}$$

(5.2)

The target of the mobile service composition problem in MSSC is to find Θ to obtain the smallest $F(\Theta)$. Thus, the problem is equivalent to the integer programming problem described in (5.1). The integer programming problem is known to be NP-hard. Then the service composition problem in MSSC is NP-Hard.

5.2.2 Approach

Integer programming algorithms can be used to cope with this problem. However, these algorithms are short of scalability, because it would cost too much time when the problem size rises. The request of runtime is important in mobile environment since the environment parameters for computation may vary much within a short time. Therefore, although the integer programming can obtain the optimal result, it is not suitable to the problem. Taking this factor into account, designing a heuristic search method to obtain a satisfactory solution in an accepted execution time is the best way to handle with the mobility-aware composition problem.

5.2.2.1 Overview

We find that Krill-Herd algorithm can reduce the search space and return high approximate optima. Thus, we propose a solution method based on the Krill-Herd algorithm to find an approximate optimal solution in polynomial time. For KH, each population consists of krill individuals; each krill represents a feasible solution. The herding of krill individuals includes two main goals: to increase krill density, and to search for food. The position of an individual krill is determined by three procedures: (1)

Table 5.1 Team matching between KH and service composition domain

Terms in KH	Terms in service composition domain
Krill individual with the best position	The optimal service composition
Krill individual	One feasible service composition
Motion induced by other krill	Learning from other service compositions
Foraging motion	Learning from the current optimal service composition

movement induced by other krill individuals, (2) foraging action, and (3) random diffusion. Table 5.1 shows the analogous term matches between the KH and service composition domains. For our mobile service composition problem, the position vector of each krill individual in the population corresponds to a feasible service composition. The KH optimization target is to find the krill individual with the best position, which corresponds to find the best mobile service composition with the shortest response time. Therefore, once the optimal krill individual is found, the best composition is obtained.

In KH, the Lagrangian model is generalized in a d-dimensional decision space as follows.

$$\frac{\mathrm{d}X_i}{\mathrm{d}t} = N_i + M_i + D_i \tag{5.3}$$

where $X_i = (x_{i1}, x_{i2}, \ldots, x_{id})$ is the position vector of the i-th krill individual (feasible services composition), d is the number of tasks in the service composition, x_{ij} is the selected candidate for the j-th task in solution X_i. N_i is the motion induced by other krill individuals; M_i is the foraging motion, and D_i is the physical diffusion of the i-th krill individual.

5.2.2.2 Method

Motion Induced by Other Krill Individuals

This step is to optimize each composition result by learning from other feasible compositions. The motion induced by other krill individuals (feasible compositions) is evaluated by three components, which are named target swarm density, local swarm density, and repulsive swarm density in the KH algorithm. For a krill individual (feasible composition), this operation can be defined as:

$$N_i^{new} = N^{max}\alpha_i + \omega_n N_i^{old} \tag{5.4}$$

where N^{max} is the maximum induced speed. According to the experimental values of the maximum induced speed, we empirically set N^{max} to 0.01 (ms^{-1}) in this work, $\omega_n \in [0, 1]$ is the inertia weight of the induced motion, N_i^{old} is the induced motion in the previous iteration, α_i is the direction of the induced motion:

$$\alpha_i = \alpha_i^{local} + \alpha_i^{target} \tag{5.5}$$

where α_i^{local} is the local effect provided by neighbor service compositions, and α_i^{target} is the target direction effect provided by the local optimal composition result.

The effect of neighbor service compositions can be regarded as an attractive tendency among the feasible compositions for a local search. The effect of neighbor service compositions is determined as:

$$\alpha_i^{local} = \sum_{j=1}^{k} \widehat{F}_{i,j} \widehat{X}_{i,j} \tag{5.6}$$

$$\widehat{F}_{i,j} = \frac{F_i - F_j}{F_{worst} - F_{best}} \tag{5.7}$$

$$\widehat{X}_{i,j} = \frac{X_i - X_j}{X_i - X_j + \varepsilon} \tag{5.8}$$

where F_{worst} and F_{best} are the worst and best response time of mobile service compositions in the current iteration, respectively. F_i represents the response time of the i-th krill individual/mobile service composition calculated by Eq. (5.2), F_j is the response time of the j-th ($j = 1, 2, \ldots, k$) neighbor service composition; and k is the number of the neighbor services compositions. For avoiding the singularities, a small positive number ε is added to the denominator. This work sets $\varepsilon = 0.0001$.

The neighbor service compositions of the i-th service composition is determined by a sensing distance (d_s) around it. The sensing distance for each service composition can be calculated in each iteration as follows:

$$d_{s,i} = \frac{1}{5N} \sum_{j=1}^{N} \|X_i - X_j\| \tag{5.9}$$

where $d_{s,i}$ is the sensing distance for the i-th service composition and N is the population size of the feasible solution set. If the Euclidean distance of two service composition vectors is less than $d_{s,i}$, they are assumed as neighbors.

To evaluate the target effect of each service composition, the optimal service composition of the current iteration with the shortest response time is taken into account by using

$$\alpha_i^{target} = C_{best} \widehat{F}_{best} \widehat{X}_{best} \tag{5.10}$$

wheres C_{best} is the effective coefficient of the service composition with the shortest response time to the i-th krill services composition. This coefficient is defined since α_i^{target} leads the solution to the local optima and it should be more effective than other service compositions such as neighbors. The value of C_{best} is determined as:

$$C_{best} = 2\left(r_a + \frac{I}{I_{max}}\right) \tag{5.11}$$

where $r_a \in [0, 1]$ is a random value to enhance exploration, I is the actual iteration count and I_{max} is the maximum number of iterations.

Foraging Motion

Besides getting knowledge from its neighbors, a krill individual also gets knowledge from the global optima, which is expressed in terms of food attraction in the foraging motion. Thus, the KH algorithm not only gets partial knowledge but also global knowledge. The foraging motion is influenced by two main factors, which are named new food locations, and previous experiences about food locations in KH algorithm. For the i-th service composition, this motion can be defined as follows:

$$F_i = V_f \beta_i + \omega_f F_i^{old} \tag{5.12}$$

where V_f is the foraging speed (empirically set to 0.02 in our study), $\omega_f \in [0, 1]$ is the inertia weight of foraging motion, and F_i^{old} is the foraging motion in the previous iteration. β_i is the direction of the foraging motion:

$$\beta_i = \beta_i^{food} + \beta_i^{best} \tag{5.13}$$

where β_i^{food} is the attractive food, and β_i^{best} is the effect of the shortest response time of the i-th service composition so far.

In KH, the virtual center of food concentration is approximately calculated according to the response time distribution of krill individuals; as it is inspired by "center of mass." It is formulated as follows:

$$X^{food} = \frac{\sum_{i=1}^{N} \frac{1}{F_i} X_i}{\sum_{i=1}^{N} \frac{1}{F_i}} \tag{5.14}$$

The food attraction for the i-th service composition can be determined as follows:

$$\beta_i^{food} = C^{food} F^{food} X^{food} \tag{5.15}$$

where C^{food} is the food coefficient. Because the effect of food in the krill herding decreases during the time, the food coefficient is determined as:

$$C_{best} = 2\left(1 - \frac{I}{I_{max}}\right) \tag{5.16}$$

The food attraction is defined to possibly attract the service composition to get close to the global optimum. Based on this definition, the service compositions normally gather around the global optima after some iterations. This can be considered as an efficient global optimization strategy to help improve the convergence of the KH algorithm. The effect of the shortest response time of the i-th krill service composition can be handled as follows:

$$\beta_i^{best} = \widehat{F}_{i,best}\widehat{X}_{i,best} \tag{5.17}$$

where $\widehat{X}_{i,best}$ is the best previously generated position of the i-th krill individual.

Physical Diffusion

This step targets at keeping the diversity of generated service compositions in each iteration and avoiding an early convergence. The physical diffusion of the service compositions is considered to be a random process. This motion can be expressed in terms of a maximum diffusion speed and a random directional vector, formulated as follows:

$$D_i = D^{max}\delta \tag{5.18}$$

where D^{max} is the maximum diffusion speed, and δ is a random directional vector with $\delta_i \in [-1, 1]$. The maximum diffusion speed is randomly generated in $[0.002, 0.01]$. The better services composition is initialized, the fewer movements are required to find the optimal answer. The effect of the induced motion from other service compositions and foraging motion gradually decreases with increasing iterations. Thus, Eq. (5.18) is modified to gradually decrease the random speed over iterations, i.e.,

$$D_i = D^{max}\left(1 - \frac{I}{I_{max}}\right)\delta \tag{5.19}$$

Position Update

In KH, defined motions frequently change the positions of krill individual/services compositions to improve their response time. The foraging motion and induced motion by other krill individuals/service compositions contain two global and two local strategies. These are working in parallel to making KH a powerful optimization algorithm. Using different effective parameters of the motion over time, the position vector of a krill individual/service composition at time $t + \Delta t$ is calculated as:

$$X_i(t + \Delta t) = X_i(t) + \Delta t\frac{dX_i}{dt} \tag{5.20}$$

where Δt is a scale factor of the speed vector and is set according to a search space. As a guideline, it can be obtained from:

$$\Delta t = C_t \sum_{j=1}^{d} \left(UB_j - LB_j \right) \tag{5.21}$$

where d is the total number of tasks in each service composition, and UB_j and LB_j are upper and lower bounds of candidate services for the j-th task, respectively. C_t is a constant number to scale the searching space. Lower values of C_t lead to the slower motion of krill individuals/service compositions, i.e., a thorough search.

5.2.3   Experiments

5.2.3.1   Optimality Evaluation

In this experiment, we evaluate how close the response time of the acquired service composition is to the actual optimal one. To assess the optimality of KMSC, we use the evaluation metric *optimality ratio* widely adopted:

$$optimality = \frac{F_{opt}}{F} \tag{5.22}$$

where F is response time value obtained by the evaluated algorithm and F_{opt} is optimal response time value that can be achieved. Note that the optimal response time value is achieved by using the integer programming algorithm [11].

Thus, we compute the *optimality ratio* of our approach and other compared algorithms versus the problem size. Because only a very few studies have investigated the problem of service selection for mobile service composition, we could not find any existing method to directly compare its results with those of KMSC. Nevertheless, because KMSC is a population-based algorithm, we chose the following population-based algorithms to implement and compare with our method.

Genetic Algorithm (GA) A search heuristic algorithm that mimics the process of natural selection. This has been used by existing service composition approaches [12]. We extend them by adding mobility.

Particle Swarm Optimization (PSO) A computational method that optimizes a problem by iteratively trying to improve a candidate solution with regard to a given measure of quality [13]. PSO has also been utilized in the service composition research [14].

Cuckoo Search (CS) CS is an optimization algorithm inspired by the obligate brood parasitism of some cuckoo species who lay their eggs in the nests of other host birds (of other species).

To evaluate the optimality of the algorithms, we plot the optimality ratio obtained by all algorithms versus increasing problem size. Figure 5.2 compares the optimality of all algorithms against the number of tasks with a fixed number (100) of services available per task. And Fig. 5.3 compares the optimality against an increasing number

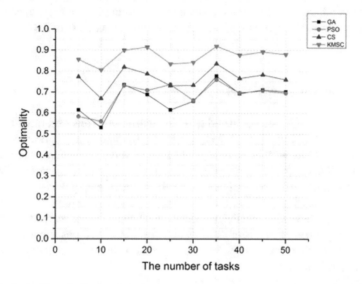

Fig. 5.2 Optimality with the number of tasks

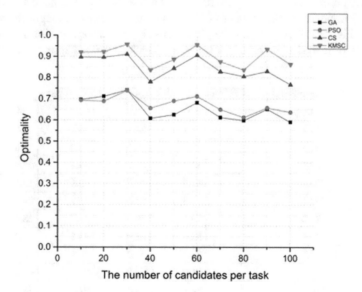

Fig. 5.3 Optimality with the number of candidates

of candidate services with a fixed number (10) of tasks. From the comparison results, we observe that KMSC has outstanding performance of solution optimality with all different task counts and candidate counts. The results indicate that the response time value achieved by our approach is close to the optimal result, i.e., the *optimal ratio* is around 90%. Furthermore, the *optimal ratio* obtained by KMSC is at least 10% higher than others. Thus, we can conclude that our approach manages to achieve an acceptable approximation ratio of the optimal solution regardless of the composition size.

5.2.3.2 Scalability Evaluation

The runtime of KMSC are compared to other algorithms in this experiment in order to assess the scalability. Table 5.2 compares the runtime of all algorithms against the number of tasks with a fixed number (100) of services available per task. We observe that the runtime of integer programming is nearly hundreds times of KMSC's. KMSC also runs fastest as compared with the other three population-based algorithms. This is because induced motion, foraging motion and physical diffusion in KMSC can be executed in parallel, whereby the efficiency of the method could reach a great improvement. In addition, we can observe that KMSC has a low algorithmic complexity, which is roughly linear with the composition size, showing a scalable feature algorithmically.

Table 5.3 compares the scalability of all algorithms against an increasing number of candidate services with a fixed number (10) of tasks. Similarly, integer programming also performs with the highest runtime. We note that the runtime of all methods is almost irrelevant to the number of services per task. Hence, all algorithms scale well in this regard. Among all the algorithms, KMSC always performs with the lowest runtime. Based on these results, we can conclude that our approach maintains

Table 5.2 Runtime milliseconds of different algorithms with the number of tasks

#Task	Integer programming	GA	PSO	CS	KMSC
5	549.2	34.4	25.1	34.8	**5.7**
10	604.3	39.3	32	40.9	**6.6**
15	662.5	50.4	44.7	54.4	**12.7**
20	700.6	61.9	49.2	60.3	**19.1**
25	739.1	69.3	53.6	71.7	**24.1**
30	829.0	79.6	59.3	81.7	**28.4**
35	872.4	83.4	62.9	91.5	**36.3**
40	957.5	88.9	66.7	95.8	**38.4**
45	995.7	91.6	76.5	96.5	**40.2**
50	1170.2	94.4	80.4	97.7	**48.3**

Table 5.3 Runtime milliseconds of different algorithms with the number of candidates

#Candidate	Integer programming	GA	PSO	CS	KMSC
10	530.1	68.7	35.4	74.0	**9.3**
20	547.0	75.3	43.4	83.0	**7.1**
30	546.1	72.3	39.2	88.0	**10.5**
40	566.2	78.4	49.0	87.0	**6.1**
50	578.0	79.5	43.7	89.9	**2.2**
60	590.8	70.6	44.2	83.1	**11.1**
70	575.0	69.3	39.4	81.2	**9.9**
80	592.1	72.8	50.3	72.5	**4.2**
90	596.2	85.1	49.1	91.0	**9.0**
100	587.7	73.8	52.6	89.0	**4.1**

acceptable performance (optimality and scalability) with large datasets for both tasks and candidates.

5.2.3.3 Reliability Evaluation

In order to verify whether user mobility should be taken into account when making a mobile composition in MSSC, we conduct extensive experiments to compare our method with the standard composition method that considers only services' individual QoS. This method selects the candidate with the optimal execution time and ignore the mobility of service providers.

The composition request of each user consists of 10 tasks, and there are 50 candidate services for each task. Then we find out the optimal solution for each composition request and compare the average quality of solutions with the two methods. In addition, we also compare their reliability, defined as follow:

$$rel = \frac{N_s}{N_t} \tag{5.23}$$

where N_s is the number of solutions found by each method, and N_t is the total number of composition requests.

The impact of mobility becomes prominent with the variation of sensing distance as we mentioned above. We plot the results versus sensing distance in Fig. 5.4. From Fig. 5.4a we can observe that the reliability of the standard method is zero when the distance is small. It is lower than KMSC's when it becomes large. Furthermore, Fig. 5.4b shows that the solution quality by the standard method is worse than that by KMSC. The results validate that traditional composition methods cannot be directly used in a mobile environment. Therefore, it is very important to take mobile user

Fig. 5.4 Comparison between the standard composition method and KMSC

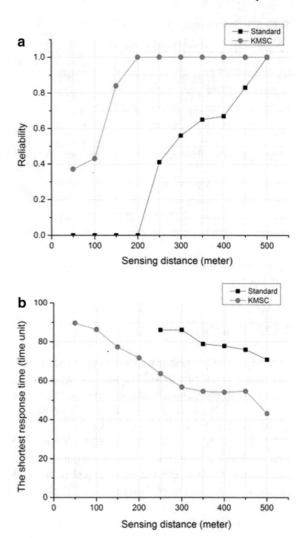

mobility into consideration when handling with service composition problems in mobile environments.

5.2.3.4   Verification in Real World

In order to verify the performance of our mobile service selection approach in the real world, we conduct series of extensive experiments by comparing the results of our method with the standard composition methods in a mobile service sharing community.

Graduate students in the College of Computer Science & Technology at Zhejiang University are chosen as project volunteers. Twenty subjects participated in the experiment. Each subject holds 10 randomly selected candidate services for a composition with 4 tasks. The execution time of services is randomly generated from 5 to 20 s, the input and output data sizes are randomly generated from 10 to 500 k. To avoid other factors affecting the experimental results, the input and output data sizes are set equal if two services have the same functionality. All the services are deployed on their smart phones and shared through Bluetooth. The subjects move in the playground of Zhejiang University with different speed. The communication network used is Bluetooth. The data transmission speed is measured by a mobile application named 360 Assistant. We utilize this application to measure the average data transmission speed of the smart phones before the experiments. The service selection algorithms are implemented as apps on the smart phones through which subjects can issue service requests.

One subject is randomly chosen as the service requester who will make a service composition request containing 4 tasks. We execute 15 trials, averaged over 5 iterations, during which each composition request is issued by the service requester at different locations. Figure 5.5 compares the response time of service compositions obtained by the standard composition method and the proposed one.

From Fig. 5.5, we can observe that our method significantly outperforms the standard one. Among the 15 trials, the composition success ratio of the standard one is only 20% while ours achieves 86.7%. Besides, the response time returned by our method is also better than the standard one. Therefore, we can conclude that standard method that consider no user mobility is not suitable for mobile environment.

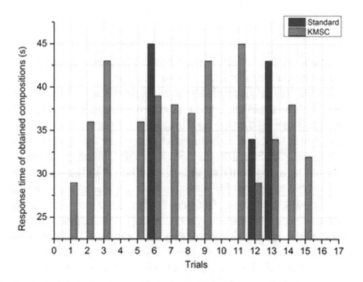

Fig. 5.5 Comparison between the standard composition method and KMSC in real-world trials (color printing is needed for clarity)

Meanwhile, our proposed one is useful to handle the service selection problem in such mobile service sharing community with the factor of mobility of end users taken into account.

5.3 Risk-Aware Mobile Service Composition

Services provided by mobile providers will be quite different from traditional stationary services. In such a highly mobile environment, the risk of service inter-action should be considered as an import issue [15]. Here, the risk of mobile services refers to their unavailability caused by out-of-range relevant movements of service requesters and providers. In mobile environment, both service requesters and providers may be subject to frequent movement. The communication among service requesters and providers are based on some wireless communication tech-nologies such as Bluetooth and WLAN. These techniques require the communication must be within a limited range. If a provider becomes unavailable when its service is being used, then the composition fails to execute successfully. Thus, a risk-aware model to describe the mobility of mobile service providers is required. In addition, to make composition, the risk of unsuccessful service interaction should be considered as well as the QoS of the composition.

5.3.1 Motivation Scenario and Problem Definition

5.3.1.1 Scenario

We use an example depicted in Fig. 5.6 to illustrate the related features of the problem of risk-aware selection for mobile service composition.

A visitor named Jack is walking in a park and he is shooting videos. Now he wants to cut a clip of the video and add some effects and speech for the video clip. But he has no such services on his own device. He can upload the video to cloud services to get the video clip, but the park is in a remote area where the signal coverage is not so good which results in the reality that the cloud services are not stable. Therefore, the video transmission may take long time or even fail. If a video processing service is provided by some nearby mobile devices, Jack can invoke such mobile services on nearby mobile devices through free near field communication techniques. If one service can't meet his requirement, several services can be composed. Due to users' mobility, the availability of service providers to Jack can vary. Thus, invoking services provided by other mobile users may face new challenges that traditional composition methods cannot handle. Jack must consider the distance between him and his nearly mobile devices and the available time he can obtain services, which cause quite a troublesome challenge.

Fig. 5.6 A motivation scenario

Firstly, there exists risk of failure that invoking services provided by mobile users. Due to the limited range of the communication among mobile devices, Jack can only invoke services provided within the required communication distance of the mobile devices. Meanwhile, the other users who are also visiting the gallery keep moving in and out the required distance uncertainly. As a result, there exists risk that the service provider moves out of range when the service is being used, then the composition fails and a re-composition is needed.

Secondly, there is limited work dealing with users' mobility when making service composition in mobile environment. Then once the generated composition solution fails when the service provider moves out of the required communication distance, it needs to recompose services for the target user, which would cost much time and communication resources.

To minimize the risk of composition fails and avoid frequent re-composition, we need to select a service provider with enough availability time for each service such that the composition can exist to finalize. We refer to a composition with such requirement as a risk-aware service composition. The difficulty for it is the mobility of service requesters and providers. For existing selection methods for service composition, only properties of candidate services are considered. But the mobility of service providers and requesters is ignored. Therefore, the risk of failure of the obtained composition is hardly controlled. Thus, it's important to solve the risk-aware selection problem for mobile service composition in the above application scenario.

5.3.1.2   Problem Definition

Firstly, definitions for all key concepts concerned with risk-aware selection problem for mobile service composition in our model are introduced clearly.

Definition 1 (*Mobile Services*) A mobile service is a triple

$$s = (id, Fun, QoS),$$

where:

(1)   *id* is the unique identifier of the service;
(2)   *Fun* is the set of functions *s* provides, a function includes the input, output, pre-condition and result of the service; and
(3) $QoS = \{q\}_{j=1}^{n}$ is a set of quality attributes, including execution cost, response time, reliability, availability, etc.

Definition 2 (*Mobile Service Provider*) A mobile service provider is a tuple

$$sp = (id, S),$$

where:

(1)   *id* is the unique identifier of the provider;
(2)   *S* is the set of mobile services *p* provides;

Definition 3 (*Services composition Plan*) A service composition plan is a tuple

$$scp = (L, G),$$

where:

(1) $L = \{l_1, l_2, \ldots l_n\}$ is a set of tasks; and
(2) $G = \{g(l_i, l_j) | l_i, l_j \in L\}$ is a set of relations between tasks in *L*.

A service composition plan is an abstract description of a business process. Each task l_i can be realized by invoking an individual service. There may be multiple services with different QoS that can be adopted to fulfill each task. *G* is used to describe the structure of the composition. $g(l_i, l_j) = 1$ represents that the inputs of l_j depend on the outputs of l_i.

Definition 4 (*Mobile Services Composition*) A mobile service composition is a tuple

$$sc = (scp, S)$$

where:

(1)   *scp* is the corresponding service composition plan; and

(2) S is the set of component services selected for each task in scp;

In terms of a mobile service composition, we care about its two properties. One is the overall QoS of the composition (e.g. response time). The other is the risk of invoking the composition in mobile environment. We firstly give the formal definition of the two properties, and then present the problem definition.

Definition 5 (*QoS of Mobile Service Composition*) The QoS of a mobile service composition sc is a tuple

$$QoS_{sc} = (Q, C)$$

where:

(1) $Q = \{q\}_{j=1}^{n}$, expressing the QoS attributes of the composite service; and
(2) $C = \{c\}_{j=1}^{n}$, expressing the integration functions for the QoS attributes. We adopt the integration functions in [16] to get the overall QoS values of sc.

Definition 6 (*Risk of Mobile Service Composition*) The Risk of a mobile service composition sc is modeled as:

$$Risk_{sc} = \max_{i=1,2...n} r_i$$

where:

(1) r_i is the risk that the service provider of the selected service for the i-th task becomes 'unavailable' during the execution of the services.
(2) n is the number of tasks for the service composition.

Note that only the service requester and provider are within the required communication distance, can the service interaction be successful. So 'unavailable' means that the service requester and provider move out of range during the interaction.

The risk of the execution of each task can be measured as follows:

$$r_i = 1 - Prob(X_i^p \geq dur_i^p) \tag{5.1}$$

where p is the service provider who provides the selected service for the i-th task; X_i^p is a random variable indicates that p keeps within the required distance to the service requester from the moment of being discovered; dur_i^p is the execution time of the i-th task if the service provided by p is selected; $Prob(X_i^p \geq t)$ is the probability distribution function representing the probability of p's staying within the required distance to the service requester, which can be obtained by some mobility prediction methods based on the signal strength detection.

The reason why we use the maximum value of all risks in each component as the risk of the composition is inspired by the cask principle. In a mobile service composition, if the execution of any one component fails, then the whole composition results in failure. Thus, the risk of a mobile services composition depends on its weakest component. Even if the other components are dependable, one component which is quite risky (i.e. the provider tends to move out of the required distance frequently) can make the whole composition failure.

Definition 7 (*Risk-Aware Selection Problem for Mobile Service Composition*) Given a mobile user wants to implement a composition plan *scp* by selecting mobile services provided by other mobile service providers *Sp* nearby. The target is to generate a feasible service composition $sc = (s_1, s_2, \ldots)$ such that:

(1) optimize the QoS of *sc*;
(2) minimize the risk of *sc*;

Thus, the objective function is as follow:

$$F(sc) = \vec{w}_q \cdot Q_{sc} + w_r \cdot Risk_{sc} \qquad (5.2)$$

where $Q_{sc} = (q_1, q_2, \ldots, q_n)$ is an n-dimension vector that specifies the value of each QoS attributes, note that all QoS attributes are transferred to negative forms (smaller the value is, better the quality is). $\vec{w}_q = \left(w_{q1}, w_{q2}, \ldots, w_{qn} \right)^T$ is an n-dimension vector that specifies the weight for each QoS attributes. w_r is the weight of $Risk_{sc}$. We set the number of QoS attributes as one for simplification. Thus, Q_{sc} is the value of a QoS attribute (e.g. response time) and we can use a real number w_q instead of $\vec{w}_q$. And $w_q + w_r = 1$. Note that the values of w_q and w_r are decided by mobile users according to their preferences.

5.3.2 MSA Approach

5.3.2.1 Optimization Problem

The risk-aware selection problem for mobile service composition (RMSC) can be formulated as a multi-objective optimization problem:

$$\begin{aligned} \min \quad & F(X) \\ \text{subject to } & x_i \in \{1, 2 \ldots, m\} \end{aligned}$$

where X is a service selection solution for the given composition plan. $i \in [1, n]$ is the index of the tasks in the composition plan. $x_i \in [1, m]$ is the index of the service candidates for the *i*-th task. $x_i = j$ if the *j*-th candidate is selected for the *i*-th task. $F(X)$ is the objective function mentioned in Eq. (5.2).

Theorem 1 *The risk-aware selection problem for mobile service composition is NP-hard.*

Proof We can reduce our studied problem RMSC to the Knapsack problem. For the RMSC problem, we always find an instance of integer programming problem such that the RMSC problem is solvable if and only if integer programming problem is solvable.

An integer programming optimization problem of finding the smallest $F(\Theta)$ with a feasible parameter vector $\Theta = (\theta_1, \ldots, \theta_n)$, which can be modeled as follows:

$$\begin{aligned} \inf \quad & F(\Theta) \\ \text{subject to } & \theta_i \in \{1, 2, \ldots, N\} \end{aligned} \tag{5.3}$$

This means the feasible set of parameter vectors is constrained by $\theta_i \in \{1, 2, \ldots, N\}$ with integer values. The optimal solution Θ^* satisfies the following conditions:

(1) Θ^* belongs to the feasible set
(2) $\forall \Theta, F(\Theta^*) \leq F(\Theta)$

Therefore, the integer programming problem is equivalent to the RMSC problem. In order to cope with such a NP-hard problem, we design a modified simulated annealing algorithm to obtain an optimal solution.

5.3.2.2   MSA Algorithm

A modified simulated annealing (MSA) method is proposed for the mobile service composition problem. Simulated annealing (SA) is a heuristic method that can avoid converging to a local optimum by accepting bad solutions during iterations [17]. SA provides an efficient way for optimization of NP-hard problems. Although it cannot guarantee to obtain the global optimum, it can find an acceptable optimum within a reasonable time [18]. The proposed MSA heuristic is discussed in detail as follows.

The Generation of a New Solution

In this problem, a solution is a permutation of mobile services to be composed. An initial solution S_0 is generated randomly in the solution space. A generating function generates a new solution S' from the current solution S. In order to facilitate subsequent calculations and new solution's acceptance, new solution is usually generated from current solution through simple transforming. The way to generate new solutions decides the neighborhood structures of current solution, which influences the annealing schedule. Different from the basic simulated annealing algorithms, new solution in MSA is produced by a mutation operator. One element of the current solution is randomly chosen and substituted by a new element with different value, which is the same as mutation in genetic algorithm.

Solution Evaluation

To compare the new solution and the current solution, we calculate the fitness value of the new solution and current solution according to the object function in Eq. (5.2), which are expressed as C' and C. The difference of fitness value between new solution and current solution is calculated by $\Delta C = C' - C$, which decides whether to accept the new solution or not.

Acceptance of New Solution

Whether a new solution is accepted or not is decided by an acceptance criterion. Metropolis criterion is the most commonly accepted one. If $\Delta C < 0$, accept S' as a new current S. Otherwise, calculate the acceptance probability function $P = exp(-\Delta C/T)$, where T is current temperature, and accept S' as a new current S with acceptance probability P. When the temperature is high, P tends to 1, and MSA accept bad S' with a high probability, which prevent MSA from converging to a local optimum. When temperature tends to 0, P tends to 0, and MSA tends to accept S' only when $\Delta C < 0$. Finally, MSA converges to an approximately global optimal solution.

Inner Iteration

At each temperature, the procedure from step (1) to step (3) is iterated several times until the fitness value of the solution keeps stable or the maximum inner iteration number is reached. Different from the basic simulated annealing algorithm, when accepting a bad solution S' with acceptance probability P, we keep the good solution S as the best solution so far (S^*). S^* is the valid solution in MSA and will be returned when MSA is terminated.

Outer Iteration

The annealing schedule starts from initial temperature T_0, then T is updated by a function $T' = T * k$ after the inner iteration is over. k is a constant number smaller than but close to 1. The bigger k is, the slower annealing schedule will be, and MSA will converge to a better solution. However, MSA will consume much more runtime with a large k. We need to find the balance between good solution and little runtime. When the temperature decreases to the limit temperature T_{min}, which is set to be 0.1 in our method, the outer iteration is terminated. Finally, the annealing schedule is terminated and the final S^* is returned as the approximately global optimal solution.

Table 5.4 The modified simulated annealing algorithm for service selection

Algorithm: MSA
01: initialize S_0, T_0 // Initialize solution.
02: while $T > 0.1$ //outer iteration
03:    while *iter < maxiter* // inner iteration
04:    | $S' \leftarrow mutate(S)$ // Generate neighbors through mutation.
05:    | $C' \leftarrow F(S')$ // Compute the fitness value
06:    | if $exp(- \Delta C/T) < 0$
07:    | | $S \leftarrow S'$
08:    | | $C \leftarrow C'$
09:    | | $S^* \leftarrow S'$ // save the best solution so far
10:    | if $exp(- \Delta C/T) > random()$
11:    | | $S \leftarrow S'$
12:    | | $C \leftarrow C'$
13:    | If C unchanged for several iterations, terminate inner loop
14:    $T \leftarrow T*cool$ //update temperature
15: return S^*

MSA Procedure

Table 5.4 shows the procedure of MSA. It starts from a solution S_0 and continues until temperature decrease to 0.1. In the inner loop, the function *mutate(S)* generate a new neighbor of a given S. If $\Delta C < 0$, accept S' as a new current S and save the best solution S^* so far. Otherwise, accept S' as a new current S with acceptance probability $P = exp(-\Delta C/T)$. The function *random()* returns a random value in the range [0, 1]. We use a terminate condition in the inner loop except for the maximum iteration number limit for the inner loop to improve the performance of MSA. The terminate condition is that if C unchanged for several iterations, terminate the inner loop. The annealing schedule obtains new temperature by the expression $T = T * k$, where k is a number smaller than but close to 1. Ultimately, approximately global optimal solution is obtained.

5.3.3   Experiments

5.3.3.1   Setup

The service compositions are generated with randomly inserted tasks and control structures. For each task, we randomly created a number of candidate services, each with a different QoS. The QoS attributes of each service were generated from a uniform distribution. The probability function of the user's staying within the required

Table 5.5 Parameters configuration

Configuration	maxiter	cool	initemp
Configuration 1	1–9	0.99	100
Configuration 2	5	0.91–0.99	100
Configuration 3	5	0.99	100–900

range follows a normal distribution $N(\mu_i, \sigma_i^2)$. The mean μ_i is generated uniformly from $[0.5RT, 1.5RT]$ in which RT is the overall response time of the composition where the worst candidates are selected for each task. The standard deviation σ_i is set $\sigma_i = 0.1\mu_i$. All the implemented algorithms are run independently 50 times in case of unprejudiced statistical results.

5.3.3.2   Impact of Parameters

There are three parameters to be adjusted to improve the MSA's performance: maximum iteration number (*maxiter*), the initial temperature (*initemp*), and the cooling rate (*cool*). To evaluate the impact of each parameter, we generated four groups of parameters configuration as in Table 5.5. For each group of parameters configuration, we tuned one parameter and fixed the other parameters.

Figure 5.7a shows the results of tuning different parameters for our approach. From Fig. 5.7a, we can observe that the fitness value of the optimal composition solution obtained by MSA descends with the increase of the maximum iteration number. This is because a larger iteration count can lead the obtained solution more approaching to the global optimum. Meanwhile, when the iteration count exceeds a certain value, for example, *maxiter* = 5, MSA does not perform with significant improvement. Therefore, an excessively large iteration count can hardly improve the performance of MSA so much but will cost more computational time.

Figure 5.7b shows the impact of the cooling rate on the obtained optimal fitness value. The fitness decreases with the cooling rate and reach smallest value at 0.99. However, the situation is different in Fig. 5.7c, the initial temperature almost has no obvious impact on the MSA when it exceeds a certain value.

5.3.3.3   Optimality Evaluation

We use the evaluation metric *optimality ratio* which has been widely adopted in literature [19] to assess the optimality of MSA:

$$optimality = \frac{F_{opt}}{F} \tag{5.4}$$

Fig. 5.7 **a** Impact of
maximum iteration number.
b Impact of cooling rate.
c Impact of initial
temperature

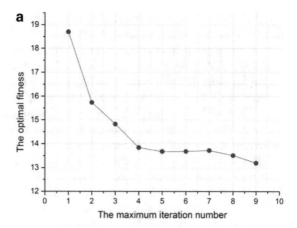

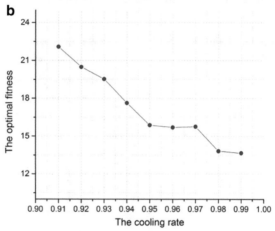

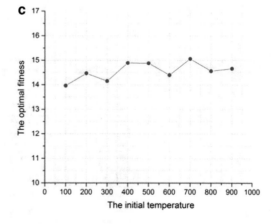

where F is fitness value obtained by the assessed algorithm and F_{opt} is optimal fitness value that can be acquired. The optimal fitness value is obtained by using the integer programming algorithm that can guarantee to get the optimal solution.

Thus, we compute the *optimality ratio* of our approach versus the problem size. Figure 5.8 plots the optimality of MSA against an increasing number of candidate services with a fixed number (3) of tasks. From the result, we observe that the fitness value achieved by our approach is close to the optimal result, i.e., the *optimal ratio* is above 97%. Thus, we can conclude that MSA manages to achieve an acceptable approximation ratio of the optimal solution.

Table 5.6 compares the runtime of MSA and the integer programming algorithm against an increasing number of candidate services with a fixed number (4) of tasks. From the result, we can observe that the runtime of the integer programming algorithm increases exponentially, while the runtime of MSA is almost irrelevant to the number of services per task. Hence, MSA scales well in this regard. Since the mobile

Fig. 5.8 Optimality ratio of MSA

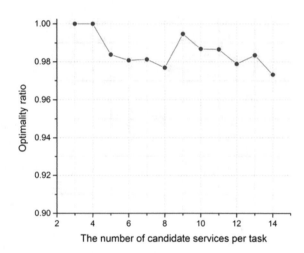

The number of candidate services per task

Table 5.6 Runtime (seconds) of different algorithms with the number of candidates

#Candidate	Integer programming	MSA
10	0.114	1.5321
20	0.325	1.6314
30	0.852	1.5357
40	1.586	1.5848
50	2.729	1.6135
60	3.823	1.5764
70	6.239	1.5521
80	9.582	1.5034
90	12.836	1.5583
100	17.443	1.6139

environment is dynamic, the requirement on runtime must be met because the environment parameters for computation may vary much within a short time. Therefore, although the Integer Programming algorithm can obtain the optimal result, it is not suitable to the problem in mobile environment due to its poor scalability. Based on these results, we can conclude that MSA maintains acceptable optimality.

5.4 Constraints-Driven Service Composition

The fast development of mobile computing and cloud computing enables people to leverage various services from their mobile devices. However, service composition with temporal and QoS constraints are becoming dramatically tough due to the mobility environment, local-time constraints and global QoS constraints as well. Therefore, it's important to form such a service composition that not only satisfies the constraints, but also ensures the composition to be executed successfully in the mobile environment.

5.4.1 Motivation Case and Problem Formulation

5.4.1.1 Study Case

Recently, Mobile cloud computing (MCC) has brought great values for wide fields through service composition in mobile environment, such as image processing, crowd computing, social networking, etc. [20]. However, there still remain several challenges for service composition in MCC.

(1) Mobility: In a highly mobile environment, both users and service providers may be subject to frequent movement. For example, mobile devices carried by customers in a restaurant form a mobile ad hoc network through Bluetooth or Wi-Fi communication. These mobile devices can provide various services, such as file downloading, GPS services, or some software. In such a mobile ad hoc network, customers may enter and leave the restaurant at different time. If a provider leaves when his service is being used, then the composition fails to execute.

(2) Temporal Constraints: Service interactions in mobile environment have more requirements in temporal constraints. For example, a foreign tourist is on the subway. As he does not understand local language, he wants to invoke two services to find the destination: first, he should invoke an optical character recognition service to extract the text of the route map; then, he needs a transition service to translate the text. It is possible that his destination is just the next stop, so the invocation of the two services should be finished in 30 s, which is the time duration before the subway reaches the next stop.

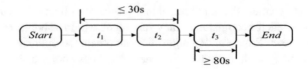

Fig. 5.9 An example of mobile service composition with constraints

(3) QoS Constraints: As the number of services keeps increasing dramatically, quality-of-service (QoS) is regarded as a significant criterion for selecting proper services from the large-scale candidate sets. Giving the growing number of candidate services that can offer same functions, the selection of the optimal combination of services satisfying users' global QoS constraints becomes very complex and time consuming.

Figure 5.9 illustrates the related features of the problem of constraints-driven service composition in mobile cloud computing.

Supposing Peter is a foreign tourist and he is on the subway, where no mobile network is available. As he does not understand local language, he cannot read the route map on the subway and does not exactly know which station he will get off, so he takes a picture of the route map and wants to seek help from the passengers on the subway. He wants to invoke three services: first, he should invoke an optical character recognition service to extract the text of the route map (9E); then, he needs a transition service to translate the text (9F) and finds the station he will get off; after that, he wants to invoke a music service to listen to some music (9G). It is possible that his destination is just the next stop, so he should find his destination stop before the subway reaches the next stop. Therefore, he claims that the duration between the beginning of 9E and the end of 9F should be shorter than 30 s. Besides, he requires a QoS constraint that the cost of the three services should not exceed 3 dollars. Each service is described with its response time and the fee that the invoker should pay to the provider. As passengers are on the subway, they will leave at different stops. As the time schedule of the subway is fixed with some deviations. Each provider can declare his leaving time by a time window.

Taking the mobility feature of mobile users and both temporal and QoS constraints into consideration at the same time, the service selection becomes a big challenge, which cannot be handled with using existing approaches. Therefore, a novel approach for constraints-driven service composition in mobile cloud computing is needed.

5.4.1.2 Problem Formulation

Firstly, we give introduction on several key concepts related to mobile service composition with constraints, then the formal problem definition based on these concepts are given.

Definition 1 (*Mobile Services*) A mobile service is a 4-tuple

$$s = (id, Fun, QoS),$$

where:

(1) *id* is the unique identifier of the service;
(2) *Fun* is the set of functions s provides, a function includes the input, output, pre-condition and result of the service;
(3) $QoS = \{q\}_{j=1}^{n}$ is a set of quality attributes, including execution cost, response time, reliability, availability, etc.

Definition 2 (*Service Composition Plan*) A service composition plan is a tuple

$$scp = (T, G),$$

where:

(1) $T = \{t_1, t_2, \ldots t_n\}$ is a set of tasks;
(2) G provides the structural information of the service composition plan, which can be specified by XML-based languages, such as BPEL.

Definition 3 (*Mobile Service Composition*) A mobile service composition is a triple

$$sc = (scp, S, QoS)$$

where:

(1) scp is the corresponding service composition plan;
(2) S is the set of component services selected for each task in scp;
(3) $QoS = \{q\}_{j=1}^{n}$, expressing the QoS attributes of the composite service.

Given a service composition sc, the QoS of sc is the aggregation of the QoS of its component services.

The service providers may move around and out of the communication range in mobile computing environment, making service composition very difficult. Once a service provider is outside the scope of service composition, the provided services cannot be obtained anymore and the application must find and reconnect to the new services. The estimated time during which the service provider will be available at the current environment can be specified. Therefore, as soon as receiving a service composition request, each service provider's estimated remaining time at the current environment will be available to the system.

Definition 4 (*Provider Mobility*) The mobility model of a service provider is modeled as a tuple

$$m = ([t_a, t_b], f)$$

where:

(1) $[t_a, t_b]$ is the time window that the service provider reports during which it may leave. That is, the provider is always available before the time $t = t_a$; it may leave during the time window $[t_a, t_b]$; after the time $t = t_b$, it will be unavailable definitely.

(2) $f = Porb(Av_i \geq t)$ is a probability distribution function that models the providers' availability during the time window $[t_a, t_b]$. Av_i is a random variable as the time by which the provider will keep available in $[t_a, t_b]$.

By involving the concept of provider mobility, a mobile service provider can be defined as follow:

Definition 5 (*Mobile Service Provider*) A mobile service provider is modeled as a triple

$$p = (id, S, m),$$

where:

(1) *id* is the unique identifier of the service;
(2) *S* is the set of mobile services *p* provides;
(3) *m* is the *p*'s mobility defined in Definition 4.

The mobility model utilized to service selection in composite services are feasible on how to obtain the stay time of a service provider. First, a service provider may report its estimated stay time to the service repository. The motivation for a service provider to provide such information is that its services may be invoked more often and create more benefit. Alternatively, the stay time of a service provider can also be obtained without explicitly requesting such information from the provider. In addition, we mainly consider two types of constraints of mobile service compositions which exert great impacts on the performance of composition. The first is the temporal constraint, which regulates the execution of the composition temporally. The second is the QoS constraint, which is required by users.

Definition 6 (*Temporal Constraint*) A temporal constraint is

$$con_t = (type, t_i, situation_i, t_j, situation, dur),$$

where:

(1) *type* means the lower constraint L or upper constraint U
(2) t_i is the pre-task
(3) *situation$_i$* is the situation of t_i, which could be the beginning (*b*) of the end (*e*) of t_i
(4) t_j is the post-task
(5) *situation$_j$* is the situation of t_j, which could be the beginning (*b*) of the end (*e*) of t_j

(6) *dur* is the constraint of time duration.

For the temporal constraint $con_t = (L, t_i, e, t_j, b, dur_i)$ as an example, it shows that the duration between the end of the task t_i and the beginning of the task t_j should be larger than dur_i.

Definition 7 (*QoS Constraint*) A QoS constraint is a 3-tuple

$$con_q = (attr, opr, threshold),$$

where:

(1) *attr* is a QoS attribute, such as execution cost, response time, reliability, and availability.
(2) *opr* represents operators such as $=, \neq, <, >, \leq, \geq, \in, \subseteq, \supseteq$;
(3) *threshold* is the constraint value of the *attr*. It can be numeric data or data set.

Note that the QoS constraints are specified on the service composition (or tasks in a process) rather than the individual services. For example, a QoS constraint $con_q = (Time, <, 500)$, expresses that the overall response time of the service composition obtained should be less than 500 time units.

Due to a large amount of candidate services which have the same functionality and different QoS values for each task, the target is to present a more precise and practical method for the selection of candidate services under temporal and QoS constraints as well as the consideration of providers' mobility.

Definition 8 (*Constraint Driven Service Composition*) Given a service composition plan *scp*, a set of providers $P = \{p_1, p_2, \ldots\}$ can provide service candidates for the tasks in *scp*. Furthermore, the temporal constraints Con_t and QoS constraints Con_q are required. The problem we focus on is to find a feasible service set from the candidates $sc = (s_1, s_2, \ldots)$ such that:

(1) The execution of *sc* should satisfy Con_t;
(2) The overall QoS of *sc* should satisfy Con_q;
(3) Maximize the success of execution of *sc*.

We define θ_i as the probability of a service provider p_i keeping available by E_j, $Prob(Av_i \geq E_j)$, where E_j is the end time of the j-th task if selecting the candidate provided by p_i. Then, the utility function of *sc* is the joint possibility that all tasks are executed successfully:

$$U(sc) = \prod_{i=1}^{n} \theta_i \tag{5.1}$$

Note that maximizing $\prod_{i=1}^{n} \theta_i$ is equivalent to maximizing

$$\ln\left(\prod_{i=1}^{n} \theta_i\right) = \sum_{i=1}^{n} \ln \theta_i$$

Thus, the utility function can be reformulated as maximizing the summation of $\ln \theta_i$ over all service providers (as in Eq. (5.2)). The reason for the reformulation of the utility function is to transfer the optimization problem to a known NP-hard problem. Then the optimization goal is to find a service composition solution that maximizes $U(sc)$.

$$U(sc) = \sum_{i=1}^{n} \ln \theta_i \tag{5.2}$$

In order to obtain the optimal solution, all candidate services should be taken into account. However, this is impracticable with the increasing number of services and constraints. Thus may increase the computation time needed to solve the service selection problem exponentially. For example, there are 10 tasks in a composition plan, 500 candidate services for each task the number of possible combinations of services is 500^{10}. However, due to the QoS and temporal constraints, not all services are potential candidates for the feasible solution. In addition, the mobility of providers increases the uncertainty of finding solutions. If selecting s_1 for the pre-task, the previous tasks end at the time 4, then p_i is available for the next task. If selecting s_2 for the pre-task, the previous tasks end at the time 8, then p_i is not available for the next task. This makes the process of finding solutions more complicated. Therefore, traditional selection methods for service composition are not suitable for the problem. Because they only consider the properties of services and ignore users' mobility which can affect service interaction experience.

5.4.2 Approach

5.4.2.1 Optimization Problem

Firstly, we model the constraint driven service composition problem to a constrained optimization problem and show that the problem is NP-hard:

$$\max \qquad U(X) = \sum_i \sum_j x_{ij} \cdot \ln \theta_i$$

subject to

(1) $\sum_i \sum_j x_{ij} = 1$

(2) $g_k(X) \leq 0 \quad 1 \leq k \leq q$

(3) $h_k(X) = 0 \quad q+1 \leq k \leq r$

where X is a service selection solution for the given composition plan. x_{ij} is a binary parameter. $i \in [1, n]$ is the index of the tasks in the composition plan. $j \in [1, m]$ is the index of the service candidates for the i-th task. $x_{ij} = 1$ if the j-th candidate is selected for the i-th task. $g_k(X)$ is an inequality constraint and $h_k(X)$ is a equality constraint.

All temporal constraints can be transferred to $g_k(X)$. For a constraint $con_t = (type, t_i, state_i, t_j, state_j, dur)$:

$$g_k(X) = (-1)^z \cdot (st + dur - ft) \tag{5.3}$$

where $z = 1$ if $type = L$, $z = 0$ if $type = U$; if $state_i = b$, st is the start time of the selected service s_{ia} for the task t_i, and if $state_i = e$, st is the end time of s_{ia}; If $state_j = b$, ft is the start time of the selected service s_{jb} for the task t_j, if $state_j = e$, ft is the end time of s_{ja}.

For a QoS constraint $con_q = (attr, opr, threshold)$, if opr is an inequality operator, it can also be transferred to $g_k(X)$:

$$g_k(X) = (-1)^z \cdot (Fun(X, attr) - threshold) \tag{5.4}$$

where $Fun(X, attr)$ is the QoS aggregation function for the QoS attribute $attr$. $z = 0$ if opr expresses less-than relation. $z = 0$ if opr expresses greater-than relation.

If opr is an equality operator, it can be transferred to $h_k(X)$:

$$h_k(X) = (Fun(X, attr) - threshold) \tag{5.5}$$

Theorem 1 *The problem of constraint driven service composition is NP-hard.*

Proof We can reduce our studied problem CDSC to the Knapsack problem, which is a classic NP-hard problem in the combinational optimization. For simplification, we consider the CDSC problem with only one constraint $g(X) \le 0$, which can be easily extended to multiple constraints. For this simple version of CDSC problem, we always find an instance of Knapsack such that the CDSC problem is solvable if and only if Knapsack is solvable.

Let s_{ij} be a service of CDSC, a_{ij} be an item of Knapsack problem with capacity W.
Let $W = threshold$;
$w(a_{ij}) = attr(s_{ij})$, the weight of item a_{ij}
$p(a_{ij}) = \ln \theta_i$, the probability of the i-th task executed successfully if s_{ij} is selected.

Then CDSC problem is to max $\sum_{s_{ij} \in O} \ln \theta_i$ with the constraint $\sum_{s_{ij} \in O} attr(s_{ij}) \le threshold$. Let O be the set of selected services.

This is equal to solve the Knapsack problem:

$$\max \sum_{a_{ij} \in O} p(a_{ij}),$$

$$\text{s.t.} \sum_{a_{ij} \in O} w(a_{ij}) \leq W$$

5.4.2.2 Constraint-Based Service Pruning

Not all services are potential candidates for the feasible solution because of the QoS and temporal constraints. Therefore, we conduct a pruning process to reduce the number of candidate services of each task, which greatly reduce the searching space. The ultimate principle of pruning candidate services is to derive the local constraints for each task based on the QoS and temporal constraints. When the local constraints are obtained, we can eliminate the service candidates not satisfying the local constraints for each task. The service pruning aims to abandon the candidate services that cannot compose a feasible solution in order to achieve faster and better performance.

QoS Constraints-Based Pruning

The target of QoS constraints-based pruning is to compute local QoS constraints for individual tasks on each QoS attribute q. If a candidate service has at least one QoS attribute that does not satisfy the local thresholds, the selection of this service will violate the global QoS constraints so that it will be pruned from the set of candidate services to reduce the search space. Due to the limitation of space, we only use the negative QoS attributes for illustration. The positive QoS attributes can be processed in an opposite way.

In order to compute the local constraints, it needs to consider the aggregation rules of different QoS attributes according to the structure of the composition plan. In the following, we first discuss the local constraint computation in basic structures (sequence, concurrent, conditional, and loop), and then present an approach for determining the local constraints in a general structure. For the following parts, the local constraint of the QoS attribute q_k for a task t_i is denoted as $LC(q_k, t_i)$; the global constraint of the QoS attribute q_k is denoted as $GC(q_k)$.

(1) Sequence flow

When only the sequence flow is involved in a service composition, there are two QoS aggregation rules: addition and multiplication. For an additive QoS attribute, the corresponding local constraint can be derived as follows:

$$LC(q_k, t_i) = GC(q_k) - \sum_{t_j \in T, t_j \neq t_i} q_{min}(t_j, q_k) \tag{5.6}$$

where $q_{min}(t_j, q_k)$ is the minimum value of this QoS attribute q_k among all the candidates for the task t_j.

Similarly, for a multiplicative QoS attribute, the corresponding local constraint can be derived as follows:

$$LC(q_k, t_i) = GC(q_k) / \prod_{t_j \in T, t_j \neq t_i} q_{min}(t_j, q_k) \qquad (5.7)$$

The computation for loop flow is the same as sequence flow, since a loop flow can be converted to a sequence flow.

(2)   Concurrent flow

In the concurrent flow, since the aggregation for additive and multiplicative attributes is the same as in the sequence flow, the local constraints can be obtained in the same way. For the max-operator attributes, the QoS constraint of each parallel path is equal to the global constraints. So that $LC(q_k, t_i) = GC(q_k)$ if each parallel path contains only one task.

(3)   Conditional flow

For a service composition that involves the conditional structure, the QoS can be aggregated as $\sum_{i=1}^{n} pr_i * q(t_i)$. In order to satisfy $sc.q_k \leq GC(q_k)$, regardless of the probability of each task, we must meet the requirement that $LC(q_k, t_i) \leq GC(q_k)$ for each task. Thus, in our approach we set the set the constraint for each conditional branch:

$$LC(q_k, t_i) = GC(q_k)$$

(4)   General structure

In a general structure where the above types of flow are all possible to appear, we firstly determine each execution path based on the concurrent or conditional structures. Assuming the number of execution paths is l, for each execution path ep, we must meet the constraints $Q(q_k, ep_j) \leq GC(q_k)j = \{1, \dots, l\}$. Then, the local constraints for tasks in each execution path are computed as sequence flow.

Temporal Constraints-Based Pruning

Although QoS constraints-based pruning eliminates some candidate services that are impossible to be a member of the feasible solutions, some useless services still need to be removed when taking into consideration the temporal constraints between services. In this subsection, we introduce how to further reduce the number of candidate services considering temporal constraints. Note that only QoS attributes (e.g. response time) that depend on the temporal properties should be taken into account. The temporal constraints can be divided into two types: upper bound constraints and lower bound constraints. We propose pruning strategies for the two kinds of temporal constraints separately.

(1) Upper bound temporal constraints.

For each upper bound temporal constraints $con_t = (type, t_i, state_i, t_j, state_j, dur)$ where $type = U$, we can regard the sub-flow between $state_i$ of t_i and $state_j$ of t_j as new composition sc'. For the sub-flow sc', it has an upper bound on response time. That is $RT(sc') \leq dur$. Thus, the problem is transformed into the QoS based pruning for the composition sc' with the global constraint on response time (not exceed to dur). Then, we can utilize the QoS based pruning method to get the local constraint on response time for each task in sc'.

(2) Lower bound temporal constraints.

For each lower bound temporal constraints $con_t = (type, t_i, state_i, t_j, state_j, dur)$ where $type = L$, we can convert the sub-flow between $state_i$ of t_i and $state_j$ of t_j to a virtual task t'. The new task t' performs with the static response time dur. sc' is the sequence flow of t_1 and t_2. Then, we utilize the QoS based pruning method for the converted composition. Thus we can get the local constraints on response time for tasks excluded in t'. Then for the converted composition with t', the global constraint on response time is 55. Since the response time of t' is always 5, the overall response time of other tasks should not exceed 50. When we utilize the QoS based pruning method, the minimum value of t' is always 5. Then, we can compute the local constraints for t_1 and t_3. For each temporal constraint, we can get the local constraints on response time for tasks related to the temporal constraint. Not that some tasks may involve in several temporal constraints, that is, some tasks may have multiple constraint values according to different temporal constraints they involve. Thus, we get the most restricted value as the final local constraint for such tasks. That means the satisfaction of the final local constraint can guarantee the satisfaction of all the temporal constraints, which shows effectiveness and feasibility.

5.4.2.3 Algorithm

We proceed to the selection of the optimal service combination after the pruning process finishes and the irrelevant candidate services are eliminated. Our method is executed on mobile devices of service requesters, so the requirement on runtime is essential since the environment parameters for computation may vary much within a short time. Therefore, although the integer programming can obtain the optimal result, it is not suitable to the problem due to its poor scalability. One possible way to obtain a satisfactory solution in an accepted execution time is to design a heuristic search method and find the near optimal solution. Therefore, our selection algorithm is based on a differential evolution algorithm which can solve the mobile service composition problem in polynomial time. The differential evolution algorithm is similar but different from the genetic algorithm. Compared to the genetic algorithm, the differential evolution algorithm focuses more on the optimal result and more operations are conducted on the objective result. Therefore, it is more suitable to be used for CDSC problem. In the following, we demonstrate the detailed procedures of our composition algorithm.

Encoding and Initialization

For the service selection problem of a composition plan, an individual in the population of the algorithm represents a composition solution and it is encoded in an array of n integers $X = (x_1, x_2, \ldots, x_n)$, where n is the total number of tasks involved in the composition plan. $x_i (1 \leq i \leq n)$ at the i-th gene position is from 1 to the number of candidate services for task t_i.

Fitness Function

Penalty function methods are the most common constraint handling technique for constrained optimization problems. They add a penalty factor into the fitness function to punish an infeasible solution so that it is less likely to survive into the next generation than a feasible solution. However, the main limitation of penalty function methods is that they require fine tuning of the penalty factors. Therefore, some researchers proposed to convert constrained optimization problems into unconstrained multi-objective optimization problems [21].

Based on this idea, the fitness function of our approach consists of two parts: (1) the utility function that represents the possibility that the solution can be execute successfully; (2) the degree of the constraint violation of an infeasible solution. For the first part, the utility function is as the same in Eq. (5.2). For the second part, the degree of constraint violation of an individual X on the j-th constraint is defined as follows:

$$G_j(X) = \begin{cases} \max\{0, g_j(X)\} & 1 \leq j \leq q \\ \max\{0, |h_j(X)| - \delta\} & q+1 \leq j \leq r \end{cases} \tag{5.8}$$

where δ is a positive tolerance value for equality constraints. Then the degree of constraint violation of the individual X is:

$$G(X) = \sum_{j=1}^{m} G_j(X) \tag{5.9}$$

Thus, the original problem is converted into a multi-objective optimization problem where two objectives are considered: the first is to maximize the original utility function $U(X)$, and the second is to minimize the degree of constraint violation $G(X)$. Thus, the fitness function is:

$$F(X) = (U(X), G(X)) \tag{5.10}$$

An important concept of multi-objective optimization is Pareto dominance [16]. An individual X_i is said to Pareto dominate another individual X_j (denoted as $X_i \prec X_j$) if $U(X_i) > U(X_j)$ and $G(X_i) < G(X_j)$. The Pareto optimal set of individuals refers to the set of individuals that are not Pareto dominated by any other member of the population. Based on the concept of Pareto dominance, all individuals in the population are assigned a level. The level of all feasible individuals is 1; the level of Pareto optimal individuals is 2; and the level of other individuals is 3.

Crossover Operation

For the crossover operation, the target individual X_i^g is mixed with the mutant vector M_i^g to form a new vector C_i^g:

$$c_{i,j}^g = \begin{cases} v_{i,j}^g & if \ rand(0, 1) \le cr \\ x_{i,j}^g & otherwise \end{cases} \tag{5.11}$$

where $i = 1, \ldots, NP$, $j = 1, \ldots, n$, $rand(0, 1)$ is a uniform random number generator, and $cr \in [0, 1]$ is the crossover control parameter.

Mutation Operation

For the mutation operation, we firstly get the best individual in the g-th generation, denoted as:

$$X_{best}^g = \left(x_{best,1}^g, x_{best,2}^g, \ldots, x_{best,n}^g \right).$$

Then, we generate NP mutant vectors $M_k^g = \left(m_{k,1}^g, m_{k,2}^g, \ldots, m_{k,n}^g \right)$ $k = 1, \ldots, NP$ according to:

$$M_k^g = X_{r1}^g + \gamma \left(X_{best}^g - X_{r1}^g \right) + \gamma \left(X_{r2}^g - X_{r3}^g \right) \tag{5.12}$$

where the random indices $r1$, $r2$, $r3$ are mutually distinct integers in $[1, NP]$ not equal to k. The scaling factor γ is a positive real-valued parameter that controls the amplification of the difference vector, and $\gamma \in (0, 1]$.

For our service selection problem, the values of the variables in a vector must be integers. Then we modified each variable in M_k^g through the following procedure:

$$v_{k,1}^g = INT \left(m_{k,1}^g \right) \tag{5.13}$$

where $INT()$ gets the integer part of the real number. Thus, NP mutant vectors $M_k^g = \left(v_{k,1}^g, v_{k,2}^g, \ldots, v_{k,n}^g \right)$ can be obtained through above procedures.

Selection Operation

After the mutation and crossover operation, we can obtain NP individual vectors C_i^g. For classic differential evolutionary algorithms, each vector C_i^g is compared against the original individual X_i^g, the better one is preserved for the next generation. However, this selection method can lead to an early converge. Therefore, we choose the method in [22], which mixes the generated vectors C_i^g and the original ones X_i^g together. Finally, the top NP individuals are preserved for the next generation.

5.4.3   Experiments

5.4.3.1   Setup

We generated our service compositions with inserted tasks and control structures. For each task, we generate a number of candidate services based on the real applications, each with a different QoS. The QoS attributes of each service were generated based on real statistics. For each composition requirement, we generated a number of QoS and temporal constraints randomly. For the providers' mobility, each service provider p_i has a random available time Av_i, which follows normal distribution $N(\mu_i, \sigma_i^2)$. We set the mean μ_i is uniformly generated from $[0.5RT, 1.5RT]$ where RT is the aggregated response time of the composition by selecting the worst candidates for each task. And the standard deviation σ_i is determined by $\sigma_i = 0.1\mu_i$. Under the 3σ rule, p_i's leaving time window $[t_a, t_b] = [\mu_i - 0.3\mu_i, \mu_i + 0.3\mu_i]$.

Note that for all the implemented algorithms, all the algorithms were run independently 50 times for unprejudiced statistical results.

5.4.3.2   Impact of Algorithm Parameters

In our approach, there are four parameters which can be adjusted to affect its performance: population size NP, maximum iteration number NI, mutation scaling factor γ and crossover probability cr. To evaluation the impact of each parameter, we generated four groups of parameters configuration as shown in Table 5.7. For each group of parameters configuration, we tuned one parameter and fixed the other parameters.

Table 5.7 Parameters configuration

Configuration	NP	NI	γ	cr
Configuration-1	10–100	500	0.3	0.6
Configuration-2	50	10–1000	0.3	0.6
Configuration-3	50	500	0.1–0.9	0.6
Configuration-4	50	500	0.3	0.1–0.9

For other variables, the number of tasks is fixed to 10 with 100 candidate services for each task and the number of constraints is set to 5.

The following figures show the consequences of adjusting different parameters in the approach. From Fig. 5.10a, we observe that with the increase of the population size, the quality of solutions is also improved (solutions with higher successful probability are found). This is because a larger population size enlarges the overall searching field and improves the probability of finding superior compositions. However, when the population size exceeds a certain value, i.e., $NP = 50$, no significant improvement is observed. Therefore, an excessively large population size has little impact on improving the performance of our approach. Similar result occurs in Fig. 5.10b, which shows the impact of the maximum number of iterations, where the quality of the best solution is increased for higher number of iterations up to a limit: $NI = 500$ in this case.

Figure 5.10c shows the impact of the mutation scaling factor. We can observe that the best performance of our approach is when $\gamma = 0.3$. As γ increases continually, the performance decreases, mainly because when γ is excessively large, high-quality chromosomes are negatively impacted. Figure 5.10d shows the impact of the crossover probability. It shows that quality of solutions is improved up to a limit ($cr = 0.6$) and then decreases afterward. This experiment shows that although higher crossover probabilities can lead to superior population diversity and their very high values lead to chaotic generation of chromosomes where offspring chromosomes do not just copy the appropriate parts of their parents.

5.4.3.3 Evaluation of Service Pruning

In order to evaluate the effectiveness of service pruning, we compare the computation time cost for making service selection with and without previous pruning process under different problem size.

Impact of Number of Tasks

This experiment is conducted with respect to the number of tasks that varies from 10 to 100 (in steps of 10) with 100 candidate services per task. The number of constraints is fixed to 5 (3 QoS constraints and 2 temporal constraints).

The results provided in Fig. 5.11 indicate that applying constraints-based pruning process significantly outperforms the basic algorithm. Furthermore, the computation time of our approach increases very slowly compared to the basic one with the increasing number of tasks.

Fig. 5.10 a Impact of
population size. **b** Impact of
maximum iteration number.
c Impact of mutation scaling
factor. **d** Impact of crossover
probability

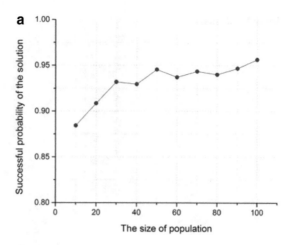

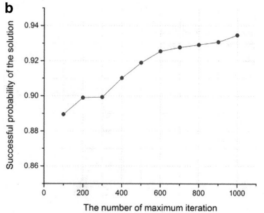

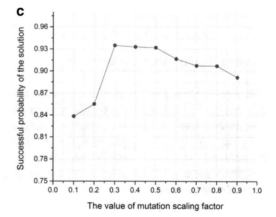

Fig. 5.10 (continued)

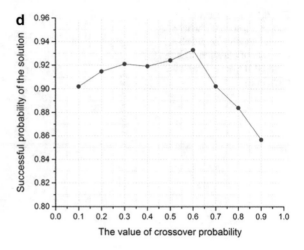

Fig. 5.11 Computation time
with different number of
tasks

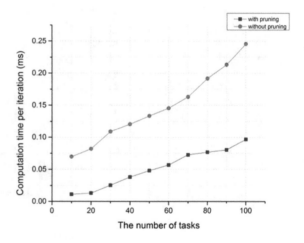

Impact of Number of Candidate Services

This experiment is conducted with respect to the number of candidate service per
task that varies from 100 to 1000 (in steps of 100) with 10 tasks. The number of
constraints is fixed to 5 (3 QoS constraints and 2 temporal constraints).

In Fig. 5.12, we give experimental results based on the computation time with
the increasing number of candidate services per task. Again, results are the same as
previously and the optimal solution can be found faster when applying constraints-
based service pruning.

Fig. 5.12 Computation time
with different number of
candidate services per task

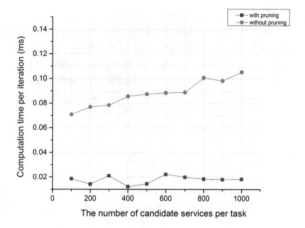

Fig. 5.13 Computation time
with different number of
constraints

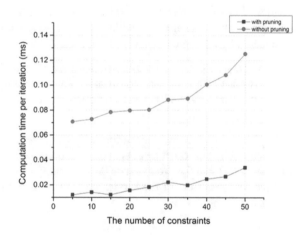

Impact of Number of Constraints

This experiment evaluates the computation time of the selection algorithms when
the number of constraints varies between 5 and 50 while the number of tasks is fixed
to 10 with 100 candidate services for each task.

The results are shown in Fig. 5.13. We can observe that the computation time of
the basic algorithm significantly increases with the increasing number of constraints
while the algorithm with pruning increases very slowly and performs better even
when the number of constraints is large. This is because when the number of
constraints increases, the number of feasible solutions decreases. Hence, more candidate services are likely to violate one or more constraints and thus they should be
pruned. However, without service pruning, more composition instances should be
checked for violation, which would cost more computation time.

From all the above experimental cases, the results show a significant improvement in performance when applying the pruning procedure compared to the algorithm that all candidate services are considered. Meanwhile, the advantage of applying pruning procedure is more obvious with problem scale increasing (i.e. the increasing number of candidate services, tasks and constraints). This is because that the number of pruned candidate services significantly increases when the number of candidate services, tasks and constraints increases.

5.4.3.4   Algorithm Comparison

Few studies have investigated the problem of service selection for constraint driven service composition in mobile cloud computing, thus the following algorithms are chosen to be compared with our method, in order to evaluate the proposed approach.

Genetic Algorithm (GA) A search heuristic algorithm that mimics the process of natural selection and has been widely used by service composition approaches. We extended it by adding constraints and mobility.

HPGA This is a GA-extended approach to select the appropriate services for service composition under temporal constraints. The hamming similarity degree is used to avoid inbreeding, and the specific pheromone is also designed to increase the searching efficiency.

To compare the above algorithms with our approach, we tuned the parameters for each algorithm to achieve its best performance. The most suitable parameters are shown in Table 5.8. To evaluate the optimality of the algorithms, we plotted the optimal response time of the service compositions found by all algorithms versus increasing problem size.

Impact of Number of Tasks

The number of tasks varies from 10 to 100 (in steps of 10), and the number of candidate services per task is fixed to 100 and the number of constraints is fixed to 10. The results are shown in Fig. 5.14. We can observe that our approach outperforms the other two. And the improvement we obtain over the HPGA is 29.79% in average. We can also observe that the successful probability of obtained solutions by all the algorithms decreases with the in- creasing number of tasks. This can be explained that there is more risk of providers' leaving when more tasks are included in a composition.

Table 5.8 Parameter setting of different algorithms

Algorithms	Parameters setting
GA	cross rate $= 0.7$, mutate rate $= 0.3$
HPGA	$p_h = 0.5, \alpha = 3, p_{p1} = 0.3, p_{p2} = 0.9, \rho = 0.95$

Fig. 5.14 Successful
probability with different
number of tasks

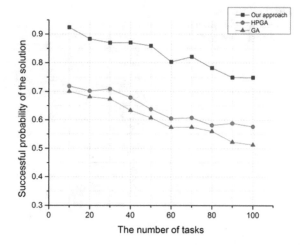

Fig. 5.15 Successful
probability with different
number of candidate services
per task

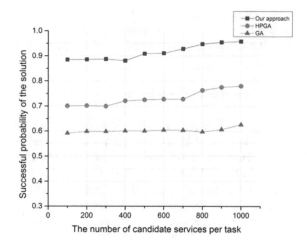

Impact of Number of Candidate Services

In the following experiment, the number of candidate services for each task varies
from 100 to 1000 (in steps of 100), and the number of tasks is fixed to 10 and the
number of temporal constraints is 10. Figure 5.15 shows the experimental results.
The improvement we obtain over HPGA is 24.93% in average. Furthermore, as
the number of candidate services per task increases, the successful probability of
obtained solutions increases. This is because more candidates can provide better
choices.

Then, the number of temporal constraints varies from 5 to 50 (in steps of 5), and
the number of tasks is fixed to 10 and the number of candidate services for each
task is 100. The experimental results are shown in Fig. 5.15. We can observe the

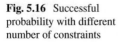

Fig. 5.16 Successful probability with different number of constraints

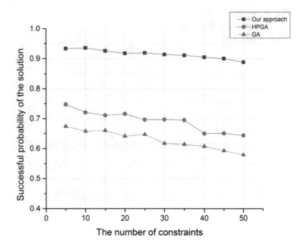

improvement we obtain over HPGA is 32.14% in average. Besides, the successful probability of obtained solutions decreases with increasing number of constraints. This is because more candidates would be filtered if there are more constraints.

Impact of Number of Constraints

The number of temporal constraints varies from 5 to 50 (in steps of 5), and the number of tasks is fixed to 10 and the number of candidate services for each task is 100. The experimental results are shown in Fig. 5.16. We can observe the improvement we obtain over HPGA is 32.14% in average. Besides, the successful probability of obtained solutions decreases with increasing number of constraints. This is because more candidates would be pruned if there are more constraints.

According to the above experiments, we can draw a conclusion that the performance of our method is better than the other two methods with different number of tasks, candidate services constraints, respectively.

Impact of Providers' Availability

In previous experiments, we set each service provider follow a normal distribution (μ_i, σ_i^2). For comparison, we set each service provider follow a uniform distribution function between the leaving time $[t_a, t_b]$. The number of tasks varies from 10 to 100 (in steps of 10) with 100 candidate services per task. The number of constraints is fixed to 5. Figure 5.17 shows the comparison results for the two distribution functions. We can observe that our approach performs worse with the cases of uniform distributions. This is because of the discontinuity of the uniform distribution. That is, under a uniform distribution between $[t_a, t_b]$, the failure probability of provider p_i has a leap

Fig. 5.17 Comparison of
different probability
distributions

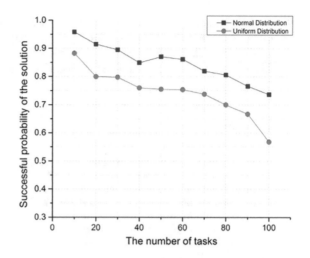

at time t_a, from 0 to a pretty large positive value; but under a normal distribution, the failure probability of p_i changes smoothly. Hence, the cases of uniform distributions are harder to deal with by our approach.

5.5 Summary

Under the situation of mobile environment, service selection and composition of mobile composite services becomes a challenge when both service requesters and providers are moving. We propose a mobile service provisioning architecture named a mobile service sharing community (MSSC). A Krill-Herd based algorithm is proposed to optimize mobile service composition in MSSC which can obtain superior performance. In addition, in order to solve the problem of risk-aware selection for mobile services, a risk model is proposed to cope with the risk of failure in the mobile service composition, which is caused by the mobility of service requesters and providers. Based on the risk model, a selection algorithm MSA is performed based on the simulated annealing algorithm. This work goes beyond existing composition approaches in order to reduce the risk of failure for the service interactions, which efficiently enhance the possibility of successful service composition for task execution in mobile environments. Constraints-driven service composition is characterized by the fully consideration of both QoS and temporal constraints simultaneously and it's significant to select the most appropriate services to form such a composition that can be executed successfully to the greatest extent. We propose an approach and it's proved with feasibility and efficiency under constraints-driven mobile service situation.

However, several certain conditions in this mobile service composition scenario are not considered well, such as the users' complex mobile trajectory in reality and different communication qualities of various regions. Considering these cases, it's important to make a mobility prediction before making service composition, which results in a more challenging problem and enables to open up many new directions and inspirations for future research on mobile service composition.

References

1. B. Liu, K. Huang, J. Li, M. Zhou, An incremental and distributed inference method for large-scale ontologies based on mapreduce paradigm. IEEE Trans. Cybern. **45**(1), 53–64 (2015)
2. P. Xiong, Y. Fan, M. Zhou, A Petri net approach to analysis and composition of web services. IEEE Trans. Syst. Man Cybern. B Cybern. **40**(2), 376–387 (2010)
3. J. Yu, Q.Z. Sheng, M. Younas, E. Shakshuki, Advances in context-aware mobile services. Pers. Ubiquit. Comput. **18**(5), 1027–1028 (2014)
4. S. Deng, L. Huang, D. Hu, Z.J. Leon, Z. Wu, Mobility-enabled service selection for composite services. IEEE Trans. Serv. Comput. https://doi.org/10.1109/tsc.2014.2365799
5. S.H. Semnani, O.A. Basir, Semi-flocking algorithm for motion control of mobile sensors in large-scale surveillance systems. IEEE Trans. Cybern. **45**(1), 129–137 (2015)
6. C.-P. Chen et al., A hybrid memetic framework for coverage optimization in wireless sensor networks. IEEE Trans. Cybern. https://doi.org/10.1109/tcyb.2014.2371139
7. K. Elgazzar, P. Martin, Mobile web services: state of the art and challenges. Int. J. Adv. Comput. Sci. Appl. **5**(3), 173–188 (2014)
8. S. Li, L.D. Xu, S. Zhao, The internet of things: a survey. Inf. Syst. Front. **17**(2), 243–259 (2014)
9. S. Deng et al., Toward risk reduction for mobile service composition. IEEE Trans. Cybern. **46**(8), 1807–1816 (2016)
10. S. Deng, L. Huang, J. Taheri, J. Yin, M. Zhou, A.Y. Zomaya, Mobility-aware service composition in mobile communities. IEEE Trans. Syst. Man Cybern. Syst. **47**(3), 555–568 (2017)
11. L. Zeng, B. Benatallah, A.H.H. Ngu et al., QoS-aware middleware for web services composition. IEEE Trans. Software Eng. **30**(5), 311–327 (2004)
12. H. Wada, J. Suzuki, Y. Yamano et al., A multiobjective optimization framework for SLA-aware service composition. IEEE Trans. Serv. Comput. **5**(3), 358–372 (2012)
13. M. Clerc, *Particle Swarm Optimization* (Wiley, Hoboken, 2010)
14. F. Tao, D. Zhao, Y. Hu et al., Resource service composition and its optimal-selection based on particle swarm optimization in manufacturing grid system. IEEE Trans. Industr. Inf. **4**(4), 315–327 (2008)
15. D.D. Wu, S.-H. Chen, D.L. Olson, Business intelligence in risk management: some recent progresses. Inf. Sci. **256**, 1–7 (2014)
16. F. Wagner, F. Ishikawa, S. Honiden, QoS-aware automatic service composition by applying functional clustering, in *IEEE International Conference on Web Services* (2011), pp. 89–96
17. S. Kirkpatrick, C.D. Gelatt, M.P. Vecchi, Optimization by simulated annealing. Science **220**(4598), 671–680 (1983)
18. W.L. Goffe, G.D. Ferrier, J. Rogers, Global optimization of statistical functions with simulated annealing. J. Econometrics **60**(1), 65–99 (1994)
19. M. Alrifai, T. Risse, W. Nejdl, A hybrid approach for efficient Web service composition with end-to-end QoS constraints. ACM Trans. Web (TWEB) **6**(2), 7 (2012)
20. H.T. Dinh, C. Lee, D. Niyato, P. Wang, A survey of mobile cloud computing: architecture, applications, and approaches. Wirel. Commun. Mob. Comput. **13**(18), 1587–1611 (2013)

21. W. Jiang, C. Zhang, Z. Huang, M. Chen, S. Hu, Z. Liu, QSynth: a tool for QoS-aware automatic service composition, in *IEEE International Conference on Web Services* (2010), pp. 42–49
22. Y. Shen, X. Yang, Y. Wang, Z. Ye, Optimizing QoS-aware services composition for concurrent processes in dynamic resource-constrained environments, in *IEEE International Conference on Web Services* (2012), pp. 250–258

Chapter 6
Mobile Service Deployment

Abstract Deploying services on edge servers even on end devices can improve the quality of mobile user experience. However, mobile devices and edge servers have limited resources compared with cloud and data center. Deploying services on edge servers even on end devices can improve the quality of mobile user experience. However, mobile devices and edge servers have limited resources compared with cloud and data center. Thus, how to organize services, deploy services on host devices and allocate resources for them become critical issues for service providers. This chapter proposes deployment methods for different types of services/applications to ensure their performance with the consideration of the trade-off between device resources and service/application performance as well as constraints.

6.1   Introduction

Mobile service/application deployment is a fundamental issue in the Mobile Edge Computing (MEC) environment. At the same time, the number of active third-party mobile apps in China reached 472 million in 2018, and the number of users in 2020 is expected to reach 485 million. In this view, mobile devices and services have successfully infiltrated into people's daily life and remold the communication between people and machines. They are emerging as flexible and powerful tools with the help of mobile clouding computing technology. People use these services for learning, entertainment, social networking and business anytime on their mobile devices. However, the limited resource of mobile devices and the instability of channels prevent the users from high efficiency and fantastic user experience—the low computational capability and energy of mobile devices restrict the popularization of complex services, and the packet losses cause external waiting time for the urgent messages. The problem will become more serious with the increase of mobile devices. Besides traditional mobile cloud computing, the development of Internet-of-Things (IoT) is also affected by many factors. Therefore, as the amount of mobile traffic increases exponentially, it is challenging to deploy applications under the circumstances of unpredictable transmission rate, the limited resource, load balance, etc. Until now, many problems have yet to be solved, e.g., how to choose edge servers

© Zhejiang University Press and Springer Nature Singapore Pte Ltd. 2020
S. Deng et al., *Mobile Service Computing*, Advanced Topics in Science
and Technology in China 58, https://doi.org/10.1007/978-981-15-5921-1_6

for deploying services or caching data, how to obtain an optimal deployment, how to ensure mobile users' quality experience while deploying, etc.

In all MEC systems, users can easily connect to the nearby edge servers via wireless network and offload their computation tasks to them. The short distance connection between users and edge servers can dramatically reduce the latency, and the computation capability of the edge servers are quite qualified to finish those conventional tasks. Additionally, the edge servers and users' tasks do not act alone in most cases. One edge server may coordinate with some other servers, e.g., it can dispatch users' requests to those servers which can handle them and send the results back to users. On the other hand, the services/applications may be complex as well. Nowadays, many influential IT companies or application vendors have adopted the microservice architecture [1–3] in their services/applications for decoupling and management. With this technique, though the developers should be more cautious about the external complexities in application development, communication controlling and failure recovering, the advantage of decomposing applications into several logically related but functionally individual microservices will bring a high degree of flexibility and reuse and makes it much easier for updating. What's more, it will be much easier for the MEC system to scale out for better performance. These microservices handle the requests in some specific orders and finally finish the tasks of applications. And with the help of Container-based techniques, these microservices can be easily deployed on edge servers.

However, the deployment scheme must be well considered, because these servers may have various computation or data storage capabilities [4, 5], while the mobile users may have different application preferences—if microservices are deployed on servers with low-level hardware or deployed on the edge servers whose connected users rarely use them, the performance of the system will not satisfy both users and vendors. More critically, there would be no doubt that the application vendors can rent lots of edge servers and deploy many instances of microservices to provide better user experience, but the cost of renting edge servers may become a major challenge. According to the report of RightScale 2, a company that specializes in cloud delivery, 26% of enterprises with more than 1000 employees are spending more than 6 million dollars a year on public cloud, but 35% of their cloud spending is wasted— the users may always overrate the resource consumption. To the contrary, the vendors always have clear demand about their applications: they want the applications to keep some key performance indicator (KPI) [6], e.g., average response time, with specific request arrival rate—the properties about request arrival rate are easy for them to summarize from history logs. In this way, we need to work out appropriate deployment schemes with less resource consumption (or cost) when some KPIs are ensured.

Currently, there are already some related studies [7–9] focusing on the above problems using MEC technologies. Zhang et al. [10] considered a scenario in which services were all deployed on edge servers, they proposed an algorithm to tell whether it was necessary to offload workload to edge servers, and which edge server to choose if migration was needed. And someone cares about the system latency, Xu et al. [11] also made use of the deployed services on edge servers by determining the services to be deployed and the tasks to be offloaded, they developed an efficient solution that optimized the latency of their edge service provisioning system.

In this chapter, we introduce three representative studies about mobile service/application deployment. The first study is about a deployment problem of microservice-based applications in MEC environment, an approach was proposed to help optimizing the cost of application deployment with the constraints of resources and requirement of performance. The second study [12] proposed an approach for formulating Data-intensive Application Edge Deployment Policy (DAEDP) that maximizes the latency reduction for mobile devices while minimizing the monetary cost for Application Service Providers (ASPs) with an edge latency deadline. The third study focused on improving the performance of the service provisioning system by deploying and replacing services on edge servers.

6.2 Microservices-Based Applications Deployment on Edges

The increasing number of mobile web services makes it convenient for users to complete complex tasks on their mobile devices. However, the latency brought by unstable wireless networks and computation failures caused by constrained resources limits the development of mobile computing. A popular approach to solve this problem is to establish a mobile service provisioning system based on a mobile edge computing (MEC) model. In the MEC model, plenty of edge servers are placed with access points via wireless networks so that the performance of applications can be optimized by deploying involved microservice instances on them. In the following, we explore the deployment problem of microservice-based applications in MEC environment and propose an approach to help to optimize the cost of application deployment with the constraints of resources and requirement of performance.

6.2.1 Motivation and Scenario

As the MEC architecture helps mobile devices to finish their tasks in proximity, the request processing will be different from that of traditional Client-Cloud mode. In this section, we will outline the scenario and motivation of our problem with an example.

The concept of "Smart City" integrates information and communication technology (ICT), and Internet of things (IoT) to optimize the efficiency of city operations [13]. It allows city officials to interact directly with both community and city infrastructure and to monitor what is happening in the city and how the city is evolving. In smart city projects of different countries, one of the most popular topics is smart policing. By deploying webcams, velometers, decibel meters along streets or inside communities, illegal behaviors like speeding and unpermitted road work can be easily detected. By equipping the policemen with portable alcometers and ID card readers, lawbreakers will get punished in time. Under this background, assume that

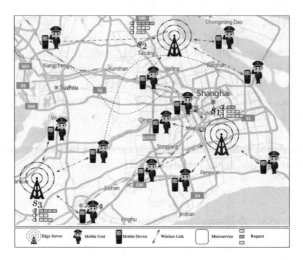

Fig. 6.1 Policemen work with portable ID card readers to find criminal suspects

an IT company SoftPoliz, which devotes itself to help simplifying policing affairs with information technology, has developed an application called *Clairvoyance*. This application aims at providing fast authentication service for grass-roots policemen, so that they can verify criminal suspects effectively. *Clairvoyance* is made up of 3 related microservices *SC = {FaceRecognizer, IllegalQuery, AutoAlarm}*. Besides packing and unpacking the data according to the communication protocol, these 3 microservices have their own function. *FaceRecognizer* is an image processing service that receives a face image and recognizes the owner, *IllegalQuery* is data access service which receives ID card number and queries the criminal database with it, *AutoAlarm* is an alarm service which receives the illegal or criminal records of someone, evaluates the danger level of him (a drug abuser may be not as dangerous as a murder with weapons), and give recommendations about what to do (e.g., wait for reinforcement or arrest on the spot) to policemen according to some laws and cases. These three microservices make up a service chain *FaceRecognizer → IllegalQuery → AutoAlarm*, and by invoking the service of the service chain in order, the task of the application will be easily finished. Therefore, the policemen can patrol the city with portable ID card readers and check whether a man is a criminal suspect by taking his photos using the application *Clairvoyance*.

It will be convenient for developers of **SoftPoliz** to deploy the related microservices on a cloud and to invoke them with RESTful APIs [14]. However, a better performance is required in this situation, because there are too many people in the overcrowded places like railway stations or airports. It is not acceptable to wait minutes for results. A good way to improve the performance is to turn to the MEC architecture. In MEC architectures, the servers in proximity work cooperatively as a platform that integrates the computation and storage capacities of them. With plenty of microservice instances deployed on the distributed nearby edge servers, the latency will be dramatically reduced. According to the experiment in [15], it shows that as much as 72% of the communication cost will be saved by taking advantage of MEC architecture in some cases. Figure 6.1 shows how it works. In this scenario, every

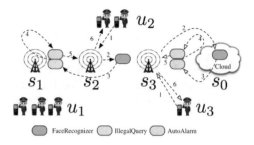

Fig. 6.2 An example of application deployment

edge server has its own serving area and resource limitation, users in different serving areas will connect to corresponding edge server to invoke the application. It is worth noting that the distribution of mobile users is location-aware. From Fig. 6.1 we can find that edge server s_1 is located near Tiesha River and its serving area covers Hangzhou Railway Station and other crowded places of Hangzhou, while s_3 will only serve residential areas. Therefore, more policemen will be assigned to the serving area of s_1, and Clairvoyance will be invoked more frequently in the serving area of s_1 than s_3. Intuitively, it will be better to deploy more microservice instances on s_1. However, it is not acceptable for **SoftPoliz** to rent all the resources of edge servers for microservice instances—the cost will be too high to afford. There must be a trade-off between the performance and operating expense.

Figure 6.2 gives an example of the deployment scheme of application *Clairvoyance*. In this case, there are 3 edge servers and a cloud server (core server). Users invoke the application from different areas, and the related microservices on different servers will be invoked in order to generate the final results.

In many cases, resources are charged by the amount of consumption. In this situation, with the system configurations shown in Fig. 6.2 we assume that the price of memory is $10/MB and the price of disk is $0.25/MB. In addition, we assume that the request rates from devices of these three areas are 20 requests per second, 30 requests per second and 50 requests per second. Then there will be many feasible deployment schemes for the application *Clairvoyance*. For example, the deployment scheme

$$\Omega_1 = \begin{bmatrix} 2 & 0 & 2 & 6 \\ 4 & 0 & 1 & 1 \\ 3 & 3 & 0 & 1 \end{bmatrix}$$ which means deploying 2 instances of *FaceRecognizer* on

s_0, 0 instance of *FaceRecognizer* on s_1, 2 instances of *FaceRecognizer* on s_2 and 6 instances of *FaceRecognizer* on s_3 etc. When we use the scheme Ω_1, the expectation of response time for the application will be 9.56 s, and the cost will be $3872.5. However, if some investigations tell that it is acceptable to wait less than

12 s, a better deployment scheme $\Omega_2 = \begin{bmatrix} 2 & 0 & 2 & 3 \\ 4 & 0 & 1 & 1 \\ 3 & 2 & 0 & 1 \end{bmatrix}$ would be worth considering because the expectation of application response time is 11.15 s and the cost can be \$3310.0. With this example, we can find out that it is important to select the deployment scheme carefully to make a trade-off between the performance and cost.

6.2.2 System Model

6.2.2.1 Servers and Network

In a typical MEC service provisioning system based on MEC paradigm, there will be a core server s_0 which acts as the typical cloud platform and n edge servers $S_1, S_2, \ldots, S_n$ distributed in different areas. These servers are available for the application developers. Considered as a major form of MEC, mobile base stations (BSs) endowed with cloud-like computing and storage capability are the most common devices that play the role of edge servers [16]. Every edge server s_j has its own serving area and U_j is the set of mobile users in this serving area. The average transmission rate between s_j and users in U_j is v_u^j. These edge servers can cooperate with each other to form a local mobile edge computing platform (sometimes it is named with "Fog Platform") to make full use of their resources. The average bandwidth between the jth edge server and the kth server is $\mathcal{B}_{j,k}$. Especially, because the edge servers can communicate with s_0, the average bandwidth between the core server and the j-th edge server is denoted with $\mathcal{B}_{0,j}$ (In general, as the edge servers in a local MEC platform may communicate with each other in a single-hop, $\mathcal{B}_{0,j}$ will always be smaller than $\mathcal{B}_{k,j}$, k > 0). The edge server s_j can provide at most L_c^j computation resource and L_d^j storage resource for deploying microservice instances.

6.2.2.2 Microservice-Based Application

A microservice ms_i is an abstract concept that describes what task it can complete with specific parameters; it has its own responsibility and scope and can be launched as instances based on container techniques. Receiving a request for ms_i whose average data size is D_i^{in} as input, an instance of ms_i on s_j can process the request with processing capacity $\mu_{i,j}$ and output the result whose average data size is D_i^{out} while it consumes $c_{i,j}$ computation resource and $d_{i,j}$ storage resource on s_j. Here we use the M/M/c queue model to describe and evaluate the running of those microservice instances, it means there are $\Omega_{i,j}$ workers serving the requests as a queue node $Q_{i,j}$ if there are $\Omega_{i,j}$ instances of microservice ms_i deployed on server s_j. We use this model because that the sojourn time of M/M/c system is less than that of c parallel M/M/1 system. This is easy to prove – if there are k jobs in system, then the M/M/c queue will

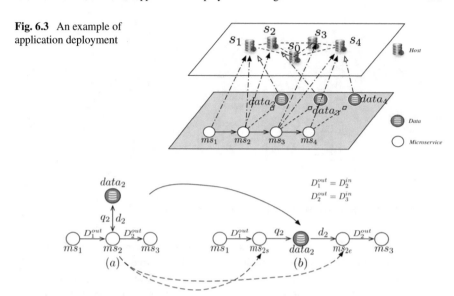

Fig. 6.3 An example of application deployment

Fig. 6.4 An example of equivalent structure transformation

process with rate $= \min\{k, c\}$ μ while the c paralleling M/M/1 system will process with rate $= j\mu$ where $j \leq \min\{k, c\}$ is the number of active queues. By fulfilling the tasks described by microservices in a service chain $SC = (ms_1, ms_2, \ldots, ms_m)$, the function declared by a microservice-based application is implemented. Though sometimes there will be data access operations in the application which may break the chain structure as shown in Fig. 6.3, we can also use the following transformation to create an equivalent service chain:

In Fig. 6.4, we can find that microservice ms_2 will access its data ($data_2$). ms_2 first sends query q_2 to tell which part of data it wants and receives the querying results d_2. The structure (a) can be transformed to (b) by adding two virtual microservices ms_{2s} and ms_{2e}—the input of ms_{2s} is D_1^{out} and the output of ms_{2s} is q_2, the input of ms_{2e} is d_1 and the output of ms_{2e} is D_2^{out}. The data microservice then becomes the successor of ms_{2s} and the predecessor of ms_{2e} in the service chain. Here the resource consumption of ms_{2s} is the same as ms_2, but ms_{2e} will not consume any resources. What's more, ms_{2s} and ms_{2e} will share the same deployment scheme as ms_2. In this way, we only focus on the chain structure, which means that the input of the application is the input of ms_1 and the output of ms_m is the required output for the application. Besides these, ms_{i+1} will use the output of ms_i as input.

6.2.2.3 Request Life Cycle

Denote the probability that server s_j dispatch requests about ms_i to s_k with $Pr_{j,k}^i$, which describes the routing policy, we can overview the life cycle of a request in

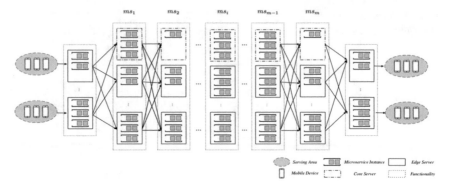

Fig. 6.5 An overview of the MEC service provisioning system

Fig. 6.5: For u in U_j, when he/she tries to use application described by SC, his/her device will first produce a request with input in_1 about it and send the request to s_j. According to the probabilities $Pr^1_{j,*}$, this request is sent to server s_{k_1} to fulfill the task declared in ms_1. The instances of ms_1 on s_{k_1} finish this task and get the output out_1, then produce a new request whose input $in_2 = out_1$ and send it to server s_{k_2} according to the probabilities $Pr^2_{k_1,*}$. Step by step, the instances of ms_m on s_{k_m} finally get the output out_m, which is the result of the application. The final result will be sent back to s_j and then to u via s_j.

As requests produced by U_j will be dynamic in one day, here we follow some previous work to divide time into discrete time periods (or time slots) in which the requests of U_j in time period t_p can be modeled with a Poisson flow whose average request arrival rate is $\lambda_j^{t_p}$. In every time period, the deployment scheme can be updated. The length of time period is not fixed, but it won't be long so that the system won't update frequently. Therefore, the deployment problem over time is divided into a series of service deployment sub-problems over time periods. In the rest of this study, we will omit the superscript t_p of $\lambda_j^{t_p}$ (namely, we will use λ_j) and focus on the service deployment scheme in a time period.

6.2.2.4 Billing Model

Different companies have their own billing models. For example, there are two types of billing models for Amazon Elastic Container Service[1]: the Fargate launch type model and the EC2 launch type model. With Fargate model, you pay for the amount of vCPU and memory resources that your containerized application requests and you pay for AWS resources you create to store and run your application in EC2 model. In this work, we mainly consider the on-demand billing in evaluating the cost of the deployment scheme—it means that the more resource is used, the more you have to pay. Without loss of generation, here we assume that the cost is proportional to the

---

[1] https://aws.amazon.com/ecs/pricing/?nc1=h_ls.

used resource, and the unit cost of computation resource and storage resource are represented by α and β respectively.

6.2.2.5 Problem Definition

With the introduction of related concepts, now we can give the problem definition clearly:

Definition 1 (*Optimal Instance Deployment Problem, OIDP*) Given the core server and edge servers $S = \{s_0, s_1, \ldots, s_n\}$, an application $\mathcal{A}$ whose service chain is $SC = \{ms_1, ms_2, \ldots, ms_m\}$, and users' average request rate for $\mathcal{A}$ on different edge servers represented with $\lambda = (\lambda_1, \lambda_2, ldots, \lambda_n)^T$ in a time period, find the deployment scheme $\Omega = \{\Omega_{i,j}\}_{i=1,j=0}^{m,n}$ with minimum cost so that the application can serve the users with an average response time no more than T^*.

6.2.3 Problem Formulation

In this section, we will clarify the objective and constraints of the problem and formulate them in a brief way.

6.2.3.1 Objective of Deployment Problem

In this work, we mainly consider the computation cost and storage cost of microservices. According to the explanation of billing model in Sect. 6.2.3, the cost of resource consumption can be represented as:

$$C(\Omega) = \sum_{i=0}^{m} \sum_{j=0}^{n} \gamma_{i,j} \Omega_{i,j} \tag{6.1}$$

If we denote $\gamma_{i,j} \triangleq \alpha c_{i,j} + \beta d_{i,j}$ as the cost of instances of different microservices. By vectorizing $\gamma_{i,j}$ and $\Omega_{i,j}$ with the order of service chain, we can get two column vectors $\gamma = (\gamma_{1,0}, \ldots, \gamma_{1,n}, \ldots, \gamma_{m,0}, \ldots, \gamma_{m,n})$ T and $\Omega = (\Omega_{1,0}, \ldots, \Omega_{1,n}, \ldots, \Omega_{m,0}, \ldots, \Omega_{m,n})^T$ whose dimension θ is $m(n+1)$. Then the cost $C(\Omega)$ can be represented as:

$$C(\Omega) = \gamma^T \tag{6.2}$$

6.2.3.2 Constraint of Application Response Time

Here we denote $\phi = (\phi_s, \phi_1, \phi_2, \ldots, \phi_m, \phi_e)$ as the request path to describe a request's life cycle, it shows the order of hosts to handle this request. Denote P_ϕ the probability of request path ϕ, and T_ϕ is the total time for requests that go through path ϕ. The average application response time can be represented as:

$$\mathbb{E}[T] = \sum_{\phi_s=1}^{n} \sum_{\phi_1=1}^{n} \cdots \sum_{\phi_m=1}^{n} \sum_{\phi_e=1}^{n} P_\phi T_\phi \tag{6.3}$$

In this way, we will investigate P_ϕ and T_ϕ respectively to calculate $\mathbb{E}[T]$.

- Probability of Request Path

With the definition of $Pr_{i,j}^t$, we can represent P_ϕ as:

$$P_\phi = Pr_{\phi_s} Pr_{\phi_s,\phi_1}^s \left(\prod_{t=1}^{m-1} Pr_{\phi_t,\phi_{t+1}}^t \right) Pr_{\phi_m,\phi_e}^e \tag{6.4}$$

Here ϕ_s means the probability that the nearby edge server is s_{ϕ_s}. Because the requests will always go back to the caller and his nearby edge server, Pr_{ϕ_m,ϕ_e}^e will not affect the value of P_ϕ. Thus, we have

$$P_\phi = Pr_{\phi_s} Pr_{\phi_s,\phi_1}^s \left(\prod_{t=1}^{m-1} Pr_{\phi_t,\phi_{t+1}}^t \right) \tag{6.5}$$

P_ϕ will be different under different service routing polices. There are many reasonable routing policies because different developers may consider different factors. For example:

Round-Robin. Under this policy, the instances of a microservice on different servers will have the same probability to receive requests—if ms_1 has 1 instance on s_1 and has 2 instances on s_2, the probability that request of ms_1 goes to s_2 is twice as much as that to s_1.

Weighted Routing. Under this policy, the processing capability is considered as another factor that can help scheduling requests, the probability an instance of microservices receives is proportional to processing capability—if ms_1 has 1 instance on s_1 whose processing capability is 200 request/s and has 2 instances on s_2 whose processing capability is 100 request/s, the probability that request of ms_1 goes to s_2 is the same as that to s_1, because $1 \times 200 = 2 \times 100$.

In this work, we will take the round-robin policy as an example to explain how we will formulate the deployment problem, so that developers can easily follow the process with their own routing policies. It is obvious that Pr_{ϕ_s} is dependent on the distribution of application requests, and because the requests will be dispatched to instances according to the amount in round-robin policy, then we have:

$$Pr_{\phi_s} = \frac{\lambda_{\phi_s}}{\sum_{i=1}^n \lambda_i}, \; Pr_{\phi_s,\phi_1}^s = \frac{\Omega_{1,\phi_1}}{\sum_{k=1}^n \Omega_{1,k}}, \; Pr_{\phi_t,\phi_{t+1}}^t = \frac{\Omega_{t+1,\phi_{t+1}}}{\sum_{k=0}^n \Omega_{t+1,k}} \tag{6.6}$$

- Response Time of Request Path

For each T_ϕ, it includes the access time, routing time, queue time and backhaul time:

$$T_\phi = T_{access} + T_{routing} + T_{queue} + T_{backhaul} \tag{6.7}$$

where the four parts can be computed as follows:

(a) **Access time.** The access time has two parts, the transmission time between mobile devices to their nearby edge server s_{ϕ_s} and the transmission time from s_{ϕ_s} to server s_{ϕ_1} which caches the instances of ms_1. Therefore, the access time is:

$$T_{access} = \frac{D_1^{in}}{v_u^{\phi_s}} + \frac{D_1^{in}}{B_{\phi_s,\phi_1}} \tag{6.8}$$

(b) **Routing time.** When any instance has finished its work, the result will be routed to the next microservice instance. Therefore, the routing time can be represented as:

$$T_{routing} = \sum_{i=1}^{m-1} \frac{D_i^{out}}{B_{\phi_i,\phi_{i+1}}} \tag{6.9}$$

(c) **Queue time.** The queue time includes the execution time and waiting time. Given the processing capacity μ_{i,ϕ_i}, the execution time T_{i,ϕ_i}^e can be represented as:

$$T_{i,\phi_i}^e = \frac{1}{\mu_{i,\phi_i}}$$

At the same time, we use T_{i,ϕ_i}^w to denote the expectation of waiting time in the queue of ms_i's instance on server s_{ϕ_i}. According to the queuing theory, T_{i,ϕ_i}^w can be represented as:

$$T_{i,\phi_i}^w = \frac{1/\mu_{i,\phi_i}}{\Omega_{i,\phi_i}\left(1 - \rho_{i,\phi_i}\right)\left[1 + \left(1 - \rho_{i,\phi_i}\right)\Upsilon_{i,\phi_i}\right]}$$

where $\Upsilon_{i,\phi_i} = \frac{\Omega_{i,\phi_i}!}{\left(\Omega_{i,\phi_i}\rho_{i,\phi_i}\right)^{\Omega_{i,\phi_i}}} \sum_{k=0}^{\Omega_{i,\phi_i}-1} \frac{\left(\Omega_{i,\phi_i}\rho_{i,\phi_i}\right)^k}{k!}$ is used here to simplify the expression.

Note that there is a parameter $\rho_{i,j}$ involved in the expression of T_{i,ϕ_i}^w. It means the serving utilization of queuing node $Q_{i,j}$. And according to the queuing theory, $\rho_{i,j}$ can be represented as

$$\rho_{i,j} = \frac{\lambda'_{i,j}}{\mu'_{i,j}}$$

here $\lambda'_{i,j}$ is the average request arrival rate of for microservice instances ms_i at node $Q_{i,j}$, and $\mu'_{i,j} = \Omega_{i,j}\mu_{i,j}$ is the processing rate. $\rho_{i,j}$ is always less than 1 so that requests will not be blocked in the queuing node.

Suppose $\lambda'_{i+1} = \left(\lambda'_{i+1,0}, \lambda'_{i+1,1}, \ldots, \lambda'_{i+1,n}\right)^{\mathrm{T}}$ is the request arrival rates for instances on different severs of ms_{i+1}. According to Burke's theorem, the request leaving rates for instances on different severs of ms_i will be equal to λ'_{i+1}. Denote $\boldsymbol{Pr}^i$ as the routing matrix for requests generated from ms_i:

$$\boldsymbol{Pr}^i = \begin{bmatrix} Pr^i_{0,0} & Pr^i_{1,0} & \cdots & Pr^i_{n,0} \\ Pr^i_{0,1} & Pr^i_{1,1} & \cdots & Pr^i_{n,1} \\ \vdots & \vdots & \ddots & \vdots \\ Pr^i_{0,n} & Pr^i_{1,n} & \cdots & Pr^i_{n,n} \end{bmatrix}$$

As the microservices are invoked one by one, the requests will go to the next microservice instances when previous tasks are fulfilled. Therefore, we can use the following equation to describe the relation between λ'_{i+1} and λ'_i:

$$\lambda'_{i+1} = \boldsymbol{Pr}^i \lambda'_i$$

While the elements of $\lambda'_{1,j}$ are initialized with

$$\lambda'_{1,j} = \sum_{k=1}^{n} Pr^s_{k,j} \lambda_k$$

By solving the equation $\lambda'_{i+1} = \boldsymbol{Pr}^i \lambda'_i$, we can get:

$$\lambda'_{i,j} = \frac{\Omega_{i,j}}{\sum_{k=0}^{n} \Omega_{i,k}} \sum_{k=1}^{n} \lambda_k$$

Therefore, the sojourn time in queue is:

$$T_{queue} = \sum_{i=1}^{m} \left(T^e_{i,\phi_i} + T^w_{i,\phi_i}\right) \tag{6.10}$$

(d) **Backhaul time.** The backhaul time has two parts as well—the transmission time between the edge server s_{ϕ_e} to connected mobile devices and the transmission time from s_{ϕ_m} to server s_{ϕ_e} ($\phi_e = \phi_s$). Therefore, the backhaul time is

$$\mathrm{T_{backhaul}} = \frac{D_m^{out}}{v_u^{\phi_e}} + \frac{D_m^{out}}{B_{\phi_m,\phi_e}} \tag{6.11}$$

- Application Response Time Estimation

As the response time of a request path is divided into four parts, and because $\mathbb{E}[X + Y] = \mathbb{E}[X] + \mathbb{E}[Y]$, the expectation of application response time $\mathbb{E}[T]$ can be represented by the sum of $\mathbb{E}[T_{access}]$, $\mathbb{E}[T_{routing}]$, $\mathbb{E}[T_{queue}]$ and $\mathbb{E}[T_{backhaul}]$. With the former equations, we can get these time costs separately. With above equations, the expectation of application response time can be represented as follows

$$\mathbb{E}[T] = \kappa \left(\lambda^T v_u^{\varnothing} + \frac{\lambda^T H \Omega}{e_1^T \Omega} \right) + \sum_{i=1}^{m-1} \frac{\Omega^T W_i \Omega}{\Omega^T J_i \Omega} + \sum_{i=1}^{m} \frac{\eta^T \Omega}{e_1^T \Omega} \tag{6.12}$$

where the auxiliary variables are denoted as follows:

$$v_u^{\varnothing} = \left(\frac{1}{v_u^1}, \frac{1}{v_u^2}, \dots, \frac{1}{v_u^n} \right)^T, \kappa = \frac{D_1^{in} + D_m^{out}}{\Lambda}, e_i = (0, .., 0, 1, \dots, 1, 0, \dots, 0)$$

$$\eta_i = \left(0, .., 0, \frac{1}{\mu_{i,0}} + T_{i,0}^w, \dots, \frac{1}{\mu_{i,n}} + T_{i,n}^w, 0, \dots, 0 \right)^T$$

$$H = \begin{bmatrix} \frac{1}{B_{1,0}} & \cdots & \frac{1}{B_{1,n}} & 0 \\ \vdots & \ddots & \vdots & \vdots \\ \frac{1}{B_{n,0}} & \cdots & \frac{1}{B_{n,n}} & 0 \end{bmatrix}_{n \times \theta}, W_i = \begin{bmatrix} & & 0 & & \\ 0 & \frac{1}{B_{1,0}} & \cdots & \frac{1}{B_{1,n}} & 0 \\ 0 & \vdots & \ddots & \vdots & \vdots \\ 0 & \frac{1}{B_{n,0}} & \cdots & \frac{1}{B_{n,n}} & 0 \\ & & 0 & & \end{bmatrix}_{\theta \times \theta},$$

$$J_i = \begin{bmatrix} 0_{(i-1)(n+1) \times i(n+1)} & 0 & 0 \\ 0 & 1_{(n+1) \times (n+1)} & 0 \\ 0 & 0 & 0 \end{bmatrix}_{\theta \times \theta}$$

As a consequence, when rewriting $\mathbb{E}[T]$ with $\mathbb{E}[T(\Omega)]$ for the decision variable Ω, the constraint of application response time can be represented as:

$$\mathbb{E}[T(\Omega)] \leq T^*$$

6.2.3.3   Constraint of Resource Consumption

Though edge servers are powerful machines with larger storage and faster computation units, they have limitations on their resources. Besides this, there is still much other application to be deployed; it is not possible to give all the resources to a specific application. Here we use $L_c = \left(L_c^0 \dots L_c^1, \dots, L_c^n \right)^T$ and $L_d =$

$(L_d^0 \ldots L_d^1, \ldots, L_d^n)^{\mathrm{T}}$ to represent the computation resource quota and storage resource quota for application $\mathcal{A}$. By denoting $\mathbf{C}_R$ the constraint matrix of resources, and L the concatenation of L_c and L_d,

$$
\mathbf{C}_R = \begin{bmatrix}
c_{1,0} & \cdots & 0 & & \cdots & \cdots & & c_{m,0} & \cdots & 0 \\
\vdots & \ddots & \vdots & & \vdots & \ddots & \vdots & & \vdots & \ddots & \vdots \\
0 & \cdots & c_{1,n} & & \cdots & \cdots & & 0 & \cdots & c_{m,n} \\
d_{1,0} & \cdots & 0 & & \cdots & \cdots & & d_{m,0} & \cdots & 0 \\
\vdots & \ddots & \vdots & & \vdots & \ddots & \vdots & & \vdots & \ddots & \vdots \\
0 & \cdots & d_{1,n} & & \cdots & \cdots & & 0 & \cdots & d_{m,n}
\end{bmatrix}
$$

Then we can describe the constraint of edge resources as

$$
\mathbf{C}_R \Omega \le L \tag{6.13}
$$

6.2.3.4 Constraint of Business Logic

As the microservices work in order to fulfill complex tasks, the absence of microservice instances for any microservice in the service chain SC will not be allowed. Therefore, we have

$$
-\mathbf{C}_B \Omega \le -1 \tag{6.14}
$$

Here the business logic constraint matrix $\mathbf{C}_B$ is denoted by

$$
\mathbf{C}_B = \begin{bmatrix}
1 & \cdots & 1 & 0 & \cdots & 0 & \cdots & 0 & \cdots & 0 \\
0 & \cdots & 0 & 1 & \cdots & 1 & \cdots & 0 & \cdots & 0 \\
\vdots & \ddots & \vdots & \vdots & \ddots & \vdots & \cdots & \vdots & \ddots & \vdots \\
0 & \cdots & 0 & 0 & \cdots & 0 & \cdots & 1 & \cdots & 1
\end{bmatrix}
$$

and $1 = (1, 1, \ldots, 1)^{\mathrm{T}}$.

6.2.3.5 Constraint of Queuing System

In queuing system, the parameter ρ means the serving utilization of the queuing node. As mentioned before, ρ should be positive and less than 1 for a stable queuing system. Otherwise, the requests will heap up so that the system cannot handle them anymore. We can represent the constraint by:

$$-\mathbf{C}_Q\mathbf{\Omega} \le -\Lambda \cdot \mathbf{1} \tag{6.15}$$

where the constraint matrix of queue system $\mathbf{C}_Q$ is denoted with:

$$\mathbf{C}_Q = \begin{bmatrix} \min\limits_{j} \mu_{1,j} & \cdots & \min\limits_{j} \mu_{1,j} & \cdots & 0 & \cdots & 0 \\ 0 & \cdots & 0 & \cdots & 0 & \cdots & 0 \\ 0 & \cdots & 0 & \cdots & \vdots & \ddots & \vdots \\ 0 & \cdots & 0 & \cdots & \min\limits_{j} \mu_{1,j} & \cdots & \min\limits_{j} \mu_{1,j} \end{bmatrix}$$

and $\Lambda = \sum \lambda_k$ is the total request arrival rate.

With the constraints and objective shown above, this problem can be formulated with:

$$P_1 : \min \qquad \boldsymbol{\gamma}^T \mathbf{\Omega}$$

$$s.t. \quad \begin{cases} \kappa\left(\lambda^T v_u^{\oslash} + \dfrac{\lambda^T H \mathbf{\Omega}}{e_1^T \mathbf{\Omega}}\right) + \sum\limits_{i=1}^{m-1} \dfrac{\mathbf{\Omega}^T W_i \mathbf{\Omega}}{\mathbf{\Omega}^T J_i \mathbf{\Omega}} + \sum\limits_{i=1}^{m} \dfrac{\eta^T \mathbf{\Omega}}{e_1^T \mathbf{\Omega}} \le \mathrm{T}^* \\ A\mathbf{\Omega} \le b \end{cases}$$

where A is the combination of $\mathbf{C}_R$, $-\mathbf{C}_B$ and $-\mathbf{C}_Q$ and b is of L, -1 and $-\Lambda \cdot 1$. In this work, we will use the primal-dual interior point method and branch-and-bound algorithm to solve this problem and call it with ID4ReE.

6.2.4 Approach and Algorithm

Therefore, searching the optimal application deployment scheme is to find the scheme $\mathbf{\Omega}^*$ from the feasible region which has the minimum cost $\boldsymbol{\gamma}^T \mathbf{\Omega}^*$. From the form of P_1 we can find that it is a nonlinear integer programming problem, which is NP-Complete. Therefore, we turn to approaches that can help to find some sub-optimums. At first, we will relax the constraint of $\mathbb{N}$ to $\mathbb{R}^0 (\mathbb{R}^0 = \mathbb{R} - \mathbb{R}^+)$ so that we can take advantage of the optimization technology for continuous problems. And then, the branch and bound technique will be adopted to find the integer solutions. Suppose b_i is the k-th element of vector b and A_k is the k-th column vector of A, and denote the constraints with:

$$c_0(\mathbf{\Omega}) = \varepsilon + T^* - \mathbb{E}[T(\mathbf{\Omega})]$$
$$c_k(\mathbf{\Omega}) = b_k - A_k\mathbf{\Omega}$$

then we can minimize an l_1-penalty function with some sufficiently large penalty factor v solve P_1:

$$\min_{\Omega \in \mathbb{R}^0} \Psi(\Omega; \upsilon) = C(\Omega) + \upsilon \sum_k \max(-c_k(\Omega), 0)$$

What's more, by smoothing this penalty function with some elastic variables w and regarding the concatenated vector $x_p = (\Omega, w)$ as points in the expanded space, we can get problem P_1's smooth version (P_2):

$$P_2 : \min_{\Omega \in \mathbb{R}^0} \Psi^S(\Omega, w; \upsilon) = C(\Omega) + \upsilon \sum_k w_k$$

$$\text{s.t.} \quad c_k(\Omega) + w_k \geq 0, w_k \geq 0$$

Thus, we can now apply the primal-dual interior point method to find the suboptimal of P_2. Namely, we need to solve a sequence of unconstrained problems (Q_t):

$$Q_t : \min_{\Omega, w} \Psi^B(\Omega, w; \tau^t, \upsilon) = \Psi^S(\Omega, w; \upsilon) - \tau^t \sum_k \log w_k - \tau^t \sum_k \log(c_k(\Omega) + w_k)$$

where the υ is the penalty factor that measures the infeasibility of subproblem Q_t and τ^t is the barrier factor that manages the constraints shown in P_2. By denoting the primal first-order Lagrange multiplier with:

$$y = \tau^t \left(C_{\text{diag}}(\Omega) + W_{\text{diag}}\right)^{-1} \vec{1}$$

$$u = \tau^t W_{\text{diag}}^{-1} \vec{1}$$

where we use vectors $c(\Omega)$ to represent the above constraints for convenience, $C_{\text{diag}}(\Omega)$ and W_{diag} are matrices that diagonalized from $c(\Omega)$ and w. Then the primal-dual function for primal vector $x_p = (\Omega, w)$ and dual vector $x_D = (y, u)$ can be represented with:

$$\Phi\left(x_P, x_D; \tau^t, \upsilon\right) = \begin{bmatrix} \gamma - J^T(\Omega)y \\ \upsilon - y - u \\ \left(C_{\text{diag}}(\Omega) + W_{\text{diag}}\right)y - \tau^t \\ W_{\text{diag}}u - \tau^t \end{bmatrix}$$

where J is the Jacobian matrix of $c(\Omega)$. Then we can find the suboptimal of the relaxed problem with Algorithm 1 (IDA4ReE).

Algorithm 1: Instance Deployment Approximation algorithm for Resource Constrained Edges

---

Algorithm 1: Instance Deployment Approximation algorithm for Resource constrained Edges, IDA4ReE

Input:
  γ: the cost vector;
  $c(\cdot)$: the constriant functions;
  τ: the initial barrier factor, $\tau \in (0,1)$
  ν: the penalty factor, $\nu > 0$
Output:
  Ω^*: the deployment scheme of instances;

1 Initialize $\Omega^0 \in \mathbb{R}^\theta$

2 Initialize $w^0 \in \mathbb{R}_+^K$ so that $c(\Omega^0) + w^0 > 0$

3 Initialize dual estimates $y^0, u^0 \in \mathbb{R}_+^K$

4 $x^t = (\Omega^t, w^t, y^t, u^t)$

5 **for** $t = 0, 1, 2, \dots$ **do**

6 $\quad$ solve linear system (42) to get δ^t

7 $\quad$ $x^{t+1} = x^t + \delta^t$

8 $\quad$ **if**

$$
\left\| \begin{bmatrix} \gamma - J^{\mathsf{T}}(\Omega^t)y^{t+1} \\ \nu - y^{t+1} - u^{t+1} \end{bmatrix} \right\| \leq \tau^{\frac{3}{2}}
$$

$$
\|(C_{diag}(\Omega^{t+1}) + W^{t+1}{}_{diag})y^{t+1} - \tau\| \leq \tau \quad (43)
$$

$$
\|W_{diag}^{t+1}u^{t+1} - \tau\| \leq \tau
$$

$$
(y^{t+1}, u^{t+1}) > 0
$$

$$
(c(\Omega^{t+1}) + w^{t+1}, w^{t+1}) > 0
$$

$\quad$ **then**

9 $\quad\quad$ $(\Omega^{t+1}, w^{t+1}, y^{t+1}, u^{t+1}) = x^{t+1}$

10 $\quad\quad$ $\Omega^* = \Omega^{t+1}$

11 $\quad\quad$ **return** Ω^*

12 $\quad$ **else**

13 $\quad\quad$ $\tau = \tau^{\frac{4}{3}}$

Algorithm 2: Branch and Bound Method in Solving the Integer Programming Problem

---

Algorithm 2: Branch and Bound, BnB

Input:
  $\Omega^\dagger$: the currently best solution;
  lb, ub: the lower and upper bound of BnB;
  $c(\cdot)$: the constraint functions;
  γ: the cost vector;
  ν: the penalty factor, $\nu > 0$
  τ: the barrier factor, $\tau \in (0, 1)$
Output:
  Ω^*: the deployment scheme of instances;

1   $Q = Queue()$
2   $Q.\text{enqueue}(c)$
3   **while** Q *is not empty* **do**
4     $c^o = Q.\text{dequeue}()$
5     $\Omega^o = IDA4ReE(\gamma, c^o, \tau, \nu)$
6     $v = \gamma^T \Omega^o$
7   **if** $\Omega^o \in N^\theta$ *and* $v \le ub$ **then**
8       $\Omega^\dagger, ub = \Omega^o, v$
9   **if** $\Omega^o \notin N^\theta$ **then**
10   **if** $v \le ub$ **then**
11         $lb = \min(lb, v)$
12         $k^* = \arg\max_{k \in [1,\theta], \Omega_k^o \notin \mathbb{Z}} \gamma_k$
13         $Ik = \lfloor \Omega_{k^*}^o \rfloor$
14         $u_k = [\underbrace{0, ..., 0}_{k^*-1}, 1, \underbrace{0, ..., 0}_{\theta-k^*}]^\mathsf{T}$
15         $c_<(\Omega) = Ik - u_k^\mathsf{T}\Omega$
16         $c_>(\Omega) = u_k^\mathsf{T}\Omega - Ik - 1$
17         $c^l(\Omega), c^r(\Omega) = \begin{bmatrix} c(\Omega) \\ c_<(\Omega) \end{bmatrix}, \begin{bmatrix} c(\Omega) \\ c_>(\Omega) \end{bmatrix}$
18         $Q.\text{enqueue}(c^l)$
19         $Q.\text{enqueue}(c^r)$

20   $\Omega^* = \Omega^\dagger$
21   **return** Ω^*

On the other hand, because the main process of the ID4ReE is the branch and bound algorithm (in Algorithm 2), it will be extremely hard to determine when the integer solutions will occur. What's more, if no bounds are available in running this algorithm, the method will degenerate to an exhaustive search. To avoid this situation, we heuristically try to solve an integer linear programming (ILP) problem whose objective is $\max \sum_i^{\theta} \Omega_i$ and constraints are $c_{1 \sim k}(\boldsymbol{\Omega}) \geq 0$. This is because the application is more likely to have smaller average response time if more microservice instances are deployed in the system. By selecting solutions that have $c_0(\boldsymbol{\Omega}) \geq 0$ from this ILP's solution set, we can roughly get the initial upper bound (in Algorithm 3).

Algorithm 3: Instance Deployment Algorithm for Resource Constrained Edges

---

Algorithm 3: Instance Deployment Algorithm for Resource Constrained Edges, ID4ReE

Input:
    $c(\cdot)$: the constraint functions;
    γ: the cost vector;
    ν: the penalty factor, $\nu > 0$
    τ: the barrier factor, $\tau \in (0, 1)$
Output:
    $\boldsymbol{\Omega}^*$: the deployment scheme of instances;
1   $\boldsymbol{\Omega}^\dagger, lb, ub = [\infty]_\theta^\top, \infty, \infty$
2   solve the following ILP, and get the solution set L:
3

$$\max \quad \underbrace{[1, 1, ..., 1]}_{\theta}^T \cdot \boldsymbol{\Omega}$$

$$s.t. \quad c_k(\boldsymbol{\Omega}) >= 0(k = 1, ..., K), \boldsymbol{\Omega} \in \mathbb{Z}^\theta$$

    for $\boldsymbol{\Omega} \in L$ **do**
4   **if** $c_0(\boldsymbol{\Omega}) \geq 0$ *and* $\gamma^\top \boldsymbol{\Omega} < ub$ **then**
5           $\boldsymbol{\Omega}^\dagger, lb, ub = \boldsymbol{\Omega}, \gamma^\top \boldsymbol{\Omega}, \gamma^\top \boldsymbol{\Omega}$

6   **return** $BnB(\boldsymbol{\Omega}^\dagger, lb, ub, \gamma, \nu, \tau)$

6.2.5 Experiments and Analysis

We have implemented the proposed algorithms in Matlab 2018b and our experiments are conducted on a machine with Intel Xeon E5-2620 v4@2.10 GHz $\times$ 2 CPU and 64 GB memory on Windows 10 operation system. Due to the lack of well-adopted platforms and datasets, we generate a dataset for configurations of services

Table 6.1 Configurations of edge service provision systems

ID #	m	n	μ qps	c MB	d MB	Lc MB	Ld GB	B MB/s	D^in MB	D^out MB	v_u MB/s	α	β
#1	2	5	[20, 50]	[100, 200]	[2, 5]	[512, 2048]	[32, 128]	[80, 100]	[1, 5]	[1, 5]	[1, 3]	10	25
#2	3	5	[20, 50]	[100, 200]	[2, 5]	[512, 2048]	[32, 128]	[80, 100]	[1, 5]	[10, 50]	[1, 3]	10	25
#3	4	5	[20, 50]	[100, 200]	[2, 5]	[512, 2048]	[32, 128]	[80, 100]	[1, 5]	[1, 5]	[1, 3]	10	25
#2	3	5	[20, 50]	[100, 200]	[2, 5]	[512, 2048]	[32, 128]	[80, 100]	[1, 5]	[1, 5]	[1, 3]	10	25
#4	3	3	[50, 60]	[100, 200]	[2, 5]	[512, 2048]	[32, 128]	[80, 100]	[1, 5]	[1, 5]	[1, 3]	10	25
#5	3	4	[50, 60]	[100, 200]	[2, 5]	[512, 2048]	[32, 128]	[80, 100]	[1, 5]	[1, 5]	[1, 3]	10	25
#6	3	5	[50, 60]	[100, 200]	[2, 5]	[512, 2048]	[32, 128]	[80, 100]	[1, 5]	[1, 5]	[1, 3]	10	25
#7	3	5	[20, 50]	[80, 100]	[2, 5]	[512, 2048]	[32, 128]	[80, 100]	[1, 5]	[1, 5]	[1, 3]	10	25
#8	3	5	[20, 50]	[100, 200]	[5, 6]	[512, 2048]	[32, 128]	[80, 100]	[1, 5]	[1, 5]	[1, 3]	10	25
#9	3	5	[20, 50]	[100, 200]	[2, 5]	[2048, 2560]	[32, 128]	[80, 100]	[1, 5]	[1, 5]	[1, 3]	10	25
#10	3	5	[20, 50]	[100, 200]	[2, 5]	[512, 2048]	[128, 160]	[80, 100]	[1, 5]	[1, 5]	[1, 3]	10	25
#11	3	5	[20, 50]	[100, 200]	[2, 5]	[512, 2048]	[32, 128]	[50, 60]	[1, 5]	[1, 5]	[1, 3]	10	25
#12	3	5	[20, 50]	[100, 200]	[2, 5]	[512, 2048]	[32, 128]	[80, 100]	[6, 7]	[1, 5]	[1, 3]	10	25
#13	3	5	[20, 50]	[100, 200]	[2, 5]	[512, 2048]	[32, 128]	[80, 100]	[1, 5]	[6, 7]	[1, 3]	10	25
#14	3	5	[20, 50]	[100, 200]	[2, 5]	[512, 2048]	[32, 128]	[80, 100]	[1, 5]	[1, 5]	[3, 4]	10	25
#15	3	5	[20, 50]	[100, 200]	[2, 5]	[512, 2048]	[32, 128]	[80, 100]	[1, 5]	[1, 5]	[1, 3]	20	25
#16	3	5	[20, 50]	[100, 200]	[2, 5]	[512, 2048]	[32, 128]	[80, 100]	[1, 5]	[1, 5]	[1, 3]	10	50

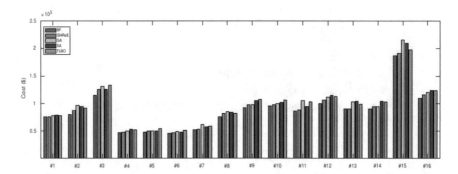

Fig. 6.6 The costs of deployment schemes generated by different approaches

and servers in a synthetic way for our experiment. Therefore, several edge service provisioning systems are created with the system configuration settings shown in Table 6.1. Though in many cases simulations are conducted on single computer, here we try to use a multi-machine environment to make the results more convincing. Meanwhile, as we also want to investigate the factors that may affect the results by keeping other factors fixed, we finally turn to a powerful simulation tool whose name is CloudSim. It can model the edge environments and measure the impact of resources, and many existing edge computing simulation platforms are built on it.

Generally, researchers prefer to adopt some heuristic algorithms to solve the constrained nonlinear integer programming problem. Therefore, we choose some of the representative approaches (GA, ID4ReE, SA and TLBO) as our baselines besides the brute-force (BF) one.

In Fig. 6.6 we can find that our approach performs better than other baselines. It means that it will cost less to deploy application microservices with our approach.

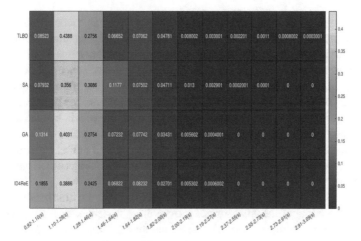

Fig. 6.7 The distribution of application response time

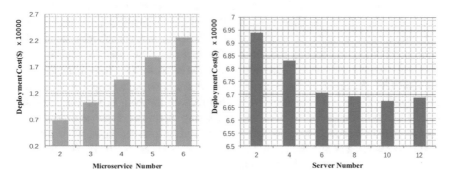

Fig. 6.8 Scheme costs for different microservice number and server number

To go a step further, we then apply the deployment schemes generated by these approaches on those provisioning systems to explore the response time of requests. Therefore, we simulate 10,000 requests for every edge service provisioning system and show the distributions of application response time for these requests for the 4 approaches with a heat-map. In the heat-map Fig. 6.7, the colored blocks stand for the distributions of the application response times. We can find that the application response times derived by our approach are more concentrated, and most of application response times are less than 1.64 s.

The number of microservices or the length of service chain determines the complexity of an application. From Fig. 6.8 and the comparison of system #01, #02 and #03, we can find that the cost of generated deployment scheme increases when the application becomes complex. Because more instances of the new microservices will be deployed to fulfill new tasks. Besides this, we can find that the cost increases when computation resource consumption or storage resource consumption of microservices becomes larger. This result is very clear because the cost is the linear weighting sum of the costs of computation resource consumption and storage resource consumption. At the same time, the cost increment caused by computation resource consumption is larger than that of storage resource consumption because of its larger unit price. Microservice instances with larger processing capacity handle the requests more efficiently, which means the execution time can be reduced dramatically. Therefore, given the requirement of response time we will need less instances to fulfill the tasks of application, as shown in Fig. 6.6 that the cost of #02 is less than that of #06. Besides these, the comparison of #12 and #13 points out that when the input and output size of microservices becomes smaller, the cost will also be less than before.

The edge server number, available resources and communication bandwidth determines the potential of the edge service provisioning system altogether, if we regard the system as a distributed machine. The number of edge server determines the complexity of system topology. It provides more possibilities for the deployment schemes. For example, if a new edge server es' which has the same parameters with es* was added to the system, the instances deployed on es* originally can be moved to es' partially without any loss while the risk resistance capacity can even increase. Not only comparing the results of #4, #5 and #6 in Fig. 6.6, we can go a step further with the result shown in Fig. 6.8. In this figure, we can find that the costs of these schemes decrease at first and then keep almost the same with the increasing of server number. This is caused by the changing of total available edge resource. At the first time, microservice instances have to be deployed on the core server because there is no enough resource for the edge servers, and to offset the response time loss for the low transmission rate between edge servers and core server. Then, when the total available resource is enough so that most of the instances can be deployed on the edge servers, the generated deployment schemes will be similar.

The requirement of response time reflects the developers' expectation for their application. In many cases, the application providers need a trade-off between performance and cost, so they should be more careful about the balance so that they can save money as well as keep the quality of experience. In Fig. 6.9, we draw the

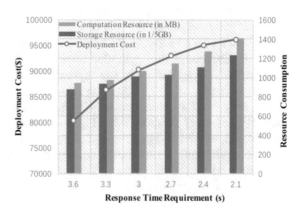

Fig. 6.9 Scheme costs for different response time requirement T*

curve for deployment schemes with different application response time requirement to show this relation (to illustrate both the computation resource consumption and storage resource consumption, here we multiply the storage resource consumption with 5 in the figure). We can find that there is an obvious trend that the cost increases when we want to have lower response time. By drawing figures for different systems, the application developers will get a general idea of the cost they have to pay for given response requirements. This will help the developers balance the cost and performance.

6.3 Data-Intensive Application Deployment on Edges

Mobile edge computing (MEC) has already developed into a key component of the future mobile broadband network due to its low latency, high bandwidth and high performance. In the MEC environment, mobile devices can access data-intensive applications deployed at the edge, which are facilitated by abundant service resources and computing resources available on edge servers. However, it is extremely difficult to handle such issues while data transmission, user mobility and load balancing conditions change constantly among mobile devices, small base stations (SBSs) and the cloud. Here we propose an approach for formulating Data-intensive Application Edge Deployment Policy (DAEDP) that maximizes the latency reduction for mobile devices while minimizing the monetary cost for Application Service Providers (ASPs) with an edge latency deadline. By automatically choosing the SBS with the best communication condition among the required-apps-deployed edge sites or selecting the only Micro Base Station (MBS) as a medium for placing data-intensive applications for execution, all mobile devices' requests can be responded to quickly with the minimum monetary cost incurred for ASPs. In particular, the problem of data-intensive application edge deployment is modeled as a Markov decision process, and a deep reinforcement learning strategy is proposed to formulate the optimal policy with the objective to maximize the long-term discount reward.

6.3.1 System Model

6.3.1.1 System Description

In Fig. 6.10, we consider an MEC environment that consists of N mobile devices equipped with energy harvesting (EH) components, M small cells (SCs) and one micro base station (MBS). Each SC is bound with a small-cell base station (SBS) equipped with a shared edge computing platform. Each SBS is interconnected via X2 Link for data transmission. As a result, application service providers (ASPs) can rent SBSs from communication facility providers (CFPs) as edge sites to deploy data-intensive applications. The MBS provides ubiquitous radio coverage and direct access to the cloud center.

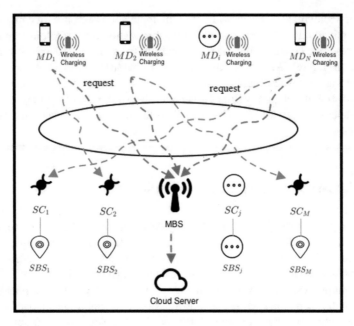

Fig. 6.10 An edge system example

From the ASP's perspective, we focus on S data-driven applications and D access data for deployment, which are denoted by $\mathcal{S}$ and $\mathcal{D}$, respectively. Each access data size is represented by $\mu_d, d \in \mathcal{D}$. Let us denote the access data set required by the sth app as $\mathcal{D}_s \in \mathcal{D}$. In each time slot $t \in \mathcal{T}$, the ASP chooses a set of SBSs from $\mathcal{M}$ for apps and access data deployment. Overlapping signal coverage is considered in our system model. Let us denote the set of SBSs covering the ith mobile device in time slot t as $\mathcal{M}_i^t$, which can vary across time slots because of the user mobility. For those mobile devices covered by more than one edge site, the SBS with the best communication condition among those required-apps-deployed edge sites is chosen automatically. For mobile devices not covered by any SBS signal covered or edge sites with the required apps, the cloud center via the MBS is chosen for offloading.

6.3.1.2 Latency Reduction Evaluation

Our objective is to rent SBSs with the minimum monetary cost to maximize the latency reduction for all mobile devices with an edge latency deadline. Let us denote the input data size (in bits) of the sth app as μ_s, which requires η_s CPU cycles. We model the mobile user's demand as an i.i.d. Bernoulli distribution [17]. Based on this model, the sth application service is requested by mobile device i with probability ρ_i^s. In addition, with probability $1 - \rho_i^s$, there is no request. We set $\mathbf{A}_i \triangleq \left\{ \times_{s \in \mathcal{S}} A_{i,s}^t \right\} \in \{0, 1\}^S$ as the request vector for the ith mobile device, i.e., $\Pr\{A_{i,s}^t = 1\} = \rho_i^s$.

As mentioned before, the service request of mobile devices can only be responded to by edge sites or the cloud center, and transmission latency will be greatly reduced if the required apps are available on the chosen edge site. For each app $s \in \mathcal{S}$ and access data $d \in \mathcal{D}$, we set $I_s^t, I_d^t \in \mathcal{M}$ as the deployment decision. For simplicity, we assume that all SBSs charge the same price for a unit time.

(1) *Latency by edge computing.* Similar to MAB, the latency comes from the wireless uplink transmission and edge computation. Let us denote the small-scale fading channel power gains from the ith mobile device to the jth SBS by $\zeta_{i,j}^t$, which is assumed to be exponentially distributed with a given unit mean [18]. According to communication theory, the corresponding channel power gain can be obtained by $h_{i,j}^t \triangleq \zeta_{i,j}^t g_0(d_0/d_{i,j}^t)^\theta$, where d_0 denotes the reference distance between i and j, $d_{i,j}^t$ denotes the real distance between i and j in the tth time slot, θ denotes the pass-loss exponent and g_0 denotes the pass-loss constant. As a result, we can obtain the achievable rate of the sth app $R_{i,j}^t(s)$ with

$$R_{i,j}^t(s) \triangleq \omega \log_2 \left(1 + I^{-1} \frac{h_{i,j}^t E_i^t(s)}{b_{i,\text{tx}}^t(s)} \right), j \in \mathcal{M}_i^t. \tag{6.16}$$

where ω represents the allocated bandwidth, I is the received average power of interference and the addictive background noise, $E_i^t(s)$ and $b_{i,\text{tx}}^t(s)$ represent the allocated energy (in energy units) and the transmission latency for the sth app, respectively. Accordingly, we have

$$R_{i,j}^t(s) b_{i,\text{tx}}^t(s) = \mu_s. \tag{6.17}$$

Besides, the latency of computing $b_{i,\text{ex}}^t(s)$ can be expressed with

$$b_{i,\text{ex}}^t(s) = \max_{d \in \mathcal{D}_s} \frac{\mu_d}{\lambda_{j,I_d^t}} + \frac{\eta_s}{f_j}, j \in \mathcal{M}_i^t. \tag{6.18}$$

where f_j represents the maximum CPU cycle frequency of edge site j, λ_{j,I_d^t} is the transmission rate from SBS j to SBS I_d^t through the X2 Link. As a result, the total latency experienced by the sth app for mobile device i is

$$b_{i,e}^t(s, j^\star) = b_{i,\text{tx}}^t(s) + b_{i,\text{ex}}^t(s). \tag{6.19}$$

where $j^\star = \text{argmax}_{j \in \mathcal{M}_i^t} h_{i,j}^t$.

(2) *Latency by cloud computing.* The latency comes from the wireless transmission, the backbone Internet transmission and the cloud computation. The achievable rate $R_{i,0}^t(s)$ for the sth app from mobile device i to MBS can be obtained in the same way as the above, with every 'j' replaced by '0'. Besides, we can obtain the transmission latency $b_{i,\text{tx'}}^t(s)$ in the same way as the above. Compared with edge computing, an additional transmission delay caused by the travel across the backbone Internet is included:

$$b_{i,\text{Int}}^t(s) = \frac{\mu_s}{\lambda} + \tau^t. \tag{6.20}$$

where λ is the backbone transmission rate and τ^t is the round trip time.
Besides, the computation latency at the cloud center $b_{i,\text{ex}'}^t(s)$ is calculated by

$$b_{i,\text{ex}'}^t(s) = \frac{\eta_s}{f_0}. \tag{6.21}$$

where f_0 represents the maximum CPU cycle frequency of the edge site which belongs to MBS.

Thus, the total latency caused by cloud computing to the sth app on mobile device i is

$$b_{i,c}^t(s) = b_{i,\text{tx}'}^t(s) + b_{i,\text{Int}}^t(s) + b_{i,\text{ex}'}^t(s). \tag{6.22}$$

Combined with $b_{i,e}^t(s, j^*)$ and $b_{i,c}^t(s)$, the total latency reduction for mobile device i is:

$$\Delta_i^t = \sum_{s \in \{s' \in S | A_{i,s'}^t = 1\}} \left(1\{I_s^t = j^*\} \cdot \left(b_{i,c}^t(s) - b_{i,e}^t(s, j^*)\right)\right). \tag{6.23}$$

6.3.1.3 Energy Harvest and Consumption

With EH component equipped in each mobile device i, E_i^t units of energy arrive at the mobile device at the beginning of the tth time slot. We set Q_i^t as the battery energy level of the ith mobile device at the beginning of time slot t. It evolves following the following equation:

$$Q_i^{t+1} = \min \left\{ Q_i^t - \sum_{s \in \{s' \in S | A_{i,s'}^t = 1\}} E_i^t(s) + E_h^t, Q^{\max} \right\}. \tag{6.24}$$

where $Q^{\max}$ is the maximum number of energy units that can be stored and E_h^t is the number of units harvested by EH components that collect energy from the wireless environment.

EH devices capture energy, such as wind energy and solar energy, then convert it to electricity. The best-known energy harvesting collectors are large solar panels and wind generators, which are the major alternative energy sources for the power grid. Note that the mobile device i drops the requests, if the battery energy is insufficient, i.e., $Q_i^t \leq 0$. In this situation, $E_i^t(s) = 0$ for every s in $\{s \in S | A_{i,s}^t = 1\}$. $E_i^t(s)$ will be an action variable that influences the entire network state in the following problem formulation.

6.3.2 Problem Formulation

As mentioned before, our goal is to rent SBSs with minimum monetary cost to maximize the latency reduction for all mobile devices with an edge latency deadline denoted by $\hbar$. We denote $\mathbf{x}_i^t = \left(\mathbf{A}_i^t, Q_i^t \right)$ as the state of the ith mobile device in time slot t. This way, the entire network state can be described by $\mathbf{x}^t = \left(\mathbf{A}^t, \mathbf{\Theta}^t \right) \in \mathcal{X} = \{0, 1\}^{N \times S} \times \{-Q^{\max}, \ldots, -1, 0, 1, \ldots, Q^{\max}\}^N$, where $\mathbf{A}^t \triangleq \{\times_{i \in \mathcal{N}} A_i^t\}$, $\mathbf{\Theta}^t \triangleq \{\times_{i \in \mathcal{N}} Q_i^t\}$. Denote $\mathbf{E}^t = \{\times_{i \in \mathcal{N}} \mathbf{E}_i^t\}$, where $\mathbf{E}_i^t \triangleq \{\times_{s \in \mathcal{S}_i} E_i^t(s)\}$ and $\mathcal{S}_i \triangleq \{s' \in \mathcal{S} | A_{i,s'}^t = 1\}$. With observation $\mathbf{x}^t$ at the beginning of the tth time slot, the edge computing system decides an action $\mathbf{y}^t = \left(\mathbf{I}_{\mathcal{S}}^t, \mathbf{I}_{\mathcal{D}}^t, \mathbf{E}^t \right) \in \mathcal{Y} = \mathcal{M}^S \times \mathcal{M}^D \times \{0, 1, \ldots, Q^{\max}\}^{S \times N}$, following a stationary control policy Φ, i.e., $\mathbf{y}^t = \Phi(\mathbf{x}^t)$, where $\mathbf{I}_{\mathcal{S}}^t \triangleq \{\times_{s \in \mathcal{S}} I_s^t\}$, $\mathbf{I}_{\mathcal{D}}^t \triangleq \{\times_{d \in \mathcal{D}} I_d^t\}$.

The reward for taking the action $\mathbf{y}^t$ under Φ in time slot t is

$$
\begin{aligned}
r\left(\mathbf{x}^t, \Phi \right) = \sum_{i \in \mathcal{N}} \Delta_i^t - \varrho \cdot \Bigg(& \phi \cdot \sum_{j \in \mathcal{M}} \left(1\{I_s^t = j\} \right. \\
& + 1\{I_d^t = i\} \Big) + \zeta \cdot \sum_{i \in \mathcal{N}} 1\{Q_i^t \leq 0\} \\
& + \kappa \cdot \sum_{i \in \mathcal{N}} 1\{b_{i,e}^t \geq \hbar\} + \xi \cdot \sum_{i \in \mathcal{N}} E_i^t(s) \cdot \left(1\{s \notin \mathcal{S}_i^t \wedge E_i^t(s) \neq 0\} \right) \Bigg)
\end{aligned}
$$
(6.25)

Taking the expectation over the network state $\mathbf{x}^t$ and the control action induced by a given policy Φ, the expected long-term reward on an initial network state $\mathbf{x}^1$ can be expressed by

$$
V(\mathbf{x}, \Phi) = \mathbb{E}_{\Phi}[(1 - \gamma) \sum_{t=1}^{\infty} \gamma^{t-1} r\left(\mathbf{x}^t, \Phi \right) | \mathbf{x}^1 = \mathbf{x}].
$$
(6.26)

where γ is the discount factor.

Therefore, the problem can be formulated as finding the optimal policy $\Phi^\star$ to obtain the maximum long-term discount reward:

$$
\Phi^\star = \operatorname{argmax}_\Phi V(\mathbf{x}, \Phi), \forall \mathbf{x} \in \mathcal{X}.
$$
(6.27)

6.3.3   DQN-Based Application Deployment

In order to maximize the latency reduction for all mobile devices while minimizing the monetary cost for ASPs with an edge latency deadline, the problem formulated in the previous section becomes an MAB problem. To solve this problem, we include the concept of status into the model, and then propose an algorithm called DAEDP for learning the optimal solution.

6.3.3.1   Optimal MDP Solution for Data-Intensive Applications Edge Deployment

The Markov Decision Process (MDP) is a basic theoretical model for reinforcement learning. In general, MDP can be represented with a quaternion which consists of state space, action space, reward function and state transition function.

Given $\Phi(\mathbf{x}^t)$, the $\{\mathbf{x}^t : t \in \mathbb{N}_+\}$ is a controlled Markov chain with the state transition probability below:

$$\Pr\{x^{t+1}|x^t, \Phi(\mathbf{x}^t)\} = \Pr\{A_i^{t+1}\} \times \Pr\{Q_i^{t+1}|Q^t, \Phi(\mathbf{x}^t)\}. \tag{6.28}$$

The optimal state-value function $\{V(\mathbf{x}), \forall \mathbf{x} \in \mathcal{X}\}$ which satisfies the Bellman's optimality equation can be represented as:

$$V(\mathbf{x}) = \max\left\{(1 - \gamma)r(\mathbf{x}) + \gamma \sum_{\mathbf{x}' \in \mathcal{X}} \Pr\{\mathbf{x}'|\mathbf{x}\} V(\mathbf{x}')\right\}. \tag{6.29}$$

where $r(\mathbf{x})$ is the reward for taking the action $\mathbf{y}$ under the state $\mathbf{x}$ and the subsequent state $\mathbf{x}'$. The size X of the state space $\mathcal{X}$ can be calculated as $X = 2^{N \times S} \times (1 + 2Q^{\max})$, where X grows exponentially as the number $N \times S$ changes. In such an extremely huge network state space of small cells, services and access data, learning the optimal solution is exponentially complex. Thus, we need to compress the dimension space with the Value Function Approximation method.

6.3.3.2   DAEDP Approach

Given the optimal action-value function $Q, \forall \mathbf{x} \in \mathcal{X}$, we have $V(\mathbf{x}) = max\|Q(\mathbf{x})$, which can be represented as:

$$Q(\mathbf{x}) = (1 - \gamma)r(\mathbf{x}) + \gamma \sum_{\mathbf{x}' \in \mathcal{X}} \Pr\{\mathbf{x}'|\mathbf{x}\} V(\mathbf{x}'). \tag{6.30}$$

If the state space is large, the matrix of $Q(\mathbf{x})$ will be large. It is often impossible to obtain enough samples to traverse each state only through repeated tests, which will inevitably lead to a failed algorithm. If we use a function to represent the value function $Q(\mathbf{x})$ and input any state so as to output the result, we can convert the problem of updating the Q matrix into a function fitting problem. Then, similar output actions can be obtained for similar states. From the aspect of data-intensive application deployment, we can formulate the optimal deployment policy based on a model-free reinforcement learning method called Q-learning. This method takes the state $\mathbf{x}$ as input and outputs the Q value of each action, which is also beneficial for the selection of actions and the Q values in the Q-learning method.

Algorithm 4: DAEDP Algorithm

Require:
  Environment E;
  Initial state $\mathbf{x}_i^0$;
  Reward discount γ;
  Learning rate α;
  Replay memory $\eth$ with a size of P;
  Action-value function Q with random weights θ;
  Target action-value function $\widetilde{Q}$ with weights $\theta^- = \theta$.
Ensure:
  The deployment strategy Φ.
1: $\theta = 0$;
2: **for** $i = 1$ to n **do**
3:   $\mathbf{x}_i^t = \mathbf{x}_i^0, \mathbf{y}_i^t = \Phi(\mathbf{x}_i) = \arg\max_{\mathbf{y}} \theta(\mathbf{x}_i^t, \mathbf{y}; \theta)$;
4:   **for** $t = 1, 2, \ldots$ **do**
5:     $r_i^t, \mathbf{x}_i^{t+1}$ is the reward and transfer status generated by action $\Phi^\varepsilon(\mathbf{x}_i^t)$ in E, respectively;
6:     $\mathbf{y}_i^{t+1} = \Phi(\mathbf{x}_i^t)$;
7:     Store transition $(\mathbf{x}_i^t, \mathbf{y}_i^t, r_i^t, \mathbf{x}_i^{t+1})$ in $\eth$;
8:     Sample a random mini-batch of transitions represented as $(\mathbf{x}_z^t, \mathbf{y}_z^t, r_z^t, \mathbf{x}_z^{t+1})$ from $\eth$;
9:     $\Phi(\mathbf{x}_z^t) = \arg\max_{\mathbf{y}} \theta^-(\mathbf{x}_z^t, \mathbf{y}, \theta^-)$;
10:    $\theta^- = \theta + \alpha \left(r_z^t + \gamma\theta^-(\mathbf{x}_z^{t+1}, \mathbf{y}_z^{t+1}; \theta^-) - \theta(\mathbf{x}_z^t, \mathbf{y}_z^t; \theta) \right)$ $(\mathbf{x}_z^t, \mathbf{y}_z^t; \theta)$;
11:    $\mathbf{x}_i^t = \mathbf{x}_i^{t+1}, \mathbf{y}_i^t = \mathbf{y}_i^{t+1}$
12: **end for**
13: **end for**

During the process of Q-learning, when updating every step, we take only one step further, estimate the target of a value function and make an improvement based on the current value function. Given the observations of the network state $\mathbf{x}^t$, the action $\mathbf{y}^t$, the reward $r(\mathbf{x}^t, \Phi)$, the request vector for the ith mobile device $\mathbf{A}_i^{t+1}$, the number of energy units harvested by the EH component, the next time slot $t+1$, the next network state $\mathbf{x}^{t+1}$ can be obtained using incremental summation:

$$Q(\mathbf{x})+ = \alpha^t \left((1 - \gamma)r(\mathbf{x}) + \gamma \sum_{\mathbf{x}' \in \mathcal{X}} \Pr\{\mathbf{x}'|\mathbf{x}\} V(\mathbf{x}') \right) \qquad (6.31)$$

where $\alpha^t \in [0,1)$ is a time-varying leaning rate. In fact, the true value function of the strategy is unknown. Due to its complex state and action space, we replace the real value function with the estimated value function using Neural Network. Algorithm 4 presents the pseudo code that summarizes DAEDP. The reward rit can be obtained from Eq. (6.25). Algorithm 4 does not need the knowledge about the entire system state. Our reinforcement learning method is model-independent and is capable of formulating the optimal control policy without any statistical information about the dynamic network.

6.3.4   Simulation Results

In order to evaluate the performance of DAEDP, we have implemented DAEDP in Python and conducted experiments on 8 CPU machines with Intel Core i5@1600 MHz and 8 GB memory, 1 GPU machine (NVIDIA Corporation GK210GL), 7 mobile devices with similar memory capacities. Due to the lack of widely acknowledged data sets, we synthesized the data sets used in the experiments based on typical mobile download scenarios.

6.3.4.1   Experimental Setup

As no standard experimental SCs, SBSs, MBS, cloud server, test data sets and data-intensive applications are available, we synthesized the experimental data to simulate real-world scenarios. Table 6.2 presents the parameter settings for the experiments. To simplify the calculation, the selected value intervals are obtained by increasing

Table 6.2 Variable assignment interval

Variable	Assignment interval/unit
Service memory size	[500, 1000]
Service instructions	[500,1000]
Input data/output data size	[0,1]
Access data size	[0,300]
SC storage	[2000,3000]
SC computing ability	[1000,2000]
Battery energy level of the mobile devices	[0,1000]
Units harvested by EH component	[0,50]
Energy allocated for apps	[0,500]

or reducing the real value intervals as a whole. This operation will not impact the accuracy of the final results.

Suppose that there are $M = 8$ *SCs*, $N = 7$ mobile devices at the edge with the cloud and MBS. The energy units harvested by *EH* components were generated randomly according to its corresponding assignment interval. We set $\omega = 106\,Hz$, $I = 10^{-3}\,W$, $Q^{max} = 1500$units, $f_0 = 3.9\,GHz$, ȟ $= 2$. For comparison, we implemented four different state-of-the-art deployment approaches, including the Simulated Annealing Algorithm (SAA) [19], the Ant Colony Algorithm (ACO) [20], the Optimized Ant Colony Algorithm (ACO v) and the Hill Climbing Algorithm [21].

6.3.4.2 Simple Scenarios

This section introduces a specific real-life example to demonstrate our goal more clearly. For the ith mobile device, a data-intensive application task which consists of 7 services and 7 access data is generated in time slot t. These services and access data need to be distributed across 8 SCs.

Two deployment plans for the data-intensive application with service size/instructions, input data, access data, SCs storage/instruction processing ability and energy allocated information are given in Table 6.3. The access data deployment information was listed in Table 6.4. The data transmission information among SCs was introduced in Table 6.5. Our objective is to deploy suitable services, data components on SCs with the aim to minimize the monetary cost for ASPs while maximizing the latency reduction for mobile devices. From the tables, we can see that there are 7 mobile users, 7 data-intensive applications and 8 SCs. For every service and access data, we have simulated two deployment scenarios where the reward values are 1.70 and 1.83 respectively. It can be seen that different deployment plans have different reward. Therefore, our motivation is to formulate the optimal deployment policy that achieves the maximum reward value.

Table 6.3 Data-intensive applications edge deployment

Mobile device	Service (size/instructions)	Input (size/unit)	Access (size/unit)	SC (storage/computing power)		Energy allocated/unit
N_0	s_0 (550/750)	u_{s0} 0.54	u_{d0} 206	SC_5 (1840/1300)	SC_1 (1600/1700)	350
N_1	s_1 (700/500)	u_{s1} 0.28	u_{d1} 319	SC_6 (1760/1900)	SC_0 (2080/1400)	150
N_2	s_2 (600/700)	u_{s2} 0.96	u_{d2} 373	SC_3 (2080/1000)	SC_1 (1600/1700)	400
N_3	s_3 (850/950)	u_{s3} 0.31	u_{d3} 204	SC_1 (1600/1700)	SC_2 (2160/1100)	400
N_4	s_4 (950/950)	u_{s4} 0.61	u_{d4} 188	SC_2 (2160/1100)	SC_3 (2080/1000)	250
N_5	s_5 (750/700)	u_{s5} 0.10	u_{d5} 161	SC_5 (1840/1300)	SC_6 (1760/1900)	300
N_6	s_6 (900/650)	u_{s6} 0.41	u_{d6} 316	SC_0 (2080/1400)	SC_5 (1840/1300)	350

Table 6.4 Access data deployment

Data set (size/unit)	SC (storage/unit)	
ud_0 (206)	SC_6 (1760)	SC_1 (1600)
ud_1 (319)	SC_6 (1760)	SC_0 (2080)
ud_2 (373)	SC_2 (2160)	SC_2 (2160)
ud_3 (204)	SC_1 (1600)	SC_3 (2080)
ud_4 (188)	SC_3 (2080)	SC_1 (1600)
ud_5 (161)	SC_5 (1840)	SC_4 (1840)
ud_6 (316)	SC_4 (1920)	SC_6 (1760)

Table 6.5 Data transmission among SCs

Transmission/ unit)	SC_0	SC_1	SC_2	SC_3	SC_4	SC_5	SC_6	SC_7
SC_0	0	3	5	3	4	6	10	7
SC_1	3	0	8	5	3	2	9	8
SC_2	5	8	0	7	5	4	8	6
SC_3	3	5	7	0	7	9	2	3
SC_4	4	3	5	7	0	5	7	9
SC_5	6	2	4	9	5	0	4	2
SC_6	10	9	8	2	7	4	0	7
SC_7	7	8	2	3	9	2	7	0

6.3.4.3 Experimental Results

This section presents and discusses the experimental results to evaluate DAEDP against the baseline approaches.

(1) *Loss convergence performance*: We set the request vector $\mathbf{A}_i^t$'s incidence probability following the distribution of Bernoulli random variables with a common parameter $\lambda_{(t)}$, the same as the number of units harvested by EH component E_h^t whose parameter is $\lambda_{(h)}$. Based on Formulas mentioned above, we plot the simulated variations in the loss function in Fig. 6.11, the results show that the degree of approximation between value function and real value function stabilizes after 1000 time slots. Thus, in the experiments, we ran the approach for at least 1,000 time slots.

(2) *Effectiveness*: We evaluated the performance of DAEDP with different reward discount γ and learning rate α. The results are presented in Fig. 6.12. From the perspective of reward discount γ, we set the learning rate $\alpha = 0.2$. The average reward in every time slot does not indicate any specific patterns. When $\gamma = 0.4$, a relatively high reward value can be obtained. From the perspective of reward discount α, we set the learning rate $\gamma = 0.4$, we can see that when α

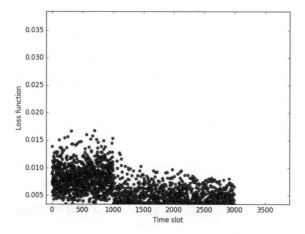

Fig. 6.11 Convergence performance of the proposed algorithm

$= 0.2$, the average reward per time slot value increases. Thus, in the following experiments, we set the reward discount $\gamma = 0.4$ and the learning rate $\alpha = 0.2$.

(3) *Comparisons*: Besides DAEDP, we also ran the four state-of-the-art approaches to obtain their average total reward performance and total latency reduction per time slot versus the units harvesting parameter $\lambda(h)$ in Fig. 6.13. The results show that DAEDP always outperforms the four state-of-the-art approaches significantly with the maximum reward value. In particular, the performance

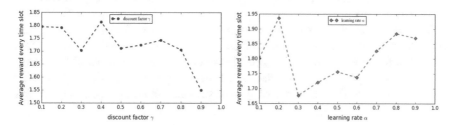

Fig. 6.12 Average reward every time slot versus discount factor and learning rate

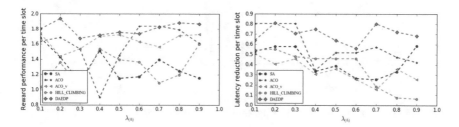

Fig. 6.13 Performance versus units harvesting parameter $\lambda(h)$

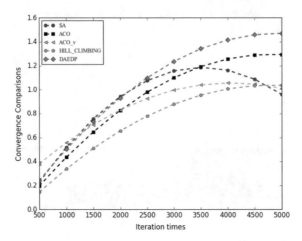

Fig. 6.14 Convergence Comparisons of different algorithms

of improved ACO_v is the closest to DAEDP and shows a relatively smooth changing trend.

(4) *Convergence Comparisons:* The objective of this experiment is to examine and compare the convergence speed of all five approaches. We set the maximum iteration times for all approaches as 5000. From Fig. 6.14, we found that the convergence speed of DAEDP was not the fastest. After about 4000 repetitions, the reward of the deployment tends to remain at a stable and relatively high value. In particular, the ACO_v has the fastest convergence except for its lower reward value.

(5) *Scalability:* We set the iteration times as 4,000, $\gamma = 0.4$ and $\alpha = 0.2$, then evaluated the effectiveness of DAEDP with data-intensive applications and SCs at different scales. We have tested 12 different edge environments, (3,3,4) means there are 3 services, 3 access data need to be deployed among 4 SCs. Figure 6.15a shows that as the system scales up in its size, the reward of large scale is always

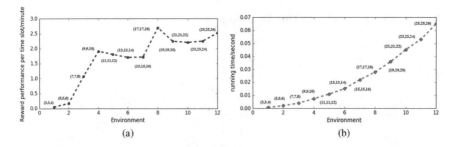

Fig. 6.15 The effectiveness of DAEDP under different scales of systems

higher than the small scales in general. Figure 6.15b shows the running time of DAEDP. As the system scales up, the running time of DAEDP increases under the above given 12 edge environments.

From the experiments, we can draw the conclusion that DAEDP can formulate deployment policies that are close to the optimal ones. The Ant Colony approach is inferior to DAEDP in terms of the reward performance. The ACO_v approach has the fastest convergence speed; however, its reward performance is not ideal. The convergence of the SA approach is the worst, its major advantage is that the highest reward value can be achieved when the number of iterations reaches 3,000. However, the SA approach cannot maintain high performance after that.

6.4 Dynamic Service Deployment and Replacement on Edges

With the rapid development of mobile computing technology, more and more complex tasks are now able to be fulfilled on users' mobile devices with an increasing number of novel services. However, the development of mobile computing is limited by the latency brought by unstable wireless network and the computation failure caused by the constrained resources of mobile devices. Therefore, people turn to establish a service provisioning system based on mobile edge computing (MEC) model to solve this problem. With the help of services deployed on edge servers, the latency can be reduced, and the computation can be offloaded. Though the edge servers have more available resources than mobile devices, they are still resource-constrained, so they must carefully choose the services for deployment. In this study, we focus on improving performance of the service provisioning system by deploying and replacing services on edge servers. Firstly, we design and implement a proto-type of service provisioning system that simulates the behaviors between users and servers. Secondly, we propose an approach to deploy services on edge servers before the launching of these servers and propose an approach to replace services on edge servers dynamically. Finally, we conduct a series of experiments to evaluate the performance of our approaches. The result shows that our approach can improve the performance of service provisioning systems.

6.4.1 Problem Definition and Description

6.4.1.1 Concepts and Definitions

Definition 2 (*Cloud Server, CS*) The cloud server in this study is an abstract of machines of a cloud platform, where the service providers can register, delegate and maintain their services on it, and users are able to send requests to these services fulfill different tasks. It can be defined by a tuple $cs = (\mu^c, v^u)$, where μc is the processing capacity that describes how many workloads it can handle per second, v^u is the average data transmission rate between mobile users and the cloud server.

Though the cloud server is made up of machines, some management systems like MESOS, Kubernetes are applied in practice. Hence, the cloud server can run in a well-organized way and provide unified API to end users.

Definition 3 (*Service, WS*) A Service is a module that fulfills a specific task, it can be defined by $ws = (func, in, out, R, \omega, vol)$, where *func* is the functionality of this service, in is the average data size of *input*, *out* is the average data size of output, R is the computation resource consumption, w is the workload of service and vol is the volume (storage resource consumption) of service.

The computation resource consumption R describes different types of resources such as memory, CPU, GPU and network. It can be represented as a vector $R = (r1,...,rn)$. And we can have $Ri > Rj$ if and only if $\forall\ rki > rkj, k = 1, 2, ..., n$. In practice, these resources are divided into several pieces for easier allocation and maintenance, e.g. 1 MB is the minimum memory allocation unit.

Definition 4 (*Edge Server, ES*) An Edge server is a computing device with stronger processing capacity and larger storage capacity (than mobile devices) that deployed on the edge of network. Generally, mobile devices can connect to edge servers via wireless network. An edge server es can be defined by a tuple $es = (loc, \mu^e, v^e, B, \rho, R^\star)$, where the loc is the location of the edge server, μ^e is the processing capacity, v^e is the data transmission rate with the mobile devices, B is the data transmission rate with cloud server, ρ is the serving area of *es*, and $R^\star$ is the resource limitation of the edge server.

In our model, the loc describes the position of edge server on; μ^e describes the capacity of es to deal with workloads; v^e is the average data transmission rate between es and the mobile users in *es*'s serving area ρ; and the parameter $R^\star$ can be represented by a vector $R^\star = (R_1^\star, R_2^\star, \ldots, R_K^\star)$, it describes the resource limitation of different types of resource of the edge server. For example, we can set $K = 2$ and $(R_1^\star, R_2^\star)$ the consumption of memory and disk if we want to consider the usage of these two types of resources. It is obvious that the resource allocated to servers cannot exceed these limitations.

6.4.1.2 Problem Description

A significant task in service provisioning system is to improve user experience and enhance user stickiness. In previous works, researchers have proposed diverse ways to measure the performance, some of them care about the cost [22], some of them care about energy [23], and most of them care about response time. In our model, we choose the average response time of services to measure it. The performance optimization task can be divided into two steps: The first step is to optimize the initial service deployment scheme, namely, determine which services are appropriate to be deployed on edges. In MEC environment, users can access services or data deployed on the edge server it connected with, and if the services or data they use are deployed or cached on the edge server, the requests for them will be accelerated. A carefully selected service deployment scheme will help the edge server hold appropriate services or data to ensure its clients good user experience in a long period. The second step is to replace the services dynamically in running time: the initial service deployment scheme gives an optimistic estimation based on request prediction, but this prediction may become inaccurate in some time periods. Hence, we need to replace the services. In our model, we endeavor to replace services by predicting their frequency dynamically with temporal and spatial factors.

(1) *Initial Service Deployment Problem*

In the initial service deployment problem, we want to find a policy to help determining which services should be deployed on the edge servers in advance. $S = (ws_1, ws_2, ..., ws_m)$ denotes the service set in the cloud server, where m is the size of the service repository which means there are m types of different services. And for every web service ws_i invoked by user u, it has two different response times T_i^c and $t_{i,j}^e$. T_i^c is the response time when ws_i is executed on the cloud server cs, and $t_{i,j}^e$ is that on the edge server es_j. We can easily estimate $t_{i,j}^e$ and T_i^c of these services with:

$$t_{i,j}^e = \frac{in_i}{v_j^e} + \frac{\omega_i}{\mu^e} + \frac{out_i}{v_j^e}$$

$$T_i^c = \frac{in_i}{v^u} + \frac{\omega_i}{\mu^c} + \frac{out_i}{v^u} \tag{6.32}$$

By denoting $x_{i,j}$ the choice of deploying service ws_i on edge server es_j or not, and $x_j = (x_{1,j}, x_{2,j}, ..., x_{m,j})$ the service deployment scheme, the average response time $\hat{r}t$ can be represented as:

$$\hat{r}t = \frac{1}{n} \sum_{j=1}^{n} \sum_{i=1}^{m} f_{i,j}\left(x_{i,j} t_{i,j}^e + (1 - x_{i,j})T_i^c\right) \tag{6.33}$$

Here $f_{i,j}$ is the invocation frequency or popularity of service ws_i on an edge server es_j, which is summarized from historical system records. Besides this, we need enough resource to enable the service deployment scheme:

$$\sum_{i=1}^{m} x_{i,j}\mathbf{R}_i \leq \mathbf{R}_j^\star, \quad 1 \leq j \leq n \tag{6.34}$$

Thus, the problem can be defined as: Given the service set $S = (ws_1, ws_2, ...,$ $ws_m)$ and edge servers $ES = (es_1, es_2, ..., es_n)$, find a service deployment scheme $X = (x_1, x_2, ..., x_n)$, $x_{i,j} \in \{0, 1\}$ to minimize the average response time $\hat{r}t$ while used resource of each edge server is less or equal than their resource limitation.

(2) *Dynamic Service Replacement Problem*

In the first step, we get an initial service deployment scheme for a good start. But requirements change over time, and the basic assumption of approximately equal invocation frequency may fail. If an edge server can never provide services to users it connects with, most of its resources will be left idle while the users have to wait longer for the long-distance communications.

Therefore, the edge server must replace the deployed services to ensure that the resources of edge servers are used adequately, at least in the next τ time slots. However, the edge server cannot conduct the service replacement anytime when a request miss occurs, because the replacement process will cause system suspending. This suspending will make parts of the server resource be unavailable until those better services are downloaded, replaced and started. Denote $x'_{i,j}$ the choice to load service ws_i on edge server es_j, while $x_j = (x_{1,j}, x_{2,j}, ..., x_{m,j})$ is the current service deployment scheme for es_j. Then, the time cost of replacing ws_i on edge server es_j can be represented as:

$$D_{i,j} = x'_{i,j}\left(1 - x_{i,j}\right)\frac{vol_i}{B_j} + \varepsilon_{i,j} \tag{6.35}$$

Here vol_i is the volume of s_i, B_j describes the average bandwidth of es_j and $\varepsilon_{i,j}$ is the disturbance term caused by other factors like service launching or system recovery. As $\varepsilon_{i,j}$ may be very small, here we omit it without loss of generation. Then the average response time $\hat{r}t(\tau)$ of services on the edge server es in the next τ time slots can be represented as:

$$\hat{r}t(\tau) = \frac{1}{n}\sum_{j=1}^{n}\sum_{i=1}^{m}\left(D_{i,j} + f_{i,j}\hat{r}_{t,j}(\tau)\right) \tag{6.36}$$

The $\hat{r}_{t,j}(\tau)$ here is the average response time of ws_i. Similarly, we need enough resource to enable the service deployment scheme:

$$\sum_{i=1}^{m}x_{i,j}\mathbf{R}_i \leq \mathbf{R}_j^\star, \quad 1 \leq j \leq n \tag{6.37}$$

Thus, the problem can be defined as: Given the service set $S = (ws_1, ws_2, ..., ws_m)$ and the current service deployment scheme $X = (x1, x2, ..., xn)$, $xi,j \in \{0, 1\}$ of edge server $ES = (es_1, es_2, ..., es_n)$, find a replacement scheme $X' = (x'_1, x'_2, ..., x'_n)$, $x'_{i,j} \in \{0, 1\}$ to minimize the average response time $\hat{r}t$ on es in next τ time slots while used resource of each edge server is less or equal than their resource limitation.

6.4.2 Approach

6.4.2.1 Problem Reduction

In the former section, we give the definition of the service deployment scheme initialization problem and the service replacement problem. It's worth noting that this problem can be simplified, because Eq. (6.33) can be transformed to:

$$\hat{r}t = \frac{1}{n} \sum_{j=1}^{n} \sum_{i=1}^{m} f_{i,j} \left(t_{i,j}^{e} - T_{i}^{c} \right) x_{i,j} + T_{i}^{c} f_{i,j} \tag{6.38}$$

and Eq. (6.36) can be transformed to:

$$\hat{r}t(\tau) = \frac{1}{n} \sum_{j=1}^{n} \sum_{i=1}^{m} \left(f_{i,j} \left(t_{i,j}^{e} - T_{i}^{c} \right) + \left(1 - x_{i,j} \right) \frac{vol_{i}}{B_{j}} \right) x_{i,j}' + T_{i}^{c} f_{i,j} \tag{6.39}$$

Then, the service deployment problem can be formulated with:

$$(\textbf{P1}) \quad \min -C^{\mathrm{T}}\mathbf{y} + C_{0}$$
$$\text{s.t.} \sum_{i=1}^{m} y_{i} \mathbf{R}_{i} \leq \mathbf{R}^{\star}, \ y_{i} \in \{0, 1\} \tag{6.40}$$

And the service replacement problem can be formulated with:

$$(\textbf{P2}) \quad \min - C'^{\mathrm{T}}\mathbf{y}_{i}' + C_{0}$$
$$\text{s.t.} \sum_{i=1}^{m} y_{i}' \mathbf{R}_{i} \leq \mathbf{R}^{\star}, \ y_{i} \in \{0, 1\} \tag{6.41}$$

It is obvious that these two problems can be reduced to the following linear integer programming (LIP) problem:

$$(\textbf{P3}) \quad \max C^{\mathrm{T}}\mathbf{y}_{i}$$
$$\text{s.t.} \sum_{i=1}^{m} y_{i} \mathbf{R}_{i} \leq \mathbf{R}^{\star}, \ y_{i} \in \{0, 1\} \tag{6.42}$$

Therefore, we propose a preprocessing algorithm (Algorithm 5) and a dynamic programming–based algorithm (Algorithm 2) called CResSA (Constrained-Resource Service Arrangement) to solve the optimization problems P3.

Algorithm 5: Preprocess

Input: C: the benefit coefficient;
                 R: the resource consumptions of services;
Output: C^+: the positive elements of C;
                 R^+: the positive elements of R;
                 $Index^+$: the service whose C_i is positive;
1: $C^+ \leftarrow []$
2: $R^+ \leftarrow []$
3: $Index^+ \leftarrow []$
4: **for** $i = 1$ **to** m **do**
5:     **if** $C_i > 0$ **then**
6:         $C^+ \leftarrow [C^+, C_i]$
7:         $R^+ \leftarrow [R^+, R^i]$
8:         $Index^+ \leftarrow [Index^+, i]$
9:     **end if**
10: **end for**

Instead of contributing to the maximization of our target, deploying service ws_i whose C_i is non-positive will bring external resource consumption on edge server. Therefore, we can take advantage of it to prune our searching space in Algorithm 5 by leaving out those services.

Algorithm 6: CResSA

Input: C: the benefit coefficient;
                 R: the resource consumptions of services;
                 $R^\star$: the capacity of resources;
Output: y: the m-dim policy vector;
1: $K \leftarrow Size(R^\star)$
2: $m \leftarrow Size(C)$
3: $F[0..m, 0..R_1^\star, 0..R_2^\star, ..., 0..R_K^\star] \leftarrow 0$
4: **for** $i = 1$ **to** m **do**
5:     **for** $r_1 = R_1^i$ **to** $R_1^\star$ **do**
6:         $\cdots$
7:         **for** $r_K = R_K^i$ **to** $R_K^\star$ **do**
8:             $F_1 \leftarrow F[i-1, r_1, ..., r_K]$
9:             $F_2 \leftarrow F[i-1, r_1 - R_1^i, ..., r_K - R_K^i] + C_i$
10:            **if** $F_1 > F_2$ **then**
11:                $F[i, r_1, ..., r_K] \leftarrow F_1$
12:            **else**
13:                $F[i, r_1, ..., r_K] \leftarrow F_2$
14:            **end if**
15:        **end for**
16:    **end for**
17: **end for**
18: $y \leftarrow Traceback(F, R, R^\star)$

In Algorithm 6 Line 1, we first capture the resource dimension K from $R^\star$, which describes the what kinds of resources are considered and the maximum resource the edge server can provide. In Line 2, we then capture the number of services need to be considered to put on edge server or not. In Line 3, we initialize the array F that records the optimal target value of the scheme. Because there are K types of resources to be considered, we use a K-layers loop for searching the optimal target value for previous i services $F[i, r_1, \ldots, r_K]$ in Line 5–16. The codes in Line 10–14 show the decision of the recursive process. Finally, with the a traceback–based algorithm (Algorithm 7), we can get the service scheme y. It can be analyzed that the time complexity of this algorithm is $O\left(m\Pi^K k = 1 R_k^\star\right)$ while the space complexity is also $O\left(m\Pi^K k = 1 R_k^\star\right)$. Compared with $O(m^{2.5})$, the time complexity of Path-following algorithm proposed by Lee and Sidford, the CResSA can handle the situations where there are many services for consideration because it's constraint is about integers.

Algorithm 7: Traceback

Input: F: the maximum value of $C^T y$;
          R: the resource consumptions of services;
          $R^\star$: the capacity of resources;
Output: y: the m-dim policy vector;
1: $y \leftarrow [0, 0, \ldots, 0]$
2: **for** $i = m$ to 2 **do**
3:     **if** $F[i, R_1^\star, \ldots, R_K^\star] = F[i - 1, R_1^\star, \ldots, R_K^\star]$ **then**
4:         $y_i \leftarrow 0$
5:     **else**
6:         $y_i \leftarrow 1$
7:         $R_1^\star, \ldots, R_K^\star \leftarrow R_1^\star - R_1^i, \ldots, R_K^\star - R_K^i$
8:     **end if**
9: **end for**
10: **if** $F[1, R_1^\star, \ldots, R_K^\star] > 0$ **then**
11:     $y_i \leftarrow 1$
12: **end if**

6.4.2.2 Initialize Service Deployment Scheme

Given the definition of the service deployment scheme initialization problem, and then we transform this problem to a service deployment problem on one edge server. However, the service frequency f_i in future is still unknown when initializing the services on edge servers. Therefore, we need to predict f_i. In this step, we assume that the frequency is approximate to the frequency of some previous periods. In this way, we can estimate f_i with

$$f_i = \frac{N_i}{\sum_{j=1}^{m} N_j} \tag{6.43}$$

where N_i is the invocation amount. Now, we can initialize the service deployment scheme with the following CRSD (Constrained-Resource Service Deployment) Algorithm 8.

Algorithm 8: Constrained-Resource Service Deployment

Input: T^c: the response time of services on cloud server
t^e: the response time of services on edge server
N: the historical invocation amount of services
R: the resource consumptions of services;
$R^{\star}$: the capacity of resources;
Output: y : the service deployment scheme
1: $m \leftarrow Size(N)$
2: $C \leftarrow \{0, 0, ..., 0\}$
3: $f \leftarrow \{0, 0, ..., 0\}$
4: $y \leftarrow \{0, 0, ..., 0\}$
5: **for** $i = 1$ to m **do**
6:      $f_i \leftarrow \frac{N_i}{\sum_{j=1}^{m} N_j}$
7:      $C_i \leftarrow f_i(T_i^c - t_i^e)$
8: **end for**
9: $C^+, R^+, Index^+ \leftarrow Preprocess(C, R)$
10: $y^+ \leftarrow CResSA(C^+, R^+, R^{\star})$
11: **for** $i = 1$ to $Index^+.size$ **do**
12:      $y_{Index_i^+} = y_i^+$
13: **end for**

6.4.2.3 Replace Service Deployment Scheme Dynamically

In this problem, the service frequency f_i in next τ time slots is still unknown, so we should carefully study the rule of service requests to find a better service replacement scheme. As researchers always use Poisson flow to model the requests without loss of generation, here we follow the principle to model them (People can easily replace the model with another one to estimate f_i).Therefore, the probability of ws_i being invoked n times in next τ time slots can be represented as:

$$P(z_i(\tau) = n) = e^{-\lambda_i \tau} \cdot \frac{(\lambda_i \tau)^n}{n!} \tag{6.44}$$

where λ_i means the average request arrival rate of ws_i in next τ time slots. Let $P_i(j;\tau)$ be the probability that ws_i being invoked j times in next τ time slots, and N_i be the expectation of service ws_i's invocation times, then we have:

$$N_i = \sum_{j=0}^{+\infty} P_i(j; \tau) \cdot j$$

$$= \sum_{j=0}^{+\infty} e^{-\lambda_i \tau} \cdot \frac{(\lambda_i \tau)^j}{j!} \cdot j$$

$$= \lambda_i \tau \qquad (6.45)$$

then we can estimate the frequency f_i with:

$$f_i = \frac{N_i}{\sum_{j=1}^{m} N_j}$$

$$= \frac{\lambda_i}{\sum_{j=1}^{m} \lambda_j} \qquad (6.46)$$

Therefore, the average response time $rt(\tau)$ can be represented as:

$$\hat{rt}(\tau) = \sum_{i=1}^{m} f_i \left(D_i + y_i' \cdot t_i + \left(1 - y_i'\right) \cdot T_i \right) \qquad (6.47)$$

6.4.3 Experiments

The hit rate and the average response time of services in different hours ($\tau = 60$ slots, 1 slot = 1 min) reflect the local provision performance of the edge servers. Figure 6.16a, c show the comparison of hit rate and average response time per hour for different replacement policies. When service replacement is not considered, the performance depends directly on the static deployment policy: the more approximate the service

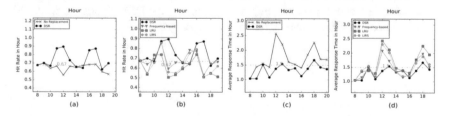

Fig. 6.16 The performance of the MEC system before and after adopting replacement policy

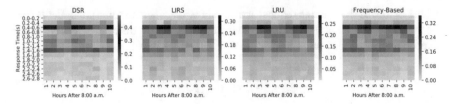

Fig. 6.17   The performance of the MEC system before and after adopting replacement policy

frequency distribution per hour is to the one used in the deployment step, the better performance it will have. In Fig. 6.16a, c, the two dashed lines reflect the performance thresholds. A good service provisioning system must adjust its provisioning policy to maintain a tolerable performance. From the performance curve, we can see that the original system can not adjust itself to improve performance when thresholds are not satisfied. As a consequence, we should adopt the Dynamic Service Replacement algorithm.

The DSR Algorithm (Algorithm 3) initializes λ spatial with similar edge servers' information, and then initialize λ temporal with requests record in previous τ time slots. Figure 6.16b, d show the curve of hit rate and average response time per hour after the replacement algorithm is adopted when choosing different types of metrics as thresholds. The hit rate threshold is set to 0.67 and the average response time threshold is set to 1.5 s. The cached services are kept the same when the threshold is satisfied, but when the server finds that threshold cannot be satisfied, it starts the DSR algorithm. In Fig. 6.16d, once the average response time in an hour grows larger than 1.5 s, deployed services will be rearranged by the edge server. As a result, the average response time decreases. But when choosing the hit rate as threshold in Fig. 6.16b, it cannot always go back to values larger than 0.67; this phenomenon is caused by the objective of the DSR algorithm. The DSR algorithm always tries to optimize the average response time not the hit rate. The reduction of average response time of services may contribute to the improvement of the hit rate, but the irregular resource cost may also counteract the contribution. Besides the hit rate and average response time in hours, another significant performance metric in the provisioning system is its 95th percentile response time. Different from the meaning of average response time, it reveals the performance variation of the system. Figure 6.17 uses a heat-map to show the distribution of response time in different hours when considering different replacement policies. In this heat-map, we can see that 95% of the service response time varies in a dense and low range when adopting the DSR algorithm, while the ones of other algorithms have larger values and ranges.

6.5 Conclusion

This chapter focused on the problem of service/application deployment in terms of latency, energy consumption and QoS correlations in mobile environments, and proposed three service/application deployment methods.

Firstly, we introduced the mobile edge computing models and highlighted the scenario of deploying microservice-based applications on the edge service provision system. Based on them, we modeled the microservice instances on servers as the queuing node and proposed an algorithm to find the optimal deployment schemes with lower cost while meeting the demand of application response time.

Then, we attempted to solve the problem of data-intensive application edge deployment with deep reinforcement learning approach. The main objective was to maximize the latency reduction for all mobile devices while minimizing the monetary cost for ASPs with an edge latency deadline. The results of extensive experimental results showed that DAEDP could formulate the deployment policies with reward performance extremely close to the optimal ones. Moreover, the performance of DAEDP could always stabilize even when the size of network space grows exponentially.

Finally, we highlighted the service deployment and replacement mechanism in MEC environment and proposed resource-constrained service management algorithms from two perspectives. It was a good attempt to give a service management mode, which was not only useful in system initialization but also helpful during system running by considering the resource limitation and temporal–spatial properties of edge servers (which are remarkable characteristics of the MEC model).

As the approaches above mentioned can generate deployment schemes for services/applications when the location-aware requests arrive, the application developers can dynamically update the deployment schemes when the request arrival signal can be predicted accurately. Therefore, we can turn to some prediction models and more practical solutions in the future work.

References

1. I. Filip, F. Pop, C. Serbanescu, C. Choi, Microservices scheduling model over heterogeneous cloud-edge environments as support for IoT applications. IEEE Internet Things J. **5**(4), 2672–2681 (2018)
2. P.D. Francesco, P. Lago, I. Malavolta, Migrating towards microservice architectures: an industrial survey, in IEEE *International Conference on Software Architecture (ICSA 2018)*, Seattle, WA, USA, 30 April–4 May 2018, pp. 29–39
3. F. Boyer, X. Etchevers, N.D. Palma, X. Tao, Architecture- based automated updates of distributed microservices, in in *Service-Oriented Computing—16th International Conference (ICSOC 2018)*, Hangzhou, China, 12–15 Nov 2018 (2018), pp. 21–36

4. M. Vögler, J.M. Schleicher, C. Inzinger, S. Dustdar, Optimizing elastic IoT application deployments. IEEE Trans. Serv. Comput. **11**(5), 879–892 (2018)
5. S. Nastic, H.L. Truong, S. Dustdar, Data and control points: a programming model for resource-constrained iot cloud edge devices, in *2017 IEEE International Conference on Systems, Man, and Cybernetics (SMC 2017)*, Banff, AB, Canada, 5–8 Oct 2017, pp. 3535–3540
6. H. Xu, W. Chen, N. Zhao, Z. Li, J. Bu, Z. Li, Y. Liu, Y. Zhao, D. Pei, Y. Feng, J. Chen, Z. Wang, H. Qiao, Unsupervised anomaly detection via variational auto-encoder for seasonal kpis in web applications, in *Proceedings of the 2018 World Wide Web Conference on World Wide Web, WWW*, Lyon, France, 23–27 April 2018, pp. 187–196
7. P. Ren, X. Qiao, J. Chen, S. Dustdar, Mobile edge computing2014a booster for the practical provisioning ap- proach of web-based augmented reality, in *2018 IEEE/ACM Symposium on Edge Computing (SEC)*. IEEE (2018), pp. 349–350
8. H. Wu, S. Deng, W. Li, M. Fu, J. Yin, A.Y. Zomaya, Service selection for composition in mobile edge computing systems, in *2018 IEEE International Conference on Web Services (ICWS)*. IEEE (2018), pp. 355–358
9. Y. Chen, S. Deng, H. Ma, J. Yin, Deploying data-intensive applications with multiple services components on edge. Mob. Networks Appl. 1–16 (2019)
10. C. Zhang, H. Zhao, S. Deng, A density-based offloading strategy for iot devices in edge computing systems. IEEE Access **6**, 73520–73530 (2018)
11. J. Xu, L. Chen, P. Zhou, Joint service caching and task offloading for mobile edge computing in dense networks, in *IEEE INFOCOM 2018-IEEE Conference on Computer Communications*. IEEE (2018), pp. 207–215
12. Y. Chen, S. Deng, H. Zhao H, et al., Data-intensive application deployment at edge: a deep reinforcement learning approach. *IEEE International Conference on Web Services (ICWS)*. IEEE (2019), pp. 355–359
13. S. Deng, Z. Xiang, J. Yin, J. Taheri, A.Y. Zomaya, Composition-driven iot service provisioning in distributed edges. IEEE Access **6**, 54258–54269 (2018)
14. A. Gamez-Diaz, P. Fernandez, A. Ruiz-Cortes, An analysis of restful a\pis offerings in the industry, in *International Conference on Service-Oriented Computing* (Springer, Berlin, 2017), pp. 589–604
15. S. Wang, C. Ding, N. Zhang, N. Cheng, J. Huang, Y. Liu, ECD: an edge content delivery and update framework in mobile edge computing. CoRR, vol. abs/1805.10783 (2018)
16. Y. Mao, J. Zhang, K.B. Letaief, Dynamic computation offloading for mobile-edge computing with energy harvesting devices. IEEE J. Sel. Areas Commun. **34**(12), 3590–3605
17. B. Dai, S. Ding, G. Wahba et al., Multivariate bernoulli distribution. Bernoulli **19**(4), 1465–1483 (2013)
18. Y. Mao, J. Zhang, K.B. Letaief, Dynamic computation offloading for mobile-edge computing with energy harvesting devices. IEEE J. Sel. Areas Commun. **34**(12), 3590–3605 (2016)
19. X. Zhihong, S. Bo, G. Yanyan, Using simulated annealing and ant colony hybrid algorithm to solve traveling salesman problem, in *2009 Second International Conference on Intelligent Networks and Intelligent Systems*, Nov 2009, pp. 507–510
20. Y. Dai, Y. Lou, X. Lu, A task scheduling algorithm based on genetic algorithm and ant colony optimization algorithm with multi-qos constraints in cloud computing, in *2015 7th International Conference on Intelligent Human-Machine Systems and Cybernetics*, vol. 2, Aug 2015, pp. 428–431
21. P. Zhou, Y. Tang, Q. Huang, C. Ma, An improved hill climbing search algorithm for rosa coupling, *in 2018 2nd IEEE Advanced Information Management,Communicates, Electronic and Automation Control Conference (IMCEC)*, May 2018, pp. 1513–1517

22. H. Gao, S. Mao, W. Huang, X. Yang, Applying proba- bilistic model checking to financial production risk evaluation and control: a case study of alibabas yue bao. IEEE Trans. Comput. Social Syst. **5**(3), 785–795 (2018)
23. M. Afrin, J. Jin, A. Rahman, Energy-delay co-optimization of resource allocation for robotic services in cloudlet infrastructure, in *International Conference on Service-Oriented Computing* (Springer, Berlin, 2018), pp. 295–303

Chapter 7
Mobile Services Computation Offloading

Abstract Aiming to reduce task transmission latency, migration latency, and execution latency, new techniques are emerging to optimize applications, servers, and users jointly during tasks that are offloading to an edge server. In this chapter, we focus on several key issues about the offloading problem. Taking into account the unstable connectivity of mobile networks, we introduce a mobility model and a trade-off fault-tolerance strategy. This strategy is designed by a modified genetic algorithm to match the structure of this model. Besides, considering the partition of data stream application and edge servers cooperation, we discuss the offloading strategy with resource-limited mobile devices and computation-intensive services. A cross-edge computation offloading (CCO) framework for partitionable applications is proposed by the Lyapunov optimization. Edge servers' clustering is also a major concern in the edge network environment to significantly improve the scheduling of network resources and satisfy the requirements of service subscribers. We designed a system that benefits from clustering edge servers based on the density of devices that connect to edge servers.

7.1 Introduction

Offloading techniques are important issues in edge computing which make calculate service closer to the source of the data. Reducing network latency and improving energy efficiency in task execution are key challenges in edge computing. Computing tasks in users' devices could adopt offloading in an edge computing network in order to save their latency and energy, due to that data-intensive or delay-intensive tasks in users' devices are offloaded to edge servers. Those tasks refer to any computing, storage, and network resources, such as cameras or smart gateways from the data source to the cloud computing center path. Applying the techniques of offloading, edge computing and cloud computing is not the opposite, on the contrary, edge computing is actually the expansion and extension of cloud computing.

The purpose of offloading terminal devices' tasks to edge servers nearby is not to replace traditional cloud computing, but to complement and extend traditional cloud computing, by providing a better computing platform for mobile computing

© Zhejiang University Press and Springer Nature Singapore Pte Ltd. 2020

S. Deng et al., *Mobile Service Computing*, Advanced Topics in Science
and Technology in China 58, https://doi.org/10.1007/978-981-15-5921-1_7

and numerous of devices called the Internet of Things (IoT). To make offloading techniques practical and efficient, the edge computing model requires the powerful computing power and support of mass storage. Traditional cloud computing also needs these techniques of offloading through edge servers to process massive data and private data to meet the requirements of real-time, privacy protection and lowering energy consumption.

Offloading in edge computing is beginning to be well known in the academia and industry. Number of papers retrieved by 'offloading' on Google Scholar grows tremendously in these ten years. In the nearing future, the main target is to deploy computing and storage resources at the edge to meet the demanding latency requirements of some applications, and to combine with emerging technologies such as 5G to achieve true edge computing by offloading terminal computations to the edges.

In our discussion, due to the development of cloud computing and virtualization techniques, mobile devices could execute very data-intensive and delay-intensive tasks by offloading these tasks to a base station nearby which is an equipped edge server. One client's device should determine whether to offload the computing task and which part of the task should be offloaded to the edge near the client. Considering the mobile computing offload problem, we give a solution that can handle multiple mobile services in the workflow to meet its complex needs to make decisions about whether the workflow should be offloaded or not. The connectivity between devices and mobile networks will be an impact on the offloading problem. Thus, proposing a robust offloading scheme to arrange mobile services is a key issue. This offloading system aims to minimize the execution time of mobile services and the energy consumption of devices with a fault-tolerance mechanism which considering the trade-off between the delay and energy. To solve this offloading problem, we need to apply a kind of heuristic algorithm, a genetic algorithm(GA), to get a near-optimal result in the studied cases. Besides this designed algorithm has almost linear algorithmic complexity to the size of problem [7].

The latency in big data transmission for users' mobile devices is a big problem in edge computing. We apply to offload thus these computation tasks could be executed on edge servers. But, in the form of mobility-aware computation-intensive services, existing offloading schemes cannot process the offloading procedure properly due to the lack of collaboration among edge servers. If we focus on the transmission latency and collaboration of edge servers, we notice that an application in the form of a data stream is partitionable if it can be used by a directed acyclic dataflow graph, which makes cross-edge collaboration possible. We propose a cross-edge computation offloading (CCO) framework especially for those tasks named partitionable applications. The transmission, execution, and coordination cost, as well as the penalty for task failure, are considered. An online algorithm based on Lyapunov optimization is proposed to jointly determine edge site-selection and energy harvesting without prior knowledge. By stabilizing the battery energy level of each mobile device around a positive constant, the proposed algorithm can obtain asymptotic optimality. Theoretical analysis of the complexity and effectiveness of the proposed framework is provided. Experimental results based on a real-life dataset corroborate that CCO can achieve superior performance compared with benchmarks where cross-edge collaboration is not allowed [19].

In an area consisting of numerous edge servers, utilizing a strategy based on the density of IoT devices and *k-means* algorithm to partition edge servers in this network could improve the Quality of Experience of service subscribers. This algorithm for IoT devices' computation offloading decisions is proposed, based on collaboration spaces formed from edge servers which efficiently handle the requests of offload IoT devices' workload. Considering edge server to choose if migration is needed and locations of edge servers with the geographic distribution of various IoT devices, this strategy can significantly improve the scheduling of network resources and satisfy requirements of service subscribers. The mathematical models in this strategy focus on whether/how/what to offload tasks from various IoT devices to edge servers. The input size of each users' device is regarded as uncertain, we model this random variable following some probability distribution based on long-term observations. Utilization with Sample Average Approximation method, the offloading strategy decides whether the tasks to be executed locally or offloaded. Based on that, an algorithm utilizing the Sample Average Approximation method is proposed to discuss whether the tasks to be executed locally or offloaded. Besides, the algorithm proposed can also help decide server relocation/migration is needed or not. Simulation results show that our algorithm can achieve 20% of global cost less than the benchmark on a true base station dataset of Hangzhou [18].

Besides, based on the initiator diversity of data offloading, some scholars have concluded these different offloading technologies for different application scenario of mobile networks, they believe that the implementation of edge computing with offloading scheme can be divided into the following four technologies as data offloading through small cell networks, data offloading through WiFi networks, data offloading through opportunistic mobile networks, and data offloading through heterogeneous networks [20]. Computational offloading is a key technology for edge computing, providing computing resources for resource-constrained devices running computationally intensive applications, speeding up calculations, and saving energy consumption. Some scholars concluded that there are three important topics which focused on the decision on computation offloading in terms of energy consumption, allocation of computing resource to minimize the delay and balance load and mobility management in edge computing [11]. In the future, innovative applications will develop rapidly at users' equipment, most of them tend to become delay-intensive and data-intensive tasks, thus saving the battery life of users' equipment and minimizing the delay become urgent issues for edge computing. The authors propose the task placement sub-problem and resource allocation sub-problem to solve a mixed-integer non-linear program about edge computing [5].

Nowadays, Alibaba Cloud officially released the Edge Container which is committed to cloud-edge-end integration and seamlessly merges the boundaries of the cloud through non-intrusive enhancement. Based on these tools, offloading techniques can be processed easily, thus they have achieved smart parking, property management, face recognition, and other scene applications, this is the first time Alibaba Cloud successfully landed in the IoT field with edge container, through the cloud-native way to improve the efficiency of DevOps in the edge computing and IoT field.

Microsoft proposed the 'Azure IoT Edge' platform which is a fully managed service built on the Azure IoT Center. Through their tools deploying some specific applications (such as artificial intelligence application and third-party services, or your business tasks) to run on the Internet of Things (IoT) or edge devices using regular containers technique becomes much convenient for clients. By offloading and migrating specific workloads to the edge from the center cloud, users' devices can reduce communication time with the cloud, speed up response to clients' requests, and even run offline reliably over long periods.

Based on the wave of edge computing is to integrating "things" into intelligent interconnection, Huawei launched the solution of the Internet of Things for Edge Computing. They provide the scheme not only supporting tremendous industrial protocols and interfaces, and widely adapts to different industry scenarios, but also satisfying the requests of intelligent data processing in different industries due to edge computing capability and cloud management architecture. It helps industries to innovate their products quickly, improve production efficiency and quality, and reduce total costs of productions.

There are several key techniques in hardware and software to support to achieve offloading technology. Intel launched NEV SDK (Network Edge Virtualization Kit) based on the idea of pooling in hardware resources and decoupling between software and hardware to help partners in the field of edge computing to accelerate the development of related applications in the field of telecommunications. In addition to focusing on the infrastructure platform of computing capabilities, NEV SDK can also provide edge computing application developers with basic software environments and rich API interfaces. It shields developers from the development work of complex telecommunication network control. Even if developers do not understand the complex telecommunication network, they can quickly develop applications. Besides, NEV SDK also provides development example program and base station/core network simulator, which can help application developers quickly build an environment close to the real network for rapid test and verification.

Security techniques are also key issues in offloading, Cisco announced that it is consolidating its security and software-defined wide area network (SD-WAN) technology to provide enterprises with more technology choices. Cisco also said that the technology maturation will be coming soon, and SD-WAN technology will promote and improve the development of cloud and edge computing. They said Cloud Edge Computing will also help Cisco complete the construction of the Internet of Things. Cisco acquired the Internet of Things business after acquiring a few years ago. Currently, Cisco's asper Control Center is one of the largest IoT platforms in the world. More than 10,000 companies have reached cooperation and covered more than 160 countries and regions. While Cisco is promoting the edge of and cloud computing, the biggest advantage of IoT construction lies in security. With the development of the network, privacy and security have become the primary factors for many consumers to consider. Cisco provides security monitoring by integrating security technologies such as firewalls into the SD-WAN. Also, Cisco's Control

Center platform integrates a range of security features to protect the Internet of Things.

We introduce three key topics about offloading for edge computing as follows: mobility of clients' devices and response time of mobile network in paper [7], the long term average of delay and parallel execution of services in paper [19], and clustering of edge servers due to the density of users' devices in the edge computing network in paper [18].

7.2 Computing Offloading in Mobile Cloud Computing

7.2.1 Mobility Model for Offloading

In this section, because we mainly consider the offloading scheme of this system to make optimal offloading decisions to minimize execution delay and energy consumption of each device for clients' services (workflows) as Fig. 7.1. Thus, the target function of the offloading strategy is defined as a weighted sum of delay in the mobile network of clients' services and their energy consumption. The formulation is as follows:

$$F(m) = w_m * L_m + (1 - w_m) * E_m \qquad (7.1)$$

L_m is execution time of service of the mth device, E_m represents the total energy of consumption of the service execution in that device. w_m represents the weight between time and energy consumption, that we can modify this value to pay more concern on the delay time or energy consumption. This value w_m in experiments was set to 0.5 to equally address the importance of both concerns.

In general, the trajectories of clients are detected by the edge computing system. The signal strength and coverage of each base station could be acquired by the system. Besides, we adopt the RWP (random waypoint) model during the simulation, it is defined as follows.

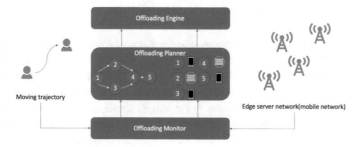

Fig. 7.1 Framework of offloading system

Fig. 7.2 A motivation
scenario

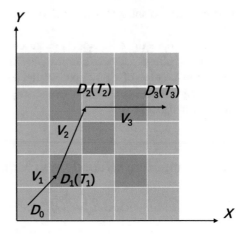

A client's moving trajectory is fixed as tuple $mt = (p_i, t_i, v_i)$, where p_i is the point in the trajectory when the client pauses at time t_i with speed v_i. Figure 7.2 explains a mobile user's trajectory in the form of RWP model.

According to RWP model, we can get the results of every part in Eq. (7.1) as follows:

$$rt_v = \frac{wl_v}{c_M} \tag{7.2}$$

where wl_v is represented the workload of the device without offloading for service v which is executed locally at a mobile device, and c_M is the CPU capacity (n MIPS) for the mobile device. the consumption of services which are executed locally is defined as follows:

$$E_v = rt_v * p_M \tag{7.3}$$

where p_M is the energy consumption rate for a device running the service. Then we define the execution time of services after offloading as follows:

$$rt_c = \frac{di}{Tx_i} + \frac{wl_c}{C_c} + Q_c + \frac{do}{Tx_o} \tag{7.4}$$

Tx_i, Tx_o represents the transmission rate (in Kbps) of the workload of input and output about the service c, To calculate Tx_i, Tx_o, we first acquire the transmission rate of each mobile device by the location using the trajectory model. wl_o is the workload need to be offloaded, d_i, d_o represents the size of data for input and output, C_c is used to indicate the CPU capacity (in MIPS) for the edge server and Q_c is the waiting time of the service c for queueing in the edge server. We defined E_c as the energy consumption of offloaded services. We can calculate the consumption by the formulation as follows:

$$E_c = \frac{di}{Tx_i} * p_{RF}^{up} + \frac{do}{Tx_o} * p_{RF}^{down} \tag{7.5}$$

where p_{RF}^{up}, p_{RF}^{down} represents the energy consumption when sending and receiving data during the offloading service c. Thus, we can change the Eq. (7.1) to the formulation as follows:

$$F(m) = w_m * L(rt_s) + (1 - w_m) * \left(\sum_l E_l + \sum_c E_c\right) \qquad (7.6)$$

where $L(rt_s)$ is the total execution time of service workload for both locally execution and execution on edge server.

7.2.2 Fault-Tolerence Offloading

Fig. 7.3 shows the states of non-offloading and offloading transition of a mobile application in edge server network. There are four different states: uploading input data (SU), offloading execution (SOE), downloading output data (SD) and failure and recovery (SFR). Assume that failure can happen during the SU, SD and SOE states for the reason that edge server being unreachable while a mobile device is moving around. The disconnection between an edge server and a mobile device is regarded as a failure, the failure recovery must detect it and restart a service immediately from the beginning.

7.2.2.1 Failure Recovery

Define R^* as the failure recovery time within the recovery process which is a period named R. Let P be the first time to the first failure after recovery, we can calculate R^* as follows:

Fig. 7.3 State transition of non-offloading and offloading

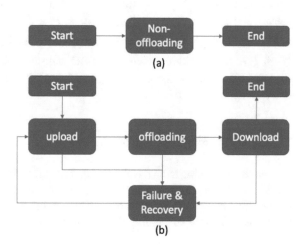

$$R^* = \begin{cases} R & if\, P > R \\ P + \hat{R} & otherwise \end{cases}$$

if $P > R$, then the recovery process will be successfully finished without nested failures during the recovery period. If $P \leq R$, a nested failure has occurred, and then a new recovery process should be carried out after P. This leads to the recovery time of $P + R$.

7.2.2.2 Offloading Without Fault-Tolerance

We define execution time of offloading with failure recovery can be calculated as:

$$rt^* = \begin{cases} rt_c & if\, P \geq rt_c \\ P + R^* + rt_c & otherwise \end{cases}$$

rt_c is the execution time without considering the mechanism of failure recovery. If $P \geq rt_c$, the service c which is offloaded could successfully finish without failures, so that the execution time would be rt_c. If $P < rt_c$, the offloading of workload in c will fail to cause a failure takes place. In this situation, a recovery time R^* is added to the process after the service execution is restarted from its beginning. Likewise, the energy consumption of an offloading the service c could be the formulation as:

$$E_c^* = \begin{cases} E_c & P \geq rt_c \\ P * p_{RF}^{up} & P < \frac{d_i}{Tx_i} \\ \frac{d_i}{Tx_i} * p_{RF}^{up} + E_c & \frac{d_i}{Tx_i} \leq P < \frac{d_i}{Tx_i} + \frac{wl_c}{cc} \\ \frac{d_i}{Tx_i} * p_{RF}^{up} + \frac{d_o'}{Tx_o} * p_{RF}^{down} + E_c & \frac{d_i}{Tx_i} + \frac{wl_c}{cc} \leq P < rt_c \end{cases}$$

If $P > rt_c$, the offloading of service c will not fail, and thus, the energy consumption would be E_c. If $P < \frac{d_i}{Tx_i}$, a failure occurs at the SU state, thus this service c will consume $P * p_{RF}^{up}$ to re-execution. If $\frac{d_i}{Tx_i} \leq P < \frac{d_i}{Tx_i} + \frac{wl_c}{cc}$, a failure occurs at the SOE state in which it will consume energy for uploading the part of data. If $\frac{d_i}{Tx_i} + \frac{wl_c}{cc} \leq P < rt_c$, a failure occurs at the SD state in which it will consume energy for uploading and downloading the part of data. d' is the data size that is already downloaded before a failure.

7.2.2.3 Offloading with Fault-Tolerance

To continue execution from the checkpoint rather than from the very beginning of the service, applying fault-tolerance techniques after the connection is recovered could be an efficient method in offloading. Thus, using the presence of fault-tolerance mechanism the total consuming time while offloading service becomes:

$$
rt_c^{FT} = \begin{cases}
r^{tc} & P \geq rt_c \\
\frac{d_i}{Tx_i} + G + R^* + \frac{d_i - d_i'}{Tx'_i} + \frac{wl_c}{c_c} + Q_c + \frac{d_o'}{Tx'_o} & P < \frac{d_i}{Tx_i} \\
\frac{d_i}{Tx_i} + G + R^* + \frac{wl_c}{c_c} + Q_c + \frac{d_o'}{Tx'_o} & \frac{d_i}{Tx_i} \leq P < \frac{d_i}{Tx_i} + \frac{wl_c}{c_c} \\
\frac{d_i}{Tx_i} + G + R^* + \frac{d_i - d_i'}{Tx'_i} + \frac{wl_c}{c_c} + Q_c + \frac{d_o' + d_o}{Tx_o} & \frac{d_i}{Tx_i} + \frac{wl_c}{c_c} \leq P < rt_c
\end{cases}
$$

P is the first time a failure occurs while offloading the service c, rt_c is the execution delay mentioned above, which is not considering the failure process, G is the delay of when disconnection happens, R^* means the recovery time after the connection is recovered, d_i', d_o' are the size of data which are already uploaded or downloaded when failure occurs, Tx'_i, Tx'_o are the rate of transmission after failure recovers.

$$
E_c^{ET} = \begin{cases}
E_c & P \geq rt_c \\
\frac{d_i}{Tx_i} * p_{RF}^{up} + \frac{d_i - d_i'}{Tx'_i} * p_{RF}^{up} + \frac{d_o'}{Tx'_o} * p_{RF}^{down} & P < \frac{d_i}{Tx_i} \\
\frac{d_i}{Tx_i} * p_{RF}^{up} + \frac{d_o'}{Tx'_o} * p_{RF}^{down} & \frac{d_i}{Tx_i} \leq P < \frac{d_i}{Tx_i} + \frac{wl_c}{c_c} \\
\frac{d_i}{Tx_i} * p_{RF}^{up} + \frac{d_o'}{Tx_o} * p_{RF}^{down} + \frac{d_o' + d_o}{Tx_o} * p_{RF}^{down} & \frac{d_i}{Tx_i} + \frac{wl_c}{c_c} \leq P < rt_c
\end{cases}
$$

P is the first time a failure occurs while Offloading with Optimized Fault-Toleranceng the service c, rt_c is the execution delay mentioned above, which is not considering the failure process, E_c is energy consumed by offloading service, which does not consider the failure recovery, d_i', d_o' are the size of data which are already uploaded or downloaded when failure occurs, Tx'_i, Tx'_o are the rate of transmission after failure recovers.

Offloading with Optimized Fault-Tolerance.

7.2.2.4 Offloading with Optimized Fault-Tolerance

It can not guarantee to save the total delay time of execution of service or energy consumption, although the fault-tolerance mechanism could avoid re-execute the service from the beginning while offloading. Therefore, we need to balance the trade-off between waiting for execution time and directly restarting a service from the beginning. Addressing this concern, we propose a following fault-tolerance mechanism.

In this Trade-off Fault Tolerance Algorithm, the time during left when the user of the mobile device to finish after the issue of their offloading workload is defined as d_c^L and it's assumed to be predicted. The system can determine if the failure occurs or not comparing d_c^L and rt_c. When a failure is about to occur, the system would make a comparison between the weighted combination of execution time and energy consumption which is calculated by directly restarting the service and executing the service with the fault-tolerance mechanism. The system also achieves the value of waiting time d_c^W till the mobile user goes into the coverage area of another base station. Then the system immediately calculates the rt', E_c' while the mobile device offloads their workload as soon as it could make a connection with the next base station.

Algorithm 1 Trade-off Fault Tolerance

1: Input:
      c - the offloaded service
      TR - the trajectory model of the mobile user
      C - attributes of the cloud server
      M - attributes of the mobile device
      S - attributes of the base stations covering TR
2: Output:
      rt_c^F - the final execution time of the service c
      E_c^F -thefinalenergyconsumptionoftheservicec
3: calculatedLc accordingtoTR, C, M, S
4: calculate rt_c without consideration of failure
5: **if** $d_c^L < rt_c$ **then**
6:    calculate $rt_c^*, E_c^*, rt_c^{FT}, E_c^{FT}$
7:    **if** $(w_m * rt_c^* + (1 - w_m) * E_c^* < w_m * rt_c^{FT} + (1 - w_m) * E_c^{FT})$ **then**
8:      $rt_c^T = rt_c^*, E_c^T = E_c^*$
9:    **else**
10:      $rt_c^T = rt_c^{FT}, E_c^T = E_c^{FT}$
11:    **end if**
12:    calculate d_c^W, rt_c', E_c'
13:    **if** $(w_m * rt_c^T + (1 - w_m) * E_c^T < w_m * (rt_c' + d_c^W) + (1 - w_m) * E_c')$ **then**
14:      $rt_c^F = rt_c^T, E_c^F = E_c^T$
15:    **else**
16:      $rt_c^F = d_c^W + rt_c', E_c^F = E_c'$
17:    **end if**
18: **end if**
19: **return** rt_c^F, E_c^F.

Finally, based on the explanation above, we could get total execution time and consumption of energy. Equation 7.6 would be changed to:

$$F(m) = w_m * L(rt_s^F) + (1 - w_m) * \left(\sum_l E_l + \sum_c E_c^F \right) \tag{7.7}$$

7.2.3   Offloading Algorithm

An improved algorithm to make the offloading plan is called a genetic algorithm based computation offloading algorithm (GACO). Basically, a genetic algorithm is an optimal method based on a population to find a globally optimized solution. [ref todo] In GACO, the chromosome consists of genes that belong to each possible solution, the strategy of offloading is encoded in an array of n integers $x_1, x_2, x_3, \ldots, x_n$ where n represents the number of services in the workload. Each gene represents

Fig. 7.4 Genetic encoding scheme

the service of the mobile device where its value means whether the execution of this service should be offloaded in encoding scheme showing in Fig. 7.4.

After we find the optimal solutions, we need to evaluate the fitness using a fitness function. In GACO, it adopts Eq. 7.7 to calculate the fitness value of each chromosome consisting of total execution time for workload and total energy consumption for execution of a mobile task, and the algorithm needs to minimize both parts.

In the initialization stage, define the population size as N, the number of iteration is I, two parameters in the algorithm mutation probability and crossover probability are p_m, p_c. Define chromosome as $X^i = (x_1^i, x_2^i, \ldots, x_d^i)$ in a population ith which $i = (1, 2, 3, \ldots, N)$. The number of services in the mobile services workflow is d, regard x_j^i as an indicator if the jth service in X^i should be offloaded.

In the selection stage, the probability of a chromosome is selected depends on the value of fitness function which can be defined as:

$$pr_i^s = \frac{F_i}{\sum_{j=1}^{S} F_j} \tag{7.8}$$

In the crossover stage, crossover operation is to combine two chromosomes to generate higher-quality offspring(chromosomes). In GACO, we propose a knowledge-based crossover operator. This method select two parents p_1, p_2 by the fitness function, and only generates one offspring c_1. To do this, first, calculate the weighted combination of execution time and energy consumption to compare the fitness:

$$f_i = w_m * rt_i^F + (1 - w_m) * E_i^F \tag{7.9}$$

The genes will apply the better local fitness to the offspring as Fig. 7.5 shows.

To slightly modify chromosomes to improve the fitness as well as avoid convergence at an early stage of iteration, GACO adopts mutation operator to extend the differs as follows:

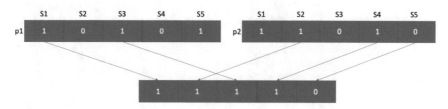

Fig. 7.5 Knowledge-based crossover

Fig. 7.6 Standard mutation

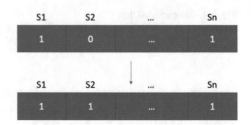

$$pr_g^m = 1 - \frac{f_g}{\sum_{j=1}^{d} f_j} \tag{7.10}$$

Thus, the mutation for services with more execution time and energy consumption is higher than the others as showing in Fig. 7.6.

7.2.4 Evaluation

Tuning different parameters for our approach will have a different impact on the evaluation results. Observing that with the increase of the population size, the quality of GACO solutions is also improved (answers with lower fitness values are found) shown in Fig. 7.7.

A similar result occurs in Fig. 7.9b, which shows the impact of the maximum number of iterations, where the quality of the best solution is increased for a higher number of iterations up to a limit: $I = 100$ in this case shown in Fig. 7.8.

Fig. 7.7 Impact of population size

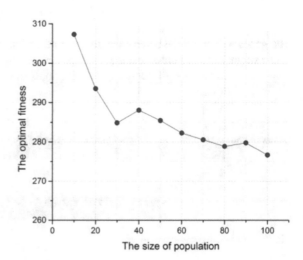

Fig. 7.8 Impact on maximum iteration

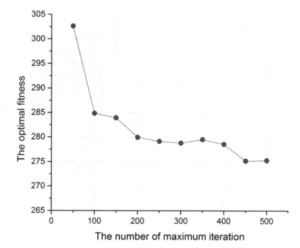

Fig. 7.9 Impact on mutation probability

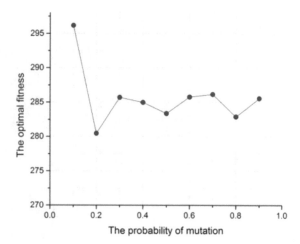

Figure 7.9 shows the impact of the mutation probability; GACO best performance is when $pm = 0.2$. As pm increases, the performance of GACO becomes unstable, mainly because when mutation probability is excessively large, high-quality chromosomes are negatively affected.

Figure 7.10 shows the impact of the crossover probability. It shows that the quality of the solutions is improved up to a limit ($pc = 0.6$) and then decreases afterward.

The evaluation is based on some benchmark algorithm as follows Algorithm 1. Our proposed method (GACO) as described above in Algorithm 2. The normal GA that uses uniform crossover and uniform mutation in Algorithm 3. A brute-force exhaustive algorithm that traverses all feasible offloading strategies to find the optimal solution.

Fig. 7.10 Impact crossover
probability

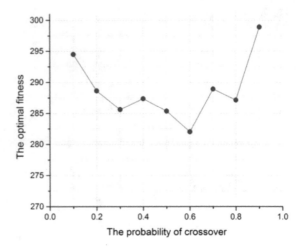

Fig. 7.11 Comparison
optimality

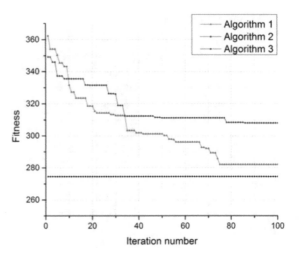

The result in Fig. 7.11 shows that, as expected, the brute-force exhaustive offloading algorithm leads to the best performance with the lowest fitness.

The evaluation is based on some benchmark algorithm as follows: Algorithm 4. There are no fault-tolerance methods involved. The execution time and energy consumption are calculated in Algorithm 5. Traditional check-pointing methods are utilized for fault-tolerance.

From the comparison results shown in Fig. 7.12, our designed fault-tolerance mechanism leads to superior solutions as compared with the other two algorithms. It also shows that GACO's trade-off fault-tolerant mechanism finds better offloading strategies when compared to a traditional check-pointing approach.

Fig. 7.12 Comparison optimality

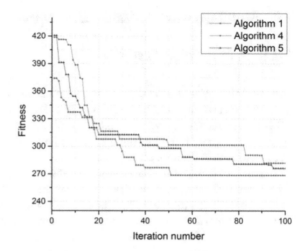

Fig. 7.13 Comparison on scalability

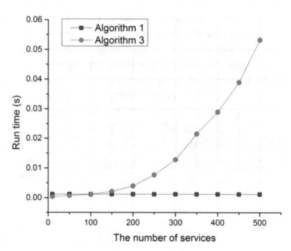

As shown in Fig. 7.13, GACO's run time is almost irrelevant to its problem size for workflows with less than 500 services, whereas the brute-force exhaustive algorithm's run time is almost exponential to the problem size even for fairly small problems.

7.3   Mobility-Aware Cross-Edge Computation Offloading

7.3.1   A Motivation Scenario

Assume MEC system consisting of N mobile devices equipped with EH (energy harvesting) hardware, indexed by $\mathcal{N}$, and M SBSs, indexed by $\mathcal{M}$. We assume that SBSs are interconnected via X2 Link for transmission of data and coordination of edge servers. Time slots with length τ, indexed by $\mathcal{T} \triangleq \{1, 2, ...\}$ is set in our system as time horizon is discretized.

Figure 7.14 demonstrates an example. The system provides autopilot and analytics for wearable devices, such as smart bracelets and intelligent glasses. Three user's devices move in the manner of the Gauss-Markov mobility model across some time slots. Each user's device generates a task offloading request with a certain probability at the beginning of each time slot. If the request can be successfully responded to *iff* it does not timeout, otherwise, the request will be dropped. Firstly, the preprocessing and packing of monitored data are carried out by the user's devices. Next, the data that are preprocessed can be divided equally and offloaded to multiple edge sites for cross-edge analytics. Assume that harvestable energy comes from light, the kinetic, wind, and other vibrations, at the beginning of each time slot. The EH components are implemented in the same manner as in [12]. Without aggregating geo-distributed data to a centralized data center, health analytics are carried out by edge sites via cross-edge Map-Reduce queries [9]. We focus on edge site selection, thus *it is assumed that* edge sites can collaborate in an appropriate match, i.e., transitions of each application phase are instantaneous without failure. The returned analytical results are much smaller compared with the offloaded data. Assume that the latency in the downlink transmission could be ignored in our system.

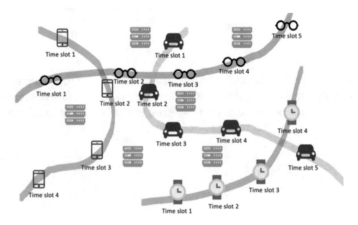

Fig. 7.14 A motivation scenario

7.3.2 Latency and Energy Consumption in Offloading

First, we construct the system model to calculate local execution latency as follows regarding the task offloading demands of mobile devices as an i.i.d. Bernoulli distribution. In each time slot, the ith mobile device's offloading demand is generated with probability ρ_i. They set $\mathbf{A}(t) \triangleq \{\times_{i \in \mathcal{N}} A_i(t)\} \subseteq \{0, 1\}^N$ as the demand vector, i.e., $\Pr\{A_i(t) = 1\} = \rho_i$. The local execution includes data preprocessing and packing. We set the data size to be processed for local execution and offloadingas μ_i^l and μ_i^r, respectively. Correspondingly, the two parts need η_i^l and η_i^r CPU cycles, respectively. For local execution, the execution latency τ_i^{lc} is η_i^l/f_i. The energy consumption of service which is locally executed is

$$\epsilon_i^l = \kappa_i \cdot \eta_i^l f_i^2, i \in \mathcal{N}, t \in \mathcal{T}, \tag{7.11}$$

where κ_i is the effective switched capacitance that depends on the chip architecture.

Second we model the latency of service which is in the duration of offloading processing.

$$\sum_{i \in \mathcal{N}} I_{i,j}(t) \leq N_j^{\max}, j \in \mathcal{M}_i(t), t \in \mathcal{T}. \tag{7.12}$$

$$R_{i,j}(t) \triangleq \omega \log_2 \left(1 + \frac{h_{i,j}(t) p_i^{tx}}{I + \varpi_0}\right), j \in \mathcal{M}_i(t), \tag{7.13}$$

$$\tau_{i,j}^{tx}(t) = \frac{\mu_i^r}{\sum_{j \in \mathcal{M}_i(t)} I_{i,j}(t)} \cdot \frac{1}{R_{i,j}(t)}, j \in \mathcal{M}_i(t). \tag{7.14}$$

$$\tau_{i,j}^{rc}(t) = \frac{\eta_i^r}{f_j \cdot \sum_{j \in \mathcal{M}_i(t)} I_{i,j}(t)}, j \in \mathcal{M}_i(t), \tag{7.15}$$

$$\tau_d \geq \max_{j \in \mathcal{M}_i(t)} \left\{\tau_{i,j}^{tx}(t) + \tau_{i,j}^{rc}(t)\right\}$$
$$+ \tau_i^{lc} + \varphi \cdot \sum_{j \in \mathcal{M}_i(t)} I_{i,j}(t), \tag{7.16}$$

Third, we calculate the battery energy level in the total consumption both of execution locally and remotely.

$$\epsilon_i^l + \sum_{j \in \mathcal{M}_i(t)} \epsilon_{i,j}^{tx}(t) I_{i,j}(t) \leq \psi_i(t), i \in \mathcal{N}, t \in \mathcal{T}. \tag{7.17}$$

$$\psi_i(t+1) = \psi_i(t) - \sum_{j \in \mathcal{M}_i(t)} \epsilon_{i,j}^{tx}(t) \cdot I_{i,j}(t) - \epsilon_i^l + \alpha_i(t), \tag{7.18}$$

where

$$0 \leq \alpha_i(t) \leq E_i^h(t), i \in \mathcal{N}, t \in \mathcal{T}. \tag{7.19}$$

7.3.3   Edge Site-Selection Problem with Parallel Execution

The overall energy consumption of the ith user's device is $\epsilon_i^l + \sum_{j \in \mathcal{M}} \epsilon_{i,j}^{tx}(t) \cdot I_{i,j}(t)$. The battery life will be affected due to excessively discharging. More importantly, there could be safety trouble. Therefore, we apply *safe discharge threshold*, i.e., the maximum transient discharge w.r.t. the ith mobile device, as ψ_i^{safe}. Thus, we have

$$\epsilon_i^l + \sum_{j \in \mathcal{M}_i(t)} \epsilon_{i,j}^{tx}(t) I_{i,j}(t) \leq \psi_i^{safe}, i \in \mathcal{N}, t \in \mathcal{T}. \tag{7.20}$$

It is a general model without specific structural assumptions. In practice, according to the types of coordination through *Multiple Criteria Decision Making*, a proper value of φ is determined. Consequently, the *Edge Site-selection Problem* can be formulated as follows:

$$\mathcal{P}_1 : \min_{\forall i, \mathbf{I}_i(t), \alpha_i(t)} \lim_{T \to \infty} \frac{1}{T} \sum_{t=0}^{T-1} \mathbb{E}\left[\sum_{i \in \mathcal{N}} \mathcal{C}(\mathbf{I}_i(t)) \right]$$

$$s.t. \quad (12), (16), (17), (19), (20).$$

7.3.4   The Cross-Edge Computation Offloading Framework

We demonstrate the details on how to obtain the asymptotic optimal solution of $\mathcal{P}_1$ by our CCO algorithm. We use a vector $\vec{\Theta}(t) \triangleq [\psi_1(t), \ldots, \psi_N(t)]$ to represent the system energy queues in the tth time slot. For a given set of non-negative parameters $\vec{\theta} \triangleq [\theta_1, \ldots, \theta_N]$, the non-negative *Lyapunov function* $L(\vec{\Theta}(t))$ is defined as follows:

$$L(\vec{\Theta}(t)) \triangleq \frac{1}{2} \sum_{i=1}^{N} (\psi_i(t) - \theta_i)^2 = \sum_{i=1}^{N} \psi_i'(t)^2, \tag{7.21}$$

where

$$\theta_i \geq \frac{V \cdot \omega \log_2(1 + \frac{h_{i,j}^{\max} p_i^{tx}}{\varpi_0})}{p_i^{tx} \mu_i^r} \left(-\frac{\mu_i^r}{\omega \log_2(1 + \frac{h_{i,j}^{\max} p_i^{tx}}{\varpi_0})} \right.$$

$$\left. + M \varrho_i - \frac{\eta_i^r}{f_j} \right) + \min\{E_{i,all}^{\max}, \psi_i^{safe}\}$$

and $E_{i,all}^{max} \triangleq \epsilon_i^l + \sum_{j=1}^{M} \epsilon_{i,j}^{max}, \epsilon_{i,j}^{max} \triangleq p_i^{tx}(\tau_d - \tau_i^{lc}), h_{i,j}^{max} \triangleq \max_{t \in \mathcal{T}: j \in \mathcal{M}} h_{i,j}(t)$.
Equation (7.21) tends to keep battery energy backlog near a non-zero value θ_i for
the ith mobile device. The conditional Lyapunov drift $\Delta(\vec{\Theta}(t))$ is define as

$$\Delta(\vec{\Theta}(t)) \triangleq \mathbb{E}[L(\vec{\Theta}(t+1)) - L(\vec{\Theta}(t))|\vec{\Theta}(t)]. \tag{7.22}$$

Notice that the lower bound of θ_i showed above is not a tightened bound. Actually,
the larger battery capacity of mobile devices, the more optimized solution can be
acquired. Because of the limited length of this section.

According to (7.18), we can acquire that

$$\psi_i'(t+1)^2$$
$$\leq \psi_i'(t)^2 + 2\psi_i'(t)\Big[\alpha_i(t) - \epsilon_i^l - \sum_{j \in \mathcal{M}} \epsilon_{i,j}^{tx}(t) \cdot I_{i,j}(t)\Big]$$
$$+ (E_{i,h}^{max})^2 + (E_{i,all}^{max})^2.$$

Consequently we have

$$\Delta(\vec{\Theta}(t)) \leq \sum_{i=1}^{N} \psi_i'(t)\Big[\alpha_i(t) - \epsilon_i^l - \sum_{j \in \mathcal{M}} \epsilon_{i,j}^{tx}(t) \cdot I_{i,j}(t)\Big] + C,$$

where $C \triangleq \frac{1}{2}\sum_{i=1}^{N}\big[(E_{i,h}^{max})^2 + (E_{i,all}^{max})^2\big]$. By Lyapunov optimization, we can obtain
the near-optimal solution to $\mathcal{P}_1$ by minimizing the upper bound of $\Delta(\vec{\Theta}(t)) +$
$V \cdot \sum_{i=1}^{N} \mathcal{C}(\mathbf{I}_i(t))$, without regard to (7.17). We define $\Delta_V^{up}(\vec{\Theta}(t))$ by

$$\Delta_V^{up}(\vec{\Theta}(t)) \triangleq \sum_{i=1}^{N} \psi_i'(t)\Big[\alpha_i(t) - \epsilon_i^l - \sum_{j=1}^{M} \epsilon_{i,j}^{tx}(t)I_{i,j}(t)\Big]$$
$$+ V\sum_{i=1}^{N} \mathcal{C}(\mathbf{I}_i(t)) + C, \tag{7.23}$$

we can solve the deterministic problem $\mathcal{P}_2$ in the every time slot t as

$$\mathcal{P}_2: \min_{\forall i, \mathbf{I}_i(t), \alpha_i(t)} \Delta_V^{up}(\vec{\Theta}(t))$$
$$s.t.\quad (12), (16), (19), (20),$$

where the constraint (7.17) is ignored due to it violates the conditions of vanilla
version of Lyapunov optimization for i.i.d. random events [15]. We set $\psi_i^{safe} \geq E_{i,all}^{max}$,
which means (7.20) can be reasonably ignored to simplify the problem. So far, we
have demonstrate the details of our CCO Algorithm, as shown in **Algorithm 1**.

The most important part of the CCO algorithm is that how to solve $\mathcal{P}_2$ asymptotic
optimally. We know that $\mathcal{P}_2$ can be divided into two sub-problems: *optimal energy
harvesting* and *optimal edge site-selection*.

Optimal energy harvesting. The optimal amount of harvested energy $\alpha_i^\star(t)$ could be acquired by solving the following sub-problem:

$$\mathcal{P}_2^{EH} : \min_{\forall i, \alpha_i(t)} \sum_{i=1}^{N} \psi_i'(t)\alpha_i(t)$$

$$s.t. \quad (19).$$

It is easy to get that

$$\alpha_i^\star(t) = E_i^H(t) \cdot \mathbb{1}\{\psi_i'(t) \le 0\}, i \in \mathcal{N}. \tag{7.24}$$

Optimal edge site-selection. The optimal decision vector $\mathbf{I}_i^\star(t)$ can be obtained by solving the following sub-problem:

$$\mathcal{P}_2^{es} : \min_{\forall i, \mathbf{I}_i(t)} \left\{ -\sum_{i=1}^{N} \psi_i'(t) \left[\epsilon_i^l + \sum_{j \in \mathcal{M}_i(t)} \epsilon_{i,j}(t) I_{i,j}(t) \right] \right.$$
$$\left. + V \cdot \sum_{i=1}^{N} \mathcal{C}(\mathbf{I}_i(t)) \right\}$$

$$s.t. \quad (12), (16), (20).$$

Algorithm 2 Cross-edge Computation Offloading (CCO)

1: At the beginning of the tth time slot, obtain i.i.d. random events $\mathbf{A}(t)$, $\mathbf{E}^h(t) \triangleq [E_1^h(t), ..., E_N^h(t)]$ and channel state information.
2: $\forall i \in \mathcal{N}$, decide $\mathbf{I}_i^\star(t)$, $\alpha_i^\star(t)$ by solving the deterministic problem $\mathcal{P}_2$.
3: $\forall i \in \mathcal{N}$, update the battery energy level $\psi_i(t)$ by (7.18).
4: $t \leftarrow t + 1$.

7.3.5 Evaluation

Optimality and stability. As shown in Fig. 7.15, the CCO algorithm outperforms the three baseline algorithms notably in overall cost $\sum_{i \in \mathcal{N}} \mathcal{C}(\mathbf{I}_i(t))$. Specifically, it outperforms RS, GSC2, and GCS1 by 36.40-42.92%, 17.83-36.96%, and 37.76-45.19%, respectively. In terms of GCS2, relatively to the computation latency which is saved through cross-edge computation offloading, the speed of communication is degraded under the condition that the allocated bandwidth is shared with a bunch of mobile devices. Therefore, GSC2 cannot outperform RS. The performance of GSC1 is worse than our CCO algorithm but better than RS and GSC2, which indicates that communication has a greater influence on the overall latency. As shown in Fig. 7.21, the battery energy level of each mobile device around θ_i and hold

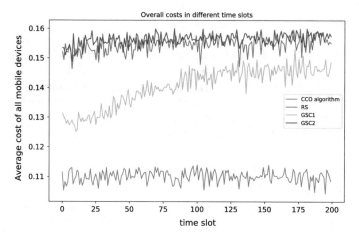

Fig. 7.15 Average cost of mobile devices

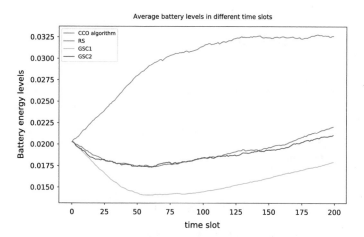

Fig. 7.16 Average battery energy level of mobile devices

$\psi_i(t) \in [0, \theta_i + E_{i,h}^{\max}]$ can be stabilised by the CCO algorithm. This result verifies **Lemma** 1. Apparently, this stability is not possessed by RS, GSC1, and GSC2 (Fig. 7.16).

Impacts of important parameters.

7.3.5.1   Impacts of Control Parameter V

As shown in Fig. 7.17a, the total cost acquired by the CCO algorithm reduces with the increase in V. But the performance of RS, GSC1, and GSC2 are not affected. Our CCO algorithm always outperforms the baseline algorithms. Inversely, as shown in Fig. 7.17c, the energy level of each mobile device increases as V increase. These results indicate that the solution acquired by the CCO algorithm is $O(\frac{1}{V})$-derivated from the optimality and the system queue size is $O(V)$, which verifies **Theorem**.

Algorithm 3 SAL-based Edge site-Selection (SES)

1: **for** $s = 1$ to S_0 **do**
2:   *Sample the sth solution* $\mathbf{I}_s(t)$ *from the feasible solution space X (denoted as* $\mathcal{U}_X$*):* $\forall j \in \mathcal{M}$, assign $\min\{N_j^{\max}, |\mathcal{N}_j(t)|\}$ connections to elements in set $\mathcal{N}_j(t)$ randomly.
3:   $\forall i \in \mathcal{N}$, update $D_i(t)$ as $\mathbb{1}\{(\max_{j \in \mathcal{M}_i(t)}\{\tau_{i,j}^{tx}(t) + \tau_{i,j}^{rc}(t)\} + \tau_i^{lc} + \varphi \cdot \sum_{j \in \mathcal{M}_i(t)} l_{i,j}(t) > \tau_d) \vee (\bar{e}_i(t) < \psi_i(t))\}$.
4:   For those mobile devices who satisfy $D_i(t) = 1$, update $\mathbf{I}_i(t)$ as $\mathbf{0}$.
5: **end for**
6: $\mathbf{I}^\star(t) \leftarrow \operatorname{argmin}_{\mathbf{I}^s(t) \in \vec{\mathcal{S}}_0(t)} G_{\mathcal{P}_2^{es}}(\mathbf{I}^s(t))$,
7: Initialize the hypothesis h_0.
8: $\mathcal{Q}_0(t) \leftarrow \varnothing$.
9: **for** $k = 1$ to K **do**
10:   *Construct the binary-labeled dataset:* For all $\mathbf{I}^s(t) \in \vec{\mathcal{S}}_{k-1}(t)$, $y^s(t) = \operatorname{sign}\{\gamma_k - G_{\mathcal{P}_2^{es}}(\mathbf{I}^s(t))\}$, $\mathcal{Q}_k(t) \triangleq \{(\mathbf{I}^1(t), y^1(t)), ..., (\mathbf{I}^{S_{k-1}}(t), y^{S_{k-1}}(t))\}$ where γ_k is the threshold for labeling.
11:   Obtain the hypothesis with a binary classification algorithm $\mathcal{L}(\cdot)$: $h_k \leftarrow \mathcal{L}(\mathcal{Q}_k(t))$.
12:   Initialize $\vec{\mathcal{S}}_k(t)$ as $\varnothing$.
13:   **for** $s = 1$ to S_k **do**
14:     *Sample with ε-greedy policy:*

$$\text{Get } \mathbf{I}^s(t) \text{ from} \begin{cases} \mathcal{H}_{h_k}, & \text{with probability } \varepsilon \\ \mathcal{U}_X, & \text{with probability } 1 - \varepsilon, \end{cases}$$

  where $\mathcal{H}_{h_k}$ is the distribution transformation of hypothesis h_k.
15:     $\vec{\mathcal{S}}_k(t) \leftarrow \vec{\mathcal{S}}_k(t) \cup \{\mathbf{I}_s(t)\}$.
16:   **end for**
17:   $\mathbf{I}^\star(t) \leftarrow \operatorname{argmin}_{\mathbf{I}^s(t) \in \vec{\mathcal{S}}_k(t) \cup \{\mathbf{I}^\star(t)\}} G_{\mathcal{P}_2^{es}}(\mathbf{I}^s(t))$.
18: **end for**
19: **return** $\mathbf{I}^\star(t)$.

7.3.5.2   Impacts of the Number of Mobile Devices N

The data fluctuation over different N is interesting. As shown in Fig. 7.17b, when N increases from 60 to 80, the average cost increases. But when N increases from 80 to 120, the average cost decreases. while N increases from 120 to 140, the average cost increases again. The total costs acquired by CCO algorithm is not monotonic

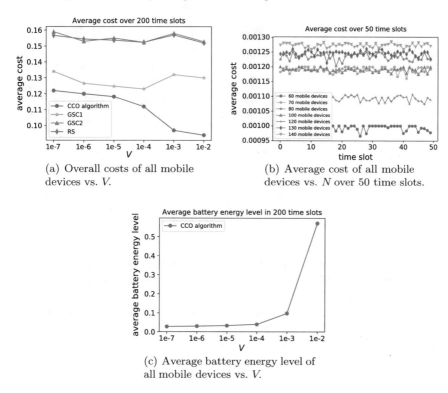

(a) Overall costs of all mobile devices vs. V.

(b) Average cost of all mobile devices vs. N over 50 time slots.

(c) Average battery energy level of all mobile devices vs. V.

Fig. 7.17 Impacts of important parameters

with N. Because of the trade-off between more intense competition on bandwidth and more efficient utilization of computing resources among mobile devices, we can observe these results.

7.4   Computing Offloading with Cooperative Edge Networks

Considering an edge computing network in one specific area with multiple IoT devices and multiple edge servers as shown in Fig. 7.18, we denote the index set of IoT devices by $\mathcal{N} \triangleq \{1, 2, \ldots, N\}$ and the index set of edge servers by $\mathcal{M} \triangleq \{1, 2, \ldots, M\}$. We apply a strategy to make classification of all edge servers in the specific region into clusters by both positions of edge servers and the devices' density in this area. By decentralizing resources and computing power of servers, it can efficiently improve the global Quality Of Service (QoS) [8] . Heavy computation task could be executed locally at IoT devices, otherwise offloaded to its nearest edge server [13]. The integrity of computation tasks can be acquired by offloading

Fig. 7.18 An edge
computing system with four
cooperative networks

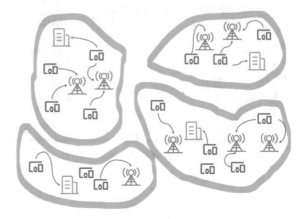

to an edge server instead of a remote cloud center because the probability of transmission failure is greatly reduced [16]. Above all, the system also needs to decide
whether to migrate its task to another edge server in their cooperative network for
better scheduling on computational resources or to execute it at the nearest edge
server without task migration. This strategic scheduling is made for obtaining the
minimized latency, i.e., the best QoE for users.

7.4.1   Edge Servers in Cooperative Networks

We classify the whole network's edge servers into k cooperative networks (clusters)
and use formulation of $A_{m,k} = 1, m \in \mathcal{M}, k \in \mathcal{K}$ to classify that the mth edge server
is attached to the kth cooperative network, otherwise 0. Thus, the matrix $\mathbf{A}$ is naturally
defined to show the inclusion relationships of edge servers and cooperative networks.

$$\mathbf{A} \triangleq \begin{pmatrix} A_{1,1} & A_{1,2} & \cdots & A_{1,K} \\ A_{2,1} & A_{2,2} & \cdots & A_{2,K} \\ \vdots & \vdots & \ddots & \vdots \\ A_{M,1} & A_{M,2} & \cdots & A_{M,K} \end{pmatrix}. \tag{7.25}$$

As we have discussed above, the overlapping of cooperative networks is disabled
and ignored. Therefore, each edge server only belongs to one specific cooperative
network, i.e., the following constraint need be satisfied:

$$\sum_{k \in \mathcal{K}} A_{j,k} = 1, j \in \mathcal{M}. \tag{7.26}$$

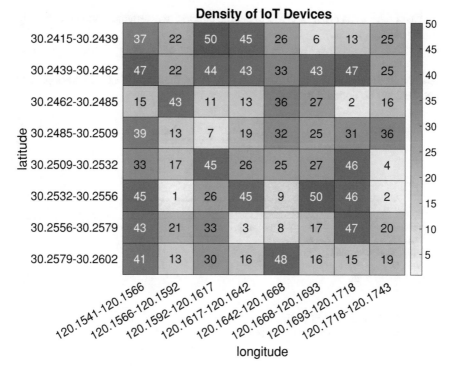

Fig. 7.19 Density of IoT Devices

we define

$$\mathcal{M}_k \triangleq \{j \in \mathcal{M} | A_{j,k} = 1\}, k \in \mathcal{K} \tag{7.27}$$

as the set of edge servers belonging to the kth cooperative network. Denote $\mathbf{z}_1, \mathbf{z}_2$ as two positions in the area of Fig. 7.19. As we have mentioned before, the value of $\Delta_{\mathbf{z}_1, \mathbf{z}_2}$ can be calculated by the formula

$$\Delta_{\mathbf{z}_1, \mathbf{z}_2} = \int_{l_{\mathbf{z}_1, \mathbf{z}_2}} f(\mathbf{z}_1, \mathbf{z}_2)dx, \tag{7.28}$$

where $l_{\mathbf{z}_1, \mathbf{z}_2}$ denotes the segment(path) between these two points, and $f(\mathbf{z}_1, \mathbf{z}_2)$ denotes the probability density function along $l_{\mathbf{z}_1, \mathbf{z}_2}$. Apparently, the bigger the devices' density, the greater the weight on the line segment of those two points.

Based on *k-means* algorithm, we first randomly initialize centroids of K cooperative networks. The centroid of the kth cooperative network is denoted as μ_k, which is a bivector representing one position on the chosen two-dimensional region. We define $\mathcal{K} \triangleq \{\bar{\ }_1, \bar{\ }_2, \ldots, \bar{\ }_K\}$ as the set of all the centroids of cooperative networks in the whole edge network.

We denote ϱ_j as the index of the specific cooperative network which the jth edge server belongs to, i.e.,

$$\varrho_j \triangleq \arg\min_{k \in \mathcal{K}} \|\mathbf{z}_j - \bar{}_k\|^2, \tag{7.29}$$

where $\mathbf{z}_j$ is the position of the jth edge server. Thus, the centroid of the kth cooperative network can be updated by

$$\mu_k \triangleq \frac{\sum_{j=1}^M \mathbb{I}\{\varrho_j = k\} \cdot \Delta_{\mathbf{z}_j, \mu_k}}{\sum_{j=1}^M \mathbb{I}\{\varrho_j = k\}}. \tag{7.30}$$

Algorithm 4 Cooperative Networks Formulation (CNF)

1: Input positions of edge servers: $\mathbf{z}_1, \mathbf{z}_2, \cdots, \mathbf{z}_M$ and IoT devices' density function: $\forall \mathbf{z}_m, \mathbf{z}_n, \Xi_{\mathbf{z}_m, \mathbf{z}_n} = f(\mathbf{z}_m, \mathbf{z}_n)$
2: Initialize K centroids $\bar{}_1, \bar{}_2, \cdots, \bar{}_K$
3: $\mathbf{A} \leftarrow \mathbf{O}$
4: **for** $k = 1$ to K **do**
5:     **repeat**
6:         $\forall j \in \mathcal{M}$, calculate ϱ_j by (7.29)
7:         $\forall k \in \mathcal{K}$, update μ_k by (7.30)
8:     **until** $\forall j \in \mathcal{M}$, ϱ_j remains unchanged
9: **end for**
10: $\forall j \in \mathcal{M}$, set $A_{j, \varrho_j} \leftarrow 1$
11: **return A**

The accuracy of our offloading strategy lies in the statistical long-term information on the density of users' devices in this area. We simplify the division of this area into grids and the distribution density of a bunch of users' devices in each grid is randomly generated for the convenience of calculation. Then, by combining with IoT devices' density (in a grid) and the actual geographic distance between them, accurate collaboration spaces are generated. The size of the grid, as an important parameter, can significantly affect the efficiency of the proposed algorithm.

7.4.2 Local and Remote Execution with Task Relocation Model

7.4.2.1 Local Execution Model

We define $\mathbf{D} = \{D_1, D_2, D_3, \ldots D_N\}^1$ as the vector consisting of random variables for input size of tasks generated by IoT devices [14]. Besides, we assume that $\forall i \in \mathcal{N}$, D_i is a random variable follows the independent and identically distributed (i.i.d.)

---

[1]Notice that d_i is a concrete realization of random variable D_i.

rule. We define L_i^l as the number of CPU cycles to process one bit of computation task in users' service at the ith IoT device locally comparing with offloading task on edge server, thus the local execution latency can be calculated by

$$c_i^{\text{local}} = \sum_{w=1}^{W_i} \frac{1}{f_i^w}, \; W_i = L_i^r \cdot d_i, \, i \in \mathcal{N}, \quad (7.31)$$

where f_i^w represents the frequency of the wth CPU cycle for the ith IoT device. However, it should satisfy the limit frequency constant:

$$0 < f_i^w \leq f_i^{\text{max}}, \, i \in \mathcal{N}, \quad (7.32)$$

where f_i^w is the CPU frequency for the wth CPU cycle [3] of the ith IoT device, which can be performed by DVFS techniques.

We defined I_i as the indicator to represent the task of the ith IoT device whether it is executed locally, i.e.,

$$I_i \in \{0, 1\}, \, i \in \mathcal{N}. \quad (7.33)$$

$I_i = 1$ if local execution is chosen, otherwise $I_i = 0$.

7.4.2.2 Remote Execution Model

When the input of computation task is transmitted from the ith IoT device to the jth edge server, the transmission power p_{ij} should satisfy the maximum transmission power constraint:

$$0 \leq p_{ij} \leq p_i^{\text{max}}, \, i \in \mathcal{N}, \, j \in \mathcal{M}. \quad (7.34)$$

Denote the small-scale fading channel power gain from the ith to the jth edge server as ζ_{ij}, which is assumed to be exponentially distributed with a given unit mean. According to communication theory [6], the corresponding channel power gain can be acquired by $h_{ij} = \zeta_{ij} \cdot g_0 \cdot (\frac{d_0}{d_{ij}})^\phi$, where d_0 represents the reference distance, d_{ij} represents the geographic distance between the ith IoT device and the jth edge server, ϕ is the pass-loss exponent, g_0 is the pass-loss constant and δ_j is the noise power at the edge server j. According to Shannon-Hartley formula [6], we can obtain the achievable rate Λ_{ij} by

$$\Lambda_{ij} = \alpha_{ij} \cdot \omega_j \cdot \log_2 \left(1 + \frac{h_{ij} \cdot p_{ij}}{\delta_j} \right), \, i \in \mathcal{N}, \, j \in \mathcal{M}. \quad (7.35)$$

where ω_j is the bandwidth of the jth edge server and α_{ij} is the proportion of bandwidth allocated for the corresponding IoT device, i.e., each connected IoT device is assigned to one sub-band with $\alpha_{ij} \cdot \omega_j$ MHz. The bandwidth allocation ratio should satisfy

$$0 < \alpha_{ij} \leq 1, i \in \mathcal{N}, j \in \mathcal{M} \tag{7.36}$$

and

$$\sum_{i \in \mathcal{N}} \alpha_{ij} \leq 1, i \in \mathcal{N}, j \in \mathcal{M}. \tag{7.37}$$

We denote the location of the ith IoT device and the jth edge server as

$$\mathbf{u}_i = (x_{u_i}, y_{u_i})^\top, \mathbf{s}_j = (x_{s_j}, y_{s_j})^\top, i \in \mathcal{N}, j \in \mathcal{M}, \tag{7.38}$$

respectively. Therefore, the distance between the ith IoT device and the jth edge server, denoted as d_{ij}, which has been mentioned before, is calculated by

$$d_{ij} = \sqrt{(x_{u_i} - x_{s_j})^2 + (y_{u_i} - y_{s_j})^2}, i \in \mathcal{N}, j \in \mathcal{M}. \tag{7.39}$$

As we have mentioned above, the computation task of the ith IoT device should be executed remotely to the nearest server for offloading, if it is decided to be offloaded.[2] Our system could identify this specific server by $j_i = \arg\min_{j' \in \mathcal{M}} \|\mathbf{u}_i - \mathbf{s}_{j'}\|_2$. Then the latency of transmission can be calculated by

$$c_{i,j}^{\text{tx}} = \frac{d_{ij}}{\Lambda_{ij}}, i \in \mathcal{N}, j \in \mathcal{M}. \tag{7.40}$$

We denote O_{ij} as the indicator to represent whether the task from the ith IoT device is going to be offloaded to the jth edge server, i.e.,

$$O_{ij} \in \{0, 1\}, i \in \mathcal{N}, j \in \mathcal{M}. \tag{7.41}$$

$O_{ij} = 1$ if task of the ith IoT device offloading to the jth edge server, otherwise 0. We can acquired that, $O_{ij} = 1$ if and only if $I_i = 1$ and $j = \arg\min_{j' \in \mathcal{M}} \|\mathbf{u}_i - \mathbf{s}_{j'}\|_2$. We define the set of all IoT devices which offload tasks to the jth edge server as

$$\mathcal{N}_j \triangleq \{i \in \mathcal{N} | O_{ij} = 1\}, j \in \mathcal{M}. \tag{7.42}$$

Each offloaded task can only be assigned to one edge server, thus

$$\sum_{j \in \mathcal{M}} O_{ij} = 1, i \in \mathcal{N}. \tag{7.43}$$

The decision for each IoT device is binary representing every computation task either be executed locally, or executed remotely at the edge server. Therefore we have

---

[2] According to [6], the shorter the geometric distance between the edge server and the IoT device, the stronger the signal of the established link between them. Therefore, the IoT device always offloads the task to the nearest edge server.

$$I_i = 1 - \sum_{j \in \mathcal{M}} O_{ij}, i \in \mathcal{N}. \tag{7.44}$$

In addition to the transmission latency, remote execution will also produce delay time. We can calculate the latency of remote execution at the jth edge server as:

$$c_{ij}^{\text{server}} = \sum_{w=1}^{W} \frac{1}{f_{j,i}^{w}}, W_j = L_j^r \cdot d_i, i \in \mathcal{N}, j \in \mathcal{M}, \tag{7.45}$$

where $f_{j,i}^{w}$ is the CPU cycle frequency of the wth CPU cycle for executing one bit of data at the jth edge server, which should satisfy

$$0 < f_{j,i}^{w} \le f_j^{\max}, j \in \mathcal{M}. \tag{7.46}$$

Besides, L_j^r is the number of CPU cycles for processing one bit of data at the jth edge server.

Define the relocation vector for the ith IoT device as $\mathbf{R}_i^{k_j}$, i.e.,

$$\begin{aligned} \mathbf{R}_i^{k_j} &= (R_{i,1}^{k_j}, R_{i,2}^{k_j}, \ldots, R_{i,|\mathcal{M}_{k_j}|}^{k_j}), \\ R_{ij}^{k_j} &\in \{0, 1\}, i \in \mathcal{N}_j, j \in \mathcal{M}_{k_j}. \end{aligned} \tag{7.47}$$

Apparently, if $R_{ij}^{k_j} = 1$, then no task relocation happens. Therefore, we can generate the following constraint[3]:

$$\sum_{j' \in \mathcal{M}_{k_j}} R_{ij'}^{k_j} = O_{ij}, i \in \mathcal{N}_j. \tag{7.48}$$

Task relocation will produce delay time, too. We can calculate the latency by

$$c_{ijj'}^{\text{reloc}} = \frac{d_i}{\Gamma_{j,j'}}, i \in \mathcal{N}_j, j, j' \in \mathcal{M}_{k_j}, \tag{7.49}$$

where $\Gamma_{j,j'}$ represents the X2 transmission rate from the jth server to the j'th server by using X2 link, which has a positive correlation with the transmission bandwidth.

Each edge server has maximum throughput limitation on executing the offloaded tasks, which can be defined as

$$\sum_{j \in \mathcal{M}_{k_{j'}}} \sum_{i \in \mathcal{N}_j} R_{ij}^{k_{j'}} \cdot d_i \le C_{j'}, j, j' \in \mathcal{M}_{k_{j'}}, k_{j'} \in \mathcal{K}. \tag{7.50}$$

---

[3] Actually, constraint (7.48) is still satisfied for $i \in \mathcal{N}_j^{\text{latent}}$, which is a set defined in subsection IV. B.

7.4.3 Latency Minimization with Uncertain of Users' Requests

All the execution and transmission latency are taken as the metrics to evaluate the strategy. Therefore, the optimization problem can be formulated to minimize the overall latency:

$$\mathcal{P}_1: \quad \min_{\Theta} \quad c^{\text{total}} = \sum_{i \in \mathcal{N}} (I_i \cdot c_i^{\text{local}} + \sum_{j \in \mathcal{M}} O_{ij} \cdot c_{i,j}^{\text{tx}}$$

$$+ \sum_{j \in \mathcal{M}} O_{ij} \cdot \sum_{j' \in \mathcal{M}_{k_j}} R_{ij'}^{k_j} \cdot c_{ijj'}^{\text{reloc}})$$

$$+ \sum_{j \in \mathcal{M}} \sum_{i \in \mathcal{N}} \sum_{j' \in \mathcal{M}_{k_j}} R_{ij'}^{k_j} \cdot c_{ij}^{\text{server}}$$

$$s.t. \quad (26), (32), (33), (34), (36), (37), (41),$$
$$(43), (44), (46), (47), (48), (50).$$

In problem $\mathcal{P}_1$, Θ is the decision vector, which consists of integer variables I_i, O_{ij}, $R_{ij'}^{k_j}$ and real variables p_{ij}, f_{ij}^w, $f_{ji}^{w'}$, $i \in \mathcal{N}$, $j \in \mathcal{M}$, $w \in \{1, \ldots, W_i\}$, $w' \in \{1, ldots, W_j\}$.

Lemma 1 *If the ith IoT device's task is executed locally, then the minimum value of c_i^{local} (denoted as $c_i^{\text{local}\star}$) is $\frac{L_i^l \cdot d_i}{f_i^{\max}}$.*

Proof ccording to basic inequality, we have $\frac{1}{\sum_{w=1}^{L_i^l \cdot d_i} \frac{1}{f_i^w}} \leq \sqrt{\prod_{w=1}^{L_i^l \cdot d_i} f_i^w} \leq \sqrt{\prod_{w=1}^{L_i^l \cdot d_i} f_i^{\max}}$,

then the minimum value can be obtained, if and only if $f_i^1 = f_i^2 = \cdots = f_i^W = f_i^{\max}$. This can be realized by DVFS technologies. $\square$

We apply the static bandwidth allocation strategy in our strategy. The bandwidth resource of the jth edge server is equally divided into several sub-bands, and every potential connected IoT device occupies one sub-band. Define the set of IoT devices whose tasks are possible to be offloaded to the jth edge server as $\mathcal{N}_j^{\text{latent}}$,[4] which can be obtained by

$$\mathcal{N}_j^{\text{latent}} = \{i \in \mathcal{N} | \arg \min_{j' \in \mathcal{M}} \|\mathbf{u}_i - \mathbf{s}_{j'}\|_2 = j\}. \tag{7.51}$$

Thus, we can obtain that

$$\alpha_{ij}^{\star} = 1/|\mathcal{N}_j^{\text{latent}}|, i \in \mathcal{N}_j^{\text{latent}}. \tag{7.52}$$

---

[4]Notice that $\mathcal{N}_j^{\text{latent}}$ is not the same with $\mathcal{N}_j$.

If $\mathcal{N}_j^{\text{latent}}$ is replaced by $\mathcal{N}_j$, then the problem formulated will be even harder to handle. Because in this way, the offloading decision is related to the bandwidth allocation, thus each IoT device decision cannot be processed individually. Besides, if we adopt the dynamic bandwidth allocation strategy for connected IoT devices, the problem formulated will become a mixed integer programming problem, which will be in-depth studied in future work.

As $\alpha_{ij}^{\star}$ can be obtained, we can calculate $c_{ij}^{\text{tx}\star}$ easily. $c_{ij}^{\text{server}\star}$ and $c_{ij}^{\text{reloc}\star}$ can be obtained in the same way.

Therefore, a new problem $\mathcal{P}_2$ can be formulated from $\mathcal{P}_1$:

$$
\mathcal{P}_2: \quad \min_{\Theta'} \quad c^{\text{total}\star} \triangleq \sum_{i \in \mathcal{N}} \Bigg(I_i \cdot c_i^{\text{local}\star} + \sum_{j \in \mathcal{M}_k} O_{ij} \cdot c_{ij}^{\text{tx}\star}
$$
$$
+ \sum_{j \in \mathcal{M}_k} \sum_{j' \in \mathcal{M}_{k_j} \backslash \{j\}} R_{ij'}^{kj} \cdot c_{ijj'}^{\text{reloc}\star}
$$
$$
+ \sum_{j \in \mathcal{M}_k} \sum_{j' \in \mathcal{M}_k} R_{ij'}^{kj} \cdot c_{ij}^{\text{server}\star} \Bigg)
$$

$$
s.t. \quad (26), (33), (41), (43), (44), (47), (48), (50).
$$

In problem $\mathcal{P}_2$, Θ' is the new decision vector consisting of $I_i, O_{ij}, R_{ij'}^{kj}, i \in \mathcal{N}, j \in \mathcal{M}$.

As we have mentioned before, the input size of the computation task of each IoT device is viewed as an uncertain random variable. It's reasonable to assume that the distribution of input size of task can be estimated from historical data, therefore we can regard the optimization target of $\mathcal{P}_2$ as expected value of $c^{\text{total}\star}$ under probability distribution P, which can be denoted as $\mathbb{E}_P[C(\Theta', \mathbf{D})]$. The decision vector Θ' can be chosen from a finite set $\mathcal{Q} \triangleq \{0, 1\}^{N+N \times M + M \times M}$. Therefore, the new target can be formulated as

$$
\min_{\Theta' \in \mathcal{Q}} \mathbb{E}_P[C(\Theta', \mathbf{D})]. \tag{7.53}
$$

Thus, the new problem $\mathcal{P}_3$ has the format of

$$
\mathcal{P}_3: \quad \min_{\Theta' \in \mathcal{Q}} \quad \mathbb{E}_P[C(\Theta', \mathbf{D})] \triangleq \sum_{i \in \mathcal{N}} \Bigg(I_i \cdot \mathbb{E}_P[c_i^{\text{local}\star}]
$$
$$
+ \sum_{j \in \mathcal{M}_k} O_{ij} \cdot \mathbb{E}_P[c_{ij}^{\text{tx}\star}]
$$
$$
+ \sum_{j \in \mathcal{M}_k} \sum_{j' \in \mathcal{M}_{k_j} \backslash \{j\}} R_{ij'}^{kj} \cdot \mathbb{E}_P[c_{ijj'}^{\text{reloc}\star}]
$$
$$
+ \sum_{j \in \mathcal{M}_k} \sum_{j' \in \mathcal{M}_k} R_{ij'}^{kj} \cdot \mathbb{E}_P[c_{ij}^{\text{server}\star}] \Bigg)
$$

$$
s.t. \quad (26), (33), (41), (43), (44), (47), (48), (50).
$$

where $\mathbb{E}_P[c_{ij}^{\text{local}\star}] = \frac{L_i^l \, \mathbb{E}_P[d_i]}{f_i^{\max}}$. $\mathbb{E}_P[c_{ij}^{\text{tx}\star}]$, $\mathbb{E}_P[c_{ijj'}^{\text{reloc}\star}]$ and $\mathbb{E}_P[c_{ij}^{\text{server}\star}]$ can be obtained in the same way.

Aiming at the average total cost of latency of all IoT devices, by Monte Carlo Sampling, with support from *the Law of Large Numbers* [4], when Θ' is fixed, the value of target can converge with probability one to the expectation $\mathbb{E}_P[C(\Theta', \mathbf{D})]$.

To solve this stochastic discrete optimization problem, the Sample Average Approximation (SAA) method can be utilized to form the target function

$$\min_{\Theta' \in Q} \hat{c}_{N'}^{\text{total}}(\Theta') \triangleq \frac{1}{N'} \sum_{q=1}^{N'} C(\Theta', \mathbf{D}^q), \qquad (7.54)$$

where N' is the number of sampling times (also called scenarios).

7.4.4   Joint Computation Offloading and Resource Management Optimization Algorithm

---

Algorithm 5 Joint Computation Offloading and Resource Management (JCORM)

1: Generate L independent solutions
2: Set up a gap tolerance ϵ
3: **for** $l = 1$ to L in parallel **do**
4:   Generate S independent scenarios
5:   Obtain the minimum value of $\hat{C}_S^l(\hat{\theta}_S^l)$ with the form of $\frac{1}{S} \sum_{l \in S} C(\hat{\theta}_S^l, \mathbf{D}^l)$ by solving problem $\mathcal{P}_2$
6:   Record the optimal solution variable $\hat{\theta}_S^l$ and optimal value $\hat{v}_S^l$
7: **end for**
8: Evaluate L independent solutions with $S' \gg S$ by scenarios $\hat{C}_{S'}(\hat{\theta}) = \frac{1}{S'} \sum_{q \in S'} C(\hat{\theta}, \mathbf{D}^q)$
9: Calculate the average value $\bar{v}_S^l = \frac{1}{L} \sum_{l=1}^{L} \hat{v}_S^l$
10: **if** the gap $\hat{C}_{S'}(\hat{\theta}_S^l) - \bar{v}_S^l < \epsilon$ **then**
11:   Choose the best solution $\hat{\theta}_S^{l\star}$ among all independent candidates
12: **else**
13:   Increase S (for drill) and S' (for evaluation), then go back to Step 2
14: **end if**
15: **return** the best solution $\hat{\theta}_S^{l\star}$

We denote $\mathcal{D}_i = [d_i^1, d_i^2, \ldots, d_i^S]$ as observations of historical scenarios (size S) for the input size of computation task generated on the ith IoT device under distribution P. We use the long-term task volume historical statistics of the device to construct the sample values in the SAA algorithm [2]. The edge servers of each area form a cooperative network by dividing the edge servers of the entire area into a unified area. The key advantage of this algorithm is that it calculates the optimization decision in one area greatly reduced, so that Algorithm 2 performs more efficiently in a relatively small area.

In our algorithm, we apply the SAA-based method (or Monte Carlo simulation-based) approach to obtain a reliable estimation of the expected discrete optimization problem. We denote $\hat{C}_S^l$ as the approximation of $C(\Theta', \mathbf{D})$ on the lth sample with S scenarios. In step 3 of Algorithm 5, we acquire S scenarios in order to obtain each sample value and calculate a feasible solution $\hat{\theta}_S^l$.[5] Setting up a precision for increasing S and S' if needed, by calculating the gap between $\hat{C}_{S'}^l(\hat{\theta}_S^l, \mathbf{D})$ and $\bar{v}_S^l$, enable our algorithm to converge with a reasonable rate [1, 10].

7.4.5 Evaluation

In the simulation, 1730 IoT devices are randomly located in the chosen area while the location of China Mobile base stations is extracted from real data. By the CNF algorithm, we divide 400 edge servers into 64 cooperative networks, as shown in Fig. 7.20. We assumed each edge server is integrated into one of the base stations. We set $M = 400$, $N = 1730$ and $K = 64$ in our simulation.

Assume the size of the task in each IoT device in the network is uniformly distributed with a mean of 16.5 Mb. Besides, the small-scale fading channel power gains are exponentially distributed with mean $g_0 d^{-4}$, where $g_0 = -40$ dB is the path-

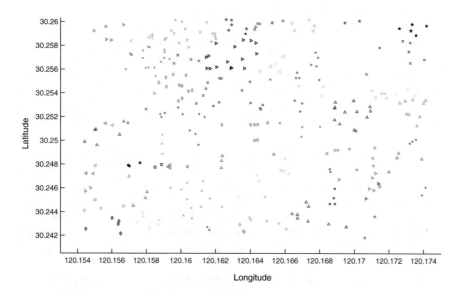

Fig. 7.20 64 cooperative networks with 400 edge servers

---

[5] θ represents approximate solution of exact solution Θ' under SAA method.

Fig. 7.21 Global latency obtained by CNF and GNF, respectively

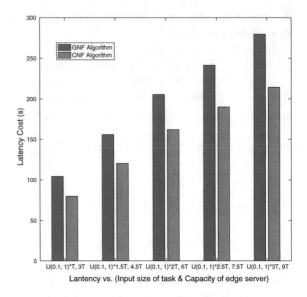

loss constant. $\forall i \in \mathcal{N}, j \in \mathcal{M}$ we set $\omega = 200\,\text{MHz}$, $\omega_r = 6\,\text{GHz}$, $\delta = 10^{-13}\,\text{W}$, $p_i^{\max} = 1.5\,\text{W}$, device CPU frequency $f_i^{\max} = 1\,\text{GHz}$, $f_j^{\max} = 3\,\text{GHz}$, $L_i = 10$, $L_j = 0.02$, $C_j = 90\,\text{Mb}$.

The input size of computation tasks generated by IoT devices follows the uniform distribution of $U(0.1, 1) \cdot T$, where $T = 3e7$bits.

We set a benchmark called **G**rids **N**etwork **F**ormulation (GNF) algorithm for comparison with CNF algorithm. The area is evenly divided into rectangular grids, and each grid is a network consisting of edge servers located by the GNF algorithm. We have evaluated on dividing the edge servers into 64 networks by CNF and GNF, respectively. Figure. 7.21 shows that although the input size of the task of each device becomes larger with a different C_j ($C_j \in \{3T, 4.5T, 6T, 7.5T, 9T\}$), the cost of the whole system obtained by the CNF algorithm is still smaller than GNF's (nearly 20%).

Simulation results demonstrated in Figs. 7.22 and 7.23 are under the same condition. Figure 7.22 verifies that the average latency of each IoT device acquired by CNF is smaller than GNF's. Figure 7.23 verifies that the variance of each IoT device's latency is much smaller under CNF. Apparently, IoT devices in each cooperative network can obtain much better service with a lower latency time for response. If the edge servers are divided by the GNF algorithm simply according to a geographical area, the important factor, i.e., the distribution of IoT devices is completely ignored comparing our proposed algorithm.

As we have discussed above, each cooperative network is an autonomous domain and capable of independently decision making. Evaluation results demonstrated in Figs. 7.24 and 7.25 is based on the following setting: From 64 cooperative networks, we randomly choose one (denoted as k) with 2 edge servers (denote as j, j',

Fig. 7.22 Average latency versus (Input size of task and capacity of edge server) under CNF and GNF, respectively

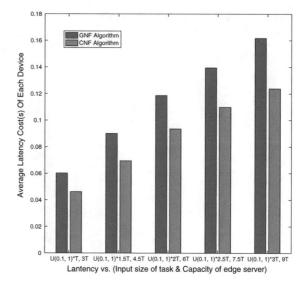

Fig. 7.23 Variance of latency under CNF and GNF, respectively

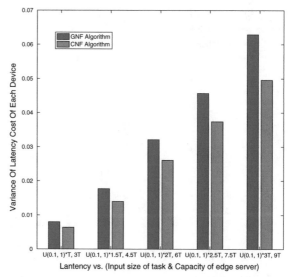

respectively). Besides, $|\mathcal{N}_j^{\text{latent}} \cap \mathcal{N}_{j'}^{\text{latent}}| = 11$. In addition, we construct a benchmark called **SAA**-based **G**reedy (SÁAG) algorithm for comparison with JCORM.

Based on the above setting, 5 controlled experiments on sample size (i.e., the number of independent solutions) of 11 IoT devices are done. Each experiment generating L independent solutions, each of which has scenarios of the same size (S and S' both). Figure. 7.24 shows that JCORM can achieve smaller latency than SAAG can do.

Fig. 7.24 Latency under different sample size under SAAG and JCORM, respectively

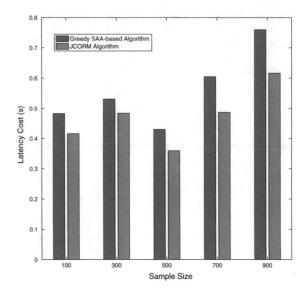

Fig. 7.25 Number of `counter`-requesting solutions under different sample sizes

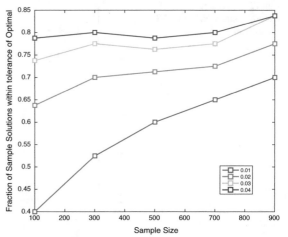

7.5   Conclusion

Related to the issues about Computing offloading in mobile cloud computing, we focus on the topics including latency of service execution and energy consumption of offloading. First, we target the problem of computation offloading for mobile services workflows, and propose mobility- enabled and fault-tolerance offloading system for making computation offloading strategies for service workflows in a mobile cloud computing environment. Based on the offloading framework, we propose an offloading algorithm based on the genetic algorithm. The experimental results show that our approach could achieve near-optimal solutions with almost near-linear algorithmic complexity about the problem size. Its work goes beyond existing approaches by considering computation offloading for service workflows where multiple services are composed together in a specific business process, while others mainly focus on single services.

Second, We designed a centralized cross-edge computation offloading framework for partitionable applications with edge site coordination costs considered. The framework can dynamically scale edge site-selection by leveraging various elastic resources. We proposed an algorithm based on the Lyapunov optimization techniques, which can obtain asymptotical optimality with a battery capacity of mobile devices stabilizing around a positive constant. Specifically, the SES algorithm is proposed with a polynomial improvement over the uniform search on the feasible solution space. The experimental results based on real-world datasets show that our algorithm outperforms three baseline algorithms. In the future, we will study typical real-world application scenarios. Besides, how to design a *distributed* cross-edge framework that lifts the heavy computation burden of MNO will be our research emphasis.

Third, we study a computation offloading strategy based on the density of IoT devices. We first apply the CNF algorithm to divide edge servers into cooperative networks, evaluating that the proposed algorithm on network division can obtain smaller global cost and variance of latency. Then We formulate a stochastic integer programming problem and propose the SAA-based JCORM algorithm to solve it, which is significantly outperforms the greedy algorithm method. Notice that the proposed algorithm is suitable for heterogeneous networks. There are several aspects we need to focus on in the future. Firstly, energy consumption for executing and transmission should be jointly considered with the overall cost of latency. Secondly, it's significant to provide an optimal offloading strategy under the premise of maintaining the stability of the time domain system. Secondly, people need to dig further on how to construct a big data platform on formed cooperative networks in practice. In our future work, grid-division will be replaced by dot density. Every small- area cooperative network only serves the devices covered by it, which greatly improves the local efficiency, and also meets the characteristics of the edge property. In our cooperative network, IoT device does not need to directly connect to the cloud center with intolerable latency or an edge server with a relatively long physical distance. The excellent characteristic above is consistent with the edge server's features for the sake of service subscribers.

At last, the offloading techniques solve the problem of migrating tasks from users' device to nearby edge servers which need heavy computation, but there are challenges that resource allocation for the selected service requests according to the available resources of a mobile device and the requirements of the tasks to be met [17]. For example, if the remaining energy of a mobile device is high and its available network bandwidth is low, it would be preferable to accept computation-intensive service requests rather than communication-intensive service requests. We will discuss issues about mobile services provisioning in the next part. Combining with service provisioning strategy, techniques of offloading will make services less latency and energy notably in edge computing.

References

1. S. Ahmed, A. Shapiro, E. Shapiro, The sample average approximation method for stochastic programs with integer recourse (Submitted for publication, 2002), pp. 1–24
2. H. Badri, T. Bahreini, D. Grosu, K. Yang, A sample average approximation-based parallel algorithm for application placement in edge computing systems, in *2018 IEEE International Conference on Cloud Engineering (IC2E)* (IEEE, 2018), pp. 198–203
3. T.D. Burd, R.W. Brodersen, Processor design for portable systems. J. VLSI Signal Process. Syst. Signal Image Video Technol. **13**(2–3), 203–221 (1996)
4. G. Casella, R.L. Berger, *Statistical Inference*, vol. 2 (Duxbury Pacific Grove, CA, 2002)
5. M. Chen, Y. Hao, Task offloading for mobile edge computing in software defined ultra-dense network. IEEE J. Sel. Areas Commun. **36**(3), 587–597 (2018)
6. T.M. Cover, J.A. Thomas, *Elements of Information Theory* (Wiley, 2012)
7. S. Deng, L. Huang, J. Taheri, A.Y. Zomaya, Computation offloading for service workflow in mobile cloud computing. IEEE Trans. Parallel. Distrib. Syst. **26**(12), 3317–3329 (2014)
8. S. Deng, L. Huang, H. Wu, Z. Wu, Constraints-driven service composition in mobile cloud computing, in *2016 IEEE International Conference on Web Services (ICWS)* (IEEE, 2016), pp. 228–235
9. L. Jia, Z. Zhou, H. Jin, Optimizing the performance-cost tradeoff in cross-edge analytics, in *2018 IEEE International Conference on Ubiquitous Intelligence Computing* (2018), pp. 564–571. https://doi.org/10.1109/SmartWorld.2018.00118
10. A.J. Kleywegt, A. Shapiro, T. Homem-de Mello, The sample average approximation method for stochastic discrete optimization. SIAM J. Opt. **12**(2), 479–502 (2002)
11. P. Mach, Z. Becvar, Mobile edge computing: a survey on architecture and computation offloading. IEEE Commun. Surv. Tutor. **19**(3), 1628–1656 (2017)
12. M. Magno, D. Boyle, Wearable energy harvesting: from body to battery, in *2017 12th International Conference on Design Technology of Integrated Systems In Nanoscale Era (DTIS)* (2017), pp. 1–6. https://doi.org/10.1109/DTIS.2017.7930169
13. Y. Mao, C. You, J. Zhang, K. Huang, K.B. Letaief, A survey on mobile edge computing: the communication perspective. IEEE Commun. Surv. Tutor. **19**(4), 2322–2358 (2017a)
14. Y. Mao, J. Zhang, S. Song, K.B. Letaief, Stochastic joint radio and computational resource management for multi-user mobile-edge computing systems. IEEE Trans. Wirel. Commun. **16**(9), 5994–6009 (2017b)
15. M.J. Neely, Stochastic network optimization with application to communication and queueing systems. Synthesis Lect. Commun. Netw. **3**(1), 211 (2010)
16. W. Shi, S. Dustdar, The promise of edge computing. Computer **49**(5), 78–81 (2016)
17. H. Wu, S. Deng, W. Li, J. Yin, Q. Yang, Z. Wu, A.Y. Zomaya, Revenue-driven service provisioning for resource sharing in mobile cloud computing, in *International Conference on Service-Oriented Computing* (Springer, 2017), pp. 625–640
18. C. Zhang, H. Zhao, S. Deng, A density-based offloading strategy for iot devices in edge computing systems. IEEE Access **6**, 73520–73530 (2018)
19. H. Zhao, S. Deng, C. Zhang, W. Du, Q. He, J. Yin, A mobility-aware cross-edge computation offloading framework for partitionable applications, in *2019 IEEE International Conference on Web Services (ICWS)* (IEEE, 2019), pp. 193–200
20. H. Zhou, H. Wang, X. Li, V.C. Leung, A survey on mobile data offloading technologies. IEEE Access **6**, 5101–5111 (2018)

Chapter 8
Mobile Service Provisioning

Abstract Deploying and executing services in close proximity to mobile users can reduce service response time, Deploying and executing services in close proximity to mobile users can reduce service response time, relieve the communication load of the core network, and reduce network congestion to a significant extent. However, both edge servers and mobile servers are still resource limited. Therefore, reasonable and efficient mobile service provisioning strategies appear to be particularly important. This chapter focuses on mobile service provisioning problems in terms of both edge servers and mobile servers, and proposes solutions for service scheduling, service catching, request dispatching, etc. in mobile environment.

8.1 Introduction

By fully utilizing the increasing number of mobile devices and their ubiquitous presence, a new architecture for mobile cloud computing (MCC) has recently been proposed [1], where the neighboring mobile devices are brought together as a cohort for resource sharing. To better distinguish the MCC architectures, we refer to the new one that enables device-residing resource sharing as NMCC hereafter in this chapter. In contrast to the powerful remote cloud servers, when accommodating excessive service requests, mobile devices may not be able to satisfy all the requests since they have limited computing capabilities and resources. In addition, the remote cloud service providers are equipped with resource-rich devices to allow them to use sophisticated solutions, e.g. machine learning and heuristic methods for processing incoming requests. As these solutions are normally associated with high computational overhead, they cannot be simply applied to mobile devices. Therefore, a new service provisioning mechanism is required to solve these problems in NMCC.

Similarly, MEC also faces some challenges. One fatal challenge is service caching. As edge servers are resource limited, they can only deploy a limited number of services and the deployed services have a high effect on the performance of edge

© Zhejiang University Press and Springer Nature Singapore Pte Ltd. 2020
S. Deng et al., *Mobile Service Computing*, Advanced Topics in Science and Technology in China 58, https://doi.org/10.1007/978-981-15-5921-1_8

servers. For an incoming service request, if a corresponding service is deployed, it will be invoked directly, otherwise, the request will be sent to other servers, causing extra time consumption and losing the advantage of edge computing. Hence, the effectiveness of a service provision system is strongly correlated to the cached service set of edge servers: the more popular services the mobile edge server caches have, the more requests from wireless devices can be optimized.

Another problem for mobile edge computing is request dispatching. Unreasonable dispatching may lead to some edge servers overloaded while some others idle. When an edge server is accommodated with excessive service requests, the execution of some requests will be delayed, which leads to the response time of these requests be extended, even exceeds the response time by invoking the services on remote cloud servers. Moreover, in MEC systems, service consumers are generally moving, which increases the difficulty of request dispatching.

In this chapter, we address the three problems mentioned above, and propose three methods correspondingly for revenue-driven service provisioning in mobile cloud computing, composition-driven service provisioning in distributed edges, and request dispatching for edge provisioning systems in Sects. 8.2, 8.3 and 8.4, respectively.

8.2   Revenue-Driven Service Provisioning in Mobile Cloud Computing

To ensure the quality of service (QoS) on the resource-constrained mobile devices, a lightweight QoS-aware service-based framework needs to be provided to (1) determine whether to accept or reject an incoming service request and (2) perform scheduling and resource allocation for the selected service requests according to the available resources of a mobile device and the requirements of the tasks to be met. For example, if the remaining energy of a mobile device is high and its available network bandwidth is low, it would be preferable to accept computation intensive service requests rather than communication intensive service requests.

Apart from enabling a lightweight QoS-aware service-based framework in NMCC, it is not hard to see that the service provisioning in such systems strongly depends on the willingness to participate of the owners of mobile devices. To further ensure the quality of services, such NMCC systems need to employ a proper incentive mechanism to motivate the resource sharing of mobile devices [2]. Mobile service requesters can always encourage resource sharing by providing some rewards (e.g. discount, credit points, etc.) to service providers, so that the mobile device owners can decide the degree of their participation to gain the corresponding revenue. We also assume that all the mobile devices have the same objective to maximize the revenue of their providing services.

In this section, we study the issue of how to incentivize user participation for addressing the resource sharing in NMCC systems. To tackle the issue, we model it as a service provisioning and resource allocation problem of mobile devices, which is generally a constrained optimization problem. Using the task scheduling technique, we designed a lightweight approach called RESP (REvenue-driven Service Provision for mobile devices) for handling all the incoming requests with the objective of maximizing the revenue of the mobile devices.

8.2.1   System Models and Problem Formulation

8.2.1.1   Mobile Cloud Architecture

Our proposed framework is designed for NMCC systems, which are composed of multiple mobile devices and a trusted broker, as shown in Fig. 8.1. The broker serves as an intermediary responsible for discovery and communication among the neighbouring mobile devices. The mobile devices are within the coverage of the broker and each one of them could act as two roles within the system simultaneously. One role is service requester who needs to offload tasks to other nearby mobile devices. The other role is service provider who has idle resources and is willing to participate in resource sharing. All mobile devices directly send their service requests and/or service provisioning information to the broker. After receiving such information, the broker performs the matching between service requesters and providers by jointly considering the requirements of the requests and the functionality and QoS of

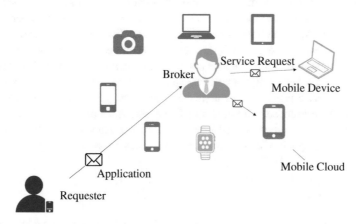

Fig. 8.1 Mobile cloud architecture

services. Once a service request is received by a mobile device, the device can choose to accept or decline it according to its current status in terms of resource utilization. If a mobile device accepts a service request, it will obtain the corresponding revenue by successfully completing the request. The result of the task will be sent back to the service requester through the broker. If a service request is declined, it will be returned to the broker for reallocation. Eventually, the service requester combines all the received results to obtain the final result.

8.2.1.2   Mobile Services and Requests

Definition 1 (*Mobile Device*) In NMCC systems, a mobile device is represented as a 3-tuple (S, A, I), where:

(1) $S = \{s_1, s_2, \ldots\}$, describing the set of services that a mobile device is able to provide;
(2) A is the function used to describe all the available resources a mobile device can share with other devices. At a given time t, the available resources are denoted as a set of 2-tuples $A_t = \{(r_i, n_i)\}_{i=1}^{m}$, where m is the total number of the types of the available resources that a mobile device can provide, and r_i and n_i denote the type and the amount of the ith kind of resource, respectively.
(3) I is a function used to describe the current idle resources of a mobile device. Idle resources refer to the resources that are available and not yet occupied by the service requests. At a given time t, it can be represented by $I_t = \{(r_i, n_i)\}_{i=1}^{m}$.

In our study, we assume that time is slotted, and the minimum time slot is a time unit. Similar to a number of existing works in MCC [3–6] and mobile computing [7], we consider a quasi-static scenario where the mobile devices remain unchanged for a period of time, which may change over consecutive periods in our work. Since most mobile devices are personal devices, the resource sharing should not disturb the predominant usage of the device owners. This hard requirement also means the available resources of mobile devices are varied over time. For example, if the owner of a mobile device wants to download some files, the available bandwidth used to share should be reduced. The amount of idle resources of a mobile device is an important factor for our proposed framework to perform service request selection and scheduling, which will be elaborated later. It can be calculated by

$$I(t, r) = A(t, r) - \sum_{q \in E_t} R_r(q) \tag{8.1}$$

where $I(t, r)$ denotes the amount of resource r that is idle at time t, $A(t, r)$ denotes the amount of resource r that is available at time t, $q \in E_t$ denotes the request executing on the mobile device at time t, and $R_r(q)$ denotes the amount of resource r that is occupied by the request q.

As mentioned before, mobile devices share their resources with others in the form of services. Mobile services can be the computing capabilities, resources, applications, data, sensors, etc. of mobile devices.

Definition 2 (*Mobile Service*) A mobile service is represented as a 5-tuple (d, R, v, F, QoS), where:

(1) d is the index of the mobile device in the NMCC systems;
(2) R describes the resources needed for the mobile device to execute the service, which can be denoted as a set of 2-tuples $R = \{(r_i, n_i)\}_{i=1}^m$, where m is the number of types of required resources, and r_i and n_i denote the type and number of the i-th kind of resource, respectively;
(3) v is the revenue the mobile device can obtain by successfully completing the service;
(4) F is the functional description of the service;
(5) QoS is a set of attributes of the requested services, including execution time t^e, which is the makespan needed for a mobile device to execute the service.

Functional description and QoS parameters are key criteria for the broker to select services for requests in the matching process. In this paper, we mainly consider the execution time of a requested service, since it plays an important role in the scheduling and resource allocation of mobile devices.

Definition 3 (*Service Request*) A service request is represented as a 4-tuple (s, d, t^a, t^d), where:

(1) s is the service that is requested;
(2) d is the index of the mobile device, to which the request is delivered;
(3) t^a is the arrival time of the request;
(4) t^d is the deadline for the request to be completed.

As introduced in Definition 3, a service request consists of information on a required service, service host and time. In the dynamic and versatile mobile environment, service requests are highly likely to express real-time requirements, so we introduce t^d to guarantee that services are completed in time. It is obvious that one request corresponds to one service. In the remaining parts of the paper, we will use the terms request and service interchangeably.

8.2.1.3   Problem Statement

Each mobile device manages an execution sequence, by which it conducts service execution, requests insertion, deletion, scheduling, and resource allocation.

Definition 4 (*Execution Sequence*) For a mobile device d, its execution sequence describes the services that will be performed on each time unit. It can be formulated as a time function $E_t = \{q_i\}_{i=1}^n$, expressing that during time unit t, a mobile device d will process n service requests including $q_1, q_2, \ldots, q_n$, simultaneously.

Fig. 8.2 Execution
sequence example

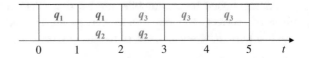

In an execution sequence, each time unit corresponds to a set of service requests
that will be processed during that time unit. For example, Fig. 8.2 shows an example
of an execution sequence, which describes the service execution of a mobile device
within the time period of 5 time units.

To describe the execution time of a service request, we let $^\bullet q$ denote the time
when request q starts to be processed and $q^\bullet$ denotes the time when q is completed.
Corresponding to a given execution sequence, there is a request sequence where the
requests involved are sorted by the time when they begin to be executed. We let $E(^*q)$
and $E(q^*)$ denote the request that is right ahead of and right behind q respectively.
Specifically, E_l denotes the last request of the execution sequence. For example,
according to Fig. 8.2, we have $E(q_1^*) = q_2$, $E(^*q_3) = q_2$ and $E_l = q_3$.

Definition 5 (*Revenue-Driven Service Provision*) Given a mobile device d, with its
available resources $A_t = \{(r_i, n_i)\}_{i=1}^m$ and idle resources $I_t = \{(r_j, n_j)\}_{j=1}^m$, and the
incoming service requests $q_1, q_2, \ldots q_n$, the revenue-driven service provision is to
select a set of service requests S from the request sequence and schedule them in the
execution sequence E to

$$\text{Maximize} \sum_{q \in S} v_q,$$

$$\text{s.t. } q^\bullet - {}^\bullet q = t_q^e, \quad \text{for each } q \in S \tag{8.2}$$

$$q^\bullet \le t_q^d, \quad \text{for each } q \in S \tag{8.3}$$

$$\forall t, \sum_{q \in E_t \cap S} R_q(r) \le A_t(r), \quad \text{for each } r \in A_t \tag{8.4}$$

It is reasonable to regard maximizing overall revenue of a mobile device as the
optimization objective for its service provisioning. Equation 8.2 implies that the
arrangement of each request is in accordance with its execution time. Equation 8.3
illustrates that each request should be completed before its deadline. Moreover, the
allocated resources should not exceed the available resources of the mobile device
at any time, as specified in Eq. 8.4. Therefore, revenue-driven service provision is
to select service requests to maximize the revenue of mobile devices, with given
dynamic resource constraints and diverse time constraints of requests.

8.2.2 RESP Approach

In this section, we present the RESP algorithm. It is a one-phase algorithm, which means that the service request selection, scheduling and resource allocation of a mobile device are made in an integrated manner. The symbols used in this paper are summarized in Table 8.1.

8.2.2.1 RESP Algorithm

Service requests are sent to mobile devices via the broker, so that mobile devices are required to deal with these requests sequentially. For each incoming request, a mobile device needs to make a decision on the following three criteria:

(1) The request can be completed before its deadline;
(2) The request can be allocated with sufficient resources;
(3) The total revenue is increased.

A service request can be accepted by a mobile device for its execution if and only if the above three criteria are all met. We first provide the definition of latest start time, which is a core element of our approach.

Table 8.1 Mathematical Notations

Symbol	Description
t_q^a	The arrival time of request q
t_q^e	The execution time of request q
t_q^d	The deadline of request q
t_q^s	The latest start time of request q
t_c	The current time
v_q	The reward for completing request q
$^\bullet q$	The time slot request q starts to process
$q^\bullet$	The time slot request q is completed
E_t	The requests in E with the same time t
$E(^*q)$	The request ahead of request q in E
$E(q^*)$	The request behind request q in e
$E(t^*)$	The request behind the time point t in e
E_l	The last request in the execution sequence E
A_t	The available resource set at time t
$A_t(r)$	The amount of the available resource r at time t
$I_t(r)$	The amount of the idle resource r at time t
R_q	The total required resources of request q
$R_q(r)$	The amount of a required resource r of request q

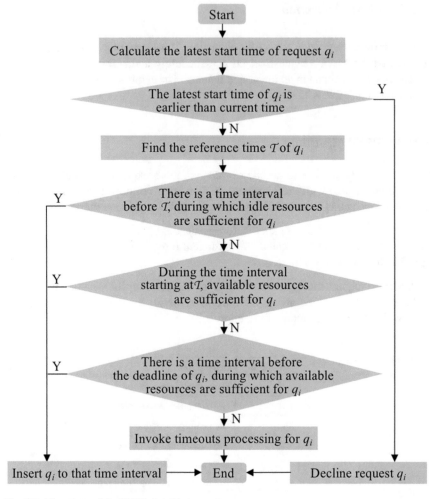

Fig. 8.3 Flowchart of the RESP algorithm

Definition 6 (*Latest Start Time*) For a given request q, its latest start time is the latest time for a mobile device to start performing it, so that it can be completed before its deadline. The latest start time can be calculated by

$$t_q^s = t_q^d - t_q^e \tag{8.5}$$

where t_q^d is the deadline of the request q, and t_q^e is the execution time of the request q.

Figure 8.3 shows the flowchart of the RESP algorithm. For a given request q_i, we first calculate its latest start time and use it to evaluate whether the request can be completed before its deadline on the device. If the latest start time of the service request is before the current time t_c, the request will not be able to complete in time and it is thus rejected. Otherwise, we schedule it with the accepted but not yet started requests located in the execution sequence E. All the requests are sorted in non-decreasing order according to their deadlines. A reference start time T will be generated for the request q_i. Next, by considering the available resource of a mobile device, we look for the actual start time of q_i. The actual start time can be before, equal to or after the reference start time T.

Algorithm 1 RESP Algorithm

Input: The execution sequence E, the available resources A, and the incoming service request q_i

Output: Updated execution sequence E

1:    $t_{q_i}^s \leftarrow t_{q_i}^d - t_{q_i}^e$
2:    **if** $t_{q_i}^s < t_c$
3:       decline request q_i
4:    **else**
5:       $T \leftarrow E_l \cdot; q \leftarrow E_l$
6:       **while** $t_{q_i}^s < t_q^s$
7:         $T \leftarrow \cdot q; q \leftarrow E(\cdot q)$
8:       $Scheduled \leftarrow N$
9:       **for** $t = t_c$ to $\min(T, t_{q_i}^s)$
10:         **if** $\forall t_0 \in (t, t+t_{q_i}^e)$ and $\forall r \in R_{q_i}, R_{q_i}(r) < I_{t_0}(r)$
11:           insert q_i to E such that $\cdot q_i = t$; $Scheduled \leftarrow Y$
12:           **break**
13:       **if** not $Scheduled$ && $T \leq t_{q_i}^s$
14:         **if** $\forall t_0 \in (T, T+t_{q_i}^e)$ and $\forall r \in R_{q_i}, R_{q_i}(r) < A_{t_0}(r)$
15:           insert q_i to E s.t. $\cdot q = T$; $Scheduled \leftarrow Y$; postpone the subsequent requests in E
16:         **else**
17:           **while** $t < t_{q_0}^s$
18:             **if** $\forall t_0 \in (t, t+t_{q_i}^e)$ and $\forall r \in R_{q_i}, R_{q_i}(r) < A_{t_0}(r)$
19:               insert q_i to E s.t. $\cdot q_i = t$; $Scheduled \leftarrow Y$; postpone subsequent requests in E
20:               **break**
21:             $t \leftarrow t+1$
22:       **if** not $Scheduled$
23:         Timeouts (E, A, q_i)

The pseudo code of the RESP algorithm is shown in Algorithm 1. For an incoming service request q_i, we first calculate its latest start time (line 1) and check whether it can be completed before its deadline (lines 2–3) compared with the current time t_c. If the request is schedulable, we determine its reference start time in the execution sequence according to its deadline (lines 5–7). To do so, we put q_i to the rear of the execution sequence (line 5). If there exists a scheduled request in the execution sequence and its deadline is behind q_i, then the reference start time of q_i should be moved forward (lines 6–7).

Once the reference start time T is determined, we will use the start time minimization technique to check whether q_i can be performed before T (lines 9–12). If there is a time interval where the mobile device has more idle resources than those required (line 10), then q_i can be safely placed into that time interval (line 11) without affecting the execution of the scheduled requests. If no such time interval exists and the latest start time of q_i is not before $\mathcal{T}$ (line 13), then we check whether q_i can be started at $\mathcal{T}$. If the mobile device has enough available resources for q_i during its execution period (line 14), then q_i should be started from $\mathcal{T}$ (line 15). If the idle resources during that interval are not enough for q_i, q_i can occupy the resources that have been allocated to other requests with later deadlines (line 15). When this step still does not provide enough resources to perform q_i, the algorithm will continue checking whether there is any time interval between $\mathcal{T}$ and the latest start time of q_i that has sufficient resources (lines 17–21). If one exists, q_i should be inserted to that interval (line 19).

After the above search process, if q_i cannot be inserted into the execution sequence, then the Timeouts algorithm will be invoked (lines 22–23), implying that the mobile device cannot accept all requests. This will lead to either q_i or some other scheduled requests being declined. For the cases that q_i is inserted to the execution sequence and thus causes one or more scheduled requests cannot being started on schedule, the timeouts algorithm needs to be used for these requests.

8.2.2.2 Timeouts Processing Algorithm

In this subsection, we present the timeouts processing algorithm, which is invoked when timeouts occurs. To better describe the algorithm, we first introduce the definition of dominance.

Definition 7 (*Dominance*) Given a service request q_i, an execution sequence E and a set of scheduled service requests S in E, q_i dominates S if and only if

$$
\exists t \text{s.t. } \forall t_0 \in \left(t, t + t_{q_i}^e \right) \quad \text{and} \quad \forall r \in R_{q_{i'}}
$$
$$
R_{q_i}(r) < I_{t_0}(r) + \sum_{q \in S \cap E_{t_0}} R_q(r) \quad \text{and} \quad v_{q_i} > \sum_{q \in S} v_q \tag{8.6}
$$

In Definition 7, constraint (8.6) illustrates that there is a time interval, during which the sum of the idle resources and the resources allocated to the requests in S exceeds the required resources of q_i. Meanwhile, the revenue for executing q_i is more than executing all requests in S. Obviously, if q_i dominates S, the requests in S can be safely replaced by q_i, with the revenue for the mobile device increased.

The timeouts process algorithm is shown in Algorithm 2. It is realized by searching for the dominated request set with the minimum price. For each time slot before the reference start time point of an incoming request q_i, the algorithm tries to find a dominated request set with less revenue (lines 2–20). The search is started from the current time to the earlier one of the reference time point and the latest start time (line 2).

Algorithm 2 Timeouts Algorithm

Input: The execution sequence E and available resources A of the mobile
Output: Updated execution sequence E

1: $M \leftarrow v_{q_i}$
2: **for** $t = t_c$ **to** min$(T, t_{q_i}^s)$
3:      $q \leftarrow E(t^*)$
4:      **if** $\forall t_0 \in (t, t + t_{q_i}^e), \forall r \in R_{q_i}, R_{q_i}(r) < I_{t_0}(r) + R_q(r)$ && $v_q < M$
5:          $Q \leftarrow \{q\}; M \leftarrow v_q; T \leftarrow t$
6:      **else**
7:          $P \leftarrow \emptyset; V \leftarrow 0$
8:          **while** $V < M$ && $\bullet q < t + t_{q_i}^e$
9:              **if** $\forall t_0 \in (t, t + t_{q_i}^e), \forall r \in R_{q_i}, R_{q_i}(r) < I_{t_0}(r) + \sum_{q \in P} R_q(r)$
10                 $Q \leftarrow P; M \leftarrow V; T \leftarrow t$
11   **break**
12   **else**
13                 $P \leftarrow P \cup \{q\}; V \leftarrow V + v_q; q \leftarrow E(q^*)$
14 **if** $M < v_{q_i}$
15   insert q_i to E such that $\bullet q_i = T$; decline the requests in Q
16 **else**
17   decline q_i

For each time point, the request starting at it is set as the first request to check (lines
1). If a request is found to be dominated by q_i and with less revenue than the previous
minimum revenue, which is represented by M in the algorithm (line 4), then it will
be assigned to the replaced request set, its revenue will be assigned to the minimum
revenue, and the time point will be marked (line 5). Otherwise, the algorithm will
check whether the following request set can be dominated by q_i and with less revenue
(lines 8–13). If it is, the algorithm will reallocate the minimum revenue, request set
and time (line 10). Otherwise, the algorithm will continue expanding the set until we
can determine that it is not qualified (line 13).

After the searching process, if the algorithm finds a dominated request with less
revenue (line 14), it will replace these requests with q_i and move the subsequent
requests accordingly (line 15), otherwise, it means that no request set dominated by
q_i is found and q_i should be rejected (line 17).

8.2.2.3 Algorithm Analysis

In the following, we prove the effectiveness of the proposed RESP algorithm, by
verifying the three conditions mentioned at the beginning of this subsection.

Theorem 1 (Effectiveness of the RESP algorithm) *If service request q_i is inserted to an execution sequence by the RESP algorithm, conditions* (1), (2) *and* (3) *hold.*

Proof If q_i is inserted to the execution sequence by Algorithm 1, we can see the algorithm confirms that q_i can be completed in time before inserting it to any part of the execution sequence (lines 9, 13 and 17), so condition (1) holds. Similarly, the algorithm confirms that the resources are sufficient before inserting q_i (lines 10, 14 and 18), so condition (2) holds. As for condition (3), if the insertion of q_i does not cause timeout of any request, it is obvious that the revenue of the mobile device has increased by v_{q_i}. If the insertion of q_i causes timeout of a request whose revenue is larger than q_i, then the request will be reinserted by Algorithm 2, which also increases the revenue. Therefore, condition (3) holds.

If q_i is inserted to an execution sequence by Algorithm 2, there must be a request set dominated by q_i. Algorithm 2 confirms that the insert time is before $t^s_{q_i}$ (line 2), so if q_i replaces the dominated request set, it can be completed in time, i.e. condition (1) holds. According to Algorithm 2 and Eq. (8.6), for each time point, the resources allocated to the dominated request set and the idle resources of the mobile device add up to exceed the required resources of q_i, and the revenue of the requests in the dominated request set adds up to exceed the revenue of q_i, therefore conditions (2) and (3) hold.

The time complexity of both the RESP Algorithm and Timeouts Algorithm are $O(lt^e n)$, where l denotes the length of the execution sequence, t^e denotes the length of the execution time of the request (the number of time units) and n denotes the number of types of available resources. It implies that the execution time of both algorithms is feasibly low, and it would not cause high overhead to mobile devices.

8.2.3   Experiments

We have implemented the algorithms in Python and our experiments are conducted on a MacBook Pro (macOS Sierra Version 10.12.5). Since no standard platforms and dataset are available, we generated our experimental data in a synthetic way. Each mobile device is equipped with three kinds of resources. Service requests are randomly generated with the revenue ranging from 1 to 10, execution time is from 1 to 6 and the required number of each resource is from 0 to 5. For each request, the time difference between its deadline and its arrival is from 1 to 10. The number of incoming requests per time unit obeys normal distribution $N(15, 5)$ and is greater than 0. All the following experiments are repeated 200 times and we adopt the average values.

8.2.3.1   Effectiveness Evaluation

To evaluate the effectiveness of RESP, we compare it with three well-known scheduling algorithms, namely, First Come First Serve (FCFS), Priority Scheduling (PS), and Genetic Algorithm (GA). FCFS performs service requests according to their arrival time. PS assigns higher priorities to the requests with higher revenue and performs them in a non-increasing order. Both FCFS and PS reject a request if no sufficient resources or time to execute it. GA is a widely used heuristic method in scheduling, and it is realised by successively iterating to generate better solutions. In the following, we vary the mean of the number of incoming requests per time unit from 5 to 40 to compare the effectiveness of the four methods. The result is shown in Fig. 8.4.

From Fig. 8.4a, the RESP approach outperforms FCFS, PS and GA in terms of revenue at all times. FCFS performs worst due to that fact it does not consider the revenue of the requests and only processes them according to their arrival sequence. PS prioritizes the requests by their revenue. To do so, it will cause all the resources to be used to perform the requests with high priorities and the requests with low priorities are ignored. As a result, the total amount of service requests drops and leads to the revenue dropping as well. GA considers both resource and revenue, so its performance is better than FCFS and PS. However, due to its algorithmic complexity, it is hard to generate the optimal solution in an online manner. With the significant performance improvement, our proposed approach does not cause the overuse of mobile devices. As shown in Fig. 8.4b, there is no obvious difference in the resource utilization rate of the four methods, which suggests that, by using the RESP approach, mobile devices can create more revenue with same amount of resources.

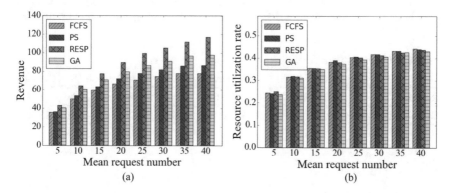

Fig. 8.4 Experimental results of effectiveness evaluation

8.2.3.2   Efficiency Evaluation

To evaluate the efficiency of RESP, we compared the execution time of the four methods. For the GA approach, we set the number of iterations from 20 to 100 with the increment interval of 20. The result is shown in Table 8.2, from which we can see that the execution time of GA is several orders of magnitude higher than the other three methods. The revenue of GA becomes stable from GA-60, but the overall revenue is still worse than our RESP method.

We further vary the length of the execution sequence, mean requests number, mean execution time and the number of the type of resources respectively to evaluate the scalability of the RESP algorithm. As shown in Fig. 8.5a–c, with the increasing of the length of execution sequence, mean requests number, mean execution time, the execution time of RESP increases almost linearly, which is in accordance with the analysis given in subsection 8.2.2. Besides, as shown in Fig. 8.5d, with the increasing number of the type of resources, the execution time of RESP decreases. This is because the increased resource number makes requests more difficult to be executed and thus decreases the length of the request sequence. Overall, the execution time of RESP is feasibly low, and it has good scalability, which demonstrates the applicability of RESP to mobile devices.

8.3   Composition-Driven Service Provisioning in Distributed Edges

The effectiveness of a service provision system is strongly correlated to the cached service set of edge servers: the more popular services the mobile edge server cache has, the more requests from wireless devices can be optimized. In this section, we

Table 8.2 Execution Time Comparison

	FCFS	PS	RESP	GA-20	GA-40	GA-60	GA-80	GA-100
Revenue	58.4	61.9	76.7	60.6	65.6	69.5	70.0	70.2
Execution time (ms)	0.59	0.62	3.06	386.82	818.80	1145.57	1487.51	1851.06

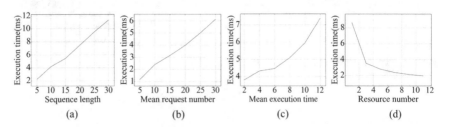

Fig. 8.5 Experimental results of efficiency evaluation

consider the cost of bringing services to the edge and assume the cost of transmitting data between edge and cloud servers negligible. What's more, with the development of Micro-Service technology [8], services will not only work individually but also will cooperate with others easily to make a composite service and finish complex tasks. Thus, some composite services may also have the capability to fulfil some simple tasks by reusing their member services. In many cases, it will help save resources if both the composite services and their member services are invoked frequently. To take all things into consideration, in this section we evaluate the performance with the average service response time (ASRT) and propose a resource consumption aware algorithm to determine how services can be placed on edge servers.

Specifically, we explore the architecture of mobile edge computing benefit of service cache and discuss the factors that may affect the performance in latency reduction of cache policies. We classify the services as composite services and atomic services and use service composition graph to describe the relation of them. By considering the resource consumption, popularity (or invocation frequency) and the service composition graph, we propose a heuristic algorithm to optimize the average service response time.

8.3.1   Problem Definition and Description

In this section, we introduce the related definitions and descriptions involved in the cache content optimization problem of MEC systems.

8.3.1.1   Concept Definition

Definition 8 (*Cloud Server, CS*) Cloud Server consists of clusters of machines. It maintains a service registry and acts as a service provision centre. Service providers can register, delegate and maintain their services on it, while users (or sensors) can query or invoke the services from it. We define $V_{u \to cs}$ the average transmission rate between cloud server and wireless users.

Though the cloud server is made up of machines, some management systems like OpenStack, Kubernetes[1] are applied in practice to manage these machines. Hence, the cloud server can run in a well-organized way and provide unified API to end users.

Definition 9 (*Web Service, WS*) A Web Service *ws* can be defined by $ws = (func, in, out, r, QoS)$, where *func* is the functionality of the web service, *in* is the input, *out* is the output, *r* is the resource consumption, and *QoS* is the quality of web service.

---

[1] https://kubernetes.io.

Fig. 8.6 An example of
Kubernetes pod YAML file

```
apiVersion: v1
kind: ReplicationController
metadata:
        name: nginx-controller
spec:
        containers:
        - image: nginx
          name: nginx
          resources:
            limits:
              memory: 200Mi
            requests:
              memory: 100Mi
```

The web service is an abstract concept that describes how a program can complete some tasks with specific parameters. It can be an instance of remote invocation based on SOAP [9], a web API provided by a software company, or a Docker[2] container/ Kubernetes pod managed by a PaaS platform. In our work, we focus on the Container-as-a-Service situation because of container's *"Build, Ship, and Run Any App, Anywhere"* properties. Edge servers can download application images from clouds and run containers to deal with different requests.

The r describes resource consumption of services such as memory, CPU, GPU or network. For example, Fig. 8.6 shows a description of the nginx-pod. QoS describes the non-functional characteristics of service, including execution time, reputation, cost, etc. [10, 11]. It varies when deployed in different environments. In our model, we focus on execution time of web services on different edge and cloud servers.

Definition 10 (*Service Composition Graph, SCG*) A Service Composition Graph reveals the relations of web services, it can be represented as a directed acyclic graph (DAG) $G_{sc} = (S, E)$, where S is the web service set, and $E = \{\langle s_i \leftarrow s_j \rangle | s_i, s_j \in S, (s_i, s_j) \in R_c\}$ is the set of graph edges. Here, R_c is the composition structure of services, in which $(s_i, s_j) \in R_c$ means that service s_j is a composite service and s_i is a member service of s_j.

The service composition technology is derived from service-oriented architecture (SOA), it tries to compose new complex services by integrating services with various functionalities provided by different service developer [12, 13]. For example, Siri[3] is one of the most famous composite applications, it integrates member services like

---

[2]https://www.docker.com.

[3]https://www.apple.com/cn/ios/siri/.

alarm clock, calendar, weather, music, etc. by recognizing human voice and responses to users by dialogs. There exist many other composite services in the service registry.[4] With well-designed UI wrappers and runtime optimization (like allocating different CPU units for parallel service execution), these composite services sometimes show better user experience and performance than invoking individual member services [14].

In the graph, the services which are made of other member services are called "*composite service*" (S_c), and the others are called "atomic service" (S_a). If a service s_i is a member service of service s_j, we denote that service s_i support service s_j.

Definition 11 (*Edge Server, ES*) Edge servers are computing devices with stronger processing power and larger storage capacity that deployed on the edge network. The edge server communicates with wireless devices (usually via wireless links), receives their requests and records the running events. An edge server es can be defined by a tuple $es = (R, V_{u \to es}, V_{cs \to es})$, where R is the provision capacity, $V_{u \to es}$ is the data transmission rate between users and edge server, and $V_{cs \to es}$ is the data transmission rate between cloud servers and edge servers.

In our model, we use average transmission rate $V_{u \to es}$ and $V_{cs \to es}$ in response time computation to reduce the computation complexity. The parameter $R = \left(R_{max}^{res_1}, R_{max}^{res_2}, \ldots, R_{max}^{res_n} \right)$ describes the maximum resource that the edge server can provide in different resource types. For example, an MEC provision system which considers only the memory resource will give the edge server a provision capacity; e.g., $R = R_{max}^{mem}$. Every service will use resources of different types, but the sum of each individual resource cannot be larger than the capacity of the edge servers.

8.3.1.2 Problem Description

A significant metric to measure the performance of a service provision system is the average service response time. Short service response time will significantly enhance user experience and can motivate users to use more services. For every web service ws_i, it typically has two different service response times T_i^c and t_i^e. T_i^c is the service response time when it is placed on the cloud server, and t_i^e is that on the edge server. They can be easily derived from the parameters of edge server and service:

$$\begin{cases} t_i^e = \dfrac{in_i}{V_{u \to es}} + QoS_{exec\_time}^{edge} + \dfrac{out_i}{V_{u \to es}} \\ T_i^c = \dfrac{in_i}{V_{u \to cs}} + QoS_{exec\_time}^{cloud} + \dfrac{out_i}{V_{u \to cs}} \end{cases} \tag{8.7}$$

---

[4]https://www.programmableweb.com/category/all/mashups.

In many cases, it is assumed that tasks will execute better on cloud because the machines of the cloud may have better hardware for computation. But things are not absolute because edge servers are also machines with good computation capability, while the cloud is made up of such machines. Therefore, we do not assume whether it takes longer on edge server or on cloud server. But in general, the transmission time when services deployed on edge servers is always larger than that on cloud, because of the short-distance communication with edge and shorter waiting time in the serving queue.

Besides invoking services from cache or cloud directly, the task of a service can also be fulfilled by invoking its member services. If service ws_i is a composite service that consists of other services $MS_i = \{s_{i1}, s_{i2}, \ldots, s_{ik}\}$, the service response time $t_i^*(y)$ can be computed recursively with the service response time of the member services (here y is the vector that describes the cache policy where $y_i = 1$ means $s_i \in$ cache and $y_i = 0$ means $s_i \notin$ cache):

$$t_i^*(y) = \begin{cases} \min\left\{t_i^e, \sum_{s_j \in MS_i} t_j^*\right\}, & y_i = 1, s_i \in S_c \\ \min\left\{T_i^c, \sum_{s_j \in MS_i} t_j^*\right\}, & y_i = 0, s_i \in S_c \\ t_i^e, & y_i = 1, s_i \notin S_c \\ T_i^c, & y_i = 0, s_i \notin S_c \end{cases} \tag{8.8}$$

Then, the ASRT $\widetilde{rt}(y)$ of S can be represented as:

$$\widetilde{rt}(y) = f_1 \times t_1^*(y) + f_2 \times t_2^*(y) + \cdots + f_n \times t_n^*(y) \tag{8.9}$$

$$= \sum_{i=1}^{n} f_i \times t_1^*(y) \tag{8.10}$$

Here f_i is the frequency of the service s_i to reflect its popularity. The frequency can be estimated by counting the invocations of different services.

In this way, with the notations and symbols shown in Table 8.3, the problem can be defined as: For an arbitrary edge server $es = (R, V_{u \to es}, V_{cs \to es})$, given the services $S = \{s_1, s_2, \ldots s_n\}$, the corresponding service composition graph $G_{sc} = (S, E)$ and the popularity $f = \{f_i\}_{i=1}^n$ of services, finding the optimal service cache policy $y = \{y_i\}_{i=1}^n$ for edge server es to minimize the average service response time $\widetilde{rt}(y)$.

$$\min \widetilde{rt}(y) = \sum_{i=1}^{m} f_i t_i^*(y) \tag{8.11}$$

Table 8.3 Symbols and Notations

Symbol	Description
cs	The cloud server
es	The edge server
$V_{u \to cs}$	The average data transmission rate between device and cloud server
$V_{cs \to es}$	The average data transmission rate between cloud server and edge server
$V_{u \to es}$	The average data transmission rate between device and edge server
s_i	A service that fulfils a specific task
S	The service set
G_{sc}	The service composition graph
S_c	The set of composite service
S_a	The set of atomic service
r_i	The resource consumption of service s_i
R	The resource limitation of edge server
f_i	The popularity (frequency) of service s_i
t_i^e	The service response time when s_i placed on es
T_i^c	The service response time when s_i placed on cs
MS_i	The set of member service of s_i
y_i	The selection indicator for s_i

$$\text{s.t.} \begin{cases} \sum_{i=1}^{m} y_i r_i \leq R \\ y_i \in \{0, 1\} \end{cases} \tag{8.12}$$

8.3.2   Approach

In this section, we will analyze the relation of services based on the service composition graph, and then propose a heuristic algorithm based on this analysis.

8.3.2.1   Service Composition Graph Analysis

The service composition graph reveals the hierarchal structure of web services. With this information, appropriate services can be selected to support more service requests using edge server caches.

Algorithm 3 Computing Service Response Time, CSRT

Input:

    $SCG\ (S, E)$: the service composition graph;
    $T = \{T_i\}_{i=1}^n$: the response time on cloud;
    $t = \{t_i\}_{i=1}^n$: the response time on edge if cached;
    y: the cache policy;

Output:

    $\{t_i^*\}$: response time with cache policy y

1	Stack $S_+ \leftarrow \emptyset$
2	**while** *not all computed* **do**
3	$S_{zero} \leftarrow \{s_i \vert s_i \in S, indegree(s_i) = 0\}$
4	**for** $s_k \in S_{zero}$ **do**
5	**if** *outdegree* $(s_k)=0$ **then**
6	**if** $y_k = 1$ **then**
7	$t_k^* = t_k^e$
8	**else**
9	$t_k^* = T_k^c$
10	**else**
11	$push\ (S_+, s_k)$
12	**for** $s_k \in S_{zero}$ **do**
13	$remove\ (G,\ s_k)$
14	$update\ G$
15	**while** $S_+ \neq \emptyset$ **do**
16	$s_k \leftarrow pop(S_+)$
17	**for** $s_k \in S_k$ **do**
18	**if** $y_k = 1$ **then**
19	$t_k^* = min\left\{\sum_{s_j \in MS_k} t_j^*, t_k^e\right\}$
20	**else**
21	$t_k^* = min\left\{\sum_{s_j \in MS_k} t_j^*, T_k^c\right\}$
22	**return** $\{t_1^*, t_2^*, ..., t_n^*\}$

To represent the service response time of all services with an analytical expression, we proposed an iterative algorithm that takes advantage of the support relations among services; it is presented in Algorithm 3. In Algorithm 3, it firstly partitions

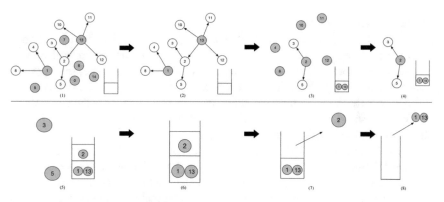

Fig. 8.7 An example of Algorithm 3

services to different levels and uses a stack to store them: the higher level a service has, the lower it will stay in the stack (Line 2–14). Then the response time is computed level by level (Line 15–21). In the worst case, there is only one path that connects all services like $s_1 \leftarrow s_2 \leftarrow s_3$, in this situation the time complexity is $O(|S|^2)$.

To illustrate the computation process, we show an example of how the response time is computed with a given policy in Fig. 8.7. In this case, there are 15 services in the service registry which are numbered from s_0 to s_{14}. In step (1), the services whose in-degree is 0 (s_0, s_1, s_6, s_7, s_9, s_{13}, s_{14}) are highlighted. In step (2), the response times of services whose outdegree is 0 (atomic services) are computed directly with the value of y, and then these services are removed from the service composition graph. In step (3), the services whose outdegree is larger than 0 (composite services) are stored in the stack and these services and their related edges are also removed from the graph. Step (4) and (5) repeat the process from (1) to (3). In step (6), all the composite services are stored in stack in their level order. In step (7), the response time of service s_2 is computed because all its member services' response time ($t_3^*(y)$, $t_5^*(y)$) are computed. When $t_2^*(y)$ is worked out, the stack will pop it. In step (8), the response times of s_1 and s_{13} are worked out, and because the stack is now empty, the computing process is over.

8.3.2.2 Cache Policy Algorithms

Inspired by the traditional knapsack problem [15], the main step of making cache policy is to decide which service is appropriate to put in cache so that the ASRT can be minimized. Furthermore, the value of policy is however not as easy to evaluate as that in the knapsack problem, because the relations here are much more complex.

(1) Enumeration Method

A direct way is to enumerate all possible policies to find the optimal one. Enumeration is a brute-force but accurate method to find the optimal solution of this NP-complete problem. As the size of the solution set is 2, this approach enumerates all policies from $y = \langle 0, 0, ..., 0 \rangle$ to $\langle 1, 1, ..., 1 \rangle$, compute and compare the ASRT in turn, the policy with minimum ASRT is the optimal one. We choose the results of it as the ground truth of our experiments.

(2) Consumption-Driven Searching Algorithm

Genetic algorithm (GA) is a kind of metaheuristic inspired by the process of natural selection. It simulates the evolution of populations with operations like *selection, crossover* and *mutation*. GA is designed to favour chromosomes with highest fitness values to produce next populations (solutions). As a result, quality of solutions for a problem is gradually improved (population by population) until the optimal answer is reached. Inspired by GA, we propose the consumption-driven searching algorithm (CDSA) with the following three steps:

Encoding. Encoding is the first step of the CDSA algorithm. In this step, the solutions of the optimization problem are represented with encoded chromosome firstly. From the problem description, the goal is to find optimal cache policy $\vec{y} = \langle y_1, y_2, \ldots, y_n \rangle$ which can minimize the ASRT. We encode the candidate policies with an n-bits-genome chromosome where 0 or 1 in the ith genome means the selection of service ws_i.

Secondly, a set of chromosomes are initialized to make a population. Typically, several hundreds or thousands of possible solutions are contained in a population, and the chromosomes of the population are generated randomly to cover a wide solutions space in increase the chance of finding the optimal solution. However, because the overuse of resources is forbidden in the provision system, random initialization may result in unrealistic solutions. Furthermore, the entire searching space will have 2^n points if it is initialized randomly without constraints, which will make it difficult for the algorithm to find the optimal solutions. Thus, in our approach, we divide the population into 2 parts. The chromosomes of the first part are initialized randomly to keep the algorithm able to escape local optimums; in the second part, we initialize the chromosomes with the resource consumption constraint according to Algorithm 4. We will prove that the generative model G can generate all valid policies that satisfy (6).

Algorithm 4 Initialization for CDSA

Input:
    $\{r_i\}_n$: the resource consumptions of services;
    R: the resource capacity of target edge server;
Output:
    $y = \{y_1, y_2, \ldots, y_n\}$: the cache policy of services;

1    $S \leftarrow \{s_1, s_2, \ldots, s_n\}$
2    $A \leftarrow \emptyset$
3   **while** $S \neq \emptyset$ **do**
4   **if** $R \leq 0$ **then**
5            $(s_w, y_w) \leftarrow pop(A)$
6            $y_w \leftarrow 1 - y_w$
7            $push\left(A, (s_w, y_w)\right)$
8        $s_k \leftarrow RandomPop(S)$
9        $y_k \leftarrow Random\{0, 1\}$
10   **if** $y_k = 1$ **then**
11         $R \leftarrow R - r_k$
12      $push\left(A, (s_k, y_k)\right)$
13 **return** y

Lemma 1 *Denote the policies generated by* Algorithm 4 *with P_g and the valid policies with P^*, then $P_g = P^*$.*

Proof To prove the equality of P_g and P^*, we only need to prove that (1) $\forall p \in P_g$, $p \in P^*$ and (2) $\forall p \in P^*, p \in P_g$.

(1) Given an arbitrary $p \in P_g, p = \{y_1, y_2, \ldots, y_n\}$, the assignment order of y_k can be described by collecting the results of pop operation in line 9 of Algorithm 4 as $O_p = \{y_{o1}, y_{o2}, \ldots, y_{on}\}$, then before the y_{oi} is assigned with 0 or 1, the policy with assigned $\{y_{o1}, y_{o2}, \ldots, y_{on}\}$ are ensured to be valid, because the available resource R in Algorithm 4 is still non-negative; It means that there are still resource to be allocated for the remaining services. For service s_{oi}, if it is

selected to be cached on edge server, the remaining resource will be $R = R - r_{oi}$. If $R \leq 0$, the allocation will be withdrawn in Line 5 of Algorithm 4. Finally, the left resource R is still non-negative, and the policy p is generated. In this way, we get $p \in P^*$.

(2) Given an arbitrary $p \in P^*$, we can replay the generating process by replacing the *RandomPop* in Line 9 of Algorithm 4 by selecting specific services. Because p is the valid policy, the remaining resource R must by non-negative after adopting p, so it is valid for every step in the generation. In this way, due to feasibility in replaying the generating process in Algorithm 4, we have $p \in P_g$.

Consequently, we can prove that $P_g = P^*$.

The initialization algorithm has the runtime complexity of $O(|S|)$ and can be easily parallelized.

Selection. During each successive generation, a portion of the existing population is selected to breed a new generation. Individual solutions are selected through a fitness-based process, where fitter solutions are typically more likely to be selected. The fitness function of GA measures the quality of generated solution. In our approach, as the objective is to minimize the ASRT with the constraint on resource consumption, the fitness function F can be defined by:

$$F(y) = \begin{cases} 1/\sum_{i=1}^{n} f \cdot t_i^*(y), & R \geq \sum_{i=1}^{n} r_i \cdot y_{i_i} \\ 0, & otherwise \end{cases} \tag{8.13}$$

In this way, a solution with smaller ASRT will have larger probability to be selected. By computing all the fitness value of chromosomes of the population, the chromosomes $y^{(k)}$ are chosen according to their probability by revolving a roulette in which the kth part occupies $P^{(k)}$ percentage of it. Here, $P^{(k)}$ is the probability to select $y^{(k)}$ to produce new chromosomes for the next generation (the selecting process is liking rotating a roulette shown in Fig. 8.8).

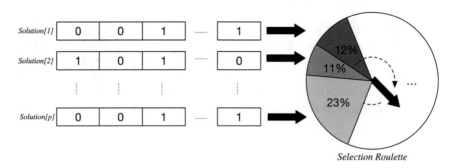

Selection Roulette

Fig. 8.8   Selecting chromosomes with a roulette

$$P^{(k)} = \frac{F\left(y^{(k)}\right)}{\sum_{i=1}^{n} F\left(y^{(i)}\right)} \tag{8.14}$$

Crossover and Mutation. With chromosomes prepared in a population, the following step is to generate the next generation of solutions. For each new solution to be produced, a pair of "parent" genomes are selected with possibility reflected in (8). Firstly, a new solution is created by sharing many of the characteristics of these "parents". It means that the selected "parents" exchange parts of their bits with each other. On the other hand, the selected "parents" may choose not to crossover, then the new "offspring" are identical to themselves. We use the parameter *crossover probability (pc)* to determine how new chromosomes are produced. The process continues until a new population of solutions of appropriate size is generated. Secondly, mutations may occur in the newborn populations. In the mutation, some genomes of a chromosome may change with a low possibility p_m called *mutation probability*. The mutation operation gives the algorithm the ability to avoid premature convergence. At last, several solutions with good fitness will stay unchanged as elites in the next generation to keep the convergence. This process finally stops when converged after 5 consecutive iterations, it results in solutions with appropriate fitness values. Choosing the one with the best fitness value from the final population, the corresponding policy will be the suboptimal of the problem.

Algorithm 5 shows the process. Firstly, the solution set or population is initialized with Algorithm 4 (Line 2–7). Secondly, The fitness of solutions or chromosomes is calculated with the *Evaluate()* function described in (7) (Line 8). Then for every generation, the algorithm will keep the elitism with good fitness and select parent chromosomes according to the probability in (8) and crossover them to generate offspring. The offspring may mutate in every generation (Line 10–25). The algorithm stops when the solution converges, or the generation number exceeds *MaxEpoch.*

Algorithm 5 Consumption-Driven Searching Algorithm, CDSA

Input:

    PopSize: the size of population;

    $rand_\%$: the percentage for random initialization;

    MaxEpoch: the maximum epoch number for evolution;

Output:

    $y = \{y_1, y_2, \ldots, y_n\}$: the cache policy of services

1    $Population_{old} \leftarrow \emptyset$

2   **while** ♣$Population_{old}$♣ $\leftarrow < \psi PopSize$ **do**

3   **if** ♣$Population_{old}$♣ $\leftarrow \lceil \leftarrow PopSize \bullet \leftarrow rand\%$ **then**

4            $chromosome \bullet \leftarrow RandInit()$

5   **else**

6            $chromosome \bullet \leftarrow CDSAInit()$

7        $Add\,(Population_{old} \,{}^\subset \psi chromosome)$

8    $fitness \bullet \leftarrow Evaluate(Population_{old})$

9    $T \bullet 0$

10   **while** $\rightarrow convergence$ or $T < \psi MaxEpoch$ **do**

11        $T \bullet T \Downarrow 1$

12        $Population_{new} \bullet \leftarrow \emptyset$

13        $Elitism \bullet \leftarrow SelectElitism(Population_{old} \,{}^\subset \psi Enum)$

14        $Add(Population_{new} {}^\subset Elitism)$

15   **while** ♣$Population_{new}$♣ $\leftarrow < \psi PopSize$ **do**

16            $father \bullet \leftarrow Select(Population_{old})$

17   *mother* •←*Select(Population$_{old}$)*

18   *child1* •←*Crossover(father^{c}mother^{c}pc)*

19   *child2* •←*Crossover(father^{c}mother^{c}pc)*

20   *child1* •←*Mutate(child1^{c}ψpm)*

21   *child2* •←*Mutate(chile2^{c}ψpm)*

22   *Add(Population$_{new}$^{c}child1)*
23   *Add(Population$_{new}$^{c}child2)*
24   *Population$_{old}$* •←*Population$_{new}$*

25   *fitness* •←*Evaluate(Population$_{old}$)*

26   *policy* •←*SelectElitism(Population$_{old}$ ^{c}ψ1)*

27   **return** *policy*

8.3.3 Experiments and Analysis

We have implemented the deploying algorithms in Python 2.7.13 and our experiments are conducted on a machine with Intel Xeon E5-2620 v4@2.10 GHz × 2 CPU and 64 GB memory on CentOS 7 operation system. Due to the lack of well adopted platforms and datasets, we generated our experimental data in a synthetic way. In our experiment, the most important data is the service composition graph to reveal the relationship among services. Figure 8.9 shows some examples of service composition graphs generated to verify our approach with different service sets. There are atomic services and composite services in every service composition graph. Different composite services can include the same member service, and every two services in the same path of the graph will not include each other. Table 8.4 shows the statistics information of the experiment data; here $|S|$ is the number of involved services, η is defined by $\frac{2|E|}{|S|(|S|-1)}$ which describes the complexity of the graph, $|S_c|_\% = \frac{|S_c|}{S}$ is the percentage of composite service, and $H_s = \frac{\max_{p\in path}|p|}{|S|}$ describes how complex the hierarchy of the composite can be.

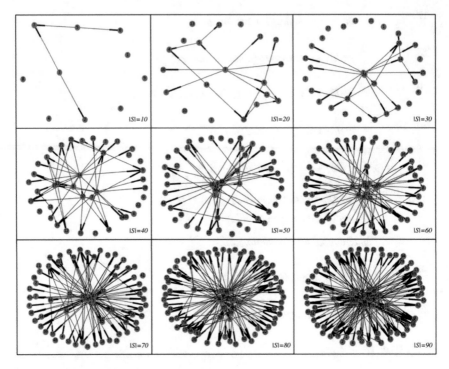

Fig. 8.9 Some service composition graphs in dataset

Table 8.4 Statistics of service composition graphs

Statistics	Min	Max	Mean
$|S|$	5	100	52.5
η	0	0.67	0.29
$|S_c|$ %	0	86.67	32.21
H_s	0	0.82	0.43

8.3.3.1 Evaluation

In this section, we conduct a series of experiments to evaluate the effectiveness of our algorithm and investigate the parameters that affect its performance.

Figure 8.10 shows the changing of average service response time during the execution of our algorithm ($|S| = 10$, $|Population| = 50$, $p_c = 0.9$, $p_m = 0.3$). With the increasing of generation, better cache policy with shorter the average service response time is found.

Figure 8.11 shows the ASRT of edge servers when adopting policies generated by the enumeration algorithm and our CDSA model. In this figure, we use a violin plot and a line chart to exhibit the comparison of our algorithm and the ground truth. In the violin plot, the width of each violin shows the diversity of distribution, the thick

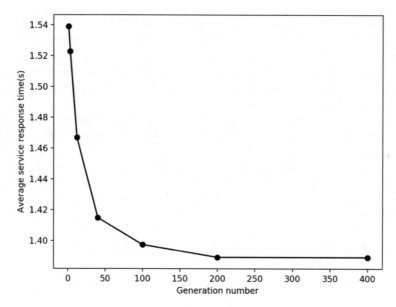

Fig. 8.10   Average service response time in different generations

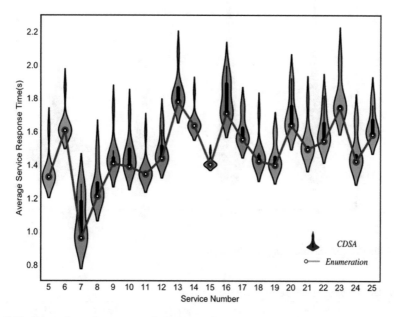

Fig. 8.11   Comparison of average service response time

vertical line in violins shows the scale of data and the hollow circle in violins shows the median of ASRT. In Fig. 8.11, the CDSA runs 100 times for every given service composition graph with a specific service number to make a candidate solution set (as the bodies of violins). We can find that the ASRT varies with the increasing or service number and the CDSA can find the optimal policy that supports the request, like using the policy generated by enumeration.

As the CDSA is an optimal evolutionary algorithm based on the constraints of the service provision system, it is necessary to evaluate the results derived from other evolutionary algorithms to check its performance. Figure 8.12 shows the results of ASRT for the service provision system when given 30 services and their composition relations with different evolutionary optimization algorithms. In our experiment, besides the generic algorithm, we also apply other evolutionary algorithms like the particle-swarm optimization (PSO) algorithm and simulated annealing (SA) algorithm to optimize the ASRT of the system. In Table 8.5 it lists the details about results when running these algorithms 300 times on a provision system with 30

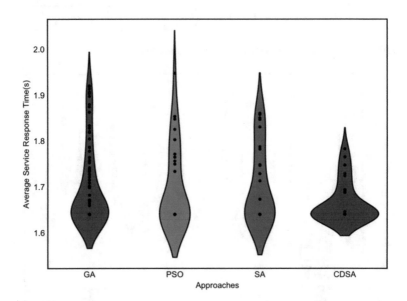

Fig. 8.12 Comparison of average service response time

Table 8.5 Statistics of different approaches

Approach	Min(s)	Max(s)	Mean(s)	Bias (%)	Opt (%)
GA	1.639	1.919	1.699	17.08	53.0
PSO	1.639	1.946	1.700	18.73	62.3
SA	1.639	1.860	1.703	13.48	55.7
CDSA	1.639	**1.782**	**1.665**	**8.72**	**73.7**

services ($|S| = 14$, $|Population| = 100$, $pc = 0.9$, $pm = 0.2$). From Fig. 8.12 and Table 8.5, we can find that all these algorithms can find the optimums of the optimization problem. However, the accuracy of them is different. In algorithm GA, PSO and SA, the maximum bias can be 17.08, 18.73 and 13.48%, while the results of CDSA is 8.72%. This comparison shows that even when algorithms cannot find the optimum, the approximate solution of CDSA will make a cache policy that have 8.72% more ASRT at last. At the same time, the table shows that in the solution set of different algorithms, 73.7% of the solutions in the results of CDSA are equal to the optimum, while those of GA, PSO and SA are 53.0, 62.3 and 55.7%. This result shows that CDSA has better robustness than others—we have a probability of 73.7% to believe that the result of running CDSA once is the optimal one. It is clear that CDSA performs better than other evolutionary algorithms in this optimization problem. The reason is that it can always initialize correctly with the resource constraint. With the reduction of search space, it becomes easier for the algorithm to find the optimums.

In Fig. 8.13, it shows how the parameter $|Population|$ can impact the generated policies of the algorithm. The CDSA is executed 100 times to calculate the bias with ground truth.

Figure 8.14 shows the impact of parameters p_c and p_m. From this figure, we can find that there is no universal p_c and p_m that work well in every scenario. When $|S|$ varies, the best (p_c, p_m) may be different. However, they have something in common to guide us to choose the parameters. The algorithm is suggested to choose a large p_c and a medium p_m. In this way, the algorithm will keep the capability to find global optimums.

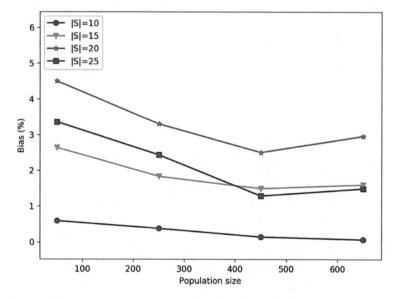

Fig. 8.13 Comparison of average service response time

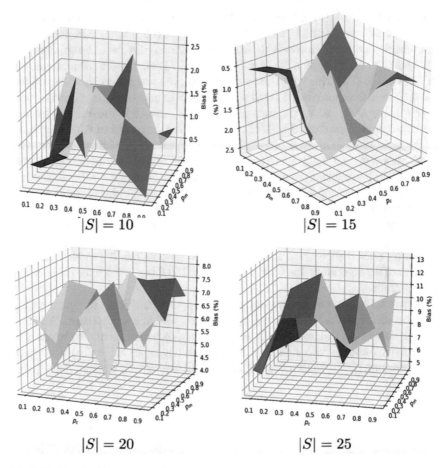

Fig. 8.14 Bias for different p_c and p_m

8.3.3.2   Efficiency

Since the deployment of services on the cache of edge servers will bring system suspending, it is of vital importance that the efficiency of the deployment algorithm must be high. Thus, in this part, we evaluate the time cost of different algorithms. As the CDSA is made up of 3 parts—encoding, selection and crossover/mutation, the time complexity of it is $O\ (|S|) + O\big((n_{population} \times |S|^2 + |S|) \times n_{epoch}\big) = O\big(n_{population} \times |S|^2 \times n_{epoch}\big)$. In Fig. 8.15, the curves show the effect of these factors. Comparing the running time of the algorithms and the ground truth in Fig. 8.15b, d, we can find that the time cost of enumeration algorithm can be as much as 600 s when the service number is only 25 as the points of searching space increase exponentially. On the other hand, the time cost of evolutionary algorithms stays less than 1.6 s even when the service number is 50. According to the analysis of the time complexity, the

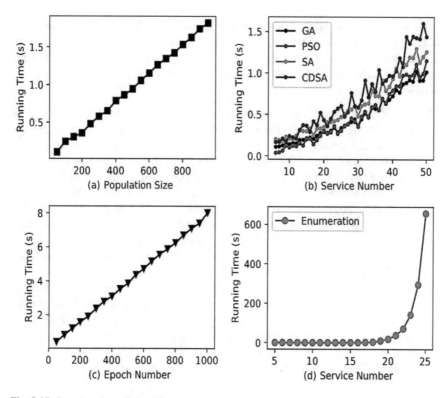

Fig. 8.15   Running time of algorithms

time cost increases linearly as the $n_{population}$ and n_{epoch} increases in Fig. 8.15a, c. The result shows that the CDSA is practical in implementation of the service provision system.

8.4   Request Dispatching for Edge Provisioning Systems

MEC not only has the advantages of MCC but can further reduce the response time of service invocations. Moreover, with service parameters transmitted directly between edge servers and mobile devices instead of through the Internet, the response time and Internet risk of service invocation are significantly reduced.

However, MEC still faces some challenges. In contrast to powerful cloud servers, edge servers are resource constrained, so when an edge server is accommodated with excessive service requests, the execution of some requests will be delayed, which leads to the response time of these requests be extended, even exceeds the response time by invoking the services on remote cloud servers. Since in MEC systems, service consumers are generally moving, it is rather important to reduce the invocation delay of services as much as possible. This task can mainly be divided into two goals as follows:

(1) Selecting an appropriate edge server or cloud server for each service request: For a service request, there may be more than one edge server that can provide the required service. These edge servers are of different capabilities, resources, accommodated service requests, as well as varied data transmission time and service execution time. When edge servers are overloaded, excessive overall response time can be induced and the advantages of edge computing are diminished. In such circumstances, remote cloud server will become a better solution ascribing to its short execution time and waiting time of service invocations. Therefore, it is a pivotal problem to balance the request processing between edge servers to avoid overload or wasted resources in any edge server, and eventually minimize the overall response time of requests.

(2) Scheduling the accommodated service requests to minimize their average response time for each edge server: For each edge server, as its resources are limited, service requests are generally waiting in queue for execution. These service requests are of different required resources and execution time. Therefore, proper scheduling is required to fully utilize the limited resources and thus minimize the overall response time of accommodated services.

In this section, we focus on minimizing service response time by jointly considering request dispatching and request scheduling in edge cloud systems. A novel heuristic approach is proposed by combing the genetic algorithm and the simulated annealing algorithm to optimize the request dispatching process. The request scheduling of edge servers is addressed by a novel request scheduling algorithm. Then, we combined these two algorithms to minimize the overall response time of service requests. Moreover, we introduced a novel solution recombination strategy, which significantly improves the efficiency of the algorithms.

8.4.1 Problem Formulation

8.4.1.1 Edge Cloud Architecture

Our proposed framework is designed for edge computing systems, which are composed of three tiers, i.e. consumer tier, edge tier and cloud tier. We assume the following properties:

- There are one cloud center and multiple edge servers in the edge computing system. Edge servers can completely cover the whole 2-D area, so when a service request is proposed, it can be sent to a nearby edge server for processing.
- For each service request, only a part of edge servers can provide corresponding services to satisfy the request, while the cloud can provide all services.
- For any two edge servers, there exists a network path connecting them, and for each edge server, there exists a network path connecting it to the cloud.
- When an edge server receives a request, it can execute the service itself only if there is a corresponding service deployed on it, while if no corresponding service is deployed on it, it can only forward the request to another edge server or the cloud for processing, and the result will be sent back after the service is completed and retransmitted to the user.
- The cloud is powerful enough to execute all incoming service requests simultaneously, which means that the services do not need to wait for execution in the cloud.

8.4.1.2 Mobile Edge Computing Models

Definition 12 (*Service Request*) A service request is represented as a 4-tuples (id, t, e, E), where:

(1) id is the unique identifier of the request;
(2) t is the time when the request is received;
(3) e is the edge server where the request is received;
(4) $E = \{e_j\}_{j=1}^n$ is the set of edge servers that can provide corresponding services for the request, and n is the number of edges in the set.

As mentioned before, for each service request, only part of edges can provide services to satisfy it, so a request can only be dispatched to the cloud server or an edge server where a corresponding service is deployed.

Definition 13 (*Service*) A service is represented as a set of 5-tuples (e, R, t, d_i, d_o), where:

(1) e is the edge server or cloud server where the service is deployed;
(2) R describes the resources needed for e to execute the service; R can be denoted as a set of 2-tuples $R = \{(r_j, n_j)\}_{j=1}^m$, where m is the number of types of required resources, and r_j and n_j denote the type and amount of the j-th kind of resource, respectively;
(3) t is the execution time, which is the makespan for e to execute the service;
(4) d_i is the data size of the input parameters;
(5) d_o is the data size of the output parameters.

Each service is deployed on a specific edge. Requests and services are matched according to their functions. There is a one-to-many relationship between requests and services. That is to say, for a service request, there may be many services deployed on different edges can satisfy it, but one request corresponds to no more than one service in each edge server. Therefore, once a request is dispatched, the corresponding service is determined, so terms request and service will be interchangeably used without causing confusion thereafter in this paper.

Definition 14 (*Edge Server*) An edge server is represented as a 4-tuple (S, A, I, L), where:

(1) $S = \{s_1, s_2, \ldots\}$, describing the set of services that the edge server can provide;
(2) A is the available resources the edge server can utilize; it can be denoted as $A = \{(r_j, n_j)\}_{j=1}^{n}$, where n is the total number of types of available resources and r_j and n_j denote the type and amount of the jth kind of resource, respectively;
(3) I is a function used to describe the current idle resources of the edge server; Idle resources refer to resources that are available and not yet occupied by service executions; At a given time t, it can be represented by $I_t = \{(r_j, n_j)\}_{j=1}^{n}$;
(4) L is the execution sequence of the edge server, which will be introduced in detail in the following definition.

Each edge server manages an execution sequence, by which it conducts service execution, request insertion, scheduling, and resource allocation. In the following, we give the definition of execution sequence.

Definition 15 (*Execution Sequence*) For an edge e, its execution sequence describes the services that will be executed on each time unit. It can be formulated as a time function $L_t = \{s_j\}_{j=1}^{n}$, expressing that during time unit t, edge e will execute n services, $S_1, S_2, \ldots, S_n$, simultaneously.

According to Definitions 12–15, for each edge server, given a time point t, we can get the following resource equation:

$$\forall r, \quad A(r) = I_t(r) + \sum_{s \in L_t} R_s(r) \tag{8.15}$$

where, $A(r)$ is the amount of available resource r of the edge server, $I_t(r)$ is the amount of the idle resource r at time t, and $R_s(r)$ is the amount of the required resource r of service s. Equation (8.15) implies that, at each time point, the amount of overall available resources equals the summation of idle resources and resources occupied by service executions.

8.4.1.3 Service Response Time Model

We aim to minimize the time delay between the moment when an edge server receives a service request to the moment when it gets the result. The detailed definition is as follows.

Definition 16 (*Service Response Time*) The response time of a service is the expected delay between the moment when a request is received and the moment when the results are got by the edge server. It can be calculated by

$$T = t_i + t_w + t_e + t_o \tag{8.16}$$

where

(1) t_i is the input parameter transmission time, which can be calculated by

$$t_i = \begin{cases} \frac{d_i}{v_{jk}}, & \text{if } e_j \neq e_k \\ 0, & \text{if } e_j = e_k \end{cases} \tag{8.17}$$

where d_i is the data size of input parameters, e_j is the edge server where the request is received, e_k is the edge or cloud server where the service is executed, and v_{jk} is the data transmission speed between servers e_j and e_k;

(2) t_w is the time delay for the service waiting to be executed in the edge server;

(3) t_e is the service execution time, which is the processing delay of the service;

(4) t_o is the output parameter transmission time, which can be calculated by

$$t_o = \begin{cases} \frac{d_o}{v_{jk}}, & \text{if } e_j \neq e_k \\ 0, & \text{if } e_j = e_k \end{cases} \tag{8.18}$$

where d_o is the data size of output parameters.

It is no doubt that if a service is executed in the same edge server where the request is received, the input and output parameter transmission time can be saved.

8.4.1.4 Problem Statement

Definition 17 (*Request dispatching problem*) Given current time t, the current states of all edges $\left\{ e_j^t = \left(S_i, A_j, I_j^t, L_j^t \right) \right\}_{j=1}^{n}$, the data transmission speed between every two servers including all edge servers and the cloud server $\{v_{ij}\}_{i,j=1}^{n+1}$, and the incoming requests $q_1, q_2, q_3, \ldots, q_m$, the request dispatching problem is to dispatch all the service requests to edge or cloud servers and schedule them to

$$\text{Minimize} \sum_{j=1}^{m} T_j$$

$$\text{s.t. } \forall j, \, s_j \in E_{q_j} \tag{8.19}$$

$$t + t_{q_j}^i \leq^{\bullet} s \tag{8.20}$$

$$s_j^{\bullet} -^{\bullet} s_j = t_{s_j}^e \tag{8.21}$$

$$\forall t' > t, \forall r, \sum_{s \in L_j^{t'}} R_s(r) + I_j^{t'}(r) \leq A_j(r) \tag{8.22}$$

where T_j is the response time of q_j, s_j is the selected service for q_j, E_{q_j} is the set of edge servers for q_j, $t_{q_j}^i$ is the input parameter transmission time of q_j, $s_j^{\bullet}$ and $^{\bullet}s_j$ are the start time and end time of service s_j, respectively, and $t_{s_j}^e$ is the execution time of s_j.

As mentioned before, it is reasonable to regard minimizing response time as the optimization objective for request dispatching. In Definition 17, it is no doubt that each request should be dispatched to a server where a corresponding service is deployed, as shown by Eq. (8.19). Equation (8.20) illustrates that services cannot start before the input data arrives. Equation (8.21) implies that the arrangement of each request is in accordance with its execution time. Moreover, the allocated resources should not exceed the available resources of the server at any time, as specified by Eq. (8.22).

It is not easy to solve this problem. In order to minimize the overall response time, we should jointly consider the global transmission delay, processing delay and waiting delay of all requests at the same time. Local edge or nearby edges are with lower transmission delay, but they are possibly not the best choice if the processing delay or waiting delay is high. In contrast, dispatching requests to remote edges or the cloud can cause high transmission delay, but the processing and waiting delay may be lower. Moreover, the dispatching of one request can affect the dispatching and scheduling of other requests, since our objective is to minimize the overall response time.

8.4.2   GASD Approach

In this section, we present our GASD approach. It is realized by combining and tailoring the genetic algorithm and simulated annealing algorithm for the proposed service request dispatching problem.

8.4.2.1   GASD Method

The genetic algorithm [16] and simulated annealing algorithm [17] are two most widely used heuristic algorithms. The genetic algorithm has powerful global opti- mizing ability, but it can easily be trapped into local optima and its efficiency is not high. The simulated annealing algorithm is with relatively reasonable selection strategy, but its global optimizing ability is rather low. Therefore, we combine the advantages of the two algorithms by introducing the temperature parameters of the simulated annealing algorithm into the genetic algorithm. The new algorithm can inherit the powerful global searching ability of the genetic algorithm, decrease the converge speed to avoid being trapped in local optima in the initial phase, and improve the convergence speed to improve efficiency in the end phase.

Table 8.6 presents the corresponding relationships between the parameters of the genetic algorithm and our request dispatching problem. Figure 8.16 shows an example of genetic encoding. In the following, we introduce the operations in detail.

Table 8.6 Term matching between the genetic algorithm and request dispatching

Genetic algorithm	Request dispatching
Chromosome	Dispatching plan
Gene	Server
Locus	Service request
Fitness	Overall response time

Fig. 8.16   Genetic encoding scheme

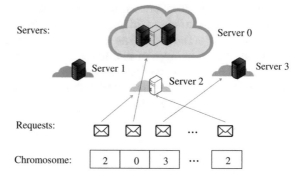

(1) Evaluation and Scheduling

Evaluation is to evaluate the fitness of chromosomes. Fitness describes how well an individual fits the environment. In our model, chromosomes with high fitness correspond to dispatching plans with short overall service response time.

As mentation before, the response time of service requests is not only determined by the dispatching of service requests, but also significantly affected by the scheduling of services inside edge servers. Therefore, given a dispatching plan, in order to calculate the overall service response time, we should give the scheduling method of services inside edge servers. Reasonable request scheduling method is also important to minimize the response time of requests. Service scheduling is a rather difficult problem, as the scheduling of one request can affect the response time of other requests executed in the same edge server. In the following, we propose a scheduling algorithm to further minimize the global response time.

Given an incoming service request q_0 and the current state of the edge server e, request scheduling is to find the optimal start time of q_0 to minimize the average response time of all service requests executed in e. According to Definitions 16 and 17, we can get conclusion that minimizing the overall response time of all requests equals minimizing the start time of q_0 plus the summation of the response time gain of all other requests dispatched to e. Therefore, we can safely transform the objective of request scheduling as Eq. (8.23):

$$\text{Min}\left(\mathcal{T}_{q_0} + \sum_{q \to e} \mathcal{T}_q \right) \Leftrightarrow \text{Min}\left({}^\bullet q_0 + \sum_{q \to e} ({}^\bullet q - {}^\bullet q') \right) \tag{8.23}$$

where $q \to e$ denotes that request q is dispatched to e, and ${}^\bullet q$ and ${}^\bullet q'$ denote the start time of q before and after the insertion of q_0, respectively. By this transformation, the complexity of the algorithm is significantly reduced, as the transmission delay and execution delay of the requests are eliminated.

Algorithm 6 shows the detailed algorithm of request scheduling. For an incoming service request q_0, we first calculate its earliest start time t_s (line 1) and then search the best insert time for q_0 (lines 3–17). The possible start time for q_0 is started from t_s to the end of the execution sequence (line 3). For each time point t, we first remove all requests that start after t (lines 4–6), then insert q_0 to its earliest possible start time (lines 7–10). The insert time should satisfy that, at each time point during the execution of q_0, each type of resource required by q_0 should be satisfied (line 8). After the insertion of q_0, we insert all transferred requests to its earliest possible start time (lines 11–15). If the current scheduling plan is better than the best plan, then it is set as the best plan (lines 16–17). Finally, the best solution is returned (line 18).

Algorithm 6 Request Scheduling Algorithm

Input:	The incoming request $q_0 = (id, t_0, e_0, E)$, the current state of the edge $\theta : (S, A, I, L)$, and the data transmission speed between e and e_0
Output:	The optimal scheduling plan

1:    $t_s \leftarrow t_0 + t_{q_0}^i$

2:    $\hat{\theta} \leftarrow \theta$

3:      **for** $t= t_s$ **to** $L^{\bullet}$

4:        **for** $q \in L_t$

5:          **if** $^{\bullet}q > t$

6:            remove q to $List$

7:        **for** $u= t$ **to** $L^{\bullet}$

8:          **if** $\forall t' \in (u, u+t_{q_0}^e)$ and $\forall r \in R_{q_0},\ R_{q_0}(r) < I_{t'}(r)$

9:            insert q_0 to e s.t. $^{\bullet}q_0 = u$

10:            **break**

11:        **for** $q \in List$

12:          **for** $u= t$ **to** $L^{\bullet}$

13:            **if** $\forall t' \in (u, u+t_q^e)$ and $\forall r \in R_q,\ R_q(r) < I_{t'}(r)$

14:              insert q to e s.t. $^{\bullet}q = u$

15:              **break**

16:        **if** $\Theta(\theta) < \Theta(\hat{\theta})$

17:        $\hat{\theta} \leftarrow \theta$

18:       **return** $\hat{\theta}$

(2) Crossover and Mutation

Crossover is an operation to recombine two parent chromosomes to generate two new child chromosomes. In a crossover process, a point is randomly chosen from the chromosome; then, the two parent chromosomes hold their genes before the point unchanged and exchange the genes after the point, thus generates two new child chromosomes. From the request dispatching perspective, crossover is to recombine two dispatching plans by interchanging corresponding objective servers to generate two new dispatching plans.

Mutation is another operation used to generate new populations. In a mutation process, a single gene is randomly chosen from the parent chromosome and randomly changed to another feasible gene. From the request dispatching perspective, mutation is to randomly choose a service request and change its objective server to another feasible sever to generate a new dispatching plan.

(3) Recombination

Recombination is to recombine the service execution sequences of edge servers according to new request dispatching plans generated by crossover and mutation operations. Algorithm 6 presents the response time calculation algorithm. However, the time complexity of the algorithm is rather high. Therefore, we propose the recombination operation to recombine the service execution sequences of edge servers to reduce the time cost of our request dispatching algorithm.

Crossover generates new chromosomes by reserving the front parts of parent chromosomes unchanged and exchanging the later parts of parent chromosomes. Accordingly, for a specific edge, the front parts of service requests dispatched to it remain unchanged and the later parts are exchanged. Therefore, we can recombine the scheduling of edge servers by simply exchanging the later dispatched requests. By this, the fitness of the newly generated child chromosomes can be simply calculated without invoking the request scheduling algorithm.

Mutation generates new chromosomes by changing one gene of parent chromosomes. Accordingly, the object server of the corresponding request is changed from one server to another. Therefore, we can recombine the scheduling of edge servers by simply deleting the request from the old objective server and inserting it to the new objective server according to the mutation operation, thus the fitness of the newly generated chromosome can be simply calculated without invoking the request scheduling algorithm.

(4) Selection

Selection performs the task to reserve superior chromosomes and to eliminate inferior chromosomes. Given a parent chromosome θ, if a child chromosome θ' is generated via crossover or mutation operation based on θ, we define $\Delta(\theta)$ as

$$\Delta(\theta) = \Theta(\theta') - \Theta(\theta) \tag{8.24}$$

where $\Theta(\theta')$ and $\Theta(\theta)$ represents the fitness of the child and parent chromosome, respectively. Then the selection is performed as follow.

If $\Delta(\theta) < 0$, it implies that the fitness of child chromosome is better, then we replace θ with θ' in the population;

Otherwise, it implies that the fitness of parent chromosome is better, then we calculate the probability

$$p = \exp - \frac{\Delta(\theta)}{K \cdot temp} \tag{8.25}$$

where K is a constant and $temp$ is the current temperature; after that, a random number rand is generated in $(0, 1)$; if $p > rand$, we replace θ with θ' in the population, otherwise, we reserve θ and discard θ'.

Equation (8.25) guarantees that chromosomes with higher fitness values have a higher probability of being selected. Therefore, a new solution can be reserved to the new generation if it is better than or close to the old one, making the new generation become better. Worse solutions are also possibly reserved to new generations, especially in earlier iterations when the temperature is high, which decreases the converge speed to avoid the algorithm being easily trapped into local optima. In later iterations, the temperature becomes low, so the possibility for worse chromosomes to replace better chromosomes becomes low, thus improves the convergence speed and the efficiency of the algorithm.

8.4.2.2 Algorithm and Analysis

Given the initial parameters, the GASD algorithm executes iteratively to search for better solutions. In each iteration process, new solutions are generated by crossover and mutation operations; then, selection is conducted to reserve superior individuals and weed out inferior individuals. As thus, superior solutions are more likely transmitted to the next generations, making the next generations fit the environment better. The detailed algorithm is presented in Algorithm 7.

Algorithm 7 GASD Algorithm

Input:	The incoming requests, the current situation of all servers with the speed among them, population size pz, crossover probability cp, mutation probability mp, initial temperature T_{max}, terminal temperature T_{min}, and cooling rate α.
Output:	An approximate optimal chromosome $\hat{\theta}$

1:          randomly compose pz chromosomes in Φ
2:          θ =random(Φ); $\hat{\theta} \leftarrow \theta$
3:          $temp=T_{max}$
4:          **while** $temp>T_{min}$
5:              **for** each θ in Φ
6:                  **if** $random.p <cp$
7:                      random select θ' from Φ
8:                      θ_1, θ_2= crossover (θ, θ')
9:                      θ= selection(θ, θ_1); θ'= selection(θ', θ_2)
10:                 **if** $random.p <mp$
11:                     θ_1= mutation (θ)
12:                     θ= selection(θ, θ_1)
13:             θ $\leftarrow$best(Φ)
14:             **if** $\Theta(\theta) < \Theta(\hat{\theta})$
15:             $\hat{\theta} \leftarrow \theta$
16:             $temp=temp * \alpha$
17:         **return** $\hat{\theta}$

The algorithm begins with initialization (line 1), where initial chromosomes are randomly generated and put into the chromosome set Φ, and a chromosome is randomly selected as the optimal chromosome (line 2). Then, the pivotal iteration steps are processed (lines 4–16). The iterations are controlled by the temperature (lines 3–4) and include operations of crossover (lines 6–9) and mutation (lines 10–12), through which more new chromosomes are generated (lines 8 and 11) and selected (lines 9 and 12). The fitness of all chromosomes in the chromosome set are compared and the current optimal one is recorded (line 13). Next, the current optimal chromosome is compared with the optimal chromosome that has ever emerged in the evolutionary history, and the better one is assigned to $\hat{\theta}$ (lines 14–15). After each iteration, the temperature is lowered (line 16) and the iteration is repeated until the temperature is lower than the lower bound. Finally, $\hat{\theta}$ is returned as the optimal chromosome (line 17).

Obviously, the time complexity of the algorithm is polynomial. Moreover, we can adjust the efficiency of the algorithm by adjusting the initialization parameters. The result may be better if one or more parameters among pz, cp, mp, mt, T_{max} and α are increased, but it will cost more time to obtain the result. In contrast, if these

Table 8.7 Variable settings

Set	Request number	Edge number
1	5–25	10
2	20	5–25

parameters are decreased, the efficiency will be improved, but the result may be suboptimal.

8.4.3 Experiments

We have implemented the algorithms in Python and our experiments are conducted on a MacBook Pro (macOS Sierra Version 10.12.5).

Since no standard experimental platforms and test data sets are available, we generated our experimental data in a synthetic way.

Service: Each service is assigned three integers as the input data size, output data size and service execution time, respectively, which are referred to [18]. Each service requires 3 kinds of resources, and the required quantity of each kind of resource is randomly generated in (2, 5).

Service request: We assume that the number of incoming service requests in each time unit is fixed. The received edge server is randomly selected for each request. The amount of available edge servers for each request ranges from 2 to 8.

Edge server: Each server has 3 kinds of resources and the available number of each resource ranges from 5 to 10. The amount of edge servers is fixed.

Speed: The data transmission speed is randomly generated from 1 to 5 for each two edge servers and the speed between each edge server and the cloud is fixed as 1.

We focus on the following two variables in the experiments:

Request number: Request number is the number of generated service requests in each time unit.

Edge number: Edge number is the number of edge servers that can provide services for each service request.

As analyzed in Sect. 8.4, the effectiveness and efficiency of the algorithm are mainly related to these two variables. We set two sets of parameters, as shown in Table 8.7. In each set, one of the two parameters is varied and the other one remains fixed. All experiments are repeated 200 times, and we use the average value as the results.

8.4.3.1 Effectiveness of GASD

In this subsection, we compare the overall response time of requests dispatched by GASD with other four widely used methods:

Table 8.8 Impact of request number on overall response time

Methods	5	10	15	20	25
GASD	274	708	1309	2051	2989
GA	280	734	1354	2104	3083
SA	277	736	1425	2256	3389
AC	305	782	1465	2307	3440
APS	397	1402	3108	5122	8200

Access Point Scheduling (APS): Access point scheduling method conducts request dispatching by simply selecting the edge server with the fastest data transmission speed.

The Genetic Algorithm (GA): GA is used to verify the effectiveness of GASD by introducing temperature factors of the simulated annealing algorithm.

The Simulated Annealing Algorithm (SA): SA is used to verify the effectiveness of the global searching ability of GASD.

The Ant Colony Algorithm (AC): AC is a widely used heuristic algorithm, which generates new solutions by assigning pheromones and performing selection according to the pheromones.

First, we examine the impact of the number of generated service requests on the overall response time of requests dispatched by the five algorithms. To this end, we set the experimental parameters according to Set 1 in Table 8.7. The results are shown in Table 8.8, from which we can see that the overall response time of all of the five methods are rising with the increasing of the service request number. As the other parameters are fixed, with the increasing of the request number, more requests will be dispatched to the edge servers, which increases the load of edge servers, therefore, the waiting time of services is increased, thus makes the response time of the requests increased. The difference between GASD and the other three heuristic algorithms becomes larger with the request number increasing, which demonstrates the superiority of our GASD method. In addition, the overall response time of service requests dispatched by APS arises more sharply, because it only considers the data transmission speed. By this, the experiment verifies the importance to consider other factors including the transmitted data size and the execution time of requests, the conditions and accommodated services of edge servers, etc.

To examine the impact of edge number on the result of request dispatching, we set the experimental parameters according to Set 2 in Table 8.7. The results are shown in Table 8.9, which shows that the overall response time of the requests is reducing with the increasing of the edge number. With the increasing of edge servers, there are more edge servers to process the service requests, which makes the waiting time of services shorter, therefore, the overall response time of service requests decreases. The difference between the results of all methods is also decreasing with the edge number increasing. Moreover, the comparison of the five methods is in accordance with the experiments before: the result of GASD is always the best, the result of

Table 8.9 Impact of edge number on overall response time

Methods	5	10	15	20	25
GASD	3033	2051	1799	1686	1590
GA	3127	2104	1853	1754	1631
SA	3525	2256	1952	1797	1681
AC	3596	2307	2004	1855	1720
APS	9950	5122	3872	3345	2790

APS is always the worst, and the gap between the result of APS and the other four methods is relatively high.

From these experiments, we can draw conclusion that our GASD method can achieve the best request dispatching over the five methods. With the resources of edge servers becoming relatively shorten, the superiority of GASD becomes more obvious. Besides, the APS algorithm performs worst, which demonstrates that the conditions of edge servers and other request-related parameters have great effect on the dispatching of service requests.

8.4.3.2 Effectiveness of Service Scheduling

In this set of experiments, we verify the importance of service scheduling on the overall response time of service requests. To this end, we design a new method, which does not account for scheduling of services in edge servers. This method processes service requests according to their arrival time. In the process of request dispatching, it adopts the GASD method to search for dispatching plans, without performing service scheduling. For an incoming service request, it simply finds the earliest time when the idle resources are sufficient for the request and do not adjust the process sequence of the requests. We name this new GASD method as NGASD.

First, we examine the impact of request dispatching with the range of request number. To this end, we set the experimental parameters according to Set 1 in Table 8.7 and implement GASD and NGASD methods. The result is shown in Fig. 8.17. It shows that, with the request number increasing, the result of NGASD raises more sharply. This is because with the request number increasing, more service requests are dispatched to edge servers, which makes the waiting time of the services lengthened.

Then, we examine the impact of service scheduling with the range of edge number. To this end, we set the experimental parameters according to Set 2 in Table 8.7. The result is shown in Fig. 8.18, from which we can see that, with the increasing of edge number, the overall response time of both methods are lowered, since the resources of edge servers are increased. Moreover, with the edge number increasing, the gap between the two methods narrows.

Fig. 8.17 Impact of service scheduling ranging request number

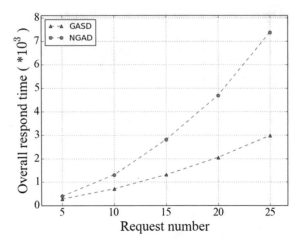

Fig. 8.18 Impact of service scheduling ranging edge number

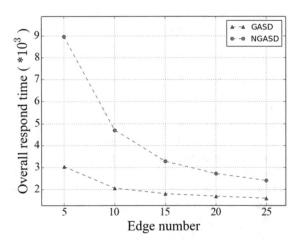

Therefore, we can draw conclusion that performing service scheduling to fully utilize the resources of edge servers performs a very important role in reducing the response time of service requests.

8.4.3.3 Efficiency Evaluation

In this subsection, we conduct two sets of experiments to examine the scalability of our method. Similarly, we also range those two parameters, i.e. request number and edge number.

Figure 8.19 shows the execution time of GASD with the ranging of request number, from which we can see that with the increasing of request number, the execution time of GASD method increases slightly. This is because the scale of the

Fig. 8.19 Impact of request number on the execution time of GASD

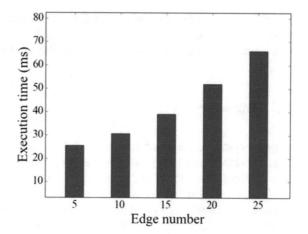

algorithm is affected by iteration numbers, which is determined by the temperature parameters in the initialization step. As the increasing of request number lengthens the chromosomes, which makes the time for crossover, mutation and selection operations become longer, there is a slight increase in the execution time of the algorithm, which is in accordance with the analysis in Subsection B of Sect. 8.4.

Figure 8.20 shows the execution time of GASD with the ranging of edge number, from which we can see that with the number of edge servers increasing, the execution time of GASD is raised slightly. This is because the increase of edge servers makes the algorithm perform scheduling for more edge servers during the dispatching process. As the number of edge servers cannot affect the iterations of the algorithm, the execution time of the algorithm does not rise sharply.

Therefore, we can draw conclusion that the scale of the request dispatching problem only has a slight effect on the execution time of our GASD algorithm,

Fig. 8.20 Impact of edge number on the execution time of GASD

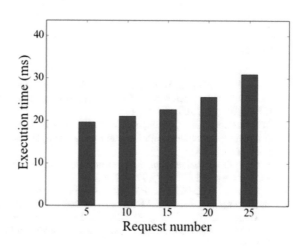

which verifies the good scalability of GASD algorithm. Moreover, the execution time of the method is in a low order of magnitude, owing to the great effort of the recombination strategy on reducing the computation complexity of the algorithm.

8.5 Summary

In this chapter, we proposed three methods for revenue-driven service provisioning in mobile cloud computing, composition-driven service provisioning in distributed edges, and request dispatching for edge provisioning systems, respectively.

First, we studied the problem of revenue-driven service provision for mobile devices. A lightweight service-based approach called RESP (revenue-driven service provision for mobile devices) is proposed to perform service request selection, request scheduling and resource allocation simultaneously, with the objective of maximizing the revenue of the mobile devices. To evaluate the performance of the approach, we have conducted a set of experiments, which demonstrated the efficacy of RESP.

Then, we introduced the mobile edge computing model and highlights the cache mechanism with composite services in MEC models. Based on them, we propose a consumption-driven searching algorithm to determine the cache policy. With the help of the cache policy, appropriate services are stored in the edge servers in proximity to support users better.

Finally, we focused on the service request dispatching problem in edge cloud systems. To further reduce the overall response time of service requests, we take service scheduling of edge servers into consideration. This problem is formally modeled, and a novel heuristic method is proposed by combining and tailoring the genetic algorithm and simulated annealing algorithm. A solution recombination strategy is proposed to improve the efficiency of the algorithm.

References

1. S. Al Noor, R. Hasan, M. Haque, Cellcloud: a novel cost effective formation of mobile cloud based on bidding incentives, in *2014 International Conference on Cloud Computing (CLOUD)*. IEEE (2014), pp. 200–207
2. M.Y. Arslan, I. Singh, S. Singh, H.V. Madhyastha, K. Sundaresan, S.V. Krishnamurthy, Cwc: A distributed computing infrastructure using smartphones. IEEE T. Mobile Comput. **14**(8), 1587–1600 (2015)
3. X. Chen, Decentralized computation offloading game for mobile cloud computing. IEEE Trans. Parallel Distrib. Syst. **26**(4), 974–983 (2015)
4. X. Chen, L. Jiao, W. Li, X. Fu, Efficient multi-user computation offloading for mobile-edge cloud computing. IEEE/ACM Trans. Netw. **24**(5), 2795–2808 (2016)
5. C. Wang, F.R. Yu, C. Liang, Q. Chen, L. Tang, *Joint Computation Offloading and Interference Management in Wireless Cellular Networks with Mobile Edge Computing* (IEEE T. Veh, Technol, 2017)

6. K. Liu, J. Peng, H. Li, X. Zhang, W. Liu, Multi-device task offloading with time-constraints for energy efficiency in mobile cloud computing. Future Gener. Comput. Syst. **64**, 1–14 (2016)
7. G. Iosifidis, L. Gao, J. Huang, L. Tassiulas, An iterative double auction for mobile data offloading, in: *2013 International Symposium on Modeling & Optimization in Mobile, Ad Hoc & Wireless Networks (WiOpt)*. IEEE (2013), pp. 154–161
8. X. Larrucea, I. Santamaria, R. Colomo-Palacios, C. Ebert, Microser- vices. IEEE Softw. **35**(3), 96–100 (2018). https://doi.org/10.1109/ms.2018.2141030
9. S. Weerawarana, F. Curbera, F. Leymann, T. Storey, D.F. Ferguson, *Web Services Platform Architecture: SOAP, WSDL, WS-Policy, WS-Addressing, WS-BPEL, WS-Reliable Messaging, and More* (Prentice-Hall, Englewood Cliffs, NJ, USA, 2005)
10. Y. Xu, J. Yin, S. Deng, N.N. Xiong, J. Huang, Context-awareQoS prediction for web service recommendation and selection. Expert Syst. Appl. **53**, 75–86 (2016). https://doi.org/10.1016/j.eswa.2016.01.010
11. R. Ghosh, A. Ghose, A. Hegde, T. Mukherjee, A. Mos, QoS- driven management of business process variants in cloud based execution environments, in *International Conference on Service-Oriented Computing (ICSOC), Banff, AB, Canada* (Springer, Berlin, 2016), pp. 55–69
12. H. Zhu, I. Bayley, On the composability of design patterns. IEEE Trans. Softw. Eng. **41**(11), 1138–1152 (2015)
13. S. Deng, L. Huang, J. Taheri, J. Yin, M. Zhou, A.Y. Zomaya, Mobility-aware service composition in mobile communities. IEEE Trans. Syst. Man, Cybern. Syst. **47**(3), 555–568 (2017)
14. S. Deng, H. Wu, D. Hu, J.L. Zhao, Services election for composition with QoS correlations. IEEE Trans. Services Comput. **9**(2), 291–303 (2016). https://doi.org/10.1109/tsc.2014.236 1138
15. S. Sahni, Approximate algorithms for the 0/1 knapsack problem. J. ACM **22**(1), 115–124 (1975)
16. D. Goldberg, *Genetic Algorithms in Search, Optimization and Machine Learning* (Addison-Wesley Publishing Company, New York, 1989), pp. 26–28
17. S. Kirkpatrick, M.P. Vecchi, Optimization by stimulated annealing. Science **220**(4598), 671–680 (1983)
18. Z. Zheng, M.R. Lyu, *QoS Management of Web Services* (Springer, Berlin, 2013)

Printed in the United States
by Baker & Taylor Publisher Services